Scottish Federalism and Covenantalism in Transition

Scottish Federalism and Covenantalism in Transition

The Theology of Ebenezer Erskine

Stephen G. Myers

PICKWICK *Publications* · Eugene, Oregon

SCOTTISH FEDERALISM AND COVENANTALISM IN TRANSITION
The Theology of Ebenezer Erskine

Copyright © 2015 Stephen G. Myers. All rights reserved. Except for brief quotations in critical publications or reviews, no part of this book may be reproduced in any manner without prior written permission from the publisher. Write: Permissions. Wipf and Stock Publishers, 199 W. 8th Ave., Suite 3, Eugene, OR 97401.

Pickwick Publications
An Imprint of Wipf and Stock Publishers
199 W. 8th Ave., Suite 3
Eugene, OR 97401

www.wipfandstock.com

ISBN 13: 978-1-55635-535-6

Cataloguing-in-Publication Data

Myers, Stephen G.

Scottish federalism and covenantalism in transition : the theology of Ebenezer Erskine / Stephen G. Myers

xxii + 258 p. ; 23 cm. Includes bibliographical references.

ISBN 13: 978-1-55635-535-6

1. Erskine, Ebezer (1680–1754) 2. Scottish Federalism. I. Title

BX9178.E77 M93 2015

Manufactured in the U.S.A.   09/14/2015

Contents

Acknowledgments | vii
Abbreviations | ix
Introduction | xiii

Chapter I
Early Life and Abjuration Oath Controversy | 1

Chapter II
The Marrow Controversy | 28

Chapter III
The Secession Crisis | 115

Chapter IV
Erskine in the 1740s | 163

Conclusion | 214

Appendix I: Text of 1712 Oath of Abjuration | 223
Appendix II: Problematic Sections | 225
Appendix III: Text of 1715 Oath of Abjuration | 226
Appendix IV: Full text of the Act of the Associate Presbytery | 228

Bibliography | 231
Index | 255

Acknowledgments

In the labors of doctoral research, as in all endeavors, the Lord gives his people tokens of his grace and favor. The years in which I undertook the following work (2004–2007) were filled with many such evidences of the Lord's care for me, and it is my joy here to recognize the goodness that God showed to me.

In the first instance, I would like to thank Professor David Fergusson, my doctoral supervisor. In the face of untold responsibilities, he never failed to make himself available to me and to offer me guidance that was always prompt and always wise. Professor Fergusson's supervision has made what could have been a tedious, soul-draining task into an endeavor that was constantly stimulating and, by God's grace, a blessing to my soul. In addition to Professor Fergusson, I have received invaluable guidance from Dr. Andrew Ross and Dr. Henry Sefton, my doctoral examiners, as well as from Dr. Susan Hardman Moore, Professor Stewart J. Brown, and Professor Jane Dawson at New College. Additionally, Professor John McIntosh from the Free Church College offered many helpful and formative insights. Finally, Principal Donald Macleod of the Free Church College provided not only encouragement, but also research accommodation that was invaluable in the completion of my work. To all of these men and women, I owe my sincerest gratitude.

Of course, I would not have reached the shores of Scotland to meet these men and women without the encouragement and support of those at home in the United States. Among those who encouraged me before I left and upheld me in prayer while I was away, I shall never forget the congregation of Coddle Creek Associate Reformed Presbyterian Church in Mooresville, North Carolina. The saints at Coddle Creek have allowed me to grow up in their midst and, in spite of all that they have seen of me, they continue to show me a love that I do not deserve. Reverend James Avery Hunt, their pastor and mine, has indelibly shaped the whole of this work; if he did not pen its words, he profoundly shaped the soul of him who did.

While in Scotland, the Lord's nourishment through his people did not cease. In the three happy years that my family and I lived in Edinburgh, not a day passed that the saints at Buccleuch and Greyfriars Free Church did not care for us and make us feel perfectly at home, even in a faraway land. The people of Buccleuch gave us a glimpse of Glory; they showed us what a congregation of the Lord's people can be. My family and I are truly humbled that we were able to be among their number for a time. In particular, I must thank the family of Neil and Mary Campbell. I have never seen Christ more clearly than I see him in their family; I have never been made to think more deeply about my research than I was by Neil's piercing questions offered casually in his home or in the church hall.

Of course, no thanksgiving would be complete without the recognition that all I have achieved is owed to my father and my mother, Mr. and Mrs. Charles Stephen Myers. Never have they failed to support me, never have they failed to encourage me, and never have they mentioned the untold sacrifices they have made to see their son succeed.

Finally, I find myself in unfathomable debt to my wife, Lisa. At the start of this entire enterprise, against all reason and against all circumstance, she believed in me. It is a debt that no words can explain and no life can repay. Along the way, she has even given me three beautiful children—Quinn Marie Myers, Charles "Cale" Stephen Myers II, and Mae Irene Myers. With each day that passes, Lisa makes God's grace more tangible, while Quinn, Cale, and Mae make his covenant more precious. It is to them all that I dedicate this work.

Above all, all thanksgiving, all glory, laud, and honor are due to the Triune God of Heaven and Earth. If there is one thing for which I would like to thank Ebenezer Erskine, it is that, day after day, he showed me the beauty of the Father, the Son, and the Holy Ghost. I doubt he would crave any other gratitude. I doubt he could think of any more appropriate conclusion than the words of a Psalm that was one of his favorites and that still echoes from the walls of Buccleuch Free Church:

> *Now blessed be the Lord our God,*
> *The God of Israel,*
> *For He alone doth wondrous works,*
> *In glory that excel.*
> *And blessed be His glorious name*
> *To all eternity:*
> *The whole earth let His glory fill.*
> *Amen, so let it be.*

Psalm 72:18–19, from the Scottish Psalter (1650)

Abbreviations

Unless otherwise noted, all quotations from original sources are given as they appear in those sources. Unconventional spellings and use of italics have been retained and will not be noted individually.

The following abbreviations will be used throughout the present work:

A&D	Associate Presbytery. *ANSWERS BY THE* Associate Presbytery, *TO* Reasons *of* Dissent, *given in to the said* Presbytery, *at* Stirling, December *23, 1742; as also, the* Representation *and* Petition *dictated to their* Clerk, *and* Reasons *of* Dissent *and* Secession, *given in to them at* Edinburgh, February *3, 1743; by the Reverend Mr.* Thomas Nairn, *Minister of the Gospel at* Abbotshall. *Together with* A Declaration and Defence *Of the* ASSOCIATE PRESBYTERY's Principles anent the present *Civil Government.* Edinburgh: T. W. and T. Ruddimans, 1744.
AD	Hadow, James. *THE ANTINOMIANISM OF THE MARROW OF* Modern Divinity *DETECTED.* Edinburgh: Mosman, 1721.
ADG	Associate Presbytery. *ACT OF THE* Associate Presbytery, *CONCERNING THE* Doctrine *of* GRACE. Edinburgh: Duncan, 1744.
ADT	Associate Presbytery. *ACT, Declaration* and *Testimony for the* DOCTRINE, WORSHIP, DISCIPLINE, *and* GOVERNMENT *of the Church of* SCOTLAND. Edinburgh: Lumisden and Robertson, 1737.
AFR	Associate Presbytery. *ACT OF THE* Associate Presbytery, *For* RENEWING *the* NATIONAL COVENANT *of* Scotland, *and the* SOLEMN LEAGUE *and* COVENANT *of the* three Nations, *IN A WAY and MANNER* agreeable *to our*

	present SITUATION, and CIRCUMSTANCES in this Period. T. W. and T. Ruddimans, 1744.
AGA	Acts of the General Assembly of the Church of Scotland, M.DC.XXXVIII.-M.DCCC.XLII. Edinburgh: Edinburgh Printing, 1843.
Answers	Queries, Agreed unto by the Commission of the General Assembly; And put to these Ministers, who gave in a REPRESENTATION and PETITION against the 5th and 8th Acts of Assembly 1720. Together with the ANSWERS Given by these Ministers to The said QUERIES. 1722.
Catechism	Associate Synod (Burgher). THE ASSEMBLY'S SHORTER CATECHISM EXPLAINED, By Way of QUESTION and ANSWER. Glasgow: Urie, 1753.
CDMD	Willison, John. THE CHURCH's Danger AND THE MINISTER's Duty Declared, in a SERMON Preach'd at the Opening of the Synod of Angus and Mearns, At MONTROSE The 16th Day of October 1733. WITH A PREFACE and POSTSCRIPT TOUCHING Some more Evils of the present Time. Glasgow: Duncan, 1733.
Declinature	Associate Presbytery. ACTS AND PROCEEDINGS OF THE MINISTERS AND ELDERS ASSOCIATE TOGETHER For the EXERCISE of CHURCH-GOVERNMENT and DISCIPLINE in a PRESBYTERIAL CAPACITY, met at Edinburgh, May 16th, 1739. Containing their DECLINATURE. Read in presence of the General Assembly, and given in to the Moderator thereof, May 17, 1739. Glasgow: Bryce and Paterson, 1758.
DNB	Matthew, H.C.G. and Brian Harrison, eds. Oxford Dictionary of National Biography. Oxford: Oxford University Press, 2004.
DSCHT	Cameron, Nigel M. de S., ed. Dictionary of Scottish Church History and Theology. Downers Grove, IL: InterVarsity, 1993.
EQ	Evangelical Quarterly
Fasti	Scott, Hew. Fasti ecclesiae Scoticanae: the succession of ministers in the Church of Scotland from the Reformation. 8 vols. Edinburgh: Oliver and Boyd, 1915–1928.

ABBREVIATIONS

FIT	Willison, John. *A Fair and Impartial TESTIMONY, Essayed in Name of a Number of Ministers, Elders, and Christian People of the CHURCH of Scotland, UNTO The laudable Principles, Wrestlings and Attainments of that CHURCH; AND AGAINST The Backslidings, Corruptions, Divisions, and prevailing Evils, both of former and present Times.* Edinburgh: Lumisden and Robertson, 1744.
"Letters"	"A copie of the letters that passed between Mr James Hadow principal of the Colledge of St. Andrews & Mr Alexr Hamilton Minister of the Gospel at Airth. Transcribed from the Authenticke copies April 27th 1717." Special Collections, New College Library, Edinburgh.
Life	Fraser, Donald. *The Life and Diary of the Reverend Ebenezer Erskine, A.M. of Stirling, Father of the Secession Church.* Edinburgh: Oliphant, 1831.
N&S	*A Narrative and State of the PROCEEDINGS of the JUDICATORIES of the Church of Scotland, Against Masters Ebenezer Erskine, William Wilson, Alexander Moncrieff, and James Fisher, late Ministers thereof.* Edinburgh: Davidson and Fleming, 1734.
Reasons	Associate Presbytery. *REASONS by Mr. EBENEZER ERSKINE Minister at Stirling, Mr. WILLIAM WILSON Minster at Perth, Mr. ALEXANDER MONCRIEFF Minister at Abernethy, and Mr. JAMES FISHER Minister at Kinclaven, Why they have not ACCEDED to the Judicatories of the Established Church.* Edinburgh: Lumisden and Robertson, 1735.
Representation	*The Representation and Petition of Several Ministers of the Gospel, to the General Assembly, Met at Edinburgh May 1721.* Edinburgh, 1721.
RoG	Hadow, James. *THE Record of God AND DUTY of FAITH Therein required.* Edinburgh: Mosman, 1719.
RSCHS	*Records of the Scottish Church History Society*
RTC	Associate Presbytery. *The Representations of Masters Ebenezer Erskine and James Fisher and of Masters William Wilson and Alexander Moncrieff to the Commission of the late General Assembly.* Edinburgh: Lumisden and Robertson, 1733.

SBET	*Scottish Bulletin of Evangelical Theology*
SCJ	*Sixteenth Century Journal*
SHR	*Scottish Historical Review*
SJT	*Scottish Journal of Theology*
TD	Associate Presbytery. *A TESTIMONY TO THE DOCTRINE, WORSHIP, GOVERNMENT, and DISCIPLINE of the CHURCH of SCOTLAND.* Edinburgh: Lumisden and Robertson, 1734.
TSP	Associate Presbytery. *THE TRUE State of the PROCESS AGAINST Mr.* Ebenezer Erskine *Minister of the Gospel at* Stirling: *SETTING FORTH The Proceedings of the Synod of* Perth *and* Stirling *against him, AND THE ACT of the late ASSEMBLY concerning him, and some other Ministers Adhering to his PROTEST.* Edinburgh: Lumisden and Robertson, 1733.
WCF	Westminster Confession of Faith. Glasgow: Free Presbyterian, 1976.
Works	Erskine, Ebenezer. *The Whole Works of the Late Rev. Ebenezer Erskine* Minister of the Gospel at Stirling *CONSISTING OF SERMONS AND DISCOURSES ON THE MOST IMPORTANT AND INTERESTING SUBJECTS.* Edinburgh: Ogle & Murray, 1871. Reprint, Glasgow: Free Presbyterian, 2001.

Introduction

IN THE STORIED FIELD of Scottish theology, Ebenezer Erskine stands as an enigma. Born on the day that a Covenanting declaration was promulgated at the town cross of Sanquhar—22 June 1680—and dying after William Robertson's Moderatism had made its presence felt in the General Assembly—2 June 1754—Erskine inhabited a tumultuous and often mysterious epoch of the Scottish Kirk. Over those decades, the Kirk would be embroiled in multiple controversies and dissensions; Erskine had a role to play in many of them, thus inextricably binding himself to the vagaries of an obscure age. In subsequent generations, Erskine would be many things to many people. In some interpretations, Erskine's evangelical warmth and the strong bond he formed with his congregations is emphasized in order to portray him as a defender of a free and gracious gospel, preparing the way not only for the revivals that swept Scotland in the eighteenth century, but also for the presbyterian mission that went out from Scotland to evangelize much of the known world.[1] In other interpretations, his sometimes contentious personality and evident inability to compromise receive attention in order to show him as the man who unleashed the destructive forces of schism within the Kirk.[2] In both disparate strands of interpretation, there is a shared tendency to see Erskine's theology as a function of, and vehicle for, his personality; what is lacking is a comprehensive theological portrait of Ebenezer Erskine that seeks to understand him as a theologian and minister driven by concrete theological commitments. It is that theological portrait that the present study will seek to present.

Traditionally, the reflections on Erskine's theology that have been offered have been marked by two themes. In the first instance, Erskine is viewed as, to greater or lesser degree, a theological antiquarian seeking to

---

1. E.g., *Life*; MacInnes, *Evangelical Movement*, 179–80; T. F. Torrance, *Theology*, 228.
2. E.g., McIntosh, *Church and Theology*, 27, hereafter, *Theology*; McIntosh, "Lessons," 6–9; Mitchell, "Erskine."

reclaim for eighteenth-century Scotland the neglected doctrine of a former era. Whether a vibrant evangelicalism or a politicized sectarianism, Erskine is seen as reviving, from the Scottish theological past, an otherwise contemporaneously-absent element. In the second instance, Erskine is perceived as a new seed in an old Kirk, introducing theological formulations and undertaking practical actions that established the precedent for disorienting changes in the century that followed his death. Most often, this discontinuity with the past is embodied in Erskine's role within the Secession of 1733; a movement in which, it is alleged, Erskine's proto-voluntaryist ecclesiology laid the foundation for multiform divisions in what previously had been the one face of the Kirk. The latent dissonance between these two themes, and the picture that emerges from them of Erskine as a "progressive antiquarian," have only exacerbated the tendency to view Erskine as a man driven as much by the whims of personality as by consistent theological commitments. Ultimately, the traditional approach of understanding Erskine's theology as either reclamation or innovation leaves Erskine as a man with ponderous force of personality, yet only very general overarching theological commitments to animate that personality.

In the recent work of scholars such as L. E. Schmidt and Margo Todd, there are intimations of a different conceptual framework for understanding Erskine's theology that presents a more coherent account of that system.[3] While the guiding principles of both Schmidt and Todd arise from their constructions of the earlier Scottish Reformation, these principles frame an important paradigm. In the work of both scholars, the theological and ecclesiastical convulsions of the Reformation created a milieu in which Scottish theologians instinctively took components of a newly-obsolete religious identity and infused them with new meaning in a new world. In this paradigm, stark notions of absolute continuity and complete discontinuity give way to the dynamic contextualization of inherited commitments. What Schmidt and Todd argue that the first generations of Scottish presbyterians did sociologically and unwittingly, Erskine did theologically and purposefully. In Erskine's lifetime, Scotland knew theological and ecclesiastical upheaval that, if less revolutionary than the change of the Reformation, was not wholly dissimilar therefrom.[4] With the Glorious Revolution of 1688, presbyterianism had shifted from a persecuted or conditionally-indulged minority opinion to the established paradigm of the nation, enjoying the

---

3. See, for example, Schmidt, *Holy Fairs*, 11–14, 16–21, 213–14; Todd, *Culture of Protestantism*, 21–23, 26, 84–98. Along with the value of such works, McIntosh's caution should be remembered. See McIntosh, *Theology*, 30.

4. For a sociological perspective on the effects of such bewildering change in this era, see Roberts and Naphy, "Introduction," 1–3.

support of both crown and parliament. With the Anglo-Scottish Union of 1707, the Kirk again transmuted from the prophet of the nation to one voice in a multi-confessional State. The Kirk of Erskine's day, then, faced an imposing challenge—how to bring the thunder of John Knox, the dominion of Alexander Henderson, and the blood of James Guthrie into post-Union Scotland. This formidable task was further complicated by the legacy of Stuart persecution under the Second Episcopate. While the Covenanting hagiography of later generations has concentrated on the martyrdom of those years, an equally troubling legacy is often ignored—the legacy of theological confusion. With the presbyterian Kirk meeting in fields and secret houses rather than in assemblies, synods, and presbyteries, varying theological emphases and strands had emerged that, when met together in one Assembly again, proved to be both dissonant with each other and individually radicalized as a result of application within extreme conditions.

Within this context of long-suppressed diversity and radicalization, Erskine forged his doctrinal system, a theological structure which rested upon two chief pillars. First, Erskine forwarded a self-consciously evangelical federalism. In his own religious experience, Erskine had known times of grave self-doubt, years of a perceived superficial adherence to doctrinal truths, and a definable moment of evidently salvific personal appropriation of those previously assented truths. In the Scotland in which he ministered, Erskine detected an insipid legalism threatening the categorical freedom of the gospel. In the federalism that Erskine crafted from the variegated inheritance of Scottish Westminster federal thought, one sees him speaking out of that personal experience, through the medium of Westminster federalism, in an effort to preserve the graciousness of the gospel in contemporary Scotland.

Secondly, Erskine asserted a system that could be termed "modified Covenantalism." Doubtlessly influenced by his father's example, Erskine maintained throughout his ministry the perpetual obligations of Scotland's Covenants, both National and Solemn League. In these documents, Scotland found both her identity and her purpose; a self-defining program that demanded national renewal. However, the Scotland which Erskine inhabited made these Covenants problematic documents filled with problematic commitments. Most pressingly, how could Covenantal commitments retain cogency in a Scotland that, after 1707, was part of a multi-confessional State under an uncovenanted magistracy? In seeking to address such a situation, Erskine drew upon the often complex Covenanting inheritance to establish the Kirk on a foundation that would anchor her upon the Covenants yet allow her to interact purposefully with the British State, seeking in every such interaction both submissive loyalty to the civil magistrate and intentional pursuit of societal reformation. In an expanding body of work, Colin Kidd has brought greater clarity to his notion of "Covenanting Whiggism," a post-Revolution incarnation of Covenanting political theory and dissent whereby Scotland's Covenant engagements were reconciled with an embrace of the uncovenanted Hanoverian State, yet the philosophical paradigm that he outlines lacks—at the very least, terminologically—the Covenantal dynamism of Erskine's thought.[5] While Erskine had adopted more modest medium-term goals in his Covenantalism than had marked the heights of seventeenth-century Covenanting theologians, his thought remained not a Covenantalism that had assimilated Whiggish commitments, but rather an unmitigated Covenantalism modified to speak intelligibly to the Scotland that Erskine providentially inhabited.

To arrive at a coherent understanding of Erskine, it is these twin theological commitments that must have interpretive pre-eminence. While both commitments tended to amplify, at varying points, differing components of Erskine's personality, it was always these underlying doctrinal priorities that guided Erskine and shaped his ministry; a prominence attested by Erskine's unwavering commitment to them even in the face of the ebbs and flows of personality and temperament. Through a theological examination of Erskine's life and ministry, it emerges that it was these commitments that unified Erskine's varying controversial engagements and that placed at the center of his proclamation and his ministry not the particularities of personality, but definable theological systems.

As Erskine's theology was equally shaped by both the tradition from which it emerged and the situation to which it spoke, an assessment of that theology must necessarily follow an historical account of Erskine's own life. Therefore, the following treatment will explore Erskine's theology as it emerged from various controversial engagements of his ministry. Neither a complete biographical narrative nor a psychological portrait will be pursued; indeed, such accounts are readily and exhaustively available in the extant secondary literature.[6] What will be presented is an account of the immediately pertinent details of Erskine's life and of those controversies that are most germane to the development and articulation of the theology that animated Erskine's well-documented personality. In the first chapter, after observing the formative influences of Erskine's early life and ministry, the Abjuration Oath controversy of 1712 will be examined for its role in shaping Erskine's modified Covenantalism. In chapter two, perhaps the

---

5. See especially Kidd, "Conditional," 1163–65.

6. The three most important such accounts are *Life*; MacEwen, *Erskines*; and Harper, *Memoir*.

most important controversy of Erskine's ministry, the *Marrow* controversy, will be considered for its disclosure of Erskine's evangelical federalism. In chapter three, Erskine's involvement in the Secession of 1733 will be explored, revealing how the modified Covenantalism that Erskine shared with many other ministers came to embody a nascent Covenantal Revolution Church. In chapter four, that Covenantal Revolution Church will be examined through the complex of controversies that the Secession Church faced in the 1740s to see if, after all of Erskine's labors, his model for a national church was even viable in post-Union, post-toleration Scotland. Finally, the conclusion will cast one last look over the whole of Erskine's controversially-developed theology and draw a few conclusions therefrom.

SOURCE CONSIDERATIONS

The nature of Erskine's controversial engagements necessitates some care in extracting his doctrinal system from the extant sources. Throughout those engagements, Erskine was consistently part of larger groups of like-minded ministers, and thus his positions were most often articulated in group and consensus documents, whether of the *Marrow* Representers in the 1720s, the Seceding Brethren in the 1730s, or the Associate Presbytery and Synod in the 1740s. As a result, it can, at times, appear difficult to differentiate between Erskine's personal views and the consensus views of the larger group that perhaps do not reflect the nuances of Erskine's own thought. However, three factors mitigate this potential complication. First, Erskine very often was responsible for the formulation of documents that later were given approval by, and issued in the name of, the larger group. For some of these documents, Erskine's responsibility is well-known; for others, it is attested by more obscure, yet equally reliable, sources. Secondly, Erskine was often the leader of the movements in which he was involved. Particularly from the first days of the Secession Crisis through the early years of the resulting Associate Presbytery and Synod, Erskine set the agenda that the remainder of the Seceders followed. Although Erskine's declining health, coupled with an influx of new Seceders, made leadership of the Secession more diffuse and thus their actions less easily equated with Erskine's personal positions from the mid-1740s, the potential confusion is removed by Erskine's authorship of a polemical pamphlet on the one controversy that occurred after those years. Thirdly, Erskine's insistence upon the freedom to exonerate his conscience from complicity in anything that erred even minutely from his own opinion meant that when Erskine dissented from a majority position, he registered that dissent. If Erskine voted for an Act or signed his name to a group document, he believed every word in it; if no dissent from Erskine is on record, it is safely assumed that the position expressed was his own.

In addition to the various group documents that elucidate Erskine's doctrine, there are many relevant works from his own personal pen. The largest body of these writings is contained in Erskine's *Whole Works*, the definitive edition of which was first published in 1761, importantly republished in 1871, and most recently reissued in 2001.[7] These *Whole Works* are chiefly sermons that Erskine preached, most of which were published during his lifetime, along with some published posthumously in accordance with Erskine's expressed desires. Of those sermons published during Erskine's lifetime, several were prefixed with lengthy and important prefaces that later were removed when the *Whole Works* were compiled. Furthermore, along with his one free-standing polemical pamphlet, Erskine authored prefatory epistles to several contemporary publications, as well as one crucially important anonymous pamphlet that is ignored in the extant secondary literature. All of these sources will be considered in an effort to construct a theology not condensed in one systematic text, but rather dispersed over a lifetime of controversial engagements.

HISTORIOGRAPHICAL CONSIDERATIONS

Along with these primary materials, there are a host of secondary materials available on Erskine. After a flurry of works, both on Erskine and on the larger Secession Church, in the mid to late nineteenth century, the last, and arguably best, in-depth study of Erskine was published in 1900 by A. R. MacEwen. While Erskine has been considered in several compendiums of important figures in the history of the Kirk, in prefaces to various republications, and in larger historical accounts since MacEwen's work, these later treatments have been little more than recapitulations of the nineteenth-century body of work and have not advanced the state of Erskine studies beyond where it stood with MacEwen.

While MacEwen represents the terminus of Erskine studies, he is of comparatively minor significance in understanding the Erskine of the secondary literature. To understand that Erskine, one must examine Donald Fraser's seminal 1831 work, *The Life and Diary of the Reverend Ebenezer Erskine, A.M. of Stirling, Father of the Secession Church*. In that work, one finds the portrait of Erskine and the narrative of his life that have retained unquestioned authority ever since their publication. Indeed, Fraser's work has been so formative that all subsequent accounts of Erskine amount to

---

7. Erskine, *Sermons and Discourses*; *Works*, respectively.

little more than extrapolations of, and reflections upon, that account. In many respects, this prominence of Fraser's work is understandable. Fraser, as Ebenezer Erskine's great-great-nephew, enjoyed unparalleled access to personal papers and family accounts of his ancestor that have long since been either lost or destroyed.[8] Among these vital sources were a series of personal diaries that Erskine sporadically kept throughout his life and multiple letters that Erskine either authored or received from others. Fortunately, Fraser recorded many of these papers *verbatim* in his account, thus providing a glimpse of Erskine that would be simply unavailable in the absence of Fraser's work.

While Fraser is thus a central asset to any Erskine scholarship, he also stands as the foremost barrier to an accurate understanding of his ancestor; a hindrance rooted in Fraser's own temporal and controversial context. In 1820, only eleven years prior to the publication of Fraser's work, the ecclesiastical descendants of the Burghers and the anti-Burghers, who split acrimoniously in Erskine's own lifetime, had reunited to form the United Associate Synod, a body that itself was defined by a "New Licht" perspective on Covenantal obligations.[9] Given Fraser's resulting synodical and personal commitments, it is perhaps not surprising to find that, in his account, Fraser offers an inaccurate picture of the Breach that produced the newly-healed rupture and wholly omits references to, and discussions of, documents that show Erskine to have held views on the Covenants and on establishment dissonant with those of the United Associate Synod.

Although Fraser's ecclesiastical setting thus corrupted his presentation of Erskine, that presentation was even more compromised by Fraser's temporal setting. As John McIntosh argues, the flood of ecclesiastical literature that emerged in the nineteenth century was fundamentally preoccupied with the burgeoning dissension within the Established Church that would lead to the Ten Years' Conflict in 1834 and, finally, the Disruption in 1843.[10] As part of this preoccupation, Church historians sought, at all costs, to establish a continuity between their personal tradition and the historic evangelical wing of the Established Church, particularly as that evangelical camp stood opposed to the Moderate party of the mid-eighteenth century, a party which historians simultaneously attempted to link to their contemporary

---

8. Even as early as 1900, these papers had become unavailable to researchers. See MacEwen, *Erskines*, 7; *Life*, 341. Fraser was the great-grandson of Ebenezer's brother, Ralph. For the exact details of Fraser's descent, see the chart in Scott, *Genealogy*, 46–47.

9. See *Life*, 446–48; M'Kerrow, *History*, I.271–72; Hamilton, "United Secession Church," 841. For the Confessional views of the United Associate Synod, see Hamilton, *Erosion*, 15–18.

10. McIntosh, *Theology*, 27–31.

adversaries. In this effort that was as much polemical as historical, nineteenth-century writers homologated eighteenth-century controversies with nineteenth-century disputes in such a way that the finer points of eighteenth-century positions were entirely obscured. For Fraser and other Secession writers, this situation was further complicated by the simple fact of the Secession. If the mounting turmoil in the Established Church were to issue in the excision of an evangelical party from the body of the General Assembly, and the United Associate Synod was to have any chance of union with that new evangelical body, there was an urgent need to present the causes and course of the Secession in such a way that that split could be easily overcome one hundred years later. To achieve this pacification of the Secession Crisis, there were few more effective means than the historiographical rehabilitation of Erskine, the *"Father of the Secession Church."* In the work of Fraser and his contemporaries, this rehabilitation chiefly assumed three characteristics. First, the *Marrow* controversy was portrayed simplistically as a decades-early adumbration of the theological fissure that would occur between evangelicals and the Moderate party later in the century.[11] Second, the place of patronage in the Secession Crisis was grossly overemphasized. Third, the Secession historians posited the existence of a pan-presbyterian evangelical identity that, even after Erskine's deposition in 1740, held out the potential of common cause, or even full reunion, between the Secession Church and the evangelicals who remained within the Established Church. By means of the first two characteristics, the Seceders were portrayed as century-long warriors against the same enemy that the Established Church evangelicals were fighting in the nineteenth century, while the third characteristic suggested that Erskine's Secession never had been so categorical as to preclude easy union a century later. That such a union was the goal of the Secession historiography was at times even made explicit.[12]

11. For an example of how this influenced later interpreters, see Watt, "Erskine," 110–11.

12. The opening note to the third edition of M'Kerrow's work clearly states: "[T]he interest thrown over the relations of church and state by the recent separation of the free church from the national establishment, upon grounds differing little if at all in principle, from those which led to the secession of last century, although under circumstances otherwise very dissimilar, and the approximation, already effected in feeling, and evidently progressing towards incorporation, betwixt these two great bodies of dissenters, have induced the publishers to put forth the present edition of the history of the secession church" (M'Kerrow, *History*, 3rd ed., xvii). Unless otherwise noted, subsequent references to M'Kerrow will be to the first, 1839, edition. The third edition was simply a republication of M'Kerrow's first two editions and a combination of a previous two-volume work into one larger volume. It is telling that M'Kerrow's work, still the definitive history of the Secession, and thus a leading authority on Erskine personally, was understood as having this end in view.

Pressed by the compulsion to both maintain and seek union with men who were the ecclesiastical sons of Erskine's opponents, Fraser repeatedly capitulated to the temptation of smoothing the edges on Erskine's rhetoric and doctrine. What makes this disingenuousness even more regrettable is that Fraser's presentation of Erskine has been imbibed unquestioningly by generations of subsequent Erskine interpreters. The view that Fraser presented, they have presented. The portions of Erskine's thought and the specimens of Erskine's writing that Fraser had omitted, whether through ignorance or by design, they have omitted.[13] As a result, the Erskine of the secondary literature is Fraser's Erskine. While theological or historical revision certainly should not be undertaken for revision's sake, the pervasive influence of Fraser's biases dictates that, at many points in the following treatment, the Erskine of the secondary literature be revised. To seek an accurate understanding of that revised Erskine, it is necessary to start at the beginning, with Erskine's earliest years and education.

Interestingly, the next major work on the history of the Secession after M'Kerrow's volume was Thomson's *Historical Sketch of the Origins of the Secession Church*, published in 1848. This work was bound together with Struthers's *The History of the Rise of the Relief Church* and published one year after the United Associate Synod and the Relief Church had united to form the United Presbyterian Church in 1847, a union that saw Confessional standards become even more relaxed than they had become in 1820. See Thomson, *Historical Sketch*; Hamilton, *Erosion*, 22–24. Secession history and analysis have ever been written under the shadow of union, and thus have been driven by historiographical concerns rather than by thorough assessment. For a succinct account of the course that church union efforts followed, see Ross, "Unions," 835–37.

13. E.g., Harper, *Memoir*, 88; M'Kerrow, *History*, 3rd ed., 818–19.

Chapter I

Early Life and Abjuration Oath Controversy

IN THE YEARS OF Erskine's early life and ministry, one detects many of the influences that would shape both the man who Erskine would become and the theology that he would promulgate. In the first instance, one sees the familial identity and the personal experience that would convince Erskine that Scotland's Covenants were hallowed entities that, in his own day, were ascending from repression to dominance. In the second instance, one encounters Erskine's pivotal conversion experience, an experience that seems deeply to have influenced the freedom that would mark his later evangelical federalism. Finally, Erskine is seen to join himself to a body of Kirk dissent that, in its re-emergence, both demonstrated and solidified Erskine's controversialist determination. In all of these glimpses into Erskine's formation, the Scotland that he inhabited would play an inimitable role.

SCOTLAND UNDER THE REVOLUTION SETTLEMENT

In 1690, Scottish presbyterians had great cause for rejoicing: after decades of persecution under the reigns of Charles II and James VII, the Presbyterian Kirk was again the legally established Church of the nation. While there was some dissatisfaction that the establishment was founded upon a mixture of the terms of 1592 and the popular will rather than upon the Covenanted heights attained by the Second Reformation, the accession of Thomas Linning, Alexander Shields, and William Boyd, the three remaining Cameronian ministers, into the pale of the establishment seemed to promise that

Scottish Presbyterianism was once again united and willing to work under an acceptable, if not ideal, arrangement.[1] Indeed, with the abolition of patronage and the purging of episcopalians from university posts, it seemed that the Kirk was well positioned for eventual victory in what still would be a long battle to remove the taint of episcopacy from the whole of Scotland.[2]

Despite the promise of 1690, there were two indications that the re-established Kirk would have to tread lightly as it sought to consolidate its power. In the first instance, William III's pragmatism on matters of establishment compelled him to desire a policy of comprehension toward all Scottish clergy—presbyterian or episcopalian—who would swear loyalty to him and renounce the Pretender.[3] Forced to accept a strictly presbyterian settlement of the Kirk, William would repeatedly seek, both overtly and covertly, to balance the presbyterians' power in order to preclude the kingdom-wide upheaval that would ensue upon an overly-zealous persecution of episcopalians.[4] Secondly, the Scots were viewed suspiciously by the "Revolution sentiment" that prevailed in England.[5] In contrast to English desires for stability following the "Glorious Revolution," the Scots' Solemn League and Covenant portended Covenanting armies crossing the Tweed and the contractual monarchy espoused in their Claim of Right seemed capable of plunging the kingdom into turmoil afresh.[6] The presbyterian Kirk was legally established, but it was also closely watched.

In the years following the Revolution, the Kirk clearly was aware of the need to proceed mildly. While efforts were made to consolidate the Kirk's establishment and to preclude future alteration thereto, the General Assembly was careful to assure William that it was acting generously toward episcopalians and presbyterian polemicists declined the supranational aspirations of the Solemn League and Covenant in favor of asserting only

---

1. See *AGA*, 224–25.

2. For the extent of the remaining battle, see Maxwell, "Presbyterian," 25–37.

3. See Glassey, "William II and the Settlement of Religion in Scotland," 317–25. Hereafter, "William II." See also Kidd, *Subverting Scotland's Past*, 51–52; Knox, "Establishment and Toleration," 336–37; and Maxwell, "William III and the Scots Presbyterians," 175. Hereafter, *Subverting*, "Toleration," and "William III," respectively.

4. See especially Glassey, "William II." On William's efforts, see Maxwell, "Church Union," 237–57. See also Burleigh, *Church History*, 263; Kidd, "Realignment," 158.

5. For the most thorough treatment of this "Revolution sentiment," see Kenyon, *Revolution Principles*, especially chapters 2 and 5. See also Knox, "Toleration," 335–36; Maxwell, "William III," 176–77. For the origins of this distrust under the Commonwealth, see Barber, "Scotland and Ireland," 195–221. See also Cowan, *Covenanters*, 25–26.

6. Kidd delineates "the black legend of Presbyterian politics" that underlay such fears. See Kidd, "Constructing," 5–6.

the particularist claims of presbytery within Scotland.⁷ Carefully and ponderously, the Kirk sought to fashion a presbyterianism that was both secure for Scotland and benign for England.⁸

ERSKINE'S EARLY LIFE AND EDUCATION

Due to a paucity of extant materials, relatively little is known of Erskine's early life and education. Born at Dryburgh on 22 June 1680, Erskine was the son of Henry Erskine, a Covenanting minister who, after being ejected from his charge under the Act of Uniformity in 1662, acquired a reputation for piety as he spent twenty-five years wandering with his family in the border regions of Scotland and England, being imprisoned several times until 1687, when he was freed from prison under the Act of Indemnity.⁹ After preaching within the bounds of Whitsome parish for several years, Henry Erskine was admitted to the parish of Chirnside in September 1690, only three years before his son Ebenezer would depart to pursue his education at the University of Edinburgh, beginning his course there in November 1693.¹⁰

The education that Erskine received at Edinburgh would have been marked by three chief characteristics. First, Erskine's education would have been self-consciously presbyterian in orientation. When Erskine matriculated in 1693, none of the six full professors on the faculty had held their posts prior to the purging of episcopalians that had accompanied presbytery's reestablishment.¹¹ Led by Gilbert Rule, Principal of the University and a noted apologist for the presbyterian cause, this new faculty would have insisted on the tenets and rights of presbytery. Secondly, Erskine's arts

---

7. For a representative exchange between the Assembly and William, see *AGA*, 222–23. For efforts at consolidation, see *AGA*, 260–61; Kidd, *Subverting*, 58–59; Kidd, "Constructing," 3; Lyall, *Presbyters*, 20. For the particularizing of presbytery's claims, see especially Kidd, *Subverting*, chapter 4.

8. See Kidd, "Protestantism," 328–29.

9. On Henry Erskine, see *Life*, 3–57; Pearce, "Erskine, Henry"; Wodrow, *Analecta*, 1:88–89.

10. *Fasti*, 2:34; Harper, *Memoirs*, 8–9. While preaching in Whitsome, Erskine was used in the conversion of the young Thomas Boston. See Boston, *Works*, 12:11–12. Sir Alexander Grant stipulates that, technically, throughout the seventeenth century, Edinburgh was a college, not a university. Grant, *University of Edinburgh*, 1:183. However, Grant's distinction is not generally followed in the literature and thus the name "University of Edinburgh" will be used throughout the present work.

11. The two senior faculty members, Gilbert Rule, Principal, and George Campbell, Chair of Divinity, had both been appointed on 26 September 1690. See Bower, *University of Edinburgh*, 1:425–27.

curriculum would have constituted a largely uniform educational experience for students of different academic years. Until the early eighteenth century, the University of Edinburgh continued to operate on the regent system wherein education progressed according to set Latin "dictations" and an underlying reliance on the orderliness of the syllogistic method.[12] Thirdly, Erskine's time at Edinburgh would have been pervaded by an emphasis upon personal piety, with both Lord's Day worship and catechism memorization fixed components of the curriculum.[13]

As Erskine and his classmates were receiving this broadly-characterized education, they would have been witnesses to an event which wins almost universal condemnation in the secondary literature. On 8 January 1697, Thomas Aikenhead, a student of divinity at Edinburgh, was executed for blasphemy due to statements he had made attacking the Trinity, the Incarnation, the authority of Scripture, and other central truths of traditional Christian orthodoxy.[14] With Aikenhead's execution still fresh in the popular imagination, Erskine graduated on 25 June 1697 and embarked upon his own course in divinity, also at the University of Edinburgh. This theological education would have followed largely the same pattern as had Erskine's undergraduate course, being structured around standard works of scholastic theology and bringing Erskine into contact with theological texts of generally accepted orthodoxy.[15] Working simultaneously as private tutor and chaplain to the family of John, Earl of Rothes, Erskine completed his divinity course and awaited an entry into the ministry as the eighteenth century dawned.[16]

---

12. During his years at the University, Erskine most likely was overseen by the regent Herbert Kennedy, of whom no record beyond his time as a regent remains. See Bower, 1:427; *Life*, 64–65. For more on the general structure of the regent system, see Shepherd, "University Life," 2, 11; Ferguson, *Scotland*, 98–99; Horn, *University of Edinburgh*, 23.

13. See Horn, *University of Edinburgh*, 23–25. As did most students, Erskine took extensive notes on both sermons and lectures that he heard. See Erskine, *Notebook 1694*. The notebook contains no continuous pagination.

14. See Devine, *The Scottish Nation*, 64; Wright, "Thomas Aikenhead."

15. See Boston, *Works*, 12:21; Ryken, "Scottish Reformed Scholasticism," 199. In a book belonging to Erskine and dated to 1699–1702, he provides a sample of some of the works he was reading: Stephen Charnock, *Discourses upon Regeneration*; Robert Ferguson, *Justification Onely upon a Satisfaction*; John Wilkins, *A Discourse concerning the Gift of Prayer*; Edward Polhill, *Speculum Theologiae*; Laurance Echard, *Ecclesiastical History*; Howell, *Elements of History from the Creation to Constantine the Great*; Edmund Calamy, *A Caveat Against New Prophets*; Turner on Providence; and Pierce, *Defence of the Dissenters in England*. See *Life*, 520–21.

16. *Life*, 65–67.

From the little that is known about Erskine's early life and education, it is possible to note two things. First, in his theological training, Erskine was exposed to a broadly uniform body of accepted Scottish theology. Unlike some contemporaries, Erskine did not receive his theological education abroad; rather, he was educated in Scotland itself, where the regent system ensured marked uniformity of exposure and restricted the influence of novelty or even of the specific personalities or predilections of individual faculty members.[17] The influences that shaped Erskine's theological education would have been shared by a large body of other ministers trained in the late seventeenth and early eighteenth centuries. Secondly, Erskine's early life and education would have instilled in him a hopeful expectation that Scotland would regain her former Covenanted glories. After being reared by a harried and wandering conventicler, Erskine went on to be educated in an Edinburgh where a resurgent presbyterianism had reclaimed the University at which he studied and the churches in which he worshipped.[18] In the actions against Aikenhead, Erskine even had seen State power employed not to persecute his father, but to dispel Socinian heresy. While a mature Erskine later would observe falterings in the Scotland of the immediate post-Revolution era, the Erskine who left Edinburgh for the parish ministry in 1703 doubtlessly entertained hopes that the positive trajectory of the nation and her Kirk would continue until the Covenanted attainments for which his father had suffered were attained afresh.

EARLY MINISTRY IN PORTMOAK

When Erskine did leave Edinburgh, he moved north to the rural parish of Portmoak, located across Loch Leven from Kinross.[19] The congregation there had voted unanimously to call Erskine on 26 May 1703 and, after an initial hesitation, he eventually acquiesced to the call and was ordained and installed on 22 September 1703.[20] Provocatively, Erskine judged that it

---

17. In the late seventeenth and early eighteenth centuries, a considerable number of Scots received their theological training abroad, particularly in Holland. For an account of the importance of Dutch influence on Scotland in that period, see Whatley, *The Scots and the Union*, 72–82.

18. MacEwen, *The Erskines*, 25.

19. The parish of Portmoak is occupied by the present-day towns of Scotlandwell and Kinnesswood.

20. Despite speculation in the secondary literature, there is no reliable indication of the reasons for Erskine's initial hesitance in accepting Portmoak's call. See *Records of the Presbytery of Kirkcaldie from October 11, 1693–April 13, 1704, Vol. 2d*, 357–58. Hereafter, *Presbytery of Kirkcaldy 1693–1704*. For common speculations, see *Life*, 73,

was in these early years at Portmoak that he was converted from a legalistic religion to the true faith of Christianity. In 1708, fully five years after his ordination, Erskine overheard a spiritual conversation between his wife, the former Alison Turpie, whom Erskine had married in 1704, and his brother Ralph and, through the agency of that overheard conversation, Erskine's heart was made to "give a consent" to Christ on 26 August 1708.[21] In Erskine's estimation, the change that occurred was so categorical that, had he died prior to that day, "I make not the least question but I had perished eternally."[22]

While all subsequent biographical accounts of Erskine's life have dated his conversion to this relatively late date, and therefore made his previous ministry little more than a spiritual fabrication, there is important primary evidence that broadens considerably one's understanding of Erskine's spiritual state in the early years of his ministry.[23] In a personal notebook, Erskine preserved, in his own hand, a letter he had received from the Reverend James Hog in 1696 in reply to a letter that Erskine had sent to him. After summarizing the content of Erskine's letter, Hog proceeded to address the central burden of that letter—Erskine's struggle with assurance. Throughout his lengthy letter, it is clear that Hog assumes himself to be writing to one who is a sincere, if young, Christian; an assumption made explicit when Hog comments that, after spending considerable time communing with Erskine, he judges that "there are fair probabilities, & (I doubt not) more than these" for believing that a saving foundation already had been laid in Erskine's heart.[24] In the estimation of a renowned pastor twenty-two years his senior, Erskine was a genuinely converted Christian as early as 1696.

Taken in tandem, Erskine's conviction of a late conversion and Hog's persuasion of a considerably earlier one present a clearer picture of Erskine's spiritual state and disposition in the formative first years of his ministry. Speaking tentatively, it is possible to suggest that as early as the mid-1690s, Erskine had been of a sincere, if weak, Christian faith and that in August 1708, he received experiential confirmation of the faith that he had had for over ten years. Heavily indebted to the Puritan conception of conversion as a protracted process culminating in a definite moment of spiritual liberty and joy, Erskine's own conversion process contained both times of spiritual

---

78; MacEwen, *The Erskines*, 31; Harper, *Memoir*, 11–12.

21. *Life*, 84. See also *Life*, 83–85.

22. *Life*, 85–86.

23. For anecdotal "proof" for a late date for Erskine's conversion, see Lachman, "Erskine, Ebenezer," in *DNB*, 18:527; Mitchell, "Ebenezer Erskine," 150–51.

24. Erskine, *Notebook 1694*.

doubting and of certainty of salvation.²⁵ Whether the definitive moment of that salvation occurred in 1708 or much earlier, one thing is certain; Erskine's own most personal religious experience would have convinced him that no amount of contact with gospel truth was salvific until it first was appropriated and applied personally.

With his ministry transformed in 1708, Erskine continued preaching and lecturing to his rural congregation, and reading broadly, while enormously important events were transpiring furth of Portmoak.²⁶

THE UNION OF 1707

In the years following the Revolution, Scotland's relationship with England, and with their shared monarch, had undergone periods of pronounced tension. Following the succession of Anne, William's heirless sister-in-law, to the throne in 1702, these tensions became focused on the question of succession and ultimately resulted in the proposal of the Treaty of Union in 1706.²⁷ In the earliest stages of debate over the Treaty, the specter of an incorporating union with episcopal England caused the Kirk to be the most potent Scottish opponent of Union.²⁸ Indeed, Kirk opposition was so sharp that some ministers' "continual preaching against union was believed in

---

25. See Pettit, *The Heart Prepared*, esp. 1–21.

26. For more on Erskine's performance of his pastoral duties, see *Life*, 186, 192; MacEwen, *The Erskines*, 37. For more on the general condition of rural Scots, like those of Portmoak, in the early eighteenth century, see Ferguson, *Scotland*, 70–74. For more on worship in the eighteenth century, see Sefton, "Revolution to Disruption," 65–78. Hereafter, "Revolution."

In his diary during these early years, Erskine periodically recorded the names of books he had found particularly profitable. The works thus listed are John Norton, *The Orthodox Evangelist*, cited on 21 December 1707; Laurance Echard, *Ecclesiastical History*, cited on 30 November 1710; John Owen, *The Glory of Christ*, cited on 22 December 1713; Blaise Pascal, *Thoughts on Religion*, cited on 26 January 1714; and Thomas Halyburton, *Life*, cited on 9 June 1714. See *Life*, 137–41.

27. Materials on the Union are legion. For a representative account, see Ferguson, *Scotland*, 36–69. For an important new modification, see Whatley, *The Scots and the Union*. On the matter of succession, see Kidd, "Protestantism," 331–34; Kidd, *Subverting*, 36–37; Knox, "Toleration," 349–50; Whatley, *The Scots and the Union* 1–3, 140–41, 206–7.

28. The Earl of Mar, a leading proponent of Union, judged that if the Treaty was rejected, it would be purely because of Kirk opposition. See *Report On the Manuscripts of the Earl of Mar and Kellie Preserved at Alloa House*, 1:315–16, 318–19. Hereafter, *Mar and Kelly Papers*.

government circles to be a threat to public order."²⁹ The image of civility that the Kirk had been cultivating since the Revolution threatened to implode.

The reasons for the Kirk's apprehension were rooted deeply in the Scottish notion of a National Church first articulated by John Knox and later systematized in the *Scots Confession*, the *First Book of Discipline*, the *Second Book of Discipline*, and the Westminster Confession of Faith.³⁰ Broadly speaking, this Knoxian view of a National Church held that the Church and the State were both divinely ordained institutions that were to work in tandem for the complete reformation of all areas of society, bringing that society into conformity with Scriptural norms.³¹ While the Church functioned as a prophet, preaching the gospel and counselling the State about the implications of God's Word, the State functioned as a righteous king, using the temporal power of the Sword to protect and advance the true Reformed religion.³² This Knoxian view of a National Church had been enshrined in the Covenants, both National and Solemn League, wherein a prophetic Church had joined with a protective State to pursue a wholly reformed society, both at home and abroad.³³ However, with the incorporating Union of 1707, this older formulation was brought to a crisis point. In its very essence, the Knoxian model was at pains to assimilate itself to a situation in which there were two National Churches competing for the ear of one civil magistrate. The simple existence of such a situation seemed to imply that neither the Church nor the State actually was fulfilling its proper function—as simply one of multiple voices, the Church could not function as an authoritative prophet, and by countenancing such a situation, the State

---

29. Devine, *Scottish Nation*, 9. See also Whatley, *The Scots and the Union*, 35, 260–61.

30. For a helpful discussion of Knox's Calvinian political thought, see Mason, ed., *John Knox on Rebellion*, Introduction. For a survey of approaches to the interaction of church and society dating back to the early church, see Fergusson, *Church*, 23–46. For an analysis of the *Scots Confession*'s stance on these issues, see Hazlett, "The Scots Confession 1560," 315–19. For an assessment of the *First Book of Discipline*, see Cameron, ed., *The First Book of Discipline*, 62–67. On the *Second Book of Discipline*, see Kirk, ed., *The Second Book of Discipline*, 57–64. For the affinity of the Westminster Confession of Faith with this tradition, see Fergusson, "Church," 118–19.

31. For a description of the breadth of this vision of reform, see Fergusson, *Church*, 114–15.

32. See Knox, *The First Blast of the Trumpet*; "A Letter to the Nobility in Scotland," in *Selected Writings of John Knox*, 371–434, 337–41, respectively.

33. The implicit presence of a Knoxian position is perhaps clearest in the National Covenant, as that document related more specifically to the relation of the church to the civil magistrate within one nation. See especially, "National Covenant," in *WCF*, 348–50.

would be failing to use its Sword to reform all aberrations in worship and discipline.[34]

The impasse thus created by the proposed Union was alleviated on 12 November 1706, when the Scottish Parliament passed the Act for the Security of the Church, or the Security Act, which made the maintenance of the presbyterian system of doctrine and government within the Church of Scotland an "essentiall Condition of any Treaty or Union to be Concluded betwixt the Two Kingdoms."[35] Almost instantaneously, pulpits that formerly were ablaze fell silent. Increasingly, ministers began to accept the reasoning that had animated many politicians since the Revolution and that William Carstares lately had been urging in support of the Union: the only sure way to prevent the return of a Stuart Pretender and combat the international ambitions of Bourbon France was to seek a closer and more formal union with England.[36] The modification to the Knoxian model that would be involved was inconsequential to the larger imperative of preserving the presbyterian structure of the Scottish Kirk. While some ministers remained opposed to the Union, the Kirk as a body was persuaded of the benefits of the Union and offered no objections when the Treaty formally went into effect on 1 May 1707.[37]

In this evolution of the Assembly's response to Union, two distinct strands within Kirk dissent emerge.[38] On the one hand, there were many ministers initially opposed to Union because of pragmatic concern for the security of Scotland's presbyterian establishment. Under the plan for Union, Scotland would relinquish her independent Parliament, which as recently as 1703 had acted as the last legislative barrier to English designs to force a measure of toleration on Scotland, thus leaving the Kirk defenseless not

---

34. Matters were worsened by the preponderance of English representation in the United Parliament, making it inevitable that the episcopal voice would be preferred if any dissonance occurred in that "united" voice. For more on the differences between a Williamite and a Scottish view of establishment that underlay some of the tension in this situation, see Knox, "Toleration." For some of the effects of the Williamite approach's pragmatism, see Allan, *Scotland*, 43.

35. In Donaldson, ed., *Scottish Historical Documents*, 277. For the legal procedures that underlay the Security Act, see Lyall, *Presbyters*, 21.

36. Such is the core of Whatley's provocative new thesis. See Whatley, *The Scots and the Union*, 5, 25, 29–30, 37–39, 58, 90–92, 264, 305. See also *Mar and Kelly Papers*, 1:315.

37. See *FIT*, 31–32; Stephen, "The Kirk and Union," 85; Burleigh, *Church History of Scotland*, 273; Whatley, *The Scots and the Union*, 36, 293.

38. For a brief, yet broad synopsis of the Kirk's reasons for opposition to the Union, see [Webster,] *A Second Defence*.

against a Catholic Pretender, but against a hostile Parliament.[39] For ministers troubled by these concerns, the Security Act was the lynchpin of Union. Without that Act, the presbyterian settlement of the Kirk was in danger and thus Union was unpalatable; with the Act, presbytery was secure and the Union could be countenanced, even with its modification of the Knoxian model for a National Church. The centrality of the Security Act to the alleviation of this concern ensured that that Act's terms would be guarded jealously in the future. The Kirk had had to extort the guarantees of the Security Act from a reluctant England, and it would be watchful in coming years to ensure that what had been given begrudgingly would not be rescinded assiduously.[40]

In addition to this protectionist concern about Union, some within the Kirk articulated an even more profound, Covenantally-based critique of the Treaty. Within this line of opposition, the initial draft of the Treaty of Union was not objectionable because it contained no guarantees for Kirk security; it was objectionable because it was a material renunciation of a Knoxian system, particularly as embodied in the Solemn League and Covenant.[41] In that Covenant, Scotland and England both had sworn to pursue the presbyterianization of the entire British Isles; under the terms of the Union, all people within the new Great Britain formally countenanced the episcopal structure of the Church of England. From this perspective, the Security Act was inconsequential; the Solemn League and Covenant had provided the framework for pan-Britannic unity and any agreement that receded from the full presbyterian unity and uniformity that it envisioned, even if it did protect Scottish presbyterianism, constituted a breach of Scotland's Covenant not only with England, but with God himself.[42] To this impulse of opposition to the Treaty of Union, there could be no remedy, and thus those

---

39. See Kidd, "Realignment," 162–63; Kidd, "Constructing," 1–2; Stephen, "The Kirk and Union," 71–72.

40. See, especially, Stephen, "The Kirk and Union". Furthermore, the anomaly of a multi-confessional state in the early eighteenth century, and thus the uncertainty that would have gripped Scottish presbyterians as to how the Union would proceed, is often overlooked. See Kidd, "Realignment," 145–46.

41. See Kidd, "Realignment," 156–57.

42. This commitment to presbyterianism, rather than a more general Protestantism, set this covenantal commitment outwith even the mainstream of religious unionism in the eighteenth century. See, for example, Colley, *Britons*, 11–54; Kidd, "Protestantism," 338–39. See also Kidd, "Conditional," 1149–50, 1153–55; Kidd, "Realignment," 156. See also Burrell, "The Apocalyptic Vision of the Early Covenanters," 21. Hereafter, "Apocalyptic."

who were animated by it remained unreconciled to the Union of 1707 long after that Union had been realized.[43]

In the actual debate over Union, these two strands of opposition to the Treaty seldom were held exclusively of each other. As demonstrated in a letter from John Logan of Alloa to the Earl of Mar, Covenantal and Constitutional strands of opposition to the Union were held and articulated in the closest of connections.[44] Rather than constituting different factions of opposition, they more properly represented differing motivations for opposition; motivations that held varying balances of influence in the opposition of individual ministers. The Kirk's eventual acquiescence in Union demonstrated that the protectionist strand was the more potent and influential basis for opposition within the Assembly.[45] The very presence of the Covenantal strand of opposition is equally important, however, for it shows that, after years of attempted civility and moderation, a voice of Covenanted dissent was once again heard within the mainstream of the Church of Scotland.[46]

THE ABJURATION OATH CONTROVERSY

While the Security Act had won the Kirk's assent to Union, cries of protest again were heard from Scotland when, in 1712, the United Parliament passed both the Toleration Act and the Patronage Act. While the latter Act's restoration of patronage in the Church of Scotland evoked strident opposition, the exact provisions of the Toleration Act caused a more immediate, and thus more prominent, crisis.[47] Under the terms of this Act, episcopalians were guaranteed freedom to worship in Scotland provided that they used the English liturgy, took the Oath of Allegiance, renounced Jacobitism, and prayed publicly for Queen Anne and the Hanoverian succession; only Roman Catholicism and blasphemy against the Trinity fell outwith the pale of legal protection.[48]

43. Whatley argues that, by the time of the Union itself, this brand of opposition was relegated to the Macmillanites. However, as will be seen, its influence was much wider than that. See Whatley, *The Scots and the Union*, 294.

44. *Mar and Kelly Papers*, 1:274–75.

45. See Kidd, "Realignment," 161–62, 165–66, 168.

46. See Kidd, "Constructing," 10.

47. For an example of opposition to the Toleration Act, see *The Case of the Church of Scotland, With Relation to the BILL for a TOLERATION to the Episcopal Dissenters*. For the roots of Scottish opinion on toleration, see Campbell, "The Scottish Westminster Commissioners and Toleration," 1–18.

48. On the Toleration Act and its precursors, see Whatley, *The Scots and the Union*, 323; Devine, *Scottish Nation*, 18–19; Ferguson, *Scotland*, 57–61, 110–11; Knox,

Despite its seemingly manifold violations of the Security Act, opposition to the entire Toleration Act began to crystallize around one specific provision thereof—the mandated swearing of the Abjuration Oath.[49] In 1708, the Abjuration had been imposed upon all Scots involved in military or civil service within the United Kingdom, and under the terms of the Toleration Act, all members of the Scottish clergy also were required to swear the Oath on or before 1 November 1712.[50] Anyone who refused to take the Oath would be removed from his charge and, if he attempted to persist therein, would be levied a fine of £500.[51] The imposition of this Oath not only threatened a confrontation between the Kirk and the State, but it also precipitated a violent division within the Kirk itself, with some non-jurant ministers refusing to take the Oath and jurant ministers arguing that it was not only permissible, but indeed requisite, that ministers comply in swearing the Abjuration.

In most secondary accounts, the Oath controversy is summarized by a synopsis of the terms of the Oath and a declaration that some ministers within the Kirk were willing to swear to those terms and some were not.[52] In actuality, however, the central issue in the Oath controversy was not whether the terms of the Oath were acceptable, but rather what the Oath actually meant.[53] As a writer of the day observed,

> Ministers only differ about the Sense of the Oath, and none take it in the Sense wherein others refuse it, nor do any condemn it

---

"Toleration," 354–55; Drummond and Bulloch, *The Scottish Church: 1688-1843*, 17–19; Burleigh, 274–75; Lyall, *Presbyters*, 21–22. To some presbyterians, the terms of the Toleration Act made it even more objectionable than the episcopalizing measures of Charles I. See *Some Thoughts, and Questions Upon the OATH of ABJURATION, and Act tolerating the English Liturgy in Scotland*, in 1712, 2. Hereafter, *Thoughts*.

49. For an example of the Abjuration being seen as representative of the entire Toleration Act, see *The Oath of Abjuration Displayed, in its sinful nature and Tendency, in its Inconsistency with Presbyterian Principles and Covenants; the Security it affords to the Church of England*, 16. Hereafter, *Oath Sinful*.

50. See [Wodrow,] *Oath*, 5–7. In 1708, many Scots had expressed scruples with the Oath that were almost identical to the ones voiced by the non-jurors in 1712. In order to allow these Scots to take the Oath in good conscience, the Parliament in 1708 had changed the wording of the Oath to remove any objections. However, when the Oath was reimposed by the Toleration Act in 1712, it was imposed using the original formulation and several attempts to use the amended version from 1708 instead of the older version were refused.

51. See *Life*, 220–22.

52. See, for example, ibid., 220–21; MacEwen, *The Erskines*, 53; Ferguson, *Scotland*, 119; Cowan, *Scottish Covenanters*, 142.

53. For a transcript of the Oath, see Appendix I.

as unlawful in the Sense wherein others declare they understand it and take it.[54]

To appreciate the nature of the Oath debate, one must examine the views of that Oath put forth by both the non-jurors and the jurors.

The Non-Juror Position

The non-jurant interpretation of the Oath, and thus their opposition to it, centered upon the word "as" in the text of the Oath.[55] In the non-jurant understanding, the Oath had the juror swear to support, maintain, and defend the succession precisely "as" that succession was stipulated in the English Acts most commonly referred to as the Limitations and the Entail. In this interpretation, the "as" was said to have a reduplicative sense, for it defined the succession as being not a succession in general, but rather the succession exactly as it was construed in the Limitation and the Entail.[56] The problem caused by this interpretation was that under the terms of those Acts, each future successor to the Throne was required to be a communicant of the Church of England and was required to swear the English Coronation Oath, in which he would swear to preserve the rights and privileges of all bishops within his realm.[57] By swearing the Abjuration, then, a presbyterian minister would be publicly aligning himself with the Church of England and vowing to not only the legitimacy, but also the supremacy, of that body.[58]

In the standard non-jurant argument, the problem with such a situation was two-fold. In the first instance, the Abjuration seemed to represent a manifest violation of the Treaty of Union's provision that Scots would not be forced to take any oath contrary to their principles. In the constitutional objection thus raised, the Oath undermined the Kirk's establishment and left no security against future, and more grievous, assaults. For many non-jurors, the Abjuration represented an undoing of the Security

---

54. *The Oath of Abjuration Considered, Both as to the Lawfulness and Expediency of its being taken by the Ministers of the Church of Scotland*, 22. Hereafter, *Oath Lawfulness*. The General Assembly realized the same thing. See *AGA*, 475.

55. See Appendix I. The "as" is placed in bold type for emphasis.

56. E.g., *Oath Sinful*; and [Wodrow,] *Oath*.

57. For a transcript of the problematic sections of the Limitation and of the Coronation Oath, see Appendix II.

58. For examples of such non-jurant argumentation, see [Wodrow,] *Oath*; *Oath Sinful*; *Some Reasons Humbly Offered, why the English Oath of Abjuration should not be imposed upon the subjects of North Britain, especially the Ministers of the Gospel there*; [Logan,] *The Oath of Abjuration Enquir'd Into*.

Act and other constitutional protections, a collapse that would leave the Kirk increasingly defenseless against an aggressive British State. In addition to this constitutional problem, there was also a Covenantal objection to the Abjuration Oath. In Scotland's Covenants, she had abjured prelacy and pledged, alongside England and Ireland, to seek the full religious uniformity of the three kingdoms under a presbyterian structure. In swearing the Abjuration, Scottish ministers thus would perjure themselves on both accounts. Not only would they countenance episcopacy by consenting that all future monarchs must be communicants in the Church of England, but they would renounce the Solemn League and Covenant's cherished goal of a pan-Britannic presbyterian uniformity. If presbyterian ministers swore that all future monarchs must be Anglican and must swear to protect the bishops, how could they then pray and labor for the day when all Britons would be presbyterian? In this Covenantal objection to the Oath, one clearly sees a festering discontent with the Union; indeed, the same objections that had been brought against the Union are recapitulated in relation to the Oath. Five years on, there was still a sentiment within the Kirk that was critical not only of the exact events of the Kirk's relationship with the State, but rather of the entire constitutional framework upon which that relationship was to proceed in a multi-confessional Britain.[59]

In most non-jurant writings against the Oath, it is these two objections that bear the weight of their argument, with the preponderance of emphasis being placed on the constitutional concerns. For the non-jurors, the situation facing presbyterian ministers if they should swear the Abjuration was dire. Constitutionally, they were endangered; Covenantally, they were perjured. In this, both an abiding, moderate, constitutionalist sensibility and a resurgent Covenantal dissent merged to array the non-jurors against the encroaching demands of the British State.

The Juror Position

In the jurant interpretation of the Oath, the exact meaning of the Abjuration was quite different. Rather than involving the juror in swearing to maintain that all future monarchs must be communicants in the Church of England, the Oath simply required them to maintain that all future monarchs must be Protestant.[60] In this construction, the "as" was seen as having a demonstra-

---

59. In his essay, Logan makes the connection between the Union and the Oath explicit. See [Logan,] *Oath of Abjuration Enquir'd Into* 1–2, 15.

60. For a representative example of the jurant position and refutation of the non-jurant position, see *Oath Lawfulness*.

tive rather than a reduplicative sense. Rather than holding that the succession to which one was swearing was the succession precisely defined in the Limitation and Entail, the "as" in the Oath merely indicated that the Protestant succession which the juror was swearing to maintain had elsewhere been addressed in those two Acts.[61] Therefore, the controversial particle, "as," was not intended to import into the Oath conditions and stipulations on the succession that were not mentioned expressly in the Oath. Rather, it was intended to indicate that the Protestant succession which the juror was swearing to maintain was nothing novel. In the jurant argument, this demonstrative sense of the Oath was necessitated by the Security Act, for any reduplicative sense to the Abjuration would be a violation of that inviolable constitutional guarantee. Thus seen in a more limited sense that was regulated by the Security Act, the Oath was not problematic and could be sworn safely by all ministers of the Church of Scotland.

The General Assembly's Decision

When the General Assembly 1712 convened, the matter of the Oath pressed upon them. In light of unrest within the Kirk over the Oath, the Commission 1711 had sent a representation to the Queen telling her that the scruples of some ministers required that they clarify the sense in which ministers would take the Oath. The Commission had then proceeded to describe the demonstrative, jurant sense of the Oath, limiting its reference to only a Protestant succession.[62] Shortly after this Representation was presented to her, Queen Anne, in her annual letter of 1712, wrote to assure the Assembly that in spite of what might be feared from the Toleration Act, "it is our firm purpose to maintain the Church of Scotland as established by law," and that the jurant sense of the Abjuration Oath described to her in the Commission's representation

> did so much manifest their loyalty and good affection to our royal person and government, and their true concern for the succession in the Protestant line, as established by law, that it could not but be acceptable to us.[63]

---

61. In *Oath Lawfulness*, 8–12, the author also demonstrates how, even if the express terms of the Limitation and the Entail were included in the Oath, they were not as offensive as the non-jurors alleged. However, the burden of his argument is to show that the fuller stipulations of these other Acts are not included in the Oath.

62. For a full transcript of the Representation, along with a similar Representation pertaining to the Patronage Act, see *AGA*, 467–71.

63. *AGA*, 460.

To many ministers, Queen Anne's letter was clear evidence that the jurors had been correct in their charitable construction of the British government's intentions and that the demonstrative, limited sense of the Oath was the only proper sense thereof.

In accordance with this perception, the Assembly voted, on 14 May 1712, to adopt the express words of the Commission, in their address to Queen Anne, as stating its own mind on the issue. In the view of the Assembly, this Address by the Commission gave a true and clear sense of the Oath that was acceptable for ministers to swear and that "appears to be intended by the said oath, as fully witnessed by her Majesty's foresaid gracious acceptation."[64] Using the Security Act as their controlling interpretive grid rather than as an instrument of protest, ministers were to swear the Abjuration in the demonstrative sense thereof.[65] However, some within the Kirk remained opposed to the Oath and to the Assembly's countenancing of it.

Erskine's Position in the Oath Controversy

Traditionally, the Erskine historiography has held that Erskine did not enter into the Oath controversy overtly outside of forced non-juration and occasional sermonic references to the matter.[66] Such a perception undoubtedly is traceable to Fraser's failure to mention any other Erskinite contributions to the controversy and his unmistakable implication that a young and timid Erskine took a stand against the Oath only out of necessity.[67] However, Erskine's involvement in the Oath controversy and his contribution to the non-jurant cause were both much more extensive than has been hitherto acknowledged.

In 1713, while the controversy was raging still, a letter written by Erskine critiquing the Oath was published anonymously and circulated widely.[68] That this pamphlet, entitled *An Essay Upon the Design, the Reference, the Penalty and Offence of the Abjuration Oath, in a Letter to a Presbyterian Minister*, is attributable to Erskine appears from the controversy that followed the much later *Marrow* affair. In 1726, an anonymous pamphlet entitled *Marrow-Chicaning Displayed; In a Letter to the Reverend Eben-Ezer*

---

64. *AGA*, 475. See also *AGA*, 460–61, 477.
65. *AGA*, 473–75.
66. E.g., *Works*, 1:15, 30.
67. See *Life*, 220–29.
68. See Marrow-Chicaning, *DISPLAYED; IN A LETTER TO THE Reverend Mr. EBEN-EZER ERSKINE, Minister of the Gospel at* Portmoak, 12. Hereafter, *Marrow-Chicaning*.

Erskine, Minister of the Gospel at Portmoak was published during the sitting of the General Assembly, attacking Erskine personally for his involvement in the *Marrow* controversy.[69] In the course of that pamphlet, reference is made twice to an earlier anti-Oath publication by Erskine. While the name of the publication is not cited, the two references to it cite exact words and heads of argumentation that it contains.[70] Both of these detailed references are to be found in the *Essay* in question.[71] Furthermore, following the publication of *Marrow-Chicaning*, both Erskine and the anonymous author of a pamphlet entitled *The Viper Shaken Off Without Hurt into the Fire* refuted *Marrow-Chicaning*'s individual charges in an effort to clear Erskine's name.[72] In both Erskine's self-defense and the anonymous *Viper*, there is no mention of *Marrow-Chicaning*'s attribution of a published non-jurant work to Erskine. In 1726, Erskine was still under judicial scrutiny for allegedly failing to show mutual forbearance to his jurant brethren in the course of the Oath controversy, and thus it is reasonable to assume that, had Erskine not authored a published work on the Oath, both he and his defender would have argued as much in order to remove any insinuation that Erskine had sought to assail his jurant brethren in print. In light of *Marrow-Chicaning*'s precise citations of a non-jurant work by Erskine and the absence of any exception to that claim in both Erskine's own advertisement and *Viper*, it appears that Erskine actually did author a published work on the controversy. As the specific references contained in *Marrow-Chicaning* coincide with the *Essay*, it appears that the *Essay* is Erskine's written contribution to the Oath debate.[73]

Although the *Essay* was not published until 1713, the contents of that work indicate that it actually was written sometime between mid-May and late October of 1712, precisely the months in which the deadline for swearing the Abjuration loomed.[74] As a means of explicating his stance on the impending Oath, Erskine explains that he will "descend particularly upon

---

69. The author of the pamphlet was widely regarded to be James Adams of Kinnaird, writing at the instruction of Alexander Anderson. See Lachman, *Marrow*, 236, 432–33.

70. See *Marrow-Chicaning*, 12, 16–17, respectively.

71. [Erskine, Ebenezer,] AN ESSAY UPON *The Design, the Reference, the Penalty and Offence of the ABJURATION OATH*, 35, 23–32, respectively. Hereafter, *Essay*.

72. Erskine's printed self-defense was included as an appendix in the anonymous work. For both, see THE VIPER *Shaken off without Hurt into the Fire*. Hereafter, *Viper*. See also Brown of Whitburn, GOSPEL TRUTH ACCURATELY STATED AND ILLUSTRATED, 110–11. Hereafter, *Gospel Truth*.

73. The English Short Title Catalogue also attributes this pamphlet to Erskine. While no reason is given for this obscure ascription, it presumably has been made for considerations similar to the ones presented here.

74. The publisher advises the reader that the letter was "*written some time ago.*" Erskine, *Essay*, 2.

such Scruples or Objections, as are most straitning and gravelling to my Conscience," scruples and objections which he says can be reduced to the four heads indicated in the title.[75] In the argumentation that follows, there is not much divergence from the standard non-jurant reasoning; if the persuasiveness of Erskine's presentation merited specific publication, the general lines of his argument most certainly did not. However, within this broad conformity to a standard non-jurant position, one detects the early formation of what later would become a robust modified Covenantalism.

In the first instance, Erskine's essay shows the young minister viewing questions of the Church-State relationship through the grid of Scotland's Covenants rather than of other constitutional guarantees. Although the normal non-jurant method of argument was to present a mixture of Covenantal and constitutional considerations against the Oath of Abjuration, with the latter normally having the pre-eminence, Erskine presents an almost wholly Covenantal argument. After establishing, at the outset of his argument, that the design of the Oath is to protect the episcopal English Church, Erskine rests the balance of his argument upon the sinfulness necessarily involved in countenancing a polity that has been abjured in Scotland's Covenants. Erskine does not concentrate his arguments upon the threat that episcopacy poses to presbyterianism, or the risk that the Church of Scotland might be under from English intentions to reintroduce episcopacy; rather, Erskine's overriding critique of the Abjuration is that it forces Scottish ministers to countenance that which they have abjured in their Covenants and even, Erskine implies, makes them active enemies to the Solemn League and Covenant's vision of a pan-Britannic presbyterianism.[76] Most often, when Erskine mentions the Treaty of Union or the Security Act, he does so either as simple recognition of diplomatic fact or in order to chide the jurant party that they are placing their trust for Church security in the fickle guarantees of man rather than in the abiding Covenant of God.[77] Although Erskine does recognize the diplomatic and constitutional realities of his situation, when he evaluates the status and the mission of the Kirk, his paradigm is almost exclusively that of the Covenants.[78]

While Erskine unreservedly embraces a Covenantal identity for the Church, this does not create in his argumentation any belligerence toward the uncovenanted British State. Although Erskine does countenance a

---

75. Erskine, *Essay*, 3.

76. See Erskine, *Essay*, 9–10, 15. For a possible, though passing, exception, see ibid., 5.

77. See ibid., 5, 23, 30.

78. See ibid., 31.

contractual view of monarchical government, both asserting that the ascent of the Hanoverians is proof that the succession is "elterable [sic—alterable] at Pleasure" and explicitly quoting from the Claim of Right, the predominant tone of his argument is much more submissive than radical.[79] Erskine freely concedes that the civil magistrate has a legitimate coercive power to which even ministers of the gospel must humbly submit "our Lives, our Estates, and every thing that pertains to us as Members of the Civil Society."[80] Indeed, within his own writing, Erskine evidences precisely such a submission to the British government, speaking deferentially of the Treaty of Union, the House of Lords, and the Hanoverian succession and asserting that disloyalty to a reigning government is the doctrine of Hobbes, Machiavelli, and Jesuits, but not of true presbyterians.[81]

At first inspection, Erskine's position can appear contradictory, coupling a primacy for the Covenants in determining the Kirk's standing in relation to the State with a deference to that State despite its uncovenanted status. However, Erskine's essay makes clear that he does not see the Covenants impinging upon questions of magisterial legitimacy. In the course of pursuing his argument concerning the reference of the Abjuration Oath, Erskine adduces the hypothetical situation of a Protestant living in Spain and thus subject to the Roman Catholic succession in that country. In considering the situation of this hypothetical Protestant, Erskine concludes that the Protestant could not justifiably swear to uphold a succession that he knew would remain Roman, yet he concedes that that same Protestant citizen could safely swear allegiance to the reigning Roman monarch.[82] In the propositions that Erskine thus adduces from his hypothetical situation, he maintains that Christian citizens must simultaneously render obedience to reigning magistrates who are hostile to the Reformed faith and use every endeavor to seek the reform of that magistracy. While this position itself is crucially important, equally important is that in his prescriptions for the Protestant Reformed Spaniard, Erskine implicitly identifies Scotland's Covenanted obligations with the biblical obligations incumbent upon all Christians. Throughout his *Essay*, Erskine's thought is permeated by the

---

79. Ibid., 11. See also ibid., 23. Erskine also repeatedly uses radical language. See, for example, ibid., 10, 17.

80. Ibid., 25.

81. See ibid., 5; 15–16; 35; 14, respectively. Erskine's reference to Hobbes likely is an appeal to "Revolution sentiment." In the post-Revolution era, Hobbes's views on government were distrusted because of their contractual, non-theistic foundation. See Kenyon, *Revolution Principles*, 16–17, 63. For more on the religious implications of Hobbes's political theory, see Tuck, Introduction to *Leviathan*, xxxviii–xliv.

82. See Erskine, *Essay*, 17–18.

assumption that Covenanted Scots must render obedience even to the uncovenanted Hanoverians, yet his opposition to the Abjuration Oath demanded that Covenanted Scots decline an Oath that would implicate them in assisting the succession of another uncovenanted monarch. In other words, Erskine consistently assumes that the Covenanted obligations of the Scots are precisely that of the Protestant Spaniard in his example; a Spaniard who is an uncovenanted Protestant living in an uncovenanted State. For Erskine, the co-existence of a Covenanted Kirk alongside an uncovenanted State was possible because the Covenants did not create extra-biblical categories of responsibility; rather, they simply added an additional solemn weight to the responsibilities that already resided upon all Christians. While the Covenants were determinative for the Church, their presence did not alter the legitimacy of the civil magistrate or the Christian's duty to submit thereto. Although Erskine did not address their provenance, the decisive factors for these matters evidently rested elsewhere.

While the overall structure provided by this nascent modified Covenantalism was thoroughly Knoxian, with the State aiding a prophetic Church in the quest for societal righteousness, Erskine's system seemed to create as many questions as it answered.[83] How could the Kirk be guided by the Covenants and yet embrace a civil magistrate that categorically rejected them? By basing such engagement upon a reduction of Scots' Covenanted obligations to a codification of pre-existing biblical obligations, was Erskine not materially altering the Covenants of the seventeenth century? If the Covenants did not influence the civil magistrate's legitimacy, from whence did that legitimacy originate? Practically speaking, while Erskine's modified Covenantalism proved to be an effective weapon of protest, was it actually coherent if called upon to guide the National Church rather than merely voice dissent from within the current, differently-structured, Kirk? As the view of Erskine and his fellow Covenantal dissidents remained a minority position within the Kirk, they were able to avoid having to articulate these and other of the finer points of their system. Rather than a cogent model for the Kirk, Erskine's modified Covenantalism represented a profoundly critical assessment of the present National Church that went beyond specific contentious issues to question both the basis for the Kirk's status as the Established Church and the ultimate goal of the Kirk's actions.

---

83. For the Knoxian emphases of Erskine's essay, see ibid., 22–25, 27–30, 34.

Erskine's Actions in the Oath Controversy

As Erskine's Covenantal opposition to the Oath seemed to make a confrontation with the government inevitable, the approach of the deadline to swear the Abjuration filled Erskine with great apprehension. This internal turmoil is evident as early as 13 April 1712 in a letter written to his sister, Jean Balderston.[84] In that letter, Erskine laments the "reeling and perplexing times" that are besetting the Kirk, judging that

> The dragon seems this day to be casting out a flood of wrath and malice against the woman, and the remnant of her seed. All the power and policy of hell is set to work for the ruin and overthrow of the Church of Scotland.[85]

In the trials that thus seem imminent, Erskine expresses his great anxiety that

> I know not how I shall be able to stand the storm itself, or how I shall do in the swellings of Jordan.... I would gladly know what our ministers are thinking or doing anent this Oath of Abjuration, which is to be imposed on us; although, through grace, I resolve not to make any man my standard, but my own light my rule in this matter. And, truly, as to any light I have as yet about it, I durst not adventure to take it, though I should be driven with my small family to beg my bread.[86]

Interpreting his current situation in the vague apocalyptic imagery of Revelation 12, Erskine clearly understood the impending confrontation over the Oath as an assault by Satan upon the Kirk; an assault that Erskine is sure will bring a persecution upon Christ's faithful servants so severe that he fears he may not be able to withstand it.[87] As the imposition of objectionable

---

84. Erskine frequently corresponded with Mrs. Balderston. While she actually was his half-sister, Erskine always referred to her simply as his sister. See Scott, *Genealogy*, 50; Harper, *Memoir*, 9.

85. *Life*, 162–63.

86. *Life*, 163.

87. Although Erskine directly equates the Oath controversy with the events of Revelation 12:13–17, it is impossible to read any apocalyptic precision into his reference. James Durham, the only authority on Revelation ever personally cited by Erskine, assigned the prophecy's reference to a time of doctrinal persecution sometime between 310 and 606 AD, while Erskine clearly is speaking of physical persecution in 1712. See Durham, *A COMMENTARIE Upon the BOOK of the REVELATION*, 445–65, 670–71. As Erskine's reference to Revelation 12:13–17 is dissonant with the interpretation of his preferred authority on Revelation, and as Erskine never applies that prophecy to the Oath controversy again, one must conclude that his description of his situation in

oaths had served as the pretext for the persecution of presbyterians during the Covenanting era, Erskine had good cause to fear that non-juration would carry a heavy cost; faced with the approach of that threat, Erskine was preparing himself for the suffering that would accompany it.[88]

On 30 October, only two days before the deadline for swearing the Abjuration, Erskine attended a meeting of presbytery at which he requested, and received, a supply to his charge until the court's next meeting.[89] Thus adopting a tactic used by other non-jurors, Erskine was able to avoid the deadline for swearing the Oath and observe how affairs would progress before preaching in defiance of the government. The situation that emerged under his watching eyes was quite surprising. In total, about one third of Scotland's presbyterian clergy refused to take the Oath.[90] Although the Kirk's detractors used this presbyterian non-juration as an occasion to accuse the Kirk of abiding political radicalism and even closet Jacobitism, London's studied unwillingness to interfere further in the affairs of a Scotland that already appeared on the brink of revolt led the government to ignore the strict penalties for non-juration and to extricate itself from the matter entirely.[91] After only one week away from his pulpit, Erskine was able to return.[92]

The government's withdrawal from the controversy transformed what had threatened to be a confrontation between Church and State into an internecine conflict within the Kirk. In this ongoing contention, Erskine continued to play an active role in the non-jurant cause, serving as part of a nationwide network of non-juring ministers who corresponded and held regular meetings in an effort to resist both the principles and designs of the Oath and those who had sworn it.[93] While the majority of ministers had sworn the Oath, the sympathies of the population largely lay with Erskine and his fellow non-jurors, and the resulting unrest threatened to

---

these terms in the present instance is intended to convey only a vague sense of Satanic assault and subsequent persecution and not a more precise apocalyptic or millenarian interpretation of contemporary events.

88. See *Life*, 221, 222.

89. *Records of the Presbytery of Kirkcaldie from April 13 1704 to Oct 1 1713*. Volume 3, 324. Hereafter, *Presbytery of Kirkcaldy 1704–1713*. See also *Life*, 222–23.

90. See *Life*, 221; Kidd, "Conditional," 1152. See also THE HISTORY AND ARGUMENT OF THE Scots Presbyterians, 4. Hereafter, *History and Argument*.

91. For Erskine's dismissal of charges of Kirk Jacobitism, see Erskine, *Essay*, 29–30, 35. See also Kidd, "Constructing," 11–12; Ferguson, *Scotland*, 61–62.

92. Such is evident from a letter written by Erskine to John, Earl of Rothes on 6 November 1712. For a transcript of the letter, see *Life*, 68–69.

93. Wodrow, *Analecta*, 2:128. At a meeting held on 5 December 1712, Wodrow estimates that there were approximately sixty ministers present. See Wodrow, *Analecta*, 2:121–28.

precipitate an open rupture within the Assembly.[94] Indeed, by 1714, popular disaffection for jurant ministers had even sparked a fledgling conventicling movement in the southwest of Scotland.[95] While annual Acts of Assembly failed to defuse the deepening antagonism between jurors and non-jurors, the course of national events precluded an open fissure.[96] With George I's accession to the throne upon Anne's death in 1714, the Jacobite Rising in 1715, and the Kirk's unflinching loyalty to the House of Hanover through such turmoil, the British State became even more prosaic on the Oath.[97] When a new version of the Oath issued in 1715 failed to remove the objections of Erskine and most other non-jurors, the government again neglected to impose the threatened penalties and seemed content to ignore the contentious matter in view of the Kirk's evident Hanoverian loyalties.[98] Internally, the Kirk soon was consumed with more alarming doctrinal matters, particularly those concerning John Simson, Professor of Divinity at Glasgow University, and thus after 1715, the Oath is not mentioned again in the formal Acts of the Assembly. While disagreement on the Oath might not have ended, open contention over it had.

The Re-Emergence of Erskine's Opposition

For Erskine, contention over the Oath was not to resurface until 1725, when he was arraigned before the Commission of the General Assembly for allegedly speaking against jurors in a sermon preached at Dysart on 7 October 1714 entitled "The Backslider Characterised; Or, the Evil and Danger of

---

94. The Assembly had detected this risk in 1712. See *AGA*, 476–77. Even the division that did exist was sufficient for Kidd to label the non-jurors as "a substantial semi-detached minority" within the establishment. Kidd, "Conditional," 1148. See also Cowan, *Scottish Covneanters*, 142; M'Kerrow, 3rd ed., 5–6.

95. See *AGA*, 489–90. See Kidd, "Conditional," 1150–51 for the abiding threat of a Covenanting rebellion.

96. See, for 1712, *AGA*, 473–75; for 1713, *AGA*, 482; for 1714, *AGA*, 489–90; for 1715, *AGA*, 499–500.

97. Erskine was among the presbyterian ministers who showed conspicuous loyalty to the Hanoverian cause even in the face of personal danger. See *Life*, 229–32.

98. When the 1715 version of the Oath was issued, Erskine initially expressed a willingness to swear it. However, he changed his mind before swearing the Abjuration and remained opposed to the Oath. For Erskine's explanation of this vacillation, see Wilson, *A DEFENCE OF THE REFORMATION-PRINCIPLES OF THE Church of* Scotland, 330. Hereafter, *Defence*. In his continued non-juration, Erskine was not unique among the original non-jurors. See *History and Argument*, 5, 11. See also MacEwen, *Erskines*, 53–54; Kidd, "Conditional," 1151–52. For the text of the 1715 version, see Appendix III.

Defection Described," and another sermon preached at Strathmiglo on 3 June 1714 entitled "God's Little Remnant Keeping Their Garments Clean in an Evil Day."[99] While other complicating factors were important in precipitating this later arraignment, the situation in 1714 to which they refer does offer insight into Erskine at this earlier point in his ministry.

In 1725, to refute the charges against him, Erskine published the full text of his contested sermons. In the preface to his sermon at Strathmiglo in particular, Erskine conceded that

> It is true, in the use of lamentation, I took notice of some who defiled themselves and the land by perjury, particularly in taking the abjuration-oath, with a design to serve the Pretender's interest. But that I spoke either of ministers taking or forbearing is false in fact; and I don't believe he will get any of that numerous company who will adventure to say so upon oath ... for my part, if the oath be a good thing, and if he took it with a good conscience, I cannot find anything in all that sermon that could militate against him, there being nothing in it so far as I know, but the pure and plain truths of God.[100]

In some respects, Erskine's protestation here is correct. In his sermon, Erskine addresses the Abjuration Oath and the sinfulness of it, yet he ascribes that sinfulness only to Jacobites who swore it with the intention of retaining their positions in the hopes of being able to aide a future return by the Pretender.[101] Presumably, sincere jurors who were opposed to the Pretender and persuaded of the demonstrative reading of the Oath were exempt from such pronouncements. However, Erskine concluded his sermon by warning his auditors that

> We should take heed to ourselves, even in the use of things that are in themselves lawful; many things are lawful, but everything lawful is not at all times expedient. Ye should shun

---

99. For the full text of these two sermons, see *Works*, 1:24–39; 1:1–23, respectively. Alexander Anderson, who brought the charges, also alleged that Erskine had preached against jurors in "The Humble Soul the Peculiar Favourite of Heaven," preached at Orwell on 27 July 1721. While that sermon contains a few references to "division," there is nothing that could be construed as applying to jurors and, given the date of that sermon, the references to "division" most certainly have a different referent. For the text of that sermon, see *Works*, 1:108–24. In 1731, Erskine's non-juration also was cited as grounds for withholding his ministerial stipend, yet such reasoning was regarded as a façade at the time. See Wodrow, *Analecta*, 4:215.

100. *Works*, 1:4–5 (preface). For Erskine's similar comments on his Dysart sermon, see *Life*, 225–28.

101. See *Works*, 1:15. Such references have in view jurant episcopalians.

EARLY LIFE AND ABJURATION OATH CONTROVERSY

every appearance of evil; do not stand in the way of temptations, or occasions of sin. And, in particular, take care to avoid evil company.[102]

Coming at the conclusion of a sermon that had clearly denounced the Abjuration Oath, the applicability here to jurors is unmistakable. Indeed, one of the standard arguments that jurors would adduce for their position was that there was nothing expressly unlawful about the Oath and thus they were free to take it.[103] Furthermore, throughout his sermon, Erskine lamented the sin of "defection," a word charged with meaning in the Covenanting idiom and, especially in light of Erskine's known Covenantal objection to the Oath, a word that could hardly be understood without reference to swearing the Abjuration, regardless of the motivations with which that Oath was taken.[104] In his sermonic references to the Oath, there is thus a level of opposition to the Abjuration that is obscured by Erskine's later self-defense. While Erskine did comply with the Assembly's calls for non-jurant ministers to invite jurant brethren to participate in communion seasons, he was also willing to preach against not only insincere jurors, but even sincere ones.[105] In Erskine's later self-defense, there is, correspondingly, a measure of disingenuity and a failure to own fully the implications of what he had preached.[106] As seen in the Oath controversy, Erskine was both resolute and potentially antagonistic in controversial matters.

IMPLICATIONS OF THE OATH CONTROVERSY

In the controversy surrounding the Abjuration Oath, three very different ideological commitments emerged within the Established Church. In the

---

102. *Works*, 1:23. Erskine also strongly implied that many who had sworn the Oath had done so in order to avoid the penalty for non-juration rather than out of true principle, thus repeating a charge he had made in his *Essay*. See *Works*, 1:17.

103. E.g., *Oath Lawfulness*, 22.

104. Harper grasps the necessary connotations of such language. See Harper, *Memoir*, 35.

105. Erskine even invited Anderson to preach at such a communion season after their disagreement. See Erskine's letter to Anderson of 20 July 1715 in *Life*, 228–29. There is no indication of whether Anderson accepted the invitation. For communion seasons' development from religious occasions to potentially divisive partisan gatherings and the implications of such development for the Oath controversy, see Schmidt, *Holy Fairs*, 21–41, 112–13, respectively.

106. The same could be said of his later biographers. See, for example, *Life*, 225. Such tendencies lend credibility to critiques of Erskine's character such as those brought by Mitchell. See Mitchell, "Ebenezer Erskine," 165–66.

majority view that was willing to swear the Abjuration, one detects a willingness to trust in the constitutional guarantees of the Treaty of Union and, based upon that trust, to permit a degree of State initiative with relation to the Church that would appear alarming in the absence of that Treaty. From this integrationist perspective, the Treaty of Union provided the secure statement of intention upon which trusting engagement with the British State could proceed. In the second ideological strand, one sees a determination to protect the Kirk against the encroachment of a British State that is viewed with a great degree of suspicion. The result of such a strand was the constitutionalist objection to the Oath. Within this constitutionalist paradigm, the guarantees of the Treaty of Union were seen as hard-won protections that must be carefully guarded or else they would be rescinded subtly by a shrewd United Parliament. In the final ideological trend, as embodied in the Covenantal objections to the Abjuration, one glimpses a far more radical critique of the Oath and of the United Parliament that had imposed it. While this Covenantal stance allowed for loyalty to the Hanoverian succession and submission to the lawful commands of the United Parliament, it fundamentally rejected the functional basis for the Union and, thus, for State interaction with the Kirk. The purpose of that interaction was not to be the maintenance of a presbyterian Kirk and a Reformed Scotland within a multi-confessional British State; the purpose was to be the furtherance of Covenanted reform, both in Scotland and in all of the United Kingdom. The specific exigencies of the Oath controversy had brought the constitutionalist and Covenantal commitments into often inextricable harmony for a considerable minority party of the Church, yet that harmony and its opposition to the integrationist commitment was by no means necessary. Indeed, the constitutionalist stance shared a more profound commonality with the integrationist predilection than with the Covenantal paradigm. In both the integrationist and the constitutionalist ideological strands, there was an acceptance of a constitutional foundation of, and goal for, the Kirk's establishment; in the Covenantal impulse, there was a fundamental rejection of this constitutional idiom in favor of stringent Covenantal foundations and Covenantal goals from which the constitutionalist position demurred.[107]

While the Erskine historiography always has regarded the Oath controversy as an insignificant event in Erskine's ministry to which he was a passive victim rather than an active participant, that controversy and its unearthing of these ideological commitments was actually a formative experience for Erskine. In those tense days of controversy, a voice of Covenantal dissent regained prominence within the Kirk and Erskine found

---

107. See Wodrow, *Oath*. See also Kidd, "Realignment," 161–62, 165–66, 168.

himself at the center of that movement, employing the Covenants and not the Treaty of Union as his controlling paradigm for critique of the State. In that critique, Erskine enunciated a clear desire to see the Kirk navigate the exigencies of eighteenth-century Scotland by means of binding Covenantal obligations, yet by perceiving those obligations as differing in degree rather than in type from the obligations that rested upon uncovenanted Christians in uncovenanted lands, Erskine was able to recognize the existential and political realities of his day and uphold the legitimacy of the uncovenanted Hanoverian State. While the nebulous modified Covenantalism that resulted lacked satisfying definition in certain areas, one can see the emergence of a paradigm that differed importantly from the prevailing, constitutionalist paradigm of the General Assembly. In the crucible of the Oath Controversy, then, Erskine was able to refine his Covenantal perspective on Kirk matters in the company of many other ministers who shared the same commitments and the same desire to see those commitments guide the Kirk in her new post-Union world, yet Erskine and his associates were delivered by their minority position within the Assembly from having to articulate the nuances of this perspective or actually implement what appeared to be a system so rife with contradiction and imprecision that it would collapse upon itself. Furthermore, although Erskine's personal correspondence shows him forcibly summoning up the courage of a martyr, he and his fellow dissenters were allowed to defy the Assembly and the State with practical impunity, thus unavoidably confirming them in their dissenting perspective.

SUMMARY

At the close of the Abjuration Oath controversy, a definitive portrait of Erskine seems to have crystallized. Sent by a formerly-persecuted father to be educated in a newly re-presbyterianized Edinburgh, the foundational and still-dynamic presence of the Covenants at the core of Scotland's identity would have suffused Erskine's mind. Several years after departing that Edinburgh for the parish ministry, Erskine underwent a definable spiritual experience that, experienced from within the pastorate, instilled within Erskine the conviction that truth, no matter how often heard, must be personally appropriated. When this Covenantally-committed, evangelical Erskine joined himself to the non-juror cause in the Abjuration Oath controversy, the minister of an obscure rural parish showed himself unrelenting in his Covenantally-delineated stances. That Erskine was simultaneously solidifying other areas of his thought would emerge in the immediately-following years.

Chapter II

The Marrow Controversy

EVEN AS ERSKINE WAS still agitating over the Abjuration Oath, the first beginnings of an even more convulsive controversy could be seen within the Kirk. In that coming *Marrow* controversy, the evangelical warmth that Erskine had sensed in 1708, and that figures so prominently in positive portrayals of Erskine's life, came to the forefront of his ministry. However, as is the overall contention of the present work, that zeal was not determinative in shaping Erskine's position in the *Marrow* controversy. Rather, that zeal was animated by, even as it enlivened, an underlying doctrinal commitment. While the controversy over the Abjuration Oath had revealed the early formation of Erskine's modified Covenantalism, the *Marrow* controversy of 1718–1723 would disclose his evangelical federalism.[1]

In the decades following the Kirk's adoption of the Westminster Confession of Faith in 1647, varying emphases within Westminster federalism had emerged, yet had lain dormant through the distractions of the Public Resolutions controversy, Stuart persecution, and anti-episcopalian polemics. Faced with the demands of the early eighteenth century, these previously-unexamined developments and divergences were brought to light as previously co-existing emphases splintered into two explosively dissonant systems. Once the resulting *Marrow* controversy is situated in its immediate

---

1. In the secondary literature, there is some discrepancy between the usage of the terms "federal theology" and "covenant theology," with the choice of terminology often implying much about the author's perspective. The present work will use the terminology of "federal theology," intending thereby both the structural complexity of David Weir's "federal theology" and the soteriological characteristics of Peter Lillback's "covenant theology." See Weir, *Origins*, 3; Lillback, *Binding*, 26–28.

doctrinal and ecclesiastical context, these two systems can be seen through a comparison of Erskine's theology with that of James Hadow, whose prominence in the initiation and prosecution of the *Marrow*'s condemnation mark his doctrine as representative of the theological commitments that led to that condemnation.[2] Based upon this comparison, it is clear that Erskine's course in the *Marrow* controversy emerged from his particular appropriation and contextual application of an inherited Scottish federalism by which he sought to address the theological exigencies of post-Union Scotland.

SIMSON, AUCHTERARDER, AND THE MARROW

Since 1710, James Webster, minister of the Tolbooth Church in Edinburgh, had been concerned with the orthodoxy of John Simson, Professor of Divinity at Glasgow University.[3] In 1714, Webster commenced a formal process that resulted in Simson being brought before the General Assembly 1715 on a libel for heresy.[4] Finally, in 1717, the protracted process concluded when the Assembly, judging that Simson indeed had adopted and taught a disparate assortment of positions that were foreign to both Reformed orthodoxy and Scripture, prohibited the professor from preaching or teaching upon such matters in the future, yet allowed him to retain his position on the Glasgow faculty.[5]

On the very day which they rendered this sentence against John Simson, the Assembly 1717 also both considered and condemned what came to be known, pejoratively, as the "Auchterarder Creed." Perceiving, in Simson's errors, a growth of legalistic tendencies in the Kirk, the Presbytery of Auchterarder had begun requiring all candidates for licensure and

---

2. Speaking in reference to the Act 1720 that condemned the *Marrow*, Thomas Boston refers to Hadow as "the spring of that black act of Assembly." Boston, *Works*, 12:327. Lachman characterizes Hadow as "the chief opponent of the Marrow Brethren." Lachman, *Marrow*, 170. See also Harper, *Memoir*, 40; Wright, "Hadow, James."

3. For a brief biography of Simson, see Reid, *Divinity Professors*, 204–40.

4. The most extensive treatment of the controversy surrounding Simson is Anne Skoczylas, *Mr Simson's Knotty Case*. Hereafter, *Simson*.

5. For a complete compendium of Webster's charges and Simson's responses to them, see Simson, *The Case of Mr John Simson*. The secondary literature often simplifies the charges against Simson by saying simply that he was accused of Arminianism; e.g., Burleigh, *Church History of Scotland*, 287–88. While Webster did speak of Simson holding Arminian doctrine, he never stopped at such classification. See, for example, Wodrow, *Correspondence*, 2:176. For the Assembly's decision, see *AGA*, 518–19. Despite Erskine's outrage at the lenity shown to Simson, Wodrow intimates that any other decision would have thrown the Assembly into turmoil. See Wodrow, *Correspondence*, 2:266–69.

ordination to subscribe several articles in addition to the Standards of the Kirk, among which was the declaration

> I believe that it is not sound and orthodox to teach that we must forsake sin in order to our coming to Christ, and instating us in covenant with God.[6]

In this "Auchterarder Creed," the Assembly detected the antinomian tendencies that long had been feared in Scottish theology and thus condemned the declaration and summoned the whole of the presbytery to the meeting of the Commission in August to answer questions upon the matter.[7]

While it was almost uniformly conceded that the "Auchterarder Creed" was worded poorly, Erskine and others within the Kirk were troubled by its condemnation.[8] Their concern was heightened by the simple fact that the Creed was both initially considered and finally condemned in the course of one Assembly session, while the process against Simson and his troubling positions had been before the Assembly for fully three years.[9] Combined, these factors evidenced to Erskine and others precisely what the Presbytery of Auchterarder had feared—an insipid legalism within the Assembly. In an effort to bring greater clarity to such matters, Thomas Boston, minister of Ettrick, recommended the book *The Marrow of Modern Divinity* to several of his associates. The esteem that this work quickly garnered in such circles

---

6. *AGA*, 519. Boston judged that the specific errors of Simson had led to this concern over legalism. See Boston, *Works*, 12:291.

7. "Antinomianism" had figured prominently in Scottish "heresy lists" for generations, a presence that is notable in light of the absence of any significant indigenous antinomian movement. However, the Scottish sensitivity to antinomianism seems attributable to the fact that the flowering of the English antinomian movement coincided temporally with the Westminster Assembly. As a result, Scottish divines who served as Commissioners to the Assembly—most notably, Samuel Rutherford—would have imbibed the concern among English Puritans about the dangers of antinomianism and brought that concern back into Scottish theology through their writings. Indeed, it is in Rutherford's work that Scottish theology had its most notable effort to combat antinomianism. See, for example, Samuel Rutherford, *A SURVEY OF THE SPIRITUAL ANTICHRIST*. In his own lifetime, Rutherford had seen Arminianism filter into Scotland from England and doubtlessly was desirous to prevent a like infiltration of antinomianism. See, Richard, "Arminianism," 16–20. Presently, most scholarly accounts of antinomianism focus on England and New England, yet such accounts contain insights helpful for the Scottish context. For the best of these, see Como, *Blown by the Spirit*; Bozeman, *The Precisianist Strain*; and Stoever, *Covenant Theology and Antinomianism*.

8. E.g., *Works*, 1:76. See also Boston, *Works*, 12:291; Macleod, *Theology*, 156–57.

9. However, Wodrow also notes the relief of the majority of the Assembly that a matter as potentially divisive as the "Auchterarder Creed" was dispensed of so quickly. See Wodrow, *Correspondence*, 2:269–71.

led to the publication of an Edinburgh edition of the book in 1718, complete with a recommendatory preface by James Hog, minister of Carnock.

The appearance of the *Marrow*, initially published in 1646 by Englishman Edward Fisher and claiming to offer a middle path between antinomianism and legalism, quickly elicited the concern of many within the Kirk.[10] Foremost among those concerned by the *Marrow* was James Hadow, Principal of St Mary's College, St Andrews. In 1719, Hadow commenced a public attack on the *Marrow*, openly preaching against its doctrine before the Synod of Fife in a sermon entitled *The Record of God and Duty of Faith Therein Required*.[11] Largely taking its cue from Hadow and his sermon, the Assembly 1720 considered the *Marrow* and eventually condemned the work, citing five heads of doctrine on which the *Marrow* was unsound and dangerous.[12] These principle grounds of objection to what became known as *Marrow* doctrine were that it held assurance to be of the essence of faith; it assumed a universal atonement; it taught that holiness was not necessary to salvation; it posited that the fear of punishment and the hope of reward were not suitable motives to obedience for a believer; and it held that the believer was not under the Law as a rule of life.[13] In response to this condemnation, a group of twelve ministers, soon to become known as the *Marrow* Brethren or the Representers, submitted a *Representation and Petition*, initially prepared by Boston and revised by Erskine, to the Assembly 1721 defending the *Marrow* doctrine from what they felt to be groundless charges and demanding a repeal of the condemnatory Act of 1720.[14] To this *Representation*, the Commission of the General Assembly responded by

---

10. For the most thorough treatment of the *Marrow* controversy published to date, see Lachman, *Marrow*. For a succinct and, unfortunately, overlooked doctrinal account, see Buchanan, *Justification*, 182–88. For important new research on the polemical origins of the *Marrow*, see Como, *Blown by the Spirit*, 1–9.

11. *RoG*.

12. Boston intimates the importance of Hadow's sermon in establishing opposition to the *Marrow*. See Boston, *Works*, 12:317. See also Lachman, *Marrow*, 207–11.

13. For the complete text of the Assembly's condemnatory Act, see *AGA*, 534–36. The Assembly also cited six "Antinomian Paradoxes" in the *Marrow* and a host of "harsh and offensive" expressions in the work, but the burden of the charges and of the following controversy centered upon the five heads of doctrine that were alleged against the book and condemned.

14. See *Representation*. On Erskine's role in the *Representation*, see Boston, *Works*, 12:325. The twelve ministers who signed the Representation were: James Hog of Carnock, Thomas Boston of Ettrick, John Bonar of Torphichen, John Williamson of Innerask and Musselburgh, James Kidd of Queensferry, Gabriel Wilson of Maxton, Ebenezer Erskine of Portmoak, Ralph Erskine of Dunfermline, James Wardlaw of Dunfermline, Henry Davidson of Galashiels, James Bathgate of Orwell, and William Hunter of Lilliesleaf.

submitting twelve queries to the Brethren in an attempt to clarify points of doctrine, to which the Brethren responded in a lengthy treatise initially prepared by Erskine.[15] In addition to such formal offerings, the debate over the Assembly's condemnation of the *Marrow* also precipitated a flood of privately-authored pamphlets and treatises. Perhaps the most influential of these was *The Antinomianism of the Marrow of Modern Divinity Detected* by Hadow, in which the Principal firmly fixed the damning label of "antinomian" on the *Marrow* and its defenders.[16] Unanswered for over six months, this work by Hadow became authoritative for many and in the wake of its influence, the Assembly 1722 officially concluded the controversy by affirming the condemnation of the *Marrow* and rebuking and admonishing the Representers before the bar of the Assembly.[17]

THE MARROW CONTROVERSY AS A FEDERALIST DISPUTE

Traditionally, one of the most pervasive and most influential assessments of the *Marrow* controversy has been shaped by the Secession and Disruption historiography of the nineteenth century. In its attempt to forge an identification between the Representers and the evangelicals of the nineteenth century, this historiography portrayed the *Marrow* Brethren as the forerunners of later evangelical theology, while presenting the General Assembly as the headwaters of a defective theology that, in the Moderate party, would engulf the Kirk by mid-century.[18] In the present day, where there is less compulsion to see a "pre-Disruption" in the eighteenth century, this analysis still enjoys abiding influence, leading many commentators to see the *Marrow* controversy as a conflict between the evangelical Christianity of the Representers and a newer strain of theology within the Kirk that was at least legalistic and perhaps even Neonomian.[19] While the Representers themselves did sense a

---

15. See *Answers*. For Erskine's role in the preparation of the *Answers*, see Boston, *Works*, 12:333.

16. See *AD*.

17. For the full text of this Act, see *AGA*, 548–56. The authoritative nature of Hadow's work was enhanced by the endorsement of both Allan Logan, a widely-respected minister, and Thomas Black, Moderator of the Assembly in 1721. For the influence of Hadow's work, see Lachman, *Marrow*, 358–61, 480. For differing reactions to the specific nature of the Assembly's disciplinary action, see *Videte Apologiam*; Mechie, "Theological Climate," 266.

18. E.g., *Life*, 233–43; Buchanan, *Justification*, 184. For the effects of this historiography, see Watt, "Erskine," 110.

19. For examples, see Macleod, *Theology*, 139–66; McGowan, *Boston*, 42–45, 159,

marked legalism within the Kirk, the lingering Secessionist interpretation of the *Marrow* controversy is compromised by three considerations.[20] First, as the following account will show, while the theology of the Assembly might have been prone to legalistic emphases at times, it was far from "Legalistic." Second, by construing the *Marrow* controversy as a rehearsal for the dissension between the Popular and Moderate parties, this reconstruction places many leading opponents of the Moderate party in the "proto-Moderate" camp, a problem typified in the person of John Willison of Dundee. Although an undisputedly evangelical minister and a leader of the Popular party in the 1740s, Willison opposed the *Marrow* and, as late as 1744, insisted that the Assembly had been right to condemn it.[21] For Willison, the *Marrow* controversy was no staging ground for the dispute with the Moderates. Third, when taken to its spiritualized extreme, such an interpretation implies that in the years 1718–1723, there were only twelve evangelical, regenerate ministers in the whole of the Kirk; a number that excluded such notable evangelicals as Willison.[22] Despite the wishes of the Secession historiography and its adherents, the *Marrow* controversy appears to have been more complex than simply a confrontation between evangelical Christianity and formalistic religion prefiguring both the Popular/Moderate dispute and the later Disruption.

While the tendency to understand the *Marrow* controversy as a conflict between nascent Neonomianism and resurgent evangelicalism has marked the majority of the secondary literature on the controversy, the work of David Lachman constitutes an important modification to this thesis which has shaped the secondary literature in more recent years. In his exhaustive analysis of the controversy, Lachman rejects the presence of a definite Neonomian camp within the Assembly and concludes that the controversy sprang from the Representers' attempt to reclaim the language and theological emphases of an earlier era, coupled with the inability of the majority within the Kirk to understand fully that terminology and those emphases.[23] To substantiate his claim, Lachman documents the reliance of the *Marrow* Brethren upon theological works and authors of the pre-Westminster and Westminster eras, and the reliance of the *Marrow*'s opponents on works of

---

208.

20. *Representation*, 20.

21. See *FIT*, 43–44, 127–28.

22. This implication is especially strong in Philip, "Marrow," 36–37.

23. See, for example, Lachman, *Marrow*, 198–200, 488–89. See also Macleod, *Theology*, 143–44; Walker, *Theology and Theologians*, 89.

later theologians. This difference of influence had bred a difference of expression and emphasis that sparked the *Marrow* controversy.

When Lachman's assessment is viewed in light of Erskine's involvement in the controversy, however, it proves to be problematic for several reasons. First, and more generally, Lachman's thesis assumes an important discontinuity between the earlier Reformed thought supposedly adopted by the Representers and the later Reformed thought of the Assembly. While Lachman never argues explicitly for a theological discontinuity within the development of Reformed orthodoxy, his thesis rests upon a vital discontinuity of terminology and emphasis that must assume at least some larger theological disjuncture.[24] While the supposition of such a theological discontinuity within the Reformed tradition has been widely accepted for some time, the recent work of Richard Muller and others has cast some doubt upon such a thesis.[25] At the very least, one is unable to assume the discontinuity that lies, unexamined, behind Lachman's thesis. When this assumed disjunction is imported into Lachman's work, it establishes the General Assembly within the progressive evolution of Scottish theology, while relegating Erskine to a position predating the decisive disjunction, and thus decades out of date in the development of Scottish thought. As the present work will demonstrate, such a positioning is dubious. Second, while Lachman offers a commendable exhibition of the varied theological influences which were shaping the respective sides in the *Marrow* controversy, he largely neglects the common influences that they shared. Erskine's own exposure to theological literature serves as a microcosm for the problem that this causes. In a book belonging to Erskine and dated to 1699–1702, he includes extracts of several authors whom he was reading as he prepared for the ministry at Edinburgh University. In this assortment of authors, there is an even mixture of those from both sides of the temporal and theological divide that Lachman suggests.[26] When one moves to consider Erskine's sporadically-kept diary, in which he would occasionally record the names of favored books, this balance remains throughout the years leading up to, and including, the *Marrow* controversy; even, in the years of that controversy, including the same authors cited by

---

24. The implicit presence of this theological discontinuity can be seen at certain points in Lachman's discussion. See, for example, Lachman, *Marrow*, 11, 199; compare 486 and 491. McGowan and Philip detect the same underlying supposition of theological discontinuity in Lachman. See McGowan, *Boston*, 200–202; Philip, "Marrow," 33–35.

25. Representatively, see Muller, "Calvin and the 'Calvinists,'" 345–75; Muller, "Calvin and the 'Calvinists' (2)," 125–60.

26. The authors listed are Charnock, Ferguson, Wilkin, Polhill, Echard, Howell, Calamy, Turner, Pierce, and Turretin. See *Life*, 520–21.

James Hadow in his defining critique of the *Marrow*.[27] Simply stated, whatever was unique about Erskine's influences, it was always both co-existent with what was uniform for many in the Kirk, and it always grew out of a prior educational experience and exposure that would have been shared by scores within the Assembly. While there was certainly discontinuity, it was always rooted in a prior and larger continuity, and something within what was shared must have given rise to what was later contested. To attribute the *Marrow* controversy to that discontinuity, while neglecting that continuity, makes Lachman's thesis ultimately incomplete.[28]

At their core, both the traditional assessment of the *Marrow* controversy and Lachman's more recent analysis rest upon different constructions of the same hypothesis—that of a fundamental discontinuity within the stream of Scottish theology. In the traditional interpretation, this discontinuity takes the form of an attempt to import a foreign legalism into a Kirk that had always been strongly evangelical; in Lachman's assessment, this discontinuity is embodied by the Representers' efforts to re-appropriate earlier emphases that, while historically legitimate, were importantly dissonant with the contemporary theology of the Kirk. In either case, the *Marrow* controversy is seen as an example of discontinuity within the Kirk, whether that be a discontinuity precipitated by importation or by reclamation.

In considering Erskine's involvement in the *Marrow* controversy, a different view of the affair presents itself. In a letter that Erskine wrote to George Gillespie of Strathmiglo on 18 September 1721, he indicated precisely why he had become entangled in the contentious dispute. In that letter, Erskine disavowed any other motivations and stated that he had initially signed the *Representation*, and thus become embroiled in the *Marrow* controversy, in order to defend five core truths of the gospel that he saw to be damaged and

---

27. The authors listed are Pascal, Norton, Echard, Owen, Halyburton, Rutherford, and Traill. See *Life*, 118, 137–41. The latest references thus given are Rutherford, in 1720, and Traill, in 1721. In *AD*, Hadow's main extrascriptural authority is Rutherford, followed by the Westminster Standards, John Owen, James Durham, and Herman Witsius.

28. This problem is highlighted by a comparison of Hadow's *Antinomianism* with his earlier writings. In his *Baptism*, Hadow cited a breadth of authors, both Continental and otherwise, that has elicited admiration from subsequent theologians. See Hadow, THE Doctrine and Practice OF THE CHURCH OF SCOTLAND, ANENT THE Sacrament of Baptism, parts 1 and 2. Hereafter, *Baptism*. See also Cunningham, *Reformers*, 282. In *AD*, however, Hadow's citations are to a much narrower field of authorities, none of whom would have been unfamiliar to Erskine and many of whom Erskine himself cited regularly.

obscured by the Act 1720.²⁹ These obscured truths, as Erskine expressed them to Gillespie, were

> . . . That believers are freed from the Law as the Covenant of Works, freed both from the *commanding* and *condemning* power of *that* Covenant . . . .
>
> . . . That there is and ought to be a difference put betwixt the Law as the Law of Works, and the Law as the Law of Christ, or the Law as a rule of obedience in the hand of a Mediator . . . .
>
> . . .That when the law as a Covenant of Works comes upon the believer with the demand of perfect obedience, as a condition of life and salvation, his only relief in this case is, to plead the perfect obedience and complete righteousness of his ever-blessed Surety; and that this plea is so far from weakening him in the study of holiness, (as the Act imports), that it is one of the principal springs thereof . . . .
>
> . . .That there is a fiducial act or appropriating persuasion in the very nature of justifying and saving faith . . . .
>
> . . . That there is a deed of gift or grant made by the Father to all the hearers of the gospel, affording warrant to ministers to offer Christ unto all, and a warrant unto all to receive him, which yet does not lead us to the Arminian camp.³⁰

If Erskine's involvement in the *Marrow* controversy is to be understood rightly, then, it must be viewed through the lens of these five "obscured truths."³¹ When such a view is taken, it becomes clear that Erskine's involvement in the *Marrow* controversy was precipitated by a fundamental dissonance between his emergent evangelical federalism and the construction of

---

29. *Christian Magazine*, 376–81. Hereafter, *Christian Magazine*. It is not certain that the letter was written to George Gillespie, but such is the common assumption and the common method of referring to the letter. See Brown, *Gospel Truth*, 122–29; *Life*, 527–31. However, it should be noted that *Christian Magazine*, which was the original publisher of the letter, makes no indication of the letter's recipient.

30. *Christian Magazine*, 377. These same five doctrinal points, and Erskine's adherence to them, were also the subject of a concurrent controversy in the Synod of Fife, thus indicating their centrality for Erskine and their resonance in the larger *Marrow* debate. See Ebenezer Erskine, *God's Little Remnant*, xii. Hereafter, *Remnant*.

31. Erskine assured Gillespie that neither an undue reverence for the *Marrow*, which he considered a flawed work, nor his admitted personal loyalty to James Hog was decisive in his involvement. See *Christian Magazine*, 378–79; *The Records of the Synod of Fife 1719-1738*, 195. Hereafter, *Synod of Fife 1719-1738*.

federal theology forwarded by James Hadow, both of which were legitimate continuations of the Scottish federalism of the early eighteenth century.

The primary pressure that brought such sharp divergence out of a common theological tradition was the process against John Simson. As embodied in Webster's enumeration of Simson's errors, the Glasgow professor's opponents perceived him as mounting a fundamental attack upon Scottish federalism.[32] As a whole, each of Simson's errors stems from either his rejection of the federal headship of Adam, his expansion of the inclusivity of the Covenant of Grace, or his particular description of incentives and conditional means within that gracious covenant. In each of these tenets, the substructure of Scottish federalism was being either directly undermined or seriously questioned by Simson's rationalism, and such challenges to Scottish orthodoxy confronted a Kirk that was already striving for greater attention to theological detail in response to a perception that heterodoxy was infiltrating the Assembly through lax and insincere Confessional subscription.[33] The concern that resulted was evidenced in the Synod of Fife, of which both Erskine and Hadow were members, where this mixture of factors coalesced to create an extended Synod-wide debate over the nature of the Covenant of Grace.[34] In short, the Kirk of the late 1710s was a crucible of theological refinement in which both Erskine and Hadow were compelled to bring greater clarity and dogmatism specifically to their covenantal thought. For Erskine, this period of refinement, coupled with his suspicion of festering legalism, bred a decidedly evangelical federalism.

While the process against Simson affected the entire Kirk in many ways, both Erskine and Hadow would have had a particular interest in, and association with, the affair. As a close friend of the outspoken James Webster, Erskine would have known of the former's concern with Simson long before the Assembly 1715.[35] For Hadow, an ongoing struggle to combat

---

32. Wodrow seems to detect covenantal foundations for certain of Simson's alleged errors. See Wodrow, *Correspondence*, 2:258–61. See also Torrance, *Theology*, 230.

33. See Colin Kidd, "Scotland's Invisible Enlightenment," 28–59. Hereafter, "Enlightenment." For an example of the results of such attention, see *AGA*, 453–56.

34. See Boston, *Works*, 12:317. For Erskine's involvement in the debate, see *Life*, 234–35. Boston's description of this ongoing debate is brief, yet he links it inextricably with the publication of the *Marrow*, which he had earlier linked just as closely with the condemnation of the "Auchterarder Creed" and the Simson process, which he saw as the catalyst for that Creed. See Boston, *Works*, 12:290–92. The chronological, rather than thematic, arrangement of Boston's *Memoirs* necessitates the separation of these events, yet Boston's handling of them indicates that he judged them all to be related.

35. See *Life*, 207–8. On 23 January 1724, almost three and one half years after the death of his first wife, Erskine married Webster's daughter, Mary. See *Life*, 312–13. Webster had died in 1720.

the appointment of Alexander Scrimgeour, a lay episcopalian suspected of Arminianism and evasive of Confessional adherence, to the Chair of Divinity at St Mary's had made him especially keen to defend the exact nuances of Reformed orthodoxy.[36] Indeed, as the 1710s progressed, one can detect both Erskine and Hadow becoming more firm in their federal constructions and more insistent upon those particular constructions.[37] It is certainly no coincidence that it was in the gathering storm of the process against Simson that Erskine's handling of certain components of federalism saw important changes, nor that Hadow's response to the *Marrow*'s theology in the years following 1718 was so much more vehement than his response to the largely similar theology of Alexander Hamilton of Airth had been in 1711. The Simson affair had led both men to bring greater definition and insistence to their federal systems, which, although drawn from the same Scottish theological inheritance, evidenced important differences. When these different constructions of federal theology collided in the *Marrow* controversy, positions that previously had been held jointly within Scottish federalism came to be irreconcilable.

In demonstrating how Erskine's involvement in the *Marrow* controversy resulted from the dissonance between his solidifying evangelical federalism and the federal structure of Hadow, the present treatment will first provide an overview of the federal thought of each man. This overview will be divided into four sections. Each section will be comprised of an account of each man's thought on a particular area of federalism, followed by an indication of germane differences, and concluded by an overview of the history of Scottish federal thought on the particular area of federalism under consideration. After following this method for each of the four sections, the five "obscured truths" cited by Erskine in his letter to George Gillespie will be considered individually in light of Erskine's and Hadow's respective federal theologies to demonstrate how the factors which led Erskine to his involvement in the *Marrow* controversy were driven by the discrepancies between his evangelical federalism and the federal thought of Hadow.

---

36. See Henry Sefton, "St Mary's," 164–65; Wodrow, *Analecta*, 2:197–98, 3:409–10; Wodrow, *Correspondence*, 2:452–53; Skoczylas, *Simson*, 346; Skoczylas, "The Regulation of Academic Society in Early Eighteenth-Century Scotland," 171–95. Hereafter, "Regulation." This battle, commencing in 1713, was ongoing at the time of the *Marrow* controversy.

37. The author of *Videte Apologiam* intimates that the excesses to which men had run in reaction to the Simson process had sparked the *Marrow* controversy. However, he does not pursue this in any detail. See *Videte Apologiam*, 16.

WORKS SELECTED

To ascertain the respective theologies of Erskine and Hadow, recourse will be had to a variety of sources. The contours of Erskine's theology can be drawn from his published sermons preached prior to the controversy, as well as from the *Representation* which he revised and the *Answers* which he authored.[38] Furthermore, consideration will be given to pertinent documents from later in Erskine's ministry, including published sermons and documents issuing from the Secession Church. In this latter group, particular attention must be afforded to two works: the *Act Concerning the Doctrine of Grace*, which Erskine co-authored for the Associate Presbytery and which took its shape from a consideration of the theological points at issue in the *Marrow* controversy, and the portions of the Associate Synod's *The Assembly's Shorter Catechism Explained* which Erskine authored.[39] While many of these documents were written posterior to the *Marrow* controversy, they provide a more complete picture of Erskine's theology that is both necessary to understanding his role in that controversy and completely harmonious with the more limited picture that emerges from his earlier writings. In ascertaining Hadow's theology, primary recourse will be had to his two influential works, *The Record of God*, preached before the Synod of Fife, and *The Antinomianism of the Marrow of Modern Divinity Detected*. While Hadow did publish other writings in relation to the *Marrow* controversy, those other works never assumed the authority of his two chief works and were almost entirely consumed with polemical and detailed argumentation relating to the positions argued by James Hog, thus rendering them less useful in constructing a view of Hadow's representative theology in itself and

---

38. Lachman asserts that Erskine did not publish any relevant material prior to the controversy. See Lachman, *Marrow*, 123. While it is true that Erskine did not publish any sermons prior to 1720, he did, in 1725, publish two very germane sermons preached prior to the controversy, one in 1714 and one in 1715.

39. *ADG*; *Catechism*. The *Catechism* was first published in two parts, with the first part being published in 1753 and the second part being issued seven years later. Work on the first part was initially undertaken jointly by Ebenezer Erskine, Ralph Erskine, and James Fisher. However, as Ralph Erskine died before the work was published, it was largely the work of Ebenezer and Fisher. Ebenezer Erskine then died shortly after the publication of the first part, leaving the composition of the whole of the second part, along with subsequent revisions and additions to the first part, to Fisher. Fraser indicates that Erskine authored the portions on questions 8–28 of the Shorter Catechism, a judgment that he bases upon his assessment that the original transcripts in his possession were in Ebenezer Erskine's shorthand for those questions. See *Life*, 494. MacEwen, on the other hand, credits Erskine with only questions 8–25. See MacEwen, *Erskines*, 137. However, MacEwen does not state the reasons for his departure from Fraser. Given Fraser's access to original documents that MacEwen himself concedes were "not now available," Fraser's assessment is adopted at present. Ibid., 7.

in comparison with that of Erskine. Furthermore, attention will be given to Hadow's correspondence with Alexander Hamilton, minister of Airth, in 1711.[40] As Hamilton's doctrine showed certain similarities with that of Erskine, many of Hadow's comments upon it will be immediately pertinent to the present discussion.

In assessing the state of Scottish federalism in regard to the matters contended in the *Marrow* controversy, a large degree of selectivity is necessary. While the secondary literature contains substantial debate concerning the time and the manner of federal theology's entrance into Scotland, there is unanimity that, by 1597, with the publication of Robert Rollock's *Tractatus de vocatione efficaci*, federalism was firmly ensconced within Scottish theology.[41] Nearly a half-century later, this federal theology received both its clearest confessional distillation and its status as the doctrinal standard of the Kirk in the Westminster Confession of Faith, and thus that Confession will serve as the starting point for the present consideration of the development of Scottish federalism.[42] While there were important works on federal theology published between the time of Rollock and the Westminster Assembly, the authoritative position held by the Confession provides not only a statement of the consensus that was reached between varying positions, but also the standard from which subsequent Scottish thought would spring.[43] As an important contemporary interpretation of the Westminster theology, consideration will also be given to *The Sum of Saving Knowledge* (1650), co-

---

40. See "Letters." Hamilton and Erskine later would be ministerial colleagues in Stirling.

41. See, for example, J. B. Torrance, "The Covenant Concept," 227; T. F. Torrance, *Theology*, 61–62; Weir, *Origins of Federal Theology*, viii; Macleod, "Covenant Theology," 214–15. For cautions regarding the attempt to trace the refinement of federal theology, see Muller, *The Unaccommodated Calvin*, 183; Philip, "'Federal Calvinism,'" 41–42. Indeed, Rollock himself played an influential role in the larger codification of federal theology. See, for example Letham, "The *Foedus Operum*," 457; McGiffert, "From Moses to Adam," 131–34; Pelikan, *The Christian Tradition*, 367–68. Generally, Rollock's federalism is ascribed to the influence of Olevianus, mediated through Robert Howie and Charles Lumsden. See Henderson, "The Idea of the Covenant in Scotland," 8–9; Bierma, "German Calvinism," 176. For varying opinions on the presence of a federal structure within Scottish theology prior to Rollock, see Torrance, *Theology*, 61–62; Kirk, *Patterns of Reform*, 72. Hereafter, *Patterns*.

42. See McWilliams, "The Covenant Theology of the Westminster Confession of Faith and Recent Criticism," 109–11; Pelikan, *The Christian Tradition*, 244, 365; Weir, *Origins of Federal Theology*, 3–5.

43. While the Confession was indelibly influenced by English Calvinism, it was also adopted by the Kirk and thus represents the agreed crystallization of the preceding fifty years of Scottish federalism. See T. F. Torrance, *Theology*, 127. See also Barth, *The Theology of the Reformed Confessions*, , 126–27, 133, hereafter, *Confessions*; Fergusson, "Predestination," 464–65; G. D. Henderson, "Idea of the Covenant," 10.

authored by David Dickson and James Durham, which itself acquired vast influence as a result of being bound with the Confession in many Scottish printings of the latter after 1650.[44] Where applicable, further explication of the thought of David Dickson will be provided by *Truth's Victory Over Error*, his itemized exposition of each chapter of the Confession.[45]

In the years of the Restoration regimes, federal thought continued to pervade Scottish theology. Perhaps the most exhaustive and the most influential work on the covenants to emerge from this period of Scottish theology was that of Patrick Gillespie. While Gillespie never completed his intended five-part exposition of the covenants, the two works that he did complete—*The Ark of the Testament Opened* (1661), which treats the Covenant of Grace, and *The Ark of the Covenant Opened* (1677), which considers the Covenant of Redemption—exercised a considerable influence within Scotland and will be considered for their disclosure of many of the important developments in Scottish Westminster federalism during the Second Episcopate.[46] In Herman Witsius' *The Economy of the Covenants Between God and Man* (1677), this federalism received a statement which became paradigmatic for Scottish thought in the late seventeenth and early eighteenth centuries through its wide use in theological education.[47] Given the prominence of Witsius' work, it too will be considered.[48] Finally,

---

44. Dickson and Durham, *The Sum of Saving Knowledge*. Hereafter, *Sum*. For an indication of Erskine's affinity for *Sum*, see Ebenezer Erskine, *Notebook*, Special Collections, New College Library, Edinburgh, ERS E3, 1–11 [no continuous pagination].

45. Dickson, *TRUTH'S VICTORY OVER ERROR*. Hereafter, *Victory*. While Dickson's *Therapeutica Sacra* was also important, it was written prior to the Westminster Assembly (although not published until thereafter). *Sum* and *Victory*, on the other hand, are self-consciously explicatory of the Westminster Confession. In seeking to ascertain the position of post-Westminster Scottish federalism, rather than pre-Westminster Dicksonian federalism, the present treatment will give preference to these two later works.

46. Patrick Gillespie, *THE ARK OF THE TESTAMENT OPENED*, 2 vols.; *The Ark of the Covenant Opened*. Hereafter, *Testament* and *Covenant*, respectively.

47. Herman Witsius. *The Economy of the Covenants Between God and Man*. While Witsius' work was originally written in Latin, it was the English translation of William Crookshank that was widely circulated in Scotland at the time of the *Marrow* controversy. See, for example, Macleod, *Theology*, 219.

48. For a reference to the influence of Witsius's work, see G. D. Henderson, "Idea of the Covenant," 12. Witsius also would have exercised a personal influence over both James Hadow and James Hog. From 1680–1698, Witsius was professor of divinity at the University of Utrecht, during which period both men were students there. See Witsius, Economy of the Covenants, 1:32–33. While Witsius authored other important works, most notably his *Irenical Animadversions*, it was his *Economy of the Covenants* that exercised the most direct influence upon Scottish theology. Due to space constraints, only that latter work will be directly considered in the present account.

attention will be given to the work of Thomas Boston, primarily in his *A Brief Explication of the First Part of the Assembly's Shorter Catechism* and *A View of the Covenant of Grace*.[49] In these representative works, one receives a contemporary account of the covenants that shows both the continuity of Erskine's thought with that of his *Marrow* brethren and certain areas of significant divergence.

FEDERAL THEOLOGICAL STRUCTURES

Foundational for the federal thought of both Erskine and Hadow were their assumptions about the nature and composition of a covenant.

Foundational Assumptions: Erskine

For Erskine, a covenant was "A mutual free compact and agreement betwixt two parties, upon express terms or conditions."[50] While there was a great deal of variation within the divine covenants that constituted God's relationship with man, they all shared a common foundation—the Law of Nature, which had been written on the human heart at the Creation.[51] Throughout his writings, Erskine refers to this Law of Nature under several different titles, such as the Law of Creation, the Moral Law, and the Royal Law, yet while the terminology sometimes varies, the concept does not.[52] The Law of Nature, which was binding upon all men due to the very fact of their Creation, dictated that "man believe whatsoever God shall reveal, and do whatever he shall command."[53] To this elemental Law of Nature, God subsequently added positive precepts, which represented the perfect Law of Nature "extending to new Objects, Occasions and Circumstances."[54]

---

49. Boston, *Works*, vols. 7–8, respectively. It is noteworthy that Boston's work on the covenant of grace is based on sermons that he preached between July 1722 and June 1724. See McGowan, *Boston*, 40. It would appear that Boston detected a federal underpinning to the controversy that had just been concluded.

50. *Catechism*, 97 (12.6). This and subsequent references will provide pagination as well as question citations for *Catechism*. The question citations, given parenthetically, will cite the number of the question in the Westminster Shorter Catechism followed by the number of Erskine's question upon that question. For example, the reference here is to Erskine's sixth question on the twelfth question of the Westminster Shorter Catechism, which appears on page 97.

51. *Catechism*, 97 (12.3).

52. See *Answers*, 29; *Works*, 1:208; and *ADG*, 70, respectively.

53. *Catechism*, 98 (12.14).

54. *Answers*, 19. See also *Works*, 1:229–30, 2:26; *Catechism*, 98 (12.14–16).

However, each positive precept represented not an expansion of the Law of God by means of addition thereto, but rather an extension of the Law of God by means of greater clarification of that all-embracing Law.[55] When the Christian viewed the entirety of this divine Law, both in its underlying Law of Nature and its specifically extrapolated positive precepts, he saw that the Law of God as a whole was nothing short of a transcript of God's Nature.[56]

Upon this substructure of the eternal and universally-binding Law of Nature, the specific divine covenants were reared. These divine covenants were simply terms and conditions superadded to the Law of Nature that dictated the method by which that Law was to be met, as well as the rewards or punishments due to either success or failure; as the Law of Nature and its applications provided a transcript of the holiness of God, the terms of each divine covenant provided the economy by which man was to attain to that holiness. The addition of these covenantal terms thus made the Law of Nature into a covenant.[57] In this sense, Erskine often spoke of the Law of Nature being delivered to man in "the form of a covenant," meaning that both the Law itself and the prescribed method for meeting the end of that Law were delivered together to man. Such a joint issuance of the Law and the applicable covenantal terms was the only way that the Law of Nature had ever been delivered to man, as even in his innocence, Adam first received the Law of Nature in the form of a covenant.[58]

Overall, Erskine saw all divine covenants as being comprised of two constituent parts—the underlying Law of Nature, replete with all of its specific applications, and the particular terms and conditions of the covenant in question. In this covenantal construction, there is room for both marked continuity and great discontinuity among the divine covenants. As each divine covenant is essentially a specific economy for meeting the one Law of God, all covenants are built upon the same Law and look to the fulfillment of that one Law.[59] However, the methods that are prescribed for seeking after this common end could vary drastically, and thus Erskine's system provided the foundation for much discontinuity in the actual outworking of each of the covenants. While each covenant shared the common ground

---

55. *Answers*, 13; *ADG*, 39–40.

56. See *Works*, 1:198, 247.

57. See *Catechism*, 101–2 (12.36; beginning with the 1765 edition of the *Catechism*, this was divided into questions 12.36–38); *Works*, 1:98; *Answers*, 24–25. In the latter, the Representers cite Durham and Burgess as agreeing with their position.

58. See *Answers*, 13, 29; *Catechism*, 97 (12.5), 103 (13.3); *Works*, 1:471.

59. See *Works*, 1:131, 146–47, 334; 2:20; *Answers*, 18–21; *ADG*, 77–78.

of the Law of Nature, the position in which man stood to that Law and the manner in which he interacted with that Law could thus be very different.[60]

Foundational Assumptions: Hadow

The foundational assumptions of James Hadow's federal theology share a great deal of commonality with those of Erskine. Hadow conceived of each of the divine covenants as comprising terms and conditions superadded upon the one Law of Nature, a Law to which Hadow referred with a terminological variety similar to Erskine.[61] However, Hadow's understanding of this Law of Nature contained a nuance that came to constitute one of the chief grounds of his disagreement with Erskine.[62] According to Hadow, the ontological distinction between God as Creator and mankind as creature meant that the Law of Nature contained necessary penal sanctions.[63] While Hadow recognized that the first covenant between God and man, the Covenant of Works, imposed penal sanctions as part of its covenantal terms, he insisted that

> a Penal Sanction is inseparable from this Royal Law of Nature, tho' no Covenant of Works had been made; and that from the Perfections of God, the Dependency of the reasonable Creature upon his Sovereign Lord Creator, and the Nature of Sin in itself.[64]

While Erskine agreed that the essential holiness of God demanded conformity to his Law and the inherent wickedness of sin necessitated its punishment, he always located the penal sanctions due to man's sin within the specific terms of each divine covenant rather than within the Law of Nature itself.[65] Hadow and Erskine were in agreement that the Law of Nature, which was a codification of the holiness of God, dictated the categories of right and wrong, yet they were in disagreement as to whether the punishment for

---

60. See *Works*, 1:204, 315.

61. For Hadow's delineation of the different senses of '"Covenant" used in Scripture, see "Letters," 59–61. See also *AD*, iv, 17, 78–80, 89–90, 127–28.

62. Hadow also differed with Erskine on whether all "positive precepts" given after the Law of Nature were extensions of that Law or additions thereto. See, for example, *AD*, 73, 123. However, this particular area of disagreement will be discussed in a subsequent section.

63. See *AD*, xii, 76–77, 126–28.

64. *AD*, 82–83. See also *AD*, 95.

65. See *Works*, 1:171, 339–40; *Catechism*, 99 (12.19); *Answers*, 29–30; *ADG*, 72–73.

wrong thus defined was to be found within the eternal Law of Creation or within the covenantal terms that were placed thereupon.

This nuance within Hadow's understanding of the Law of Nature proves to be highly problematic, for it represents a categorical confusion between a law and a covenant, even upon Hadow's own definition of each concept. Hadow agreed with Erskine that each divine covenant was comprised of terms and conditions superadded to the underlying Law of Nature; in other words, a covenant was the addition of promises and threatenings to the Law of Nature. However, in positing that the Law of Nature carries with it inherent penal sanctions, Hadow left no substantial distinction between the Law of Nature and a proper covenant. For Hadow, the Law of Nature was a codification of the holiness of the Creator-God that brought punishment for any violations thereof and, at least by implication, brought the blessing of continued communion with God for conformity thereto. Simply stated, Hadow's Law of Nature was a covenant, not a law.[66] This was particularly problematic given Hadow's agreement with Erskine that the Law of Nature ran through and underlay each of the divine covenants. By thus bringing the Law of Nature to bear upon each subsequent divine covenant, Hadow essentially imported a covenant, complete with penal sanctions, into every other divine covenant. In reality, each of Hadow's divine covenants was thus a double covenant, for even outwith the specific covenantal terms and conditions of the covenant in question, one had to address the penal sanctions that necessarily attached to the Law of Nature that underlay it.[67]

Foundational Assumptions: Doctrinal Context

On the pressing question of necessary penal sanctions within the Law of Nature, the testimony of Scottish federalism is decidedly ambiguous. While the Westminster Confession never addresses the question directly, it conceives of the Law as being given to Adam as a covenant rather than as an abstract Law, thus being friendly to a reading that sees punishable guilt as necessarily following on from violation of the Law, yet locates specific penal sanctions within covenantal terms rather than within the nature of the Moral Law itself.[68] This faint witness was quickly clouded, however, by *The*

---

66. Erskine seemed to recognize this. See *Works*, 1:101–2. Furthermore, Hadow himself seemed to realize that the Representers saw his notion of the Law of Nature as synonymous with a proper covenant, yet he attributed this to their alleged antinomianism rather than to any categorical confusion on his part. See *AD*, 171.

67. For example, see *AD*, 16–17, 73–74, 76–77, 89–90, 104, 127–28, 139.

68. *WCF*, 6.6, 7.1, 19.1.

Sum's oblique suggestion that Adam was bound to obedience within the Covenant of Works under pain of death not only by the specific terms of that covenant, but also by the Law of Nature itself.[69] However, *The Sum* was far from unequivocal in its statement; a fact evidenced by Dickson's evident dismissal of necessary penal sanctions within the Moral Law in *Truth's Victory*.[70] Such duality of statement continued to mark Scottish theology during the Second Episcopate. In his *Ark of the Testament*, Gillespie posits that the Law of Nature *was* the Covenant of Works, exclusive of any other positive laws or terms, and God's writing of the Law upon Adam's heart marked the formal contracting of that covenant.[71] In such a position, one is practically forced to locate all penal sanctions within the Law of Nature which is, itself, the covenant. However, Gillespie then almost immediately locates the Covenant of Works' threatening of death in the positive law of Genesis 2:17.[72] Overall, Gillespie must be read as a summary of the situation within the Scottish theology of his day—the Moral Law inherently imparted penal guilt to sin, yet the exact penal sanctions for that guilt were imparted by the covenantal terms superadded to that Law.

In Witsius, one sees the climax of this confusion over the presence of necessary penal sanctions in the Moral Law. In his discussion of the penal sanction of the Covenant of Works, Witsius distinguishes between the penal guilt of sin and the specific penal sanction of eternal death that was attached to that guilt under the Covenant of Works.[73] After a detailed discussion of the matter, Witsius concludes that while sin's liability to punishment is a necessary result of the holiness of God, the specific character of the eternal death that was the sanction of that sin under the Covenant of Works could have been different had God so chosen. From this discussion, one is justified in concluding that while the holiness of God, as expressed in the Moral Law, imparts penal guilt to sin, the specific penal sanctions prescribed for that guilt are determined by the covenantal terms superadded to the Law.[74] However, much later in his work, Witsius unequivocally states that the Law, considered absolutely, is

> A command of the supreme ruler, binding every one to obedience under the threatening of eternal death . . . .[75]

69. *Sum*, 323.
70. Dickson, *Victory*, 138–39.
71. Gillespie, *Testament*, 1:183–84.
72. Ibid., 1:184–85.
73. For the following, see Witsius, 1:82–104.
74. Similarly, see ibid., 1:82.
75. Ibid., 2:179. Similarly, see ibid., 1:62.

In this forthright statement, Witsius locates a definite penal sanction—eternal death—within the Law itself rather than in the covenantal terms that were added to it. If Witsius' discussion of the penal sanction of the Covenant of Works countenanced Erskine's dismissal of necessary penal sanctions within the Moral Law, his consideration of the abstract Law provided equal validation to Hadow's supposition of those necessary penal sanctions.

Viewed as a whole, the Scottish federalism of which Erskine and Hadow were both heirs bore a divided witness on the question of necessary penal sanctions within the Moral Law. In the earliest works under consideration, the matter seemed wholly marginal and thus received only oblique attention. In the later works under consideration, especially in Witsius, the matter received a treatment that was void of the consistency that marked the consideration of other theological matters. Overall, one is left with the distinct impression that the question of definite penal sanctions inherent in the Moral Law was not considered with any great attention prior to the *Marrow* controversy. As a result, the federal system of the Kirk contained the theological suppositions and assertions necessary to build the contrasting positions of both Erskine and Hadow.

THE COVENANT OF WORKS

When one moves to consider Erskine's and Hadow's perceptions of the specific divine covenants, there continues to be both marked similarity and important dissimilarity. In seeking to delineate the divine covenants, it is this dissimilarity that first emerges, as Erskine and Hadow each asserted a different number of such covenants. While Hadow spoke of three covenants—the Covenant of Redemption, the Covenant of Works, and the Covenant of Grace—Erskine spoke of only two—the Covenant of Works and an expansive Covenant of Grace that comprehended what Hadow denominated under both the Covenant of Redemption and the Covenant of Grace.[76] As there was such a foundational dissonance between Erskine and Hadow on matters relating to the Covenant of Redemption and the Covenant of Grace, their evidently more consonant positions on the Covenant of Works will be considered first.

---

76. For Erskine's most direct statement of a bi-covenantal view, see *Catechism*, 97 (12.7). Erskine judged that the Noahic Covenant was an outworking of the Covenant of Grace. See *Works*, 1:355.

The Covenant of Works: Erskine

There is nothing exceptional about the details of Erskine's doctrine of the Covenant of Works; a covenant that Erskine saw to be fundamentally gracious in its promise of eternal life upon the condition of an obedience that Adam owed to God, due to his creation, even outwith any promised covenantal blessings.[77] However, Erskine's overall federal theology was importantly shaped by his notion of the two-fold purposefulness of the Covenant of Works. In the first instance, the Covenant of Works was intended to provide man, a finite creature, with a way whereby he could obtain eternal life.[78] As the Covenant of Works was not made with man as sinner, but rather with man as man, it was not at all concerned with justification, for justification was needed by guilty sinners, not man in his innocence. The graciousness of the Covenant of Works was not that it promised justification to a sinner, but rather that it promised eternal life to a creature.[79] Secondly, the Covenant of Works was intended to point forward to the Covenant of Grace. In Erskine's estimation,

> when God gave the law to Adam in innocence, in the form of a covenant, he never designed that man's happiness should stand upon that footing; no, the covenant of works was only designed as a scaffold for rearing up a more glorious building of grace and mercy, which God has said 'shall be built up for ever,' Ps. lxxxix. 2.[80]

The purpose, then, of the Covenant of Works was not that it should be fulfilled by man; the purpose of the Covenant of Works was to open an avenue whereby finite man could obtain infinite life and then, in the subsequent closing of that avenue by the breach of the covenant, to point to the necessity of the Covenant of Grace.[81]

---

77. *Catechism*, 100–101 (12.28, 30–31, 33), 130 (19.4), 131 (19.6), 155 (20.114); *Works*, 1:248. Such an emphasis, while central to Erskine's federal structure, was not unique thereto. See, for example, WCF, 7.1; *Sum*, 323; Gillespie, *Testament*, 1:221; Witsius, *Economy of the Covenants*, 1:70, 402.

78. See, for example, *Catechism*, 155–56 (20.117); *Works*, 1:228. This will become more clear in subsequent sections.

79. See *ADG*, 56–57. On the rare occasion that Erskine speaks of "justification" in relation to the Covenant of Works, he is comparing that covenant with the Covenant of Grace and thus using the term "justification" for reasons of accommodation rather than of theological precision. See, for example, *Works*, 1:446. When theological precision is his concern, he steadfastly avoids speaking of "justification" in relation to the Covenant of Works.

80. *Works*, 1:471. See also *Works*, 1:298–99, 460.

81. See *Catechism*, 141 (20.28), 156 (20.119); *Works*, 1:125, 140, 151, 386, 425, 449,

While Erskine's discussion of the Covenant of Works is largely guided by his views of the nature and purpose of that covenant, one must also note his perception of the post-Fall status of the covenant. Due to Adam's transgression of the Covenant of Works, no man is able to attain to life by the terms of that covenant, yet man's inability to satisfy the Covenant of Works does not mean that it is no longer binding upon him in full.[82] Each individual born after the Fall is subject to both the terms imposed by the Covenant of Works and the curse suffered because of the failure to meet those terms.[83] The covenant thus remains binding in full upon the individual and will do so eternally unless he enters into the Covenant of Grace.[84] In Erskine's system,

> though the Law of Works be a *broken*, yet it is a perpetually *binding* Law; and though the Sinner be an *insolvent* Debtor, yet the Debt, both of Obedience and Satisfaction, *lies upon his Head*, as long as he is under the Law, and not under Grace . . . .[85]

The Covenant of Works: Hadow

While Hadow's conception of the Covenant of Works is largely synonymous with Erskine's, his doctrine of that covenant contains a crucial divergence. Throughout his treatment of the Covenant of Works, Hadow evidences a highly nuanced understanding of man's relationship to that covenant. Prior to the Fall, Adam was under the terms of the Covenant of Works, while after the Fall, Adam was subject to both the terms and the curse of the covenant. All of Adam's posterity are born under this double obligation to the Covenant of Works, an obligation both to fulfill its terms and to suffer its curse.[86] However, when a sinner hears the gospel proclamation, he is advertised therein of covenantal terms that are "opposite and inconsistent"

459–60; *ADG*, 57.

82. Erskine argues that the Covenant of Works has never been abrogated, whether by man's sin and apostasy, man's weakness, Christ's work, or faith. See *Catechism*, 102 (12.37–42), 104–5 (13.11–12), 124–25 (18.15), 131 (19.9–10), 156 (20.119); *Works*, 1:314, 437, 439, 448, 471–72.

83. See *ADG*, 57; *Catechism*, 123 (18.9); *Works*, 1:446–47, 477–79.

84. See *Answers*, 20, 32–33; *Works*, 1:55, 398. The Representers cited the Westminster Confession 19.6 and John Owen's "On Justification" as supporting this contention that only believers are in any manner freed from the Covenant of Works. See *Answers*, 31–32, 33–35, respectively.

85. *ADG*, 57.

86. See "Letters," 61–62.

with the terms of the Covenant of Works; rather than seeking justification through perfect personal obedience, the sinner under the preaching of the gospel is told of the new way whereby justification is to be sought and thus the old terms of the Covenant of Works are "abrogated or antiquated."[87] The sinner is thus no longer under the terms of the Covenant of Works, but only under its curse.[88] The sinner who has heard the gospel proclamation continues in this relationship to the Covenant of Works—freed from its terms but laboring under its curse—until such time as he may enter into the Covenant of Grace. If that entrance into the Covenant of Grace should occur, the sinner is then freed from the curse of the Covenant of Works, thus wholly and finally extricating himself from that former covenant.[89] As Hadow stated the situation:

> the Covenant of Works, as to its formal Obligation, *Do and live*, is not still standing in full force, but abrogated, with Respect to all to whom the Gospel is sent . . . the Unregenerate are under the standing Curse, and penal Sanction of this broken

---

87. *AD*, 66, 67, respectively. Much of the disagreement on this point rested on the fact that Hadow judged the Covenant of Works had been given to bring justification, while, as discussed previously, Erskine held that the Covenant of Works promised eternal life, not justification. See *AD*, 122, 124.

88. See *AD*, 124. The Representers argued that merely living under an external dispensation of the gospel did not at all alter a man's relationship to the Covenant of Works. See *Answers*, 32–33.

Due to length considerations, the six Antinomian Paradoxes that were advanced by the *Marrow*, condemned by the Assembly, and defended by the Representers cannot be specifically considered in the present treatment. However, it should be noted that this particular view of Hadow concerning the unregenerate sinner's freedom from the terms of the Covenant of Works seems to have been the primary factor in his opposition to these paradoxes. According to Hadow, the paradoxes are antinomian because the relationship between the believer and the Covenant of Works that these paradoxes assume—namely, freedom from the obligation of obedience to that covenant—is also true of the non-believer. Based upon this assumption, Hadow proceeds through the six paradoxes, showing them to be truly antinomian by using the method of keeping "mostly the Words of the *Marrow*, P. 200, 201. only putting *Unbelievers* for *Believers*." *AD*, 125. Hadow, then, has used his particular understanding of the unregenerate sinner's relationship to the terms of the Covenant of Works as the foundation for asserting that what the *Marrow* says about believers in these paradoxes, it also says about nonbelievers, for it has based its assertions upon a freedom from the terms of the Covenant of Works that is as true of the latter as it is of the former. It is thus little wonder that these paradoxes prove to be openly antinomian rather than provocatively orthodox. However, the underlying assumption of Hadow's critique of these paradoxes, and the cause of his eventual condemnation of them, is his supposition that believers and nonbelievers stand in the same relation to the terms of the Covenant of Works; a supposition that Erskine and the other Representers did not share. See *AD*, 124–25.

89. See *AD*, 16, 75, 89, 122.

Covenant, and ... they are not freed from it, till, in Obedience to the Gospel Call, they fly to the Mediator's Righteousness for their Relief.[90]

In this, Hadow envisioned the movement of the sinner from being under both the terms and the curse of the Covenant of Works to being wholly freed from that covenant as a graduated movement.

The Covenant of Works: Doctrinal Context

While the Covenant of Works had been a prominent feature in Scottish federalism since the days of Robert Rollock, there had never been any explicit discussion of the post-Fall status of that covenant in the precise terms of the difference that arose between Erskine and Hadow. The pattern for the oblique nature of most of the discussion in this area was both mirrored and further solidified in the Westminster Confession. In chapter 6 of the Confession, all sin is construed as transgression of the Law of God. By this legal transgression, the individual sinner brings guilt upon himself and, because of that guilt, relegates himself to the wrath of God and the curse of the Law.[91] In this view of sin and its punishment, the imposition of the curse of the Covenant of Works is clearly understood as a function of man's failure to meet the abiding terms of that covenant; the connection between the terms of the law and the curse thereof is such that the latter cannot be retained, or even accrued, without the presence of the former. This notion of the connection between the terms and the curse of the law continues throughout *The Sum*, which likewise founded the inescapability of the curse upon the individual's continual violation of the law's terms; terms which Christ alone, and not simply the gospel proclamation, would obviate.[92]

While Gillespie's discussion of the post-Fall status of the Covenant of Works does not differ in substance from that of the Confession and *The Sum*, the greater detail of that discussion makes it more revelatory of the confusion that could arise from the standard Scottish position. On the one hand, Gillespie clearly holds that all men, by nature, are under the Covenant of Works in the fullest sense; a burden that they can escape only by, and not at all prior to, their entrance into the Covenant of Grace.[93] However, in

---

90. *AD*, 67. See *AD*, 64–67.
91. *WCF*, 6.6.
92. *Sum*, 327–28, 331, 339, 341. See also Dickson, *Victory*, 138.
93. E.g., Gillespie, *Testament*, 1:273–74.

discussions of such matters, Gillespie would speak of the believer's freedom from the Covenant of Works as that covenant being

> abrogated and abolished to the Believer, not only as a court of righteousnesse and life, or a way of Justification and Salvation, in which respect it is also abrogated to the unbeliever; for ever since God brought in a contrary and quite opposite way of Justification and Salvation by Faith in Jesus Christ, the Covenant of Works is thus far antiquated, and doth cease to be a possible way of righteousnesse to any sinfull flesh . . . but the Covenant of Works is abrogated also to the Believer, who by faith hath accepted the Covenant of Grace in point of death and condemnation, he is thence forward free from the penalty and forfaulture of that Covenant . . . .[94]

In this representative passage, Gillespie evidences a duality of expression that could produce the positions of both Hadow and Erskine. On the one hand, Gillespie speaks of the Covenant of Works being both "abrogated" and "antiquated" even in respect to the non-believer, an abrogation and antiquity that he founds upon that covenant's present inability to bring salvation. In this, Gillespie is little, if at all, distant from Hadow's supposition that the hearing of the gospel proclamation obviates the power of the terms, although not of the curse, of the Covenant of Works in the life of the unregenerate gospel auditor. On the other hand, Gillespie elsewhere expounds what he intimates here—this abrogation and antiquation of the Covenant of Works is purely functional.[95] Properly speaking, the terms of the Covenant of Works have not been abrogated and antiquated; rather, the ability of man to meet them has been abrogated and antiquated. Even in the quotation cited above, Gillespie clearly implies that the Covenant of Works is applicable to the non-believer "in point of death and condemnation" because of "the penalty and forefaulture of that Covenant." In other words, the Covenant of Works still binds the unregenerate over to a death that arises from their failing to meet the covenant's terms; terms that thus, by definition, must still be in force. For all of the similarity between Gillespie's and Hadow's modes of expression at points, then, there remains a crucial difference. While both men saw the Covenant of Works as utterly incapable of saving, Gillespie held that it was yet still that covenant in full, both its curse and its terms, that condemned the unregenerate, while Hadow posited that

---

94. Ibid., 1:273.
95. E.g., ibid., 1:275.

it was only the curse that abided and that thus served as the channel for the unregenerate's condemnation.[96]

In Witsius, one finds a doctrinal position very similar to that of Gillespie. While the advent of the Covenant of Grace did necessitate a certain abrogation of the Covenant of Works, this was not an abrogation that transferred the unregenerate out from under the terms of that covenant; rather, it was an abrogation that rendered him impotent to meet the full covenant terms that still rested upon him.[97] Indeed, the presence of these covenantal terms was still so real that Witsius was able to hypothesize that if a man was able to meet them as Christ did, he would acquire eternal life.[98] The terms of the covenant, then, were still in force; only man's ability to meet them had been truly abrogated.[99]

Viewed as a whole, the Scottish federalism which Erskine and Hadow inherited evidently had never directly addressed the applicability of the terms of the Covenant of Works to the unregenerate gospel auditor. The tangential character of this question to previous federalism is seen most clearly in the dissonance between the doctrine that that federalism imparts and the vocabulary which it uses to express that doctrine. As a body, Scottish federalism taught that each individual sinner would be condemned not by an abstract curse of the Covenant of Works, but rather by his personal transgression of concrete covenantal terms. However, that body of federal thought also uniformly held that salvation by the terms of the Covenant of Works was no longer possible for any man, and most writers expressed this inability using the language of "abrogation" and even "antiquation." Scottish federal theology leading up to the 1720s, then, spoke of "abrogation," yet logically demanded continuation. Clearly, no theological debate had arisen to cause the Kirk to consider this dissonance; such a debate awaited the *Marrow* controversy. In that controversy, Erskine and Hadow each would focus upon varying components of the Scottish federal system and arrive at starkly different conclusions.

---

96. See ibid., 1:217, 275 (a typographical error in the work lists the page as "775").
97. Witsius, *Economy of the Covenants*, 1:151–52, 156, 158–61.
98. Ibid., 1:159, 402.
99. See Macleod, "Covenant Theology," 215.

THE COVENANT OF REDEMPTION

The Covenant of Redemption: Erskine

Erskine's rejection of a distinct Covenant of Redemption is so absolute that it almost invariably takes the form of curt dismissal rather than detailed refutation. Negatively, this dismissal is based upon a lack of Scriptural warrant for such a covenant.[100] Positively, Erskine rejects the notion of a distinct Covenant of Redemption because Scripture explicitly states that there are only two divine covenants and, as these covenants are manifestly the Covenant of Works and the Covenant of Grace, such a declaration is tantamount to a direct denial of a separate Covenant of Redemption.[101] At every point, Erskine's rejection of a distinct Covenant of Redemption is founded entirely upon Scriptural argumentation, the terseness of which indicates Erskine's conviction of its decisiveness.

As one considers the entire corpus of Erskine's work, there appears to be a certain amount of development prior to this final rejection of a Covenant of Redemption. In a sermon preached on 3 June 1714, Erskine asserts that

> God the Father gave a remnant unto Christ of the posterity of Adam, in the covenant of redemption, to be ransomed and redeemed by him, from that woe and wrath, into which Adam, by his apostasy, had involved himself and all his posterity.[102]

Here, Erskine not only uses the language of "covenant of redemption," but he also describes the contents of that covenant in a standard manner. However, this reference is the only time in all of Erskine's writings that he thus refers approvingly to a "covenant of redemption." In sermons preached in 1715 and 1717, Erskine clearly has in view the redemptive and contractual components that he had earlier denominated as "the covenant of redemption," yet he omits the covenantal language that he had earlier employed.[103]

---

100. *Catechism*, 144 (20.50).

101. See *Catechism*, 144 (20.51–52). To this end, Erskine cites Galatians 4:24. Galatians 4 was formative in Erskine's overall federal theology. See, for example, *Works*, 1:445–46.

102. *Works*, 1:3. In this instance, Erskine cites John 17, especially verse 6, as proof of this gifting of the elect to Christ. With two notable exceptions, Erskine's subsequent sermonic references to John 17, either in part or in full, pertain to the work that Christ did for the elect or the privileges that the elect enjoy without making any reference to the Covenant of Redemption. The two exceptions to this will be addressed below.

103. See *Works*, 1:48; 1:62, respectively.

By the time of the *Marrow* controversy, Erskine's failure to use the language of "Covenant of Redemption" had lost any appearance of inadvertent omission. In a sermon preached on 4 June 1721, Erskine first conspicuously omits such language when discussing the pre-temporal redemptive contract between the Father and the Son and then, for the first time in his extant writings, uses the language of "the council of peace" to refer to the pre-temporal intra-Trinitarian compact that others might denominate as the Covenant of Redemption.[104] Indeed, in his subsequent uses of this term, Erskine ascribes to that council what he had ascribed to the "covenant of redemption" in 1714—the giving of the Son, by the Father, to be a surety for the elect—and does so by making use of the same Scripture references.[105] Erskine's conception of precisely what had transpired in that compact had not changed, yet his manner of referring to it had.[106]

Since Erskine's approbation of the terminology "covenant of redemption" in 1714 is unique among all of his extant writings, and since his description of that "covenant" is indistinguishable from his later descriptions of the compact that he insistently referred to as "the council of peace," it is impossible to assert definitively that Erskine held to a distinct Covenant of Redemption in his earlier ministry. What is certain is that Erskine's apparent willingness to use such terminology waned in the following years and, in the midst of the *Marrow* controversy, was replaced by the use of a term whose recurrence in subsequent years indicates that Erskine intentionally chose it to evidence his unwillingness to condone the theological implications that were coming to be attached to the language of "covenant of redemption." Language that had been acceptable previously was no longer acceptable in light of the *Marrow* controversy.[107] While Erskine's understanding of exactly what had transpired in the pre-temporal intra-Trinitarian compact had

---

104. See *Works*, 1:98–99 for the omission; 1:101 for the language of "council of peace."

105. In the 1714 sermon in which he had spoken of the "covenant of redemption," Erskine had referred generally to John 17. In 1734, Erskine would cite John 17 in reference to the Council of Peace; in 1738, he would cite John 17:2 in reference to the work that Christ undertook in accordance with the Council of Peace. See *Works*, 2:228, 479, respectively.

106. Erskine's understanding of the exact contents of the Council of Peace will be detailed below.

107. Erskine's refusal to use the term "Covenant of Redemption" is especially remarkable given that Boston, who likewise held a bi-covenantal view, was perfectly willing to use the phrase as long as it was properly nuanced. See Boston, *Works*, 7:39–40; 8:396–98, 427–28. Almost twenty years after Erskine discontinued any use of the term "Covenant of Redemption," Boston was still willing to use it, perhaps illustrating a less visceral antipathy to the notion.

clearly not changed, the relationship of that compact to the other areas of his theology that could be inferred from his language had. If there was any development in Erskine's thought on the Covenant of Redemption, it was only in relation to the placement of this compact within Erskine's theological system and not in relation to the contents thereof.

The Covenant of Redemption: Hadow

Contrary to Erskine, Hadow fully accepted the notion of a distinct Covenant of Redemption, which he conceived of as "God's constituting and appointing His only begotten Son to be the Mediator, Redeemer, aad [sic—and] Saviour of Sinners."[108] In his writings, Hadow always assumes the independence and validity of the Covenant of Redemption and seldom offers either a defense of that validity or a full discussion of the covenant itself.[109] Indeed, Hadow's most extended treatment of the Covenant of Redemption comes in relation to the Covenant of Grace. Speaking of the Covenant of Grace, Hadow writes

> This Federal transaction betwixt God the father and his own son the mediator & surety, doth presuppose the eternal decree of election; wherein a certain definite number of mankind, were chosen & appointed unto eternal life & salvation. As also it supposeth the eternal counsel of grace, wherein all the ways & means were fixed & determined for bringing about the elects salvation, unto the praise of glorious free grace, which counsel of grace is in Scripture represented in the form of a covt betwixt the father & the son (tho' the parties contracting have not different free wills)...[110]

From this, three essential elements of Hadow's Covenant of Redemption are clear. First, that covenant presupposes a prior decree of election and proceeds upon the categories of election created thereby. Second, the Covenant of Redemption is an independent covenant distinct from the Covenant of Grace. In this particular passage, Hadow refers to the covenant as "the eternal counsel of grace," yet he also asserts that this counsel "is in Scripture represented in the form of a covt betwixt the father & the son."[111] In his later writings, Hadow would refer to this covenant as the "Covenant

---

108 *AD*, 131.

109. Hadow's normal method is to argue from the Covenant of Redemption rather than to argue for it. See, for example, *AD*, 36–37, 131–32.

110. "Letters," 62.

111. Hadow does not offer any Scriptural citations for such a representation.

of Redemption."[112] Third, Hadow asserts that the Covenant of Grace functions only upon the presumption of both the decree of election and this Covenant of Redemption.[113] These two prior realities establish the channel in which that later covenant will run, determining both what that covenant will do and the group for whom it will be done. For Hadow, the Covenant of Redemption, which established the means by which God would save the previously defined and delineated group of the elect, is the starting point for any consideration of the Covenant of Grace.

THE COVENANT OF GRACE

Covenant of Grace: Erskine[114]

The most prominent and the most important characteristic of Erskine's Covenant of Grace is that it is an expansive Covenant of Grace, essentially collapsing into one covenant what others separate into two covenants, a Covenant of Redemption and a Covenant of Grace.[115] For Erskine, there is only one Covenant of Grace, wherein God both purposes and accomplishes the redemption of fallen men.[116] Consistently speaking of the covenant in legal and contractual terms, Erskine asserted that the two contracting parties to the eternal Covenant of Grace were the Father and the Son; the elect were considered in the Covenant of Grace not as parties thereto, but only insofar as they were in Christ.[117] Clearly, then, there are two essential compo-

112. E.g., *AD*, 131–32.

113. E.g., "Letters," 68.

114. A discussion of the history and status of the Covenant of Redemption in Scottish federalism will be deferred until the specifics of Erskine's expansive Covenant of Grace have been described, thus allowing for a more cogent discussion of the influences of that history and status upon both Erskine and Hadow.

115. Erskine frequently cited Question 31 of the Westminster Larger Catechism as supporting him in this construction of an expansive Covenant of Grace. See, for example, *Catechism*, 145 (20.57); *Works*, 1:357. At times, Erskine simply would refer to "the standards of the Church of Scotland" as supporting him. E.g., *Works*, 1:358.

116. For Erskine's two most complete treatments of the Covenant of Grace, see *Catechism*, 137–56 (20.1–20.120); and *Works*, 1:354–92.

117. *Catechism*, 143 (20.41), 149–50 (20.81), 154–55 (20.112); *Works*, 1:38, 357–58. See also *Catechism*, 139–42 (20.16–27, 29, 40). As scriptural evidence for the Covenant of Grace being made with Christ rather than with the elect in any sense, Erskine cites Isaiah 42:6; Hebrews 8:6, 13:20; and Luke 23:35. See *Catechism*, 140–41 (20.22, 29). See also *Catechism*, 137–38 (20.3–4), 153 (20.101–3). In light of Karl Barth's critique of federalism, two things must be observed in this statement. First, the elect, while not parties to the Covenant of Grace, were present at the Council of Peace. Second, the elect were present federally in Christ their Head, not metaphysically in Christ their Brother.

nents to Erskine's Covenant of Grace—the covenant as it stands between the Father and the Son and the covenant as it stands between the Son and the elect who are in him. Realizing the need to differentiate these two elements of the covenant, Erskine distinguished between the federal disposition of the Covenant of Grace and the testamentary disposition of the Covenant of Grace. Speaking in terms of this distinction, Erskine argued

> A *federal* disposition is made upon an *onerous* cause, or proper condition; but a *testamentary* disposition is a deed, or conveyance, of *grace* and bounty, *without all conditions*, properly so called. Thus the Father's federal disposition, of all covenant benefits to Christ, was on condition of his making *his soul an offering for sin*; but Christ's testamentary disposition to sinners, who have nothing, is *without money, and without price*. Isa. liii. 10. and lv. 1.[118]

To conflate terminology, Erskine's federal disposition of the Covenant of Grace was a covenant of redemption, while his testamentary disposition of the Covenant of Grace was a covenant of grace. For Erskine, both elements of redemption were part of one Covenant of Grace.

The foundational component of Erskine's Covenant of Grace is the pre-temporal, intra-Trinitarian Council of Peace, wherein the Father freely chose the elect and gave them to the Son, the Son consented to purchase their redemption with his active and passive obedience, and the Holy Spirit agreed to apply the redemption that the Son had thus purchased.[119] It was this element of the Covenant of Grace that Erskine denominated as the federal disposition thereof, for the Council of Peace contained the requisite

---

See Barth, *Church Dogmatics*, IV/1:64–66. Hereafter, *CD*.

118. *Catechism*, 152–53 (20.100; beginning with the 1765 edition, this was divided into questions 20.100–101).

119. See *Catechism*, 140–41 (20.27); *Works*, 1:359; 3:339. For Erskine's most complete sermonic treatment of the Council of Peace, see *Works*, 3:322–37. Erskine's descriptions of the Council of Peace are thoroughly Trinitarian in both language and emphasis, as are his descriptions of both election and the overall redemption of the Covenant of Grace. See, for example, *Catechism*, 137–138 (20.2, 7–9), 140 (20.20–22), 149 (20.77), 156 (20.120); *Works*, 1:98–99, 276, 333, 357, 395. In his Trinitarian understanding of election, Erskine seems to offer a response to T. F. Torrance's critique that federalism creates a crisis within the doctrine of God by presenting the Father solely as Lawgiver to the neglect of the love of the Father. See Torrance, *Theology*, 227–28. In Erskine's Covenant of Grace, the Father and the Son are both "Love" and are both "Lawgiver." See, for example, *Works*, 1:53, 98, 104. In this, there is a unity of purpose and no appearance of the potential for opposite wills within the Godhead, as Barth fears to be nascent in an intra-Trinitarian covenant. See Barth, *CD* IV/1:64–66.

"*onerous* cause, or proper condition"; namely, the righteousness of Christ.[120] By consenting to render perfect obedience to the Law of God, both actively and passively, Christ undertook a definite set of conditions that had to be met and, in meeting them, actually procured the promised benefits of the covenant.[121] Indeed, Erskine's writings make clear that the exact shape of this covenantal purchase was virtually synonymous with the covenantal disposition that was later offered to Adam in innocence under the Covenant of Works.[122] In his overall covenantal system, Erskine was clear that the Covenant of Grace was prior to the Covenant of Works, yet the correspondence between Christ's work in the Covenant of Grace and the terms enjoined upon Adam in the Covenant of Works, coupled with the greater clarity given to the latter in Scripture, led Erskine to speak often of the Son's role in the Covenant of Grace as an undertaking of the Covenant of Works on behalf of his people.[123] In the Council of Peace, the Son consented to enter into the "Covenant of Works" as the representative of the people whom the Father had given to him in that same Council and, in fulfilling that "Covenant of Works," the Son purchased and became the legal possessor of eternal life; the Council of Peace first created the elect and then effectually secured their redemption through the Son.[124]

Flowing from this federal disposition of the covenant was the testamentary disposition of the Covenant of Grace, the element of that covenant wherein the blessings and benefits that had been procured by Christ were dispensed unilaterally and graciously by him to his people.[125] In keeping with Erskine's understanding of a testamentary disposition, there were no conditions, precepts, penalties, or terms of any kind within this portion of the Covenant of Grace; what was given was given freely and unconditionally.[126] While the federal disposition of the covenant had been made from

120. *Works*, 1:228. See also *Catechism*, 155 (20.114), 156 (20.120); *Works*, 1:373.

121. This underlying Law of God was the eternal Law of Nature. See, for example, *ADG*, 74; *Catechism*, 142 (20.35–36), 146 (20.60), 155 (20.114); *Works*, 1:140, 228, 336, 362.

122. E.g., *Catechism*, 146 (20.62).

123. See *Catechism*, 141 (20.28), 146 (20.59), 149 (20.80; a typographical error in the text numbers this as question "88." Future references will cite "20.80" without noting the error); *Works*, 1:98, 100, 140, 314, 336, 479; 3:329.

124. Erskine asserts that the entirety of the *ordo salutis* was secured in the Council of Peace, with its great end being the establishment of the Church. See *Works*, 1:357, 485–86. Erskine's Council of Peace also contained a positive decree of reprobation, although he seldom mentioned it. See *Works*, 1:303–4.

125. *Whole Works*, 1:314, 462–63; 3:345; *Catechism*, 152 (20.99).

126. Even fatherly chastisements and threats are numbered among the promissory components of the Covenant of Grace. See *Catechism*, 150–51 (20.86–89), 155

all eternity, Christ's administration of this testamentary portion of the covenant began in time. Upon Adam's breach of the Covenant of Works, Christ commenced the testamentary disposition of the eternal and prior Covenant of Grace, therein dispensing to his people "all the benefits of the covenant, even HIMSELF, and ALL THINGS in and with him."[127] In every respect, this testamentary disposition of the Covenant of Grace was wholly promissory, becoming essentially an economy for freely distributing the eternal life that Christ had already definitively purchased.[128] Indeed, Christ's purchase in the federal disposition of the covenant was so definitive, that only this testamentary disposition of the covenant remained to confront sinners as an active entity in the gospel offer; thus this testamentary disposition could be referred to simply as "the Covenant of Grace," even though, strictly speaking, it was only half of that covenant.[129]

While the lack of conditions upon Christ's distribution of the covenant's blessings to the elect was thus a function of the testamentary character of that portion of the covenant, it was also a logical necessity of Erskine's expansive notion of the Covenant of Grace. As detailed above, Erskine understood a covenant to be a mutual agreement between two parties based upon certain terms and conditions. In the Covenant of Grace, those two parties were the Father and the Son and the terms and conditions upon which they had agreed had been met by the Son in the federal disposition of the covenant. Thus, the conditional elements of the Covenant of Grace, while a necessary component thereof, had been met already and there was no room for any further conditions in the testamentary disposition of the covenant. If conditions were introduced to that portion of the covenant, Erskine's one Covenant of Grace would become two covenants, with two sets of contracting parties and two sets of terms and conditions. For Erskine's

---

(20.115); *Works*, 1:19–20.

127. *Catechism*, 154 (20.106). See also *Catechism*, 153–54 (20.101–3, 106–8), 156 (20.118); *Works*, 1:101, 363. Erskine insisted that the righteousness that Christ secured in the Council of Peace did not have any existential being outwith the purpose of God until the incarnation; in the incarnation, however, the eternally-secured righteousness that would be imputed to the elect became concretized. It is in this sense that one must understand Erskine's comment elsewhere that Christ's "sacrifice was *laid* on the altar, in the first moment of his incarnation," *Catechism*, 182 (25.23). This provocatively-worded statement by Erskine thus speaks to the temporal manifestation of an eternally-secured, limited redemption; it does not contain intimations of a doctrine of incarnational atonement, as T. F. Torrance supposes. See Torrance, *Theology*, 245–46. Boston uses very similar language, yet he does so in connection with other language that is not without potential problems. See Boston, *Works*, 8:429–30.

128. See *Catechism*, 149 (20.78, 80), 156 (20.120); *Works*, 1:277.

129. E.g., *Works*, 1:172–73, 358–59, 406, 483.

one Covenant of Grace to cohere, the testamentary disposition thereof had to be free of all conditionality.

While Erskine was thus adamant that the Covenant of Grace was entirely promissory in relation to man, his notion of that covenant also contained certain elements that firmly enjoined duty upon those who had received the wholly gracious promises.[130] Throughout his considerations of both the Covenant of Works and the Covenant of Grace, Erskine always distinguished two components—duty and privilege. Both duty and privilege could be found in both covenants and, by their placement relative to each other in each covenant, gave the respective covenants their distinctive character. Indeed, at a practical level, Erskine saw the Covenant of Works and the Covenant of Grace as being distinguished almost wholly by the relative priority of either duty or privilege.[131] In the Covenant of Works, man first performed duty in order to obtain privilege; in the Covenant of Grace, man was first graciously given privilege and then was enjoined by that privilege to go on to perform duty. In large part, Erskine did not see the distinction between the Covenant of Works and the Covenant of Grace in terms of a mercenary versus a gracious covenant, for Erskine firmly believed that both covenants were gracious. Instead, the distinction between the covenants was to be found in the relative priority of duty and privilege, two elements that lay at the heart of each covenant. For Erskine, duty for man was not absent from the Covenant of Grace, it was simply posterior to privilege received and was to be performed only out of gratitude for that previous privilege.[132]

Perhaps most provocatively, Erskine applied this temporally posterior role even to the "duty" of faith.[133] While it was faith that united an individual to Christ, that faith was exercised only posterior to the sovereignly-given and received privilege of regeneration. Faith, as a requisite duty flowing from the gracious privilege of the covenant, was an instrument rather than a condition.[134] In this instrumental role, faith enabled the believer to partake of the blessings of all of the divine covenants. Via the Covenant of Grace, the sinner was reconciled to God through Christ and, in that reconciliation, freely received the eternal life that Christ had procured from the "Covenant

---

130. The presence of meaningful duty within Erskine's theological system obviates the concerns of Macleod, "Covenant Theology," 216.

131. *Works*, 1:126, 207–8. If the relative order of privilege and duty was changed, the covenant itself was changed; thus it would appear as if the only ultimate difference between the two covenants was precisely that order.

132. This duty was understood as obedience to the Law of Nature, particularly as codified in the Decalogue. See, for example, *Works*, 1:35–36, 362, 376–77, 431–32.

133. See, for example, *Works*, 1:361–62, 376–77, 461, 463.

134. See *Catechism*, 148 (20.72–74), 154 (20.107–8); *Works*, 1:245–46, 346, 359.

of Works"; through God's covenantal method, the finite sinner's sin was given righteousness in the Covenant of Grace and his finitude was given infinite life in the "Covenant of Works."[135] In this, redemption was complete, for a finite sinner had been brought into eternal life in the presence of a holy God; the scaffolding of the Covenant of Works and the building of the Covenant of Grace had realized their divinely-intended purpose.[136]

The Covenant of Grace: Hadow

In comparison to Erskine's expansive Covenant of Grace, Hadow posited a much more "restricted" covenant, a restriction clearly necessitated by his holding to a Covenant of Redemption that was distinct from, prior to, and foundational for his Covenant of Grace. However, while the contents of Hadow's Covenant of Grace were thus limited, he in no way saw the graciousness thereof as being similarly restricted. Indeed, in the redemption of his people, God

> is not moved thereto from the Consideration of any good Thing in us, but of his own Love and Mercy he gives eternal Life. It is his free Gift.[137]

The Covenant of Grace, which brought this free gift, was contracted between the Father and the Son, who acted therein as the representative of the elect, and it effectually redeemed the elect group strictly delineated in the prior Covenant of Redemption.[138]

It is in relation to this matter of the parties to the covenant that some of the distinctives of Hadow's Covenant of Grace begin to emerge. First, one clearly sees the importance of the prior Covenant of Redemption to Hadow's Covenant of Grace, an importance that Hadow himself freely recognized. In the very actions of the Covenant of Grace, Hadow conceives of the Son entirely in terms of that previous covenant; from the outset of the Covenant of Grace, Christ acts as the representative of the group created and defined by the Covenant of Redemption.[139] Clearly, as Hadow stated, the Covenant of Grace thus construed presupposes the existence of

---

135. In this, the Covenant of Works and the Covenant of Grace worked in tandem to redeem finite sinners. See *Catechism*, 154 (20.111); *Works*, 1:209, 228.

136. See *Works*, 1:298–99.

137. *RoG*, 9.

138. See "Letters," 65, 68.

139. E.g., ibid., 62–63, 68.

the Covenant of Redemption.[140] Furthermore, this necessary presupposition creates perhaps the most important element of Hadow's Covenant of Grace—the notion of gracious precepts. In the making of the Covenant of Grace, Christ acted as the representative of the elect, undertaking the duties of the Covenant of Works on behalf of that group and offering his righteousness and satisfaction as the only proper condition of the Covenant of Grace.[141] However, Christ thus undertook to represent the elect "without any previous commission or consent given by the Elect unto Jesus Christ to be their representative & Surety."[142] Therefore, the elect stand as legal beneficiaries of all of the blessings of the Covenant of Grace without having done anything to secure the representation of Christ that has alone won those blessings on their behalf.[143]

In order to render a legal consent to this representation of Christ and thus to enter formally into the bond of the covenant, the elect are called to perform certain "requirements."[144] Most notably, the elect are required to exercise repentance and faith.[145] As repentance and faith are thus necessitated and enjoined by the Covenant of Grace, Hadow spoke of the commands to repent and to believe as "gospel commands."[146] These commands of the Covenant of Grace, then, were necessitated by the realities of the distinct Covenant of Redemption; obedience to these precepts was required to give consent to one's membership in the elect, the group whom Christ had acquired in the Covenant of Redemption and had eyed in all of his activities in the Covenant of Grace.[147] As Christ had not thus contracted on behalf of this distinguishable group of the elect in any other covenant, these precepts were new to the Covenant of Grace.[148] However, Hadow also conceived of

140. See ibid., 62–63.

141. Ibid., 63–64, 75.

142. Ibid., 64. See also ibid., 67.

143. Speaking anachronistically, Hadow here seems to recognize a validity to Barth's fifth critique of federalism. See Barth, CD IV/1:64–66.

144. See "Letters," 64, 73–75. Almost without exception, it is in relation to this notion of the elect "entering into the bond of the covenant" that Hadow speaks of conditionality in relation to the elect.

145. See AD, ix–xi; RoG, 13, 15–16. This was a longstanding component of Hadow's theology. See, for example, Hadow, Baptism, 1:15. Often, it appears as if Hadow's notion of the requisite faith stops short of the *fiducia* element thereof. See, for example, RoG, 15.

146. E.g., AD, 131. In some contexts, Hadow would speak of the repentance and faith thus required as "conditions" or "means." See, for example, "Letters," 65–66, 73; RoG, 11.

147. "Letters," 59–61, 73.

148. Hadow also argued that the commands to repent and believe were novel to the

other, older precepts as having a role in the Covenant of Grace. The eternal Law of Nature, which underlay all divine covenants, came into the Covenant of Grace and, while this Royal Law was thus mediated through Christ, such mediation did not divest it of any of its divine authority, and thus it continued to bring with it its necessary penal sanctions.[149]

The believer under the Covenant of Grace, then, was beholden to two different sets of precepts.[150] First, he had to render obedience to the Gospel Precepts of repentance and faith in order to ratify his membership in the group for whom Christ had undertaken the Covenant of Grace. Second, he had to render obedience to the eternal Law of Nature, which yet still represented the duty that man owed to God as his Creator.[151] In both of its aspects, this obligation resting upon the believer could be spoken of as the Law of Christ.

> NOT the Moral Law only, but all Gospel Commands, as was observed before, belong unto the Law of Christ. For they are given forth by God in Christ, reconciling the World to himself, and are founded upon the Covenant of Redemption, and God's constituting and appointing His only begotten Son to be the Mediator, Redeemer aad [sic—'and'] Saviour of Sinners. And these Gospel Commands and Institutions are Christ's Laws; seeing to Him as such, all Power in Heaven and in Earth is given, and all Judgment committed: And by this his Power and Authority, He gives them out in the Gospel as his Commands. . . . The Gospel then is the Law of Christ unto all who hear it, enjoining them to receive, believe and observe what Things soever He hath commanded.[152]

In this description of the Law of Christ, Hadow indicates two things that should be noted. First, the Gospel Commands are firmly rooted in Hadow's distinct Covenant of Redemption. The Son's appointment to the office of Mediator in that covenant establishes the foundation for the commands, and the mediatorial power that he acquires thereby invests those commands with their authority. The Gospel Commands, then, find both their origin and their authority in Hadow's distinct Covenant of Redemption. Second, in spite of its developments and its nuances, Hadow's Law of Christ remains, essentially, the eternal Law of Nature, with Hadow describing the former in

---

Covenant of Grace because such duties could not be deduced from the Law of Nature in its "Primitive Constitution." *AD*, 73.

149. See especially *AD*, 127. See also *AD*, xi–xii; 76.
150. See *AD*, 126–27.
151. See *AD*, 16.
152. *AD*, 131–32.

precisely the same terms in which he had previously described the latter. Given the comprehensiveness of the Law of Nature, its inherent penal sanctions, and its continued presence in Hadow's Covenant of Grace, the Gospel Commands are essentially dissolved into it and it remains little more than it was to Adam in innocence—a command to believe whatever God said and to do whatever he commanded upon pain of definite penal sanctions. This identification of the Law of Christ with the Law of Nature is furthered by Hadow's assertion that it is binding upon all men.[153] Just as was the Law of Nature, the Law of Christ is thus binding upon the believer not necessarily because of his redemption, but rather because of his creation. Through the Covenant of Redemption, Christ comes to proclaim the eternal Law of Nature as his own, augmenting it with clearer commands and not derogating at all from its binding authority.

While Hadow thus saw precepts as lying at the heart of the Covenant of Grace, he also saw grace as lying at the heart of the precepts. From the very outset of his consideration of the Gospel Precepts, Hadow is very insistent that whatsoever God has required of the elect, he has also freely and graciously provided.[154] If God has required repentance and faith in order to number an individual among the elect whom Christ represented in the Covenant of Grace, than God has also freely given to the elect the repentance and the belief that he has required of them. In this, the Covenant of Grace is truly and thoroughly gracious. Indeed, Hadow was ever insistent that an understanding of redemption in which man did anything of his own strength to win his justification was "legalism."[155] Rather than offering man a way by which to obtain any justifying merit, the Gospel Precepts were divinely intended to humble man by showing him his weakness and his utter need of Christ.[156]

Hadow's notion of the Covenant of Grace, while different from Erskine's, was thus self-consciously gracious. At every point, Hadow was very concerned to assert and protect both the gracious divine provision of all that has been required of the elect and the complete monergism of God in all aspects of the redemption of his people. Although the salvation of elect sinners through the Covenant of Grace involved Gospel Precepts, the provision of all that those precepts demanded made the precepts and the covenant gracious. From the very outset of the Covenant of Grace, God's

---

153. See also *AD*, 135.

154. This provision is given for the entirety of the Law of Christ. See *AD*, x–xi, 41, 44, 75; "Letters," 62–63, 64–66; *RoG*, 11, 13.

155. See *AD*, 66.

156. See *AD*, xi, 55.

purpose had been to redeem the elect and he alone had undertaken all that was required to win that redemption.

The Covenant of Grace: Emerging Issues

In light of these brief descriptions of Erskine's and Hadow's notions of the Covenant of Grace, two important differences emerge between those understandings of the covenant. These two differences are both fundamentally rooted in the two men's different positions on the independence of the Covenant of Redemption and produce a dissonance between the resulting Covenants of Grace that created a great deal of the discord of the *Marrow* controversy.[157]

The first difference to emerge between Erskine and Hadow in their conceptions of the Covenant of Grace is the distinction between an immediate and a mediate graciousness.[158] Within their own systems, both men assumed and argued that the Covenant of Grace was truly a gracious covenant. However, Erskine and Hadow entertained very different conceptions of how this graciousness was imparted from God to man. For Erskine, that graciousness was given immediately from God to man via the testamentary disposition of the Covenant of Grace; for Hadow, that graciousness was realized mediately via the gracious Gospel Precepts that were part of the Covenant of Grace. Both men recognized that the end product of the Covenant of Grace was that God gave salvation to the elect; Erskine judged that that salvation was given as a gift, while Hadow argued that it was given

---

157. While the secondary literature almost universally recognizes the difference between a bi-covenantal and a tri-covenantal view, it is always held to be an inconsequential semantic. See, for example, Lachman, *Marrow*, 138. However, the supposition that this difference is, in the end, negligible seems to arise from commentators' propensity to consider its implications on a limited theological question rather than examining its conceptual shaping of the entire Covenant of Grace. For examples of such limited considerations, see McGowan, *Boston*, 14–16, 40–41; Bell, *Calvin and Scottish Theology*, 155–57; Bruggink, "The Theology of Thomas Boston," 177–84. While Macleod does not pursue the matter, he notably hints that the differences between a bi-covenantal and a tri-covenantal perspective underlay some of the confusion of the *Marrow* controversy. See Macleod, *Theology*, 147–48.

158. Often, this difference between the views of the Representers and of the opponents of the *Marrow* is described as the difference between an absolute and a conditional Covenant of Grace. However, such terminology is declined presently due to its oversimplification. See, for example, *Catechism*, 145 (20.58). If such terminology of "absolute" and "conditional" surfaced at times during the controversy—as it certainly did—it was due to concerns of polemics rather than precise theological clarity. Even in such polemical contexts, a degree of ambiguity was recognized in such language. See, for example, Boston, *Works*, 8:461.

through the means of the elect's divinely-enabled obedience to the Gospel Commands. In the former, grace came immediately; in the latter, it was mediated through the Gospel Precepts.

The importance of the immediacy of grace in Erskine's Covenant of Grace was most often expressed through the language of "promise." Throughout his writings, Erskine reiterated that the Covenant of Grace was a wholly promissory covenant, that it contained only promises and no precepts.[159] The conditions of the Covenant of Grace having been met by Christ in the federal disposition of the covenant, the blessings of the covenant were freely given to the elect in the testamentary disposition thereof. Viewed in its testamentary disposition, the Covenant of Grace could be subsumed under the idea of "promise," for in it, Christ promised to his people what he had sovereignly procured by his active and passive obedience. This identification of the Covenant of Grace with "promise" was so strong for Erskine that he was even able to interchange the language of "promise" and "covenant" in his offhand citations of Scripture.[160] In proclaiming the Covenant of Grace, Erskine saw himself as proclaiming a testamentary promise, a promise of benefits already fully secured and thus bequeathed immediately.[161]

The second vital difference to emerge between Erskine's and Hadow's notion of the Covenant of Grace is the distinction between an indefinite and a definite covenant.[162] For Erskine, the Covenant of Grace, in its initial making, viewed mankind indefinitely. Prior to the Council of Peace, which was part of the Covenant of Grace, there were no categories of "elect" or

---

159. See *Works*, 1:358.

160. *Works*, 1:358–59. Here, in a direct reference to Acts 2:39, Erskine says: "'To you is the word of this salvation sent: The promise (or covenant) is unto you." Acts 2:39 is one of the most frequently cited verses in Erskine's writings and he does not always make this verbal substitution. The change here has been deliberate. Similarly, Erskine would often speak of the Covenant of Grace as "God's Covenant of Grace and Promise." *ADG*, 74.

161. The strength of Erskine's emphasis upon the immediacy of grace is highlighted when compared with the writings of Thomas Boston. See Boston, *Works*, 7:39, 8:474; 8:558–59; 8:589–90; 8:435–36, 555. For Boston, the emphasis was on the orderliness in which immediate grace came. See Boston, *Works*, 8:425. For Erskine, the emphasis was on the immediacy of that ordered grace.

162. The sense in which the present treatment uses the terminology of an "indefinite" Covenant of Grace, as explained below, must be carefully distinguished from the eighteenth-century use of that term to describe a view of the divine election of attributes rather than of individuals. As will be seen below, this is not the sense in which Erskine's Covenant of Grace was "indefinite." While the possibility for confusion is regrettable, the distinction between "indefinite" and "definite" simply is the best description of the distinction between Erskine's and Hadow's Covenants of Grace on this point, and thus it will be used in the present account.

"reprobate"; all mankind was considered as a uniform and undifferentiated group—sinners. When God thus contracted in the Covenant of Grace to save sinners, it was an indefinite covenant that resulted. As the Covenant of Grace unfolded, through the purchase of redemption in its federal disposition and the application of redemption in its testamentary disposition, it acquired an undeniable definiteness. In Erskine's most detailed description of the Council of Peace, one sees precisely this movement from indefiniteness to definiteness. At the outset of the Council of Peace, the Triune God sought "a way how *sinners* might be saved," while the end result of that Council of Peace was the Holy Ghost's agreement to apply redemption "to *an elect world.*"[163] While salvation was purchased and applied only in reference to the elect, this definiteness was something that the Covenant of Grace unilaterally created, not a supposition upon which it operated. Specifically, the Covenant of Grace did not commence, in the initial Council of Peace, with reference to categories such as "elect" and "reprobate"; rather, in its outworking, the Covenant of Grace created those categories, thus making the differentiation and the redemption of the elect covenantally identical.[164] In this, the Covenant of Grace was an indefinite covenant for Erskine; it was forged in an indefinite milieu, with no distinction made among men, and proceeded toward definition.[165]

In contrast, Hadow conceived of the Covenant of Grace as an exceedingly definite covenant. As Hadow stated, the Covenant of Grace presupposed the existence of both the decree of election and the Covenant of Redemption. Even before the establishment of the Covenant of Grace, then, there was an inescapable differentiation made among man, for each individual sinner was either an elect sinner or a reprobate sinner, and it was in terms of this divine distinction that the Covenant of Grace viewed man, a fact frequently asserted by Hadow.[166] Simply stated, the differentiation of the elect was covenantally distinct from the redemption of the elect.[167] Hadow's Covenant of Grace did not create salvific categories; it imported them

---

163. *Works*, 1:333; emphasis mine.

164. In the secondary literature, it is sometimes suggested that the Brethren held to an Amyraldian construction of the covenants. See, for example, Kidd, "Enlightenment," 49. However, this redemptive unity that is created by Erskine's indefinite, expansive Covenant of Grace precludes any such accusations. In one covenant, Christ is sent to redeem and redemption is effectually applied to specific, elect individuals. Interestingly, Boston argued that it was a tri-covenantal perspective that opened the door to an Amyraldian universalism. See Boston, *Works*, 8:404–5; McGowan, *Boston*, 40.

165. See *Catechism*, 143 (20.46).

166. E.g., "Letters," 65–66, 68–71, 77.

167. See, for example, *AD*, 131.

from the Covenant of Redemption and operated upon the framework that they provided. In this, Hadow's Covenant of Grace was a definite covenant; when it was first made, man already was considered in definite categories and its intention was to secure salvation for mankind within one of those categories.[168]

This distinction between Erskine's and Hadow's Covenant of Grace is vitally important when one turns to the matter of the gospel offer. For Erskine, the gospel offer was simply an "exhibition" of the Covenant of Grace; essentially, to offer the gospel was to describe God's Covenant of Grace.[169] In Erskine's system, this meant that the Covenant of Grace was to be exhibited, and thus offered, indiscriminately to all persons.[170] In making the Covenant of Grace, God had acted sovereignly, without reference to salvific categories, and by his actions in that covenant, had created definitive salvific categories and won salvation in terms of those categories. For Erskine, then, the Covenant of Grace was to be proclaimed to all men, to men considered only as sinners, and, in this proclamation, the gospel would create categories of election and reprobation.[171] In exhibiting the Covenant of Grace, Erskine refused to exhibit it in terms of the categories of election, for those were categories created by the covenant, not anterior to it. Just as it had in its formation, so the Covenant of Grace was to function in Erskine's preaching—it was to go forth into an indefinite milieu of men considered as sinners and,

---

168. In the Covenant of Grace, God is "willing to be reconciled to Elect sinners." "Letters," 63.

169. See, for example, *Works*, 358–59. Such had long been the Scottish view. See, for example, *Sum*, 334–35.

170. See, for example, *Catechism*, 151 (20.90–94). In this instance, the unlimited offer of the gospel is grounded in "the *intrinsic sufficiency* of Christ's obedience and death, for the salvation of all." While it is certainly important that Erskine offers this specific rationale for an indefinite gospel offer, such explicit arguments for the extent of the gospel offer already receive much attention in the secondary literature. What is under consideration here, and what is entirely neglected in the secondary literature, is the implicit conceptual difference between how the Covenant of Grace was approached and viewed by both Erskine and Hadow. It was this conceptual difference, it is contended, that made Erskine and Hadow unable to reach any agreement even though they would have both affirmed the same explicit statements. Indeed, such is the case here. While both would have agreed on the sufficiency of Christ's death for all, they would starkly disagree on how the Covenant of Grace that contained that sufficient death confronted humanity. Did it confront the human as sinner, thus giving warrant to all to receive it, or did it confront the human as elect sinner, thus offering a warrant that was limited to a select group?

171. See, for example, *Works*, 1:245–46, 342, 427.

in that going forth, it was to create salvific categories and either save or condemn accordingly.[172]

For Hadow, the situation was markedly different. While Hadow essentially concurred with Erskine's definition of the gospel proclamation as being a description of the Covenant of Grace, the Covenant of Grace that was thus described was quite different; as the Covenant of Grace was a definite covenant, the exhibition of it was to be definite, as well.[173] In its first making, the Covenant of Grace had considered man in the categories of elect sinners and reprobate sinners, categories created by the prior Covenant of Redemption. Therefore, the exhibition of the Covenant of Grace was to consider men in terms of the same categories; in speaking of the Covenant of Grace, the preacher was able to speak in terms of election and reprobation, for those terms had definitive content and meaning even before the Covenant of Grace was made. The exhibition of the Covenant of Grace, then, exhibited precisely the salvation that the Covenant of Grace intended to secure from its inception—salvation for the elect, but not for the reprobate.[174]

At a conceptual level, then, Erskine's and Hadow's different notions of the definiteness of the Covenant of Grace necessitated very different views of the gospel offer. For Erskine, the gospel offer was the proclamation of the Covenant of Grace to a homogeneous group that, in its proclamation, created eternal distinctions between the elect and the reprobate. Just as did the Covenant of Grace itself, the proclamation of that covenant first encountered man indefinitely and moved inexorably to eternal definiteness. For Hadow, the gospel offer was the proclamation of the Covenant of Grace to a heterogeneous group that, even in its first proclamation, operated on previously existing categories of election. Just as did the Covenant of Grace itself, the proclamation of that covenant first encountered each individual man as a member of one of two groups and dealt with him accordingly. For Erskine, the gospel was proclaimed to a "promiscuous multitude," for all the hearers of the gospel were sinners; for Hadow, the gospel was proclaimed to a "mixed multitude," for each hearer of the gospel was either an elect sinner or a reprobate sinner.[175] In both instances, the milieu in which the Covenant of Grace had been made in eternity governed the milieu in which that Covenant of Grace is to be proclaimed in time.

---

172. See especially Erskine's illustration on *Works*, 1:172, where he exhorts his hearers to "Let the indefinite and absolute nature of the covenant of grace be your warrant for embracing the Lord Jesus." See also *Works*, 1:363.

173. "Letters," 67–68.

174. "Letters," 67–68.

175. E.g., "Letters," 75–76.

The Covenant of Grace: Doctrinal Context

In seeking to establish the historical precedent for Erskine's and Hadow's differing views of the Covenant of Grace, three different issues must be considered. First, is the "Covenant of Redemption" to be subsumed under the Covenant of Grace or distinguished therefrom? Second, is the graciousness of the Covenant of Grace mediate or immediate? Third, is the Covenant of Grace a definite or an indefinite covenant? These three matters shall be considered in turn.

Distinct Covenant of Redemption

The first issue that must be clarified within the trajectory of Scottish federalism is the existence of a distinct Covenant of Redemption. Within the theology which Erskine and Hadow inherited, there was an increasing tendency to speak of a "Covenant of Redemption," yet this growing consensus of expression masks a great deal of variety regarding the specific issues in contention between the two men.

Within the Confession of Faith, the notion of a distinct Covenant of Redemption is neither affirmed nor denied, and this evident studious avoidance of the matter has led many to suppose that the Confession does not support either side of the question.[176] However, the Confession contains all of the ingredients of a bi-covenantal position, even if it does not contain the explicit terminology thereof. Throughout chapter 7, the Confession speaks of the Covenant of Grace as a testament; in chapter 8, Christ's purchase of redemption and his application of the same to the elect are covenantally linked; and when there is a distinction made between the purchase and the application of redemption in chapter 11, that distinction is purely temporal rather than covenantal.[177] In each of these chapters, the Confession speaks of the purchase and the application of redemption in such a way that the latter is an organic climax, rather than a causal result, of the former. In this, the Confession could be classed tentatively as a bi-covenantal document that has not entered into polemic with a tri-covenantal perspective. However, such a classification certainly must take account of the simple fact that the Confession was commonly bound with *The Sum* without any supposition of contradiction. That ancillary work, *The Sum*, is very self-consciously tri-covenantal in perspective, consistently differentiating between the Covenant of Redemption, which purchases salvation, and the Covenant of

---

176. E.g., McWilliams, 116n29.
177. *WCF*, 7.2–4; 8.1, 3, 8; 11.4.

Grace, which applies it; arguing that the former is the necessary and causal foundation of the latter; and viewing man as a party-contractor to the Covenant of Grace.[178] In *The Sum*, one thus sees an impulse to bring greater logical precision to the more nebulous statements of the Confession; if this impulse is not pursued as rigorously as it would be in subsequent treatises, it nonetheless helped establish the foundation for such inquiries.[179]

In Patrick Gillespie's work, the notion of a discernible Covenant of Redemption received a more exhaustive and more detailed treatment than it had in most previous Scottish theology. Within that considerable body of work, there are four observations that are immediately germane to the present issue. First, the simple fact of Gillespie's work and the organizational structure thereof is evidence of a growing tendency within Scottish federalism to distinguish terminologically between the Covenant of Redemption and the Covenant of Grace.[180] Indeed, Gillespie often framed this distinction in terms of the Covenant of Redemption serving as the foundation of the Covenant of Grace.[181] Secondly, however, Gillespie's work also manifests the very closest of connections between these two differentiated covenants.[182] While the covenants are to be distinguished, they jointly represent "one continued tract of Covenant-grace, one current of the water of life."[183] Thirdly, as Gillespie elucidates his doctrine of a Covenant of Redemption, it is clear that his concern is not, fundamentally, the distinction of that covenant from the Covenant of Grace. Rather, Gillespie is primarily concerned to assert the eternality and intra-Trinitarian nature of the Covenant of Redemption. Indeed, throughout his exposition of a tri-covenantal system, Gillespie says little that differs from Erskine's bi-covenantal system, with the former's "Covenant of Redemption" being almost indistinguishable from the latter's "Council of Peace."[184] Fourthly, as Gillespie seeks to assert this pre-temporal intra-Trinitarian covenant, it becomes quite evident that he is driven by

---

178. See *Sum*, 324; 324, 331, 335, 338; 332–33, 334–35, 343, respectively. Interestingly, *Sum* also uses the Covenant of Redemption as both an explanation of the graciousness of the Covenant of Grace and a warrant for sinners to believe in Christ. See *Sum*, 335, 338, respectively. For the influence of Dickson's and Durham's tri-covenantal views, see Richard, "Arminianism," 157.

179. At times, *Sum* conspicuously fails to reference the Covenant of Redemption. See, for example, *Sum*, 326. Furthermore, in *Victory*, Dickson fails to mention the Covenant of Redemption at all, even though ample opportunity to do so is present.

180. See Gillespie, *Covenant*, 1–2, 7, 26.

181. E.g., ibid., 1, 3

182. See ibid., 5, 44–45, 113–28; ibid., 2:150.

183. Ibid., 125. Provocatively, Boston uses almost identical imagery to describe his bi-covenantal system. See Boston, *Works*, 8:475.

184. See especially Gillespie, *Covenant*, 1–50, 118, 125–27

anti-antinomian polemical concerns. In opposition to the Antinomians, who eviscerated the Law in the life of the believer by freeing him from any covenantal duties, Gillespie was concerned to assert a Covenant of Redemption, distinguishable from the Covenant of Grace, that left room for duties to reside upon believers as parties to the Covenant of Grace.[185]

In Herman Witsius' presentation of the Covenant of Redemption, there is much similarity with Gillespie. Although Witsius avoids the term "Covenant of Redemption," he does consistently distinguish between the covenant made between the Father and the Son and the covenant made between God and the elect, with the latter covenant being founded explicitly upon the former.[186] Also, like Gillespie, Witsius appears more concerned to establish the eternality of the intra-Trinitarian covenant than to assert its abstract distinction from the Covenant of Grace.[187] Furthermore, Witsius also marshals his tri-covenantal scheme to polemical duty; namely, the refutation of Socinian and Arminian doctrine.[188] However, what is particularly notable about Witsius is the closeness of the connection in which he holds the covenant between the Father and the Son and the covenant between God and the elect.[189] The essential foundation of this connection for Witsius is that in his covenant with the Father, Christ satisfied the condition upon which the blessings of the Covenant of Grace were contingent, thus leading to the effectual bestowal of those blessings upon the elect.[190] In seeking to answer those who might suppose that such an arrangement makes the covenant between God and the elect to be less than a proper covenant, Witsius argued that

> there is no absurdity, should we maintain, that that disposition of the new covenant, which was made to the Surety, retained the proper notion of a covenant, signifying a compact between two parties of mutual faith; but that the other disposition made *to us*, comes nearer to the form of a testament, and is rather unilateral, or appointed by one party.[191]

Here, in seeking to explicate his Tri-Covenantal scheme, Witsius presents a view that is virtually indistinguishable from Erskine's bi-covenantal scheme.

---

185. E.g., ibid., 2, 5; Gillespie, *Testament*, 2:154.
186. See Witsius, *Economy of the Covenants*, 1:165, 263–64, 281.
187. See ibid., 1:291.
188. See ibid., 1:166. This will be pursued further in following sections.
189. In the structuring of his work, Witsius even treats both of these covenants under the rubric of the Covenant of Grace. See ibid., book II, chapters 1–2.
190. See ibid., 1:165–66, 189–90, 284.
191. Ibid., 1:287. See also ibid., 2:187.

Witsius speaks of two dispositions of the new covenant, one being made to Christ and retaining the character of a proper covenant, the other being made to the elect and of a testamentary character.[192] In this description, there is nothing different from Erskine's expansive Covenant of Grace, composed of both a federal and a testamentary disposition.[193] While Witsius holds to both a covenant between the Father and the Son and a covenant between God and the elect, they are here held in such an organic unity that they appear as different aspects of the same covenant.[194]

Overall, the Scottish federalism which Erskine and Hadow inherited had undeniably adopted a distinction between the Covenant of Redemption and the Covenant of Grace.[195] However, this distinction was driven not by a desire to abstract the two covenants from each other, but rather by a concern to assert the eternal, intra-Trinitarian foundation of the redemption that was realized in time.[196] In this situation, both Hadow and Erskine could find countenance for their covenantal schemes. Hadow could clearly claim the precedent of asserting a distinct Covenant of Redemption. That this covenant had previously been used in polemic against an antinomian rejection of it would only further Hadow's conviction that Erskine's denial of the Covenant of Redemption was driven by antinomian commitments. However, despite this rejection of a distinct Covenant of Redemption, Erskine could plead fidelity to the commitments that had produced the distinction that he declined, for in his expansive Covenant of Grace, complete with his robust Council of Peace, there was undeniably an eternal, intra-Trinitarian foundation for human redemption. If Erskine rejected the language that had previously been used against Antinomians, he certainly embraced the concerns that had driven that polemic. Both Erskine's and Hadow's covenantal

---

192. At times, Witsius refers to this latter component as a "testamentary disposition." See, for example, ibid., 1:165. See also ibid., 1:284–85. As such terminology is not prominent in the literature of the time, it seems likely that Erskine's characteristic use of it is attributable to Witsius's influence.

193. Witsius's descriptions of the covenant between the Father and the Son are strikingly similar to Erskine's description of the Council of Peace. See ibid., 1:165–66, 168–69.

194. Bruggink notes an affinity between Witsius and a bi-covenantal scheme, yet offers no discussion or substantiation of such a claim. See Bruggink, "Theology of Thomas Boston," 183.

195. Macleod, however, affords this distinction more historical precedent than it is perhaps due. See Macleod, *Theology*, 147–48.

196. See Richard, "Arminianism," 151–55. Such a concern had been present in Reformed theology long before the distinction of a separate Covenant of Redemption was adopted to assert it. See, for example, Bierma, *German Calvinism*, 107; Lillback, *Binding of God*, 101, 213–14; Helm, "Calvin and the Covenant," 80–81.

structures, then, were legitimate continuations and developments of the inheritance of Scottish federalism.

Mediate versus Immediate Graciousness

In the matter of whether the graciousness of the Covenant of Grace is given mediately or immediately, it again appears that Erskine's and Hadow's refinement of federal theology had introduced tension between different emphases that had previously been held in tandem in Scottish federalism. In the Westminster Confession's distillation of this federal system, there are intimations of grace coming both mediately, as through means that God had appointed to lead to salvation, and immediately, as being bequeathed by Christ in his testament.[197] These positions are asserted in startling proximity in *WCF* 7.3, which states that God

> freely offereth unto sinners life and salvation by Jesus Christ, requiring of them faith in Him that they may be saved and promising to give unto all those that are ordained unto life His Holy Spirit, to make them willing and able to believe.[198]

Here, the Confession asserts both Erskine's immediate graciousness in the contention that salvation is freely offered, and Hadow's mediate graciousness in the contention that God both requires and bestows the faith that is the means through which that salvation is given. For the Confession, there is no contradiction or tension in holding both that grace is freely given, and that it is thus given through the divinely-appointed and divinely-enabled means of faith.

This balance that the Confession evidences between a mediate and an immediate graciousness is not so evident in *The Sum*. While *The Sum* retains some echoes of an immediate graciousness—most notably, in several references to Christ being "a gift"—the dominant emphasis therein is upon the mediation of grace, primarily through divinely-commanded and divinely-enabled faith and repentance.[199] Indeed, the significant contribution that *The Sum* makes to Scottish federalism in this regard is its self-conscious description of Gospel Commands. For *The Sum*, the command to believe in Christ "is a command of the gospel, posterior to the law, given for

---

197. For the former, see *WCF*, 19.7. For the latter, see *WCF*, 7.4.

198. *WCF*, 7.3. See *WCF*, 3.6 for another example of such duality of statement.

199. For the notion of Christ as a gift, see *Sum*, 333. For the mediation of grace, see, for example, *Sum*, 324–26, 328.

making use of the remedy of all sins."[200] It is by his gracious and sovereign provision of the faith that he has required that God ushers individuals into the Covenant of Grace.[201] In this, *The Sum* maintains an insistence that the Covenant of Grace is a truly gracious covenant, yet it also insists that that graciousness is mediated through divinely-enabled obedience to Gospel Commands. Dickson would maintain the same dual emphasis in *Truth's Victory*, arguing both against a meritorious Gospel Law and for the presence of commands within the Gospel.[202]

While the presence of Gospel Commands is already easily discernible in *The Sum*, they become even more prominent in Gillespie. Throughout his exposition of the covenants, Gillespie makes repeated reference to "Gospel Commands and Conditions," which he sees as comprising the commands to believe, to repent, and to work out one's own salvation with fear and trembling.[203] While Gillespie thus insists on the presence of these Gospel Commands, he is simultaneously adamant that the ability to obey these commands and meet these conditions is given by God with such unilateral sovereignty that the salvation to which they are means can be conceived of as absolutely dispensed.[204] For Gillespie, the graciousness of the Covenant of Grace was mediated in such a way that neither God's unilateral bestowal of the ability to meet the Gospel Conditions, nor the individual's personal activity in utilizing that ability, was to be diminished.[205] The grace of Gillespie's Covenant of Grace was thus undoubtedly a mediate graciousness.

In Gillespie, a growing emphasis within Scottish federalism on the mediate nature of grace within the Covenant of Grace reached its apex; in Witsius, that emphasis was almost entirely muted. In Witsius' notion of the

---

200. *Sum*, 336. See also *Sum*, 337.

201. See *Sum*, 325

202. See Dickson, *Victory*, 148–51; 146–47, respectively. In his support for gospel commands, Dickson is writing in polemic against antinomian doctrine.

203. Gillespie, *Testament*, 2:58. See also ibid., 2:50–53. For Gillespie's enumeration of these commands, see *Covenant*, 121. While Gillespie does not argue, with Hadow, that obedience to these gospel commands renders the elect sinner's consent to Christ's representation of him in the Covenant of Redemption, one can detect in Gillespie the ground from which such a position might have arisen. See Gillespie, ibid., 122–23.

204. See Gillespie, *Testament*, 1:351, 367–68; 2:45, 61–62; Gillespie, *Covenant*, 43. At times, Gillespie speaks of this connection in terms of the instrumentality of faith. See Gillespie, *Testament*, 1:247–48. In his most intriguing description of the divine bestowal of the ability to meet the gospel conditions, Gillespie speaks of that ability coming by way of testamentary, absolute disposition. See ibid., 1:315, 332. In this, Gillespie was able to speak of grace coming both via testament and through means.

205. Gillespie, *Covenant*, 122; Gillespie, *Testament*, 1:260–61, 272. For a similar view in Olevianus, see Bierma, "The Role of Covenant Theology in Early Reformed Orthodoxy," 459–61. Hereafter, "Covenant Theology."

Covenant of Grace, that covenant was wholly promissory, containing no conditions and no commands whatsoever.[206] At times, Witsius seems to break from this overriding emphasis and to speak of a progression within the bestowal of grace that could intimate a certain mediateness to grace.[207] However, the orderliness that Witsius sees within the Covenant of Grace is derived from the order in which God bestows his promises, not from a system of divinely-enabled obedience to Gospel Commands.[208] Indeed, Witsius obviates any notion of Gospel Commands, clearly asserting that all promises are to be placed within the gospel and all commands or injunctions to duty are to be relegated to the law.[209] For Witsius, the graciousness of the Covenant of Grace was an immediate, ordered graciousness.

By the end of the seventeenth century, Scottish federalism contained strong notes of both Hadow's mediate graciousness and Erskine's immediate graciousness. The balance of the Scottish witness, however, was undoubtedly with Hadow's system. In Gillespie's federal scheme, *The Sum*'s positing of Gospel Commands had been brought to such a prominent position that there is no discernable difference between Gillespie's doctrine and Hadow's mediate graciousness. In Gillespie, there is decided precedent for Hadow's doctrine. However, in Witsius, a remarkably strong emphasis upon the promissory nature of the Covenant of Grace, and thus the immediate nature of the graciousness thereof, was injected into the Scottish scene. While it is possible to see Hadow's system as faithful to Witsius' insistence upon the orderliness of immediate grace, the preponderance of Witsius' support lies with Erskine's immediate graciousness. Just as strongly as Hadow could claim Gillespie's support on this question, Erskine could claim Witsius'. Both positions were firmly entrenched within the inheritance of Scottish federalism.

Definite versus Indefinite Covenant of Grace

The point of contention that arose between Erskine and Hadow on whether the Covenant of Grace is given definiteness by the prior Covenant of

---

206. See Witsius, *Economy of the Covenants*, 1:49–50, 165, 283–84, 286, 288; 2:187. For a refutation of the conditionality of faith in particular, see ibid., 1:411–15. When Witsius does speak of conditions within the Covenant of Grace, he is insistent that they are conditions to be performed by Christ, not by the elect. See ibid., 1:165, 286.

207. Witsius even speaks of "means" to salvation. See ibid., 1:409.

208. See ibid., 1:270, 283–84, 286–89, 338–39. It is most likely this emphasis on the orderliness of immediate grace that influenced Thomas Boston.

209. Witsius held, with Erskine, that the gospel simply revealed new objects for the duties previously disclosed in the law. See ibid., 1:290–91, 410.

Redemption, or whether the Covenant of Grace itself provides that definition, seems to have not been considered at all in the previous course of Scottish federal theology. The commencement of this ambiguous situation is clearly seen in *The Sum*. In expositing Isaiah 55:1–5, *The Sum* asserts that

> the Lord promises, that this offer being received, shall quicken the dead sinner; and that, upon the welcoming of this offer, he will close the covenant of grace with the man that shall consent unto it, even an indissolvable covenant of perpetual reconciliation and peace. . . . Which covenant, he declareth, shall be in substance the assignation, and the making over, of all the saving graces which David (who is Jesus Christ, Acts xiii. 34.) hath bought for us in the covenant of redemption . . . .[210]

In this one statement, the Covenant of Grace is portrayed as both indefinite and definite. In the first portion of its statement, *The Sum* conceives of the offered Covenant of Grace considering men as dead sinners. With the covenant thus offered to all men, some consent to it and others do not, and thus the covenant itself produces definiteness; a definiteness that comes posterior to the gospel proclamation rather than anterior thereto.[211] In this, *The Sum* seems to hold a view of an indefinite Covenant of Grace that is not substantially different than that of Erskine. However, in the second portion of the quoted excerpt, *The Sum* undeniably speaks of the Covenant of Grace as a covenant limited by the prior Covenant of Redemption. Indeed, this definiteness of the Covenant of Grace is so pronounced that that covenant becomes little more than the bestowal of the blessings that had already been secured in the Covenant of Redemption. In this situation, the specification of grace has occurred covenantally prior to the Covenant of Grace, thus making that covenant a definite covenant. In this, one receives a paradigm for the whole of *The Sum* on this matter—the Covenant of Grace, limited by a prior Covenant of Redemption, could itself be seen as confronting an indefinite milieu and introducing definiteness thereto.[212]

The Sum's ability to jointly assert both a Covenant of Redemption and an indefinite Covenant of Grace continued to mark Scottish federalism in the following decades, as evidenced in the work of Gillespie and Witsius. Indeed, *The Sum*'s ambivalence on this matter reaches even greater heights in Gillespie, who on the very same page of his treatise on the Covenant of Redemption is able to speak of the Covenant of Grace first as definite and

---

210. *Sum*, 333. See also *Sum*, 324–25, 328, 332, 342.
211. See also *Sum*, 333, 338.
212. See also *Sum*, 335.

then as indefinite.²¹³ For Witsius, the source of ambiguity can be glimpsed when, speaking of man as a contracting party to the covenant between God and the elect, he writes that

> here men are considered, 1st. As *sinners* . . . 2dly. As *chosen* by God . . . 3dly. As those for whom Christ engaged or made satisfaction: for this ought to be considered as necessary, before ever it could be worthy of God to make mention of his grace to sinful man.²¹⁴

Here, Witsius asserts that the foundational view that the covenant between God and the elect takes of man is of man as sinner, yet he also posits that the subsequent view taken of man as chosen sinner is necessary before anyone can speak of God being gracious to man viewed as sinner. In other words, Witsius' "covenant of grace" is both indefinite and definite, and he is thus able to speak of it in terms indicative of both views.²¹⁵

Overall, the system of Scottish federalism that Erskine and Hadow inherited contained little that was definitive on whether the Covenant of Grace was a definite covenant or an indefinite covenant. In various contexts, the authorities could speak of the Covenant of Grace as both. However, two germane trends do emerge. First, when the Covenant of Grace is presented as a definite covenant, it is almost invariably coupled with a presentation of the Covenant of Redemption as an indefinite covenant. In such contexts, where covenantal differentiation occurs, the idea of an indefinite covenant is not absent; it simply is assigned to the Covenant of Redemption rather than the Covenant of Grace. Secondly, when the Covenant of Grace is presented as an indefinite covenant, it is almost invariably in contexts in which the author in question is speaking of the entire course of God's redemptive work. In these contexts, as the Covenant of Redemption is subsumed implicitly under God's redemptive purposes as expressed in the Covenant of Grace, that latter covenant takes on the limiting functions of the former. In this, both Hadow and Erskine could find fodder for their respective views. If the former trend lent approval to Hadow's notion of a definiteness to the Covenant of Grace, the latter trend countenanced Erskine's insistence that definiteness occurred through, rather than prior to, his expansive Covenant of Grace. What previous generations of Scottish federal theologians had held together, Erskine's and Hadow's greater refinement would tear asunder.

---

213. Gillespie, *Covenant*, 127. See also ibid., 118–19, 123.
214. Witsius, *Economy of the Covenants*, 1:282.
215. See ibid., 1:49–50, 165, 168–69, 261, 416–17.

ERSKINE'S "OBSCURED TRUTHS"

At length, having acquired a familiarity with the federal structures of both Erskine's and Hadow's theologies, the important differences that arise between those structures, and the connection that both men's systems had with the current of Scottish federalism, one is able to proceed to a consideration of the five "obscured truths" whose defense prompted Erskine's involvement in the *Marrow* controversy. As each of these truths, as well as both Erskine's and the General Assembly's notions of them, are examined, one realizes that the catalyst for Erskine's involvement in the controversy was the dissonance between his and Hadow's federal structures.

Obscured Truth 1

The first truth that Erskine judged to be obscured by the Act 1720 was the truth

> That believers are freed from the Law as the Covenant of Works, freed both from the *commanding* and *condemning* power of *that* Covenant....[216]

Erskine and the other Representers argued that this truth had been slighted when the Act specifically condemned the *Marrow*'s proposition

> *That as the Law is the Covenant of Works, Believers are altogether and wholly set free from it: Set free both from the Commanding and Condemning Power of the Covenant of Works.*[217]

In examining this condemned proposition, it is possible to distinguish two separate clauses within it: first, that believers are freed from the covenantal terms of the Covenant of Works and, second, that believers are set free from the commanding and condemning power of the Covenant of Works. When this two-fold proposition is viewed from within the respective covenantal systems of Erskine and Hadow, two very different perceptions of what is being asserted emerge.

From Erskine's covenantal perspective, the condemned proposition was a single assertion, with the second clause thereof being simply a parallel restatement of the first. In Erskine's understanding, to assert, in the first instance, that believers are freed from the Law as the Covenant of Works and, in the second instance, that believers are set free from the commanding

---

216. *Christian Magazine*, 377.
217. *Representation*, 5–6. See *AGA*, 535.

and condemning power of that covenant is really to assert the same truth twice—that believers are free from the terms of the Covenant of Works; terms that both made the Moral Law a covenant and alone gave it a coercive authority.[218] This particular understanding of the matter was made evident when the Representers stated, in reference to the condemned proposition, that the Law, in respect of believers, is

> divested of it's Promise of Life and threatening of Death . . . as it really is, since they are not under it to be thereby Justified, or Condemned, we cannot comprehend how it continues any longer to be a Covenant to them, or as such to have a Commanding Power over them.[219]

The Moral Law acquired both its covenantal status and its commanding and condemning power from the covenantal terms and conditions superadded to it; the removal of those terms meant the removal of both covenantal status and coercive authority. While the believer was not freed from the Moral Law in an absolute sense, he was free from the commanding and condemning power imparted to it by the terms of the Covenant of Works.[220] For Erskine, then, the Assembly's condemnation of the *Marrow*'s unified proposition was the very worst of legal doctrine, for it was a condemnation of the simple declaration that believers are free from the Covenant of Works.

From within Hadow's covenantal paradigm, the matter was quite different. For Hadow, the condemned proposition was actually a double assertion, with the second clause thereof constituting a subtle antinomian extension of the first. In Hadow's conception of the Covenant of Works, the commanding and condemning power of that covenant emanated from a double source—first, from the specific terms of the Covenant of Works and, second, from the divine origin of the Law of Nature that underlay it. Therefore, the disputed proposition from the *Marrow* made a double assertion. First, the *Marrow* asserted that the believer was free from the Law as the Covenant of Works, thus positing that the believer was free from the terms of the Covenant of Works. Second, the *Marrow* asserted that the believer was freed from the entirety of the commanding and condemning power of the Covenant of Works, thus positing that the believer was also free from the intrinsic authority of the Law of Nature. If all of the commanding and condemning power of the Covenant of Works was obviated, then both sources of that authority must be rendered obsolete to the believer. The

---

218. See *ADG*, 60.
219. *Representation*, 6.
220. See, for example, *Answers*, 20–21.

Marrow's proposition, then, first declared the believer free from the terms of the Covenant of Works and then declared him liberated from the Moral Law.

That Hadow thus understood the double nature of the *Marrow*'s proposition, finding the first assertion wholly acceptable and the second wholly contemptible, is evident in Hadow's admission that

> I should have made no Quarrel with the *Marrow*, had he said, That a Believer is not under the Obligation of the Law, as it had the Form of the Covenant of Works put upon it, requiring perfect Obedience as the Condition of Eternal Life: And owned, That he is still under the standing Obligation of the Moral Law, which was the Matter of the Covenant of Works. . . . Doth the assumption of the Moral law into the Gospel Dispensation, deprive it of its Original Binding Power on the Believer, as he is a Man, a reasonable Creature? Or doth the Grace of Christ exempt a Believer from Subjection to the perpetual Law of Nature?[221]

The commanding and condemning power that the Covenant of Works had as a result of its covenantal terms was indeed removed in respect of the believer, yet the commanding and condemning power that it had as a result of the Moral Law that underlay it was still binding, requiring submission even from the believer under the Covenant of Grace. For Hadow, the condemned proposition was a double assertion. By supporting it, Erskine and his fellow Representers were first making a wholly orthodox proposition and then subtly seeking to import a wholly antinomian tenet in its wake. In this, Erskine was guilty of "sly antinomianism" at its worst—the importation of antinomian doctrine as a supposed extrapolation of orthodox theology.[222]

When one thus views the first of Erskine's "obscured truths," it is evident that the disagreement surrounding that "truth" stemmed from the different constructions of federal theology held by Erskine and Hadow.[223] Viewed from within Erskine's covenantal scheme, the condemnation of the *Marrow*'s proposition truly was abject legalism. As the commanding and condemning power of the Covenant of Works sprang solely from the terms of that covenant, the Assembly's assertion that some such commanding and condemning power remained for believers was an effective relegation of believers to the Covenant of Works. Viewed from Hadow's covenantal sys-

---

221. *AD*, 89.

222. Hadow often referred to the *Marrow* as the work of a "sly Antinomian." See, for example, *AD*, 122.

223. Further, see the exchange on the Commission's second Query in *Answers*, 20–21; *AGA*, 554.

tem, on the other hand, Erskine's support of the *Marrow*'s proposition was undoubtedly antinomian. As the commanding and condemning power of the Covenant of Works stemmed both from the terms of that covenant and the divine origin of the Law of Nature that underlay it, Erskine's assertion that the believer was wholly freed from the commanding and condemning power of the Covenant of Works was a declaration of the believer's wholesale liberty from the Moral Law. For Erskine, Hadow and the Assembly were legitimately guilty of legalism; for Hadow, Erskine was legitimately guilty of antinomianism. In these disparate conclusions, Erskine and Hadow were each led by the differing positions that they had adopted from a shared, early eighteenth-century Scottish federalism.

Obscured Truth 2

The second truth that Erskine judged to be obscured by the Assembly's Act 1720 was

> That there is and ought to be a difference put betwixt the Law as the Law of Works, and the Law as the Law of Christ, or the Law as a rule of obedience in the hand of a Mediator . . . .[224]

For Erskine and his brethren, "the Law as the Law of Works" referred to the Law within the Covenant of Works, while "the Law as the Law of Christ" referred to the Law within the Covenant of Grace.[225] Therefore, in contending for this "obscured truth," Erskine was urging that a distinction be made between the functioning of the Law of God within these two divine covenants. However, in the Act 1720, the Assembly had declared such a distinction to be "altogether groundless"; a dismissal that Erskine judged to be an effective casting of believers back upon the Covenant of Works as a means of obtaining eternal life.[226] If there was no distinction made between the functioning of the Law under the two covenants, than salvation came by obedience thereto under both covenantal dispensations.[227] While the Assembly 1722 accepted the Brethren's understanding of what was implied by "the Law as the Law of Works" and "the Law as the Law of Christ," they objected that the Act 1720 had not intended the errors imputed to it, but rather had acted to

---

224. *Christian Magazine*, 377.

225. See *Answers*, 79–80.

226. *AGA*, 536. The Assembly had thus declared the distinction groundless specifically in reference to the six Antinomian Paradoxes. However, the ensuing debate on the distinction did not consider it in this more narrow application. See *Representation*, 6–8.

227. See *Answers*, 79–81.

prevent a latent antinomianism that would have eviscerated the Law under the Covenant of Grace.[228]

While this area of debate within the *Marrow* controversy was marked by much disagreement, at least the exact question under debate was uniformly understood. According to the *Marrow*, there was a vital two-fold distinction between the functioning of the Law under the Covenant of Works and the functioning of the Law under the Covenant of Grace: first, under the latter, the Law held only non-salvific rewards and punishments for obedience or disobedience thereto, and second, the Law under the Covenant of Grace applied only to believers, to the exclusion of non-believers. Both the proponents and the opponents of the *Marrow* agreed that the acceptability of this two-fold distinction was the matter under debate, with Erskine and the Brethren holding that the *Marrow*'s distinction was vital to the gospel and Hadow and the Assembly arguing that it was destructive of the same. In examining this "obscured truth," one must note two previously noted distinctions between Erskine's and Hadow's federal theologies—the distinction between an immediate and a mediate graciousness within the Covenant of Grace and the different views entertained of the post-Fall status of the Covenant of Works.

In considering Erskine's and Hadow's different positions on the *Marrow*'s limitation of the Law of Christ to only non-salvific rewards and punishments, one is confronted with their views of the immediate graciousness of the Covenant of Grace and the mediate graciousness of the Covenant of Grace, respectively. Within Erskine's system, the immediate nature of this graciousness was evidenced by the necessary priority of privilege received over duty performed. In other words, when the Christian first considered the question of obedience to the Law of Christ, he had already received the salvific blessing of eternal life. Therefore, while Erskine maintained that obedience to the Law of Christ was a matter of vital importance to the Christian, obedience or disobedience to that Law did not carry the salvific implications of determining one's salvation or damnation. Such matters had been settled prior to the Christian's obedience or disobedience to the Law.

Within Hadow's Covenant of Grace, the functioning of the Law of Christ was markedly different. In Hadow's system of mediate graciousness, God sovereignly gave to the elect both the repentance and faith that he required and the eternal life that he had promised upon condition of that repentance and faith. In Hadow's system, these Gospel Commands of repentance and faith, along with the Law of Nature, comprised the Law of Christ. Therefore, Hadow could state decisively that the Law of Christ,

---

228. See *AGA*, 554.

> as it is to be obeyed, is a Rule by which He will judge all to whom it is sent; and the not obeying of it, shall be a Ground of their Condemnation....[229]

In this, Hadow was simply restating his position of mediate graciousness. As individual men either obeyed or disobeyed the Gospel Commands, they received either salvation or damnation, respectively. In a very real sense, then, the Law of Christ carried salvific implications. Obedience to that Law brought eternal life; disobedience to that Law brought eternal damnation. That the requisite obedience could be rendered only by God's gracious enablement did not alter either the necessity of that obedience or the Law's reference to salvific reward.

When one moves from Erskine's and Hadow's disagreement over whether the Law of Christ contains salvific implications to their disagreement over whether that Law applies to believers only or to all men, one is confronted with their different views of the post-Fall status of the Covenant of Works. In Erskine's federal system, all non-believers still stood under both the terms and the curse of the Law as it was the Law of Works, obliged to render legal duty before they could receive salvific privilege. The only thing that could change this relationship between an individual and the Law of God was one's entrance into the Covenant of Grace. Upon that entrance, one stood in relation to the Law not as the Law of Works, but as the Law of Christ, a Law that offered instruction not in how to obtain privilege, but in how to show gratitude for privilege that had already been received. Therefore, the Law of Christ only applied to believers. To the non-believer, who was under the Covenant of Works, the Law was the Law of Works; to the believer, who was under the Covenant of Grace, it was the Law of Christ.

In Hadow's federal system, the post-Fall status of the Covenant of Works is much more complex. As detailed above, Hadow posited that when a sinner heard the gospel, he became subject not to the precepts of the Covenant of Works, but rather to the Gospel Commands to repent and believe. These Gospel Commands, which Hadow identified with the Law of Christ, were thus binding upon all who heard them, both believers and non-believers. Indeed, the Law of Christ had to be binding upon the unregenerate, for it was only through the means of divinely-enabled obedience to that Law that men were able to enter into the bond of the Covenant of Grace.

When Erskine's and Hadow's positions on the immediate/mediate graciousness of the Covenant of Grace and the post-Fall status of the Covenant of Works are thus considered, the men's respective positions on the *Marrow*'s distinction within the Law of God become much clearer. For

---

229. *AD*, 132. Hadow cites 2 Thess 1:8 and 1 Pet 4:7.

Erskine, this distinction was vital to the very nature of the gospel. If the Law of Christ carried salvific implications for obedience or disobedience thereto, than legal duty still had a necessary priority over salvific privilege, an ordering of duty and privilege that Erskine viewed as the hallmark of the Covenant of Works. Furthermore, if both believers and non-believers were equally under this Law, than there was certainly no privilege imparted by the gospel and all men were uniformly bound to a covenantal economy that they were intrinsically unable to fulfil. Without the *Marrow*'s distinction, then, Erskine was left with a sort of universal Pelagianism wherein all men clamored to offer means to obtain a graciousness that could only be received immediately, and thus salvation was not possible for anyone. For Hadow, the *Marrow*'s distinction was just as destructive to the Covenant of Grace as it was vital to the same for Erskine. In the first instance, if such a distinction were imported into Hadow's system, none would be bound to obey the Moral Law. Unregenerate gospel-hearers were delivered from any obligation to the Law as the Law of Works by their hearing of the gospel proclamation and from any obligation to the Law as the Law of Christ by their unbelief, thus leaving them in abject licentiousness. Believers were similarly left without a real compulsion to obey the Law, for that Law was sorely enervated, only having reference to non-salvific, and thus presumably trifling, matters. What is even more, the *Marrow*'s distinction, if taken into Hadow's system of mediate graciousness, made salvation impossible for everyone. For the non-believer, the acquisition of salvation became impossible, for he was no longer under the Law of Christ that alone both revealed and, for the elect, provided the means through which God graciously and sovereignly brought salvation. For the believer, the real possession of salvation was likewise rendered impossible, for even though he was bound by the Law of Christ, the repentance and faith that it commanded were divested of the power to impart salvific reward, for the Law of Christ only pertained to non-salvific rewards and punishments. For both the unregenerate and the regenerate, then, the means through which grace was mediated evaporated, leaving no binding and effectual conduit of God's grace.

When one thus views Erskine's second "obscured truth" through the federal paradigms of Erskine and Hadow, the true nature of their disagreement emerges. From within Erskine's covenantal system, the rejection of the *Marrow*'s distinction created a legalism that bound all men to the Covenant of Works and thus made salvation impossible for everyone. From within Hadow's covenantal system, the acceptance of the *Marrow*'s distinction fostered an antinomianism that separated all men from both a compulsion to obey the Law and an ability to receive the salvific grace that God mediated through divinely-enabled obedience to that Law. For both men, then, the

Marrow's distinction within the Law was a serious matter and their disagreement over that distinction was deeply rooted in their differing refinements of a common Scottish federalism.

Obscured Truth 3

Among the many expressions from the *Marrow* that the Assembly condemned in its Act 1720 were the statements

> *For in Christ I have all Things at once, neither need I any Thing more, that is necessary unto Salvation. . . . Christ is my Righteousness, my Treasure, and my Work. I confess, O Law, that I am neither godly nor righteous, but yet this I am sure of, that he is godly and righteous for me.*[230]

In the estimation of Erskine and his brethren, the Assembly's condemnation of these expressions implied that a sinner needed something additional to Christ's imputed righteousness to obtain justification.[231] This apprehension is evident in Erskine's third "obscured truth," in which he expresses concern that the Act 1720 distorted the truth

> That when the law as a Covenant of Works comes upon the believer with the demand of perfect obedience, as a condition of life and salvation, his only relief in this case is, to plead the perfect obedience and complete righteousness of his ever-blessed Surety; and that this plea is so far from weakening him in the study of holiness, (as the Act imports), that it is one of the principal springs thereof . . . .[232]

When the Assembly 1722 responded to such allegations from the Brethren, they objected that the Act 1720 was not guilty of the error imputed to it. Rather, the Act had sought to assert that

> though good works be excluded from being the ground of justification, yet they are necessary in the justified, in order to their obtaining the enjoyment of eternal salvation; and this doth no way cut off or condemn the believer's only plea, in answer to the

---

230. *Representation*, 9. The Act 1720 had condemned the whole of pages 150–53 of the 1718 edition of the *Marrow*, where these expressions are found, citing only a very few excerpts from that section in the actual text of the Act. In the *Representation*, the Brethren fixated particularly on these sentences and thus a good portion of the ensuing debate was conducted in reference to them. See *AGA*, 535.

231. See *Representation*, 9.

232. *Christian Magazine*, 377.

law demands of perfect obedience, for justification and title to eternal life, as the Representation alleges.[233]

In the estimation of the Assembly 1722, the Act 1720 had not wrongly held that good works were necessary for justification, but rather had rightly asserted that good works were necessary, in the justified, to obtain salvation.

As the debate surrounding this third "obscured truth" unfolded over the course of the *Marrow* controversy, matters became extremely complex. Given the logical and emotional centrality of justification and salvation to any doctrinal system, the debate quickly expanded to include a considerable number of related theological issues.[234] While these side-issues created much heated debate, they remained precisely that—side-issues. In order to arrive at a coherent analysis of this particular factor in Erskine's involvement in the *Marrow* controversy, one must focus his attention upon the central matter that bred all of the subsequent disagreement—the salvation of a condemned sinner. In particular, one must realize how both Erskine and Hadow understood the condemned sinner's salvation, with that salvation being viewed as his entrance into the bond of the Covenant of Grace.[235] To arrive at this understanding, one has to ask three questions of each man's theological system. First, precisely what plea does the condemned sinner need in order to realize this salvation? Second, is this salvation instantaneous, or is it gradual? Third, when the formerly-condemned sinner has realized this salvation, what is his resulting relationship to the Law of Christ? It is to these three questions that one must turn.

The first matter under consideration is the identification of the precise plea that Erskine's and Hadow's federal systems each required of the condemned sinner in order to free him from his legal burdens and allow him to enter into the bond of the Covenant of Grace. Of course, to arrive at this identification, one must take into consideration the exact Law to which the sinner finds himself bound, for if the sinner is to be freed from his pre-salvific bondage and allowed to enter into the bond of the Covenant of Grace, he must render a plea commensurate with the demands of the Law that binds him. In Erskine's covenantal system, the Law that thus bound

---

233. *AGA*, 553.

234. Erskine himself saw the matter of justification as one of the keys to the *Marrow* controversy. See *Works*, 1:506.

235. As will be seen below, a considerable amount of the controversy on this "obscured truth" concerned the different definitions of "salvation" used by the Representers and the Assembly. While both Erskine and Hadow certainly would have desired to define "salvation" more precisely, the current definition is adopted because it is vague enough to have won the assent of both men.

the guilty sinner was the Law as the Law of Works.[236] In order to realize his salvation from this bondage, the sinner needed the imputed righteousness of Christ, which answered the Law's dual demand of obedience to its precept and satisfaction of its penalty.[237] With this imputed righteousness received and pled, however, the sinner had realized his salvation, being fully delivered from all demands binding upon him.[238] This exact identification between freedom from the Covenant of Works and proper salvation is evident even in the wording of Erskine's third "obscured truth," in which Erskine has a legal scene in view, yet he speaks of "salvation" rather than "justification." For Erskine, forensic justification according to the Covenant of Works and proper salvation were synonymous.[239]

Within Hadow's theological system, the plight of the condemned sinner was different. When a sinner heard the gospel proclamation, he found himself under both the curse of the Covenant of Works and the Law of Christ, which included both the Law of Nature and the individual Gospel Commands. In order to be freed from these obligations, then, the sinner needed a double plea.[240] In the first instance, the sinner's salvation required the plea of the imputed righteousness of Christ for his justification.[241] Furthermore, the sinner needed the plea of obedience to the Law of Christ, particularly to the Gospel Commands to repent and believe.[242] Until the sinner was able to render both of these pleas, he was still bound under law and thus had not fully entered into the bond of the Covenant of Grace.

In comparing Erskine's and Hadow's positions on precisely what plea the condemned sinner needs in order to be delivered from his pre-salvific legal bondage, one thus detects both an important similarity and an important difference. In the first instance, Erskine and Hadow both argue that the sinner needs the imputed righteousness of Christ. For both men, this

---

236. *Works*, 1:477.

237. See *ADG*, 45; *Representation*, 9–10; *Works*, 1:98–99, 140. In this, the imputation of Christ's righteousness to an individual assumes the imputation of that individual's sin to Christ.

238. Erskine was insistent that one's actual justification did not occur until his conversion. See *Works*, 1:99.

239. See also *Representation*, 10.

240. See, for example, *AD*, 134–35.

241. *AD*, vi. See also *RoG*, 11. For the Assembly's statement to the same effect, see *AGA*, 553. The effect of Hadow's view of the abiding validity of the terms of the Covenant of Works on his understanding of justification was not always consistent. For a thorough statement of Hadow's doctrine of justification, see *AD*, iii–iv, v–viii.

242. See, for example, *AD*, 165.

imputation and the deliverance that it wrought was understood as justification.[243] In many ways, then, Erskine and Hadow have similar understandings of the contents of justification. However, in addition to this similarity, an important dissonance between the two men's systems is introduced by Hadow's requiring that the sinner also render a plea of obedience to the Law of Christ in order to extricate himself fully from his pre-salvific legal obligations. Given that Hadow viewed the Law of Christ as comprehending not only the Gospel Commands, but also the entirety of the Law of Nature, this requisite conformity is little different from an entire sanctification. For Erskine, the sinner's full salvation from pre-salvific legal bondage and entrance into the bond of the Covenant of Grace required the plea of his justification; for Hadow, it required the plea of both the sinner's justification and his sanctification.[244]

The second matter that must be addressed is whether the salvation that is realized by the rendering of these respective pleas is either instantaneous or gradual. In Erskine's system, the salvation that is realized by the plea of justification through the imputed righteousness of Christ is an instantaneous salvation. Even though more remained to be accomplished in the Christian's life—most notably, his sanctification—his salvation was actual and instantaneous upon his justification through the imputed righteousness of Christ.[245] The instantaneous nature of this salvation is closely related to Erskine's insistence upon the immediate graciousness of the Covenant of Grace. Since God bestows the crowning grace of salvation without reference to means, as soon as deliverance from the legal obligations of the Covenant of Works is given, the sinner knows actual and full salvation. As the sinner does not lack any means requisite to actual salvation, he does not lack any of the actual salvation itself.

While Erskine's salvation was instantaneous, the salvation of Hadow's system was a gradual process. Even after a sinner had been justified through the imputed righteousness of Christ, his full salvation still awaited his sanctification, a process that was not completed until the sinner's death. As a result, salvation in Hadow's system was a life-long process that included even the final perseverance of the believer.[246] Hadow did not argue that ev-

---

243. This was also true for the Assembly at large. See *AGA*, 554–55. There, justification by the imputed righteousness of Christ is affirmed, yet it is not at all prominent.

244. See, for example, *AD*, 155–56. There, Hadow speaks of "all Things necessary to Salvation" as including both justification and sanctification. See also *AD*, 158–59, 165–66.

245. See, for example, *Representation*, 10; *ADG*, 41–42. In the latter, 2 Tim 2:10, 1 Pet 1:9, and 1 John 3:36 are cited. See also *Works*, 1:314.

246. The Assembly explicitly numbered "perseverance" among the things requisite

erything necessary for salvation was not in Christ; he simply argued that Christ did not give all things necessary to salvation at once.[247] Rather, God had appointed means to the great end of salvation, and the end was had only when all of the means—sanctification among them—had been secured.[248] However, the God who had graciously given justification would also graciously give all the requisite means and, finally, the salvation that was the desired end. In this, Hadow's salvation was a gradual process whose outcome, because divinely controlled, was certain.

In comparing Erskine's and Hadow's positions on the matter of whether a condemned sinner's salvation is either instantaneous or gradual, one again notes both a similarity and a difference. For both men, justification through the imputed righteousness of Christ was a guarantee of salvation. However, Erskine and Hadow differed on whether the receipt of this guarantee and the actual realization of salvation were simultaneous or distinct.[249] For Erskine, salvation came simultaneously with justification itself, for that justification freed the sinner from the only pre-salvific legal demand placed upon him, and thus fully ushered him into the Covenant of Grace. For Hadow, justification was an important component of a process that inexorably would bring salvation, yet the justified sinner still needed the plea of sanctification to realize his salvation and thus he had to await the completion of that certainly efficacious process.[250] Therefore, the receipt of salvation's guarantee and the actual realization of salvation could be distinguished in Hadow's system.

---

to "salvation." See *AGA*, 553. This was not altogether novel within Scottish theology. See, for example, *Sum*, 326.

247. E.g., *AD*, 155.

248. See *AD*, 165–66, for a discussion of the "means" of salvation.

249. This difference bred the correlative debate over whether good works are a walking in the way of eternal happiness or the way itself. To use the implied imagery, if the Christian begins his journey at "justification" and walks toward "glorification" via the path of "sanctification," at what point on that journey can he be described as "saved"? In Erskine's system of instantaneous salvation, the Christian is "saved" at the start of his journey and thus his sanctification is a walking in the way charted by his salvation; in Hadow's system of gradual salvation, the Christian is not "saved" until he reaches "glorification," and thus his sanctification is itself the way to salvation. For a sample of this debate, see *Representation*, 15.

250. See *AD*, 165–66. This difference between Erskine and Hadow fueled the ongoing debate over whether fear of punishment and hope of reward were suitable motivations to Christian duty. Erskine perceived of Hadow's gradual salvation as compelling post-justification obedience out of mercenary interests; Hadow construed Erskine's rejection of such motivations as an antinomian disregard for the Law. See, for example, *ADG*, 51–52. It would appear as if neither man accurately grasped the other's motivations.

The third issue that must be addressed is the relationship of the formerly-condemned sinner to the Law of Christ upon his realization of salvation. Within Erskine's system, the saved sinner is obligated to obey the Law of Christ. Having received the privilege of salvation from the Law of Works, the saved sinner is enjoined to render duty to the Law of Christ; a law that has become a guide to help the Christian live in accordance with the new nature that is also his covenant privilege.[251] As the saved sinner grows in this sanctified conformity to the Law of Christ, he knows the increasing completeness of the salvation that he actually and truly possessed upon his justification. Indeed, the intrinsic unity of the believer's actual salvation in his justification and his complete salvation in his sanctification guarantees that that sanctification will occur, even though that occurrence is a flowering of actual salvation rather than a component thereof.[252]

For Hadow, the salvation of a sinner fostered a markedly different relationship to the Law of Christ. Prior to his salvation, the sinner in Hadow's system stood under legal obligation to both the curse of the Covenant of Works and the Law of Christ, and thus his salvation required his deliverance from both of those obligations. As a result, when a sinner realized his salvation, he was necessarily delivered from any legal obligation to the Law of Christ. In order to be delivered from his pre-salvific obligations, the sinner had had to render obedience to the Law of Christ and in rendering this obedience, he had freed himself from the obligation of that Law. In Hadow's system, a saved sinner was freed from any obligation to the Law of Christ, satisfaction of that Law being a necessary precondition of his very salvation.[253] On this matter of the saved sinner's relationship to the Law of Christ, then, there is no agreement between Erskine and Hadow.

In light of this brief analysis of their respective understandings of the salvation of a condemned sinner, one is able to arrive at an understanding of Erskine's and Hadow's positions on the third of Erskine's "obscured truths." In the relevant passages that had been condemned by the Act 1720, the *Marrow* had taught that all that was necessary for salvation was to be had, imputatively, through Christ. Within Erskine's covenantal system, this was true.[254] As the condemned sinner stood only under the curse and the terms

251. See, for example, *ADG*, 51–52; *Works*, 1:446–47.

252. See, for example, *ADG*, 44; *Answers*, 39; *Representation*, 15.

253. While Hadow never provides a detailed discussion of this, it forms the foundation for his denunciations of the *Marrow* as antinomian. Chiefly, those critiques assume that a full salvation involves both freedom from the Covenant of Works and freedom from the obligation of the Law. See, for example, *AD*, 160–62.

254. Hadow's misunderstanding of Erskine's doctrine at this point gave rise to his allegations that the Brethren taught an imputed sanctification. See, for example, *AD*,

of the Covenant of Works, the imputed righteousness of Christ brought actual salvation.[255] Within Hadow's system, however, the *Marrow*'s doctrine was incomplete. As the condemned sinner stood under both the curse of the Covenant of Works and the terms of the Law of Christ, he needed obedience to the Law of Christ to satisfy the latter demand as much as he needed Christ's imputed righteousness to satisfy the former. The *Marrow*'s doctrine was not simply incomplete within Hadow's federal paradigm, however; it was also dangerous. As salvation involved one's meeting the obligation of the Law of Christ, in declaring that the justified sinner instantaneously possessed actual salvation upon his justification, the *Marrow* taught the antinomian error that all Christians were under no obligation to the Law of Christ.[256]

In opposition to such fallacious doctrine, Hadow posited an alternative formulation which made use of a distinction within the salvation of a condemned sinner. In his justification through the imputed righteousness of Christ, the sinner had a right and title to salvation. As the sinner's justification was inextricably linked to his final salvation by the unity and efficacy of God's decree, that justification did impart a definitive right to salvation. However, the actual possession of that salvation awaited the sinner's satisfaction of the Law of Christ. When that satisfaction had been rendered by means of obedience to the Gospel Commands of repentance and faith, as well as a life lived in holy conformity to the Law of Nature, the justified sinner could finally be said to possess salvation.[257] In this distinction, Hadow did not intend to introduce any sort of legalism into salvation. Rather, he sought to assert both the certain connection between justification and salvation, and the continued obligation of the Christian to observe the Law of Christ. From within Erskine's system, however, such a distinction within the sinner's salvation appeared as legalism.[258] If the sole burden resting upon the sinner prior to his entrance into the Covenant of Grace was his obligation to the Covenant of Works, than to speak of anything being necessary to obtain salvation after having received a title to it in the imputed righteousness of Christ implied that man's obedience to the Covenant of Works had to be

---

155–59. However, by keeping the entire matter of sanctification posterior to salvation rather than making it a portion thereof, Erskine remains well clear of the doctrinal position Hadow alleges against him.

255. See *Answers*, 37–39; *Catechism*, 153–54 (20.106).

256. See *AD*, 149–54, 160–62, 165.

257. See, for example, *AD*, vi, xi–xii. See also *AGA*, 555.

258. See *Works*, 1:193–94. There, Erskine asserts that the tendency latent in Hadow's theology is a fundamental rejection of the gospel. As support for this charge, he quotes at length from John Owen's commentary on Hebrews 5:7.

added to Christ's own righteousness in order fully to extricate the sinner from that covenant.[259]

When one thus views Erskine's third "obscured truth" through the respective federal theologies of Erskine and Hadow, the actual nature of the two men's disagreement becomes clear. Contrary to appearances, Hadow's rejection of the *Marrow*'s doctrine that everything necessary for salvation was to be had, imputatively, in Christ was not caused by an insipid legalism within his theology. Hadow undeniably held to the forensic nature of justification and the complete graciousness and divine monergism of the entirety of a sinner's salvation. Nonetheless, from within Erskine's federal system, Hadow's rejection of the *Marrow*'s teaching did leave salvation as a legalistic affair that had as much to do with man's obedience as it did with Christ's righteousness. From Hadow's perspective, on the other hand, Erskine's acceptance of the *Marrow*'s position was both a denigration of the grand sweep of salvation and a thinly-veiled antinomianism that would leave all Christians without any care for the Law of Christ. For both men, the teaching of the *Marrow* on this point was of grave importance, and the exact nature of this importance was inextricably linked with each man's formalization of positions that previously had been ambivalent within Scottish federal theology.

Obscured Truth 4

In Erskine's estimation, the Act 1720 gave further cause for alarm in its obscuring of the truth

> That there is a fiducial act or appropriating persuasion in the very nature of justifying and saving faith . . . .[260]

Erskine's concern over this fourth "obscured truth" stemmed from the Assembly's condemnation of the *Marrow*'s exhortation to sinners to

---

259. See *Answers*, 27; *AD*, v–vi. Erskine's and Hadow's differing perceptions in this area underlay the debate over the eighth Act of the Assembly 1720. For the text of the Act, see *AGA*, 538. While that Act, and the subsequent interpretation of it by the Assembly 1722, saw matters in light of Hadow's distinction between a title to salvation and the possession thereof, such a distinction appeared as legalism to the Brethren. See, for example, *AGA*, 554–55; *ADG*, 42–44; *Answers*, 41–42; *Representation*, 19–20. See also *Works*, 1:219, 229–30.

Erskine also traced this alleged legalism to Hadow's declaration that the commands to repent and believe were Gospel Commands rather than inherent in the Law of Nature, a position that Erskine judged led to Neonomianism and Pelagianism. See *Answers*, 16; *ADG*, 40.

260. *Christian Magazine*, 377.

be verily persuaded in your heart that Jesus Christ is yours, and
that you shall have life and salvation by him; that whatsoever
Christ did for the redemption of mankind, he did it for you.[261]

According to Erskine and his brethren, in condemning these and similar words, the Assembly was destroying the element of personal appropriation that distinguished true faith from the "doubtsome faith" of Roman Catholicism, and was doing so in direct contradiction to the stream of Reformed divines who had held that assurance was of the essence of faith.[262] In their verdict on the matter in the Act 1722, the Assembly judged that the Brethren could not legitimately charge the Act 1720 with teaching a doubtsome faith,

> Nor can they charge the Assembly with denying, that a belief
> and persuasion of the mercy of God in Christ, and of Christ's
> ability and willingness to save all that come to him, is necessary unto justifying faith; but they do, and must maintain, with
> our Confession and Catechisms, that a true believer is not at all
> times, even when he is acting faith unto salvation, assured of his
> present being in a state of grace, and that he shall be saved; but
> that he may wait long before he obtain this assurance.[263]

In the judgment of the Assembly, the condemnation of the *Marrow* passages in question did not destroy a true understanding of assurance. While both the *Marrow* and the Representers taught that there was an assurance in the direct act of faith, the Assembly held that the only assurance possible for Christians came as a result of the reflex act of faith.[264]

In Erskine's fourth "obscured truth," one receives a distillation of the *Marrow* controversy's debate on assurance. While Erskine and his associates held that there was an assurance in the direct act of faith, Hadow and the balance of the Assembly judged that there was not, and the dissonance between these two positions produced one of the most pervasive and vitriolic components of the entire controversy.[265] Chiefly, this dissonance centered

---

261. *AGA*, 534.

262. See *Representation*, 11–13. For similar arguments concerning the consensus of older Reformed divines, see *ADG*, 34–36; *Answers*, 58–59. Also, see Boston's comments in his preface to the *Marrow* in Boston, *Works*, 7:147–48. For representative dismissals of such arguments, see *AD*, 1–13; Dunlop, *A COLLECTION OF* Confessions of Faith, cxxxvii.

263. *AGA*, 552.

264. See *Answers*, 49–72.

265. The *Marrow*'s doctrine of assurance was the first aspect of that work to be directly attacked by Hadow, with a critique of that doctrine forming the substance of *RoG*. See Lachman, *Marrow*, 9.

upon Erskine's and Hadow's different positions on whether faith, in its direct act, is either personal or general. It is to a consideration of this issue, through the respective federal paradigms of Erskine and Hadow, that one must turn.

For Erskine, the direct act of faith was decidedly personal, being the act whereby an individual sinner personally believed and applied the offer of salvation that was extended to all men in the gospel proclamation.[266] Indeed, in Erskine's system, the personal nature of this first act of faith was a necessary component thereof.[267] Speaking of the personal persuasion of faith's direct act, Erskine could state that

> there can be no true Faith without this Persuasion in some Measure or Degree . . . without this Persuasion, that *we shall* have Life and Salvation by Christ, we do not set to our Seal that God is *true*, nor give that Answer of Faith, which the Lord points out, as the only suitable Answer unto his Call of *looking unto him for Salvation*.[268]

This emphasis upon the necessity of a personal appropriation in the direct act of faith was intimately tied to Erskine's expansive notion of the Covenant of Grace. In that covenant's process of indefiniteness moving inexorably toward definiteness, the personal appropriation of the promises that were held out to all sinners in the gospel was vital, for it was only in that personal appropriation that an indefinite salvation was made efficacious in the life of an individual. In his preaching, Erskine used many illustrations to evidence this necessity, such as the imagery of a rope being cast into a company of drowning men.[269] In this and many other illustrations, Erskine's point was clear—when an offer of blessing is framed in reference to an indefinite group as a group, in order for that blessing to be effectual in the life of any one member of that group, it must be grasped individually. If it is not, the blessing is lost and the one who offered that blessing is offended.[270]

Even more foundationally than making the personal nature of faith's direct act necessary, Erskine's expansive Covenant of Grace made that

---

266. See *Representation*, 11; *Works*, 1:219–20, 2:28–29.

267. Similarly, see Witsius, *Economy of the Covenants*, 1:409.

268. *ADG*, 33–34. In this context, Erskine cites Acts 15:11 and Micah 7:7, arguing that both passages show the people of God expressing themselves in terms of this personal persuasion of faith.

269. See, for example, *Works*, 1:172. Erskine adopts this illustration directly from Norton. See Norton, *The Orthodox Evangelist*, 84–85. That Erskine was so fond of Norton is somewhat surprising. See Stoever, "A Faire and Easy Way to Heaven," 108–9, 194, 207n6.

270. See, for example, *Works*, 2:307.

personal nature of faith possible. As the leading promise of the Covenant of Grace was "God will save sinners," all that was required in order to number an individual among the group who had access to those promises was that he be a sinner. As Erskine repeatedly urged in his preaching, Christ's

> visits and offers of grace in the gospel are to sinners, to 'men, and to the sons of men;' and, if thou find thy name there, thou hast no reason to exclude thyself.[271]

In this, the indefinite nature of Erskine's Covenant of Grace provides the necessary foundation for the individual sinner personally appropriating the promise of salvation, and that foundation is not based upon the universality of any aspect of redemption proper, but rather upon the universality of the Fall.[272] Given the indefinite nature of the Covenant of Grace, a personal appropriation within the direct act of faith was both possible and necessary.[273]

For Hadow and the Assembly 1722, the direct act of faith was just as decidedly general as it was personal for Erskine. In Hadow's estimation, this general nature of the direct act of faith was necessitated by Scripture's silence on the identity of the specific recipients of God's grace; the direct act of faith must have its object revealed in Scripture and, since no one individual's personal salvation is guaranteed in Scripture, a personal appropriation of the promise of salvation cannot be included in the direct act of faith.[274] Clearly, this supposition of the necessarily general nature of faith's direct act is rooted in Hadow's notion of a definite Covenant of Grace. In that federal construction, in order to be assured of one's access to the promise of the Covenant of Grace, an individual had to ascertain his election, for that covenant, in its first making, distinguished among men based upon categories of election and reprobation and was made for the exclusive salvation of "elect sinners."[275] If a sinner was not an "elect sinner," he had no interest in the covenant. As Scripture did not testify to any individual's membership in that group, however, there was no object for such a belief in the direct act of faith. Hadow's definite Covenant of Grace, then, made a personal persua-

---

271. Ibid., 1:342. See also ibid., 3:58–59; *ADG*, 36.

272. Such a line of reasoning can even be found in *Sum*, 329–30.

273. See, for example, *ADG*, 28; *Answers*, 61–62.

274. *RoG*, 30–31. Hadow consistently posited that the ground of faith was only the veracity of God's revelation, often framing such an assertion in opposition to the rationalism of Simson. See, for example, *RoG*, 15. See also *Answers*, 60.

275. Hadow was not novel in seeing a connection between assurance and a knowledge of one's election. See, for example, *Sum*, 343; Witsius, *Economy of the Covenants*, 1:341–43. Barth sees the interest in such a connection embedded within the Westminster Confession. Barth, *Confessions*, 143–44, 215–16. Barth bases this entirely upon chapter eighteen of the Confession. See below.

sion of access to the promise of the Covenant of Grace within the direct act of faith impossible.[276]

Given these differences in how they understood the nature of the direct act of faith, it is clear that Erskine and Hadow would have viewed the *Marrow*'s statements relative to assurance quite differently. Broadly speaking, the *Marrow* taught that an individual sinner would be saved if he believed that what Christ had done to redeem men, he had done on his behalf, thus making personal assurance essential to faith. Within Erskine's covenantal system, this teaching was true. When Christ had undertaken his redemptive work in the Covenant of Grace, he had done so in order to save "sinners." That the progress of the Covenant of Grace created categories of election and reprobation, effectually saving the elect and effectually damning the reprobate, did not categorically alter the group which God had eyed in making the covenant; it simply gave greater definition. Therefore, in order for an individual to number himself among the group for whom Christ had undertaken his redemptive work, he simply had to be convinced that he was a "sinner."

From within Hadow's covenantal paradigm, conversely, the *Marrow*'s doctrine was heretical. Prior to the Covenant of Grace, the Triune God had viewed mankind in the categories of either "elect sinners" or "reprobate sinners," and when Christ had undertaken his redemptive work in the Covenant of Grace, he had done so on behalf of the elect exclusively. Therefore, if an individual was to be convinced that he was among the group for whom Christ had undertaken his work of redemption, he had to be convinced of his personal election. If personal assurance were essential to faith, this would mean that an individual, in his first act of faith, would have to believe that he was elect. However, since knowledge of one's election was thus made prior to one's first act of faith, that election had to be evidenced by something other than faith. Simply stated, election had to apply to men as a function of their humanity; Christ's redemptive work had to apply to all men. In Hadow's opinion, in order for assurance to be essential to faith, one had to advocate the universalism of an unlimited atonement.

On one matter, Erskine and Hadow were in agreement; in order for assurance to lie in the essence of faith, each individual man must be able to know, prior to his faith in Christ, that he is among the group that God eyed in contracting the Covenant of Grace. In Erskine's system, this group was man as "sinner." If an individual was persuaded of his sinfulness and thus came to Christ, he would be saved; the proclamation of salvation for

---

276. For an interesting example of this, see *RoG*, 31–32; compare with *ADG*, 28.

"sinners" would bring the salvation of the elect.[277] In Hadow's system, the group that God had eyed in contracting the Covenant of Grace was man as "elect sinner." If assurance were essential, and thus prior, to faith, this meant that all men must be "elect sinners." An assured faith necessitated an unlimited atonement. For Erskine, the *Marrow*'s doctrine of assurance was the gospel; for Hadow, it was heresy.

As the *Marrow* controversy unfolded, Erskine and his brethren repeatedly attempted to exonerate themselves from this heresy alleged against them by further clarifying their doctrine of assurance. The chief clarification that they articulated to this end was a distinction between an assurance of faith, which came upon the direct act of faith, and an assurance of sense, which was a function of the reflex act of faith.[278] Simply stated, Erskine's assurance of faith looked outside of the sinner and found its basis in the promise of Christ's sufficiency, while his assurance of sense looked within the sinner and found its basis in the sinner's own experience of the regeneration that came through that external sufficiency of Christ.[279] In Erskine's judgment, it was the assurance of sense that chapter eighteen of the Westminster Confession of Faith denied to be essential to faith; a denial with which Erskine earnestly agreed.[280] The assurance of faith, on the other hand, was necessary to the direct act of faith, a position countenanced by chapter fourteen, section two of the Confession's approbation of "resting upon Christ . . . by virtue of the covenant of grace."[281] In terms of this distinction, the Brethren could agree with everything that the Assembly had said about assurance, as long as it was applied to the assurance of sense and the importance and centrality of the assurance of faith was affirmed.

277. This implied no disingenuity in the gospel proclamation. See, for example, *Works*, 1:359–60.

278. Erskine gave his fullest treatment of this distinction, as well as other distinctions within his doctrine of assurance, in *The Assurance of Faith Opened and Applied*. See *Works*, 1:205–73. This work, which was a revised compilation of sermons on Hebrews 10:22, remained Erskine's most substantial treatise on the doctrine of assurance. Erskine had been exposed to an embryonic form of this distinction between an assurance of faith and an assurance of sense as early as 1696. In the aforementioned letter received by Erskine that year from James Hog concerning Erskine's doubts about his conversion, the elder Hog enunciated a notion of faith and assurance remarkably similar to that later espoused and detailed in the *Marrow* controversy. See Erskine, *Notebook 1692*, item VII. From this, it appears that the doctrine of assurance that Hog forwarded in the *Marrow* controversy was not as much of a personal innovation as Lachman alleges it to have been. See Lachman, *Marrow*, 133–34, 156, 221–22.

279. See *ADG*, 27–28; *Answers*, 69–70.

280. e.g., *Representation*, 11–13.

281. See, for example, *Works*, 1:374. Erskine also saw Question 86 of the Westminster Shorter Catechism as supporting this position. See ibid., 1:212, 313.

Although Erskine and his associates gave great attention to articulating this distinction within assurance, it did nothing to alleviate their controversy with the Assembly. Seen in light of Erskine's and Hadow's differing federal paradigms, this failure of Erskine's distinction to resonate with Hadow and the Assembly is seen to have been unavoidable. Indeed, it is only in light of Erskine's view of an indefinite Covenant of Grace that his distinction within assurance can be understood, thus rendering the distinction incoherent to Hadow.[282] Within Erskine's system, when an individual sinner was confronted with the proclamation of the Covenant of Grace, he encountered an indefinite promise that God would save "sinners." In this proclamation, the sinner was told that there was full salvation, in Jesus Christ, offered to a group of which that same proclamation declared him to be a member. If the individual in question truly believed this—that he was a sinner and that God saves sinners in Christ—then he had the assurance of faith, an assurance rooted in his belief of the promise that God really would save sinners, a category into which he fit. In this sense, Erskine could refer to the assurance of faith as

> the *Assurance of the Promise* of Salvation; or, an assured Faith of Righteousness and Salvation in Christ Jesus, as held forth to every Sinner of *Adam*'s Race, to whom the Gospel comes, to be received and applied by them, for their *own Benefit* . . . .[283]

In this, the assurance of faith was founded upon the indefinite nature of Erskine's Covenant of Grace.[284] Just as Erskine's indefinite Covenant of Grace moved to definiteness, so the assurance of faith moved to the assurance of sense. In this reflexive assurance of sense, the saved sinner found comfort in the personal manifestation of the indefinitely-offered salvation of the covenant. In this sense, Erskine could describe the assurance of sense as "an Assurance that the Faith which *we have*, is indeed the Faith of God's *Elect*."[285] The assurance of sense thus offered assurance to the individual that as the indefinite Covenant of Grace narrowed into eternal specificity, he still maintained an interest in it. In this, the connection between the assurance

---

282. While the secondary literature widely recognizes Erskine's distinction between an assurance of faith and an assurance of sense, the integral foundation of this distinction within Erskine's view of an indefinite Covenant of Grace is never explored. As a result, Erskine's distinction is most often seen as a utilitarian, and perhaps even invalid, appendage to his theology rather than a coherent component of his overall thought. See, for example, Bell, 166; Lachman, *Marrow*, 441–42.

283. *ADG*, 28.

284. See *ADG*, 28–29, where this connection is made very clear. Also, see, for example, *Works*, 1:177, 255–56, 262.

285. *ADG*, 28.

of faith and the assurance of sense, and the movement from the former to the latter, was a microcosm of Erskine's Covenant of Grace. In the believer's progression from the assurance of faith to an assurance of sense, he would experience in his own soul the covenantal movement from indefiniteness to definiteness; the movement from a conviction that he stood in the path of the graciousness of the Covenant of Grace to the assurance that he was one who had actually and effectually received that grace.

As Hadow's Covenant of Grace was definite from its inception, Erskine's assurance of faith, being founded upon an initial indefiniteness to the Covenant of Grace, was entirely unintelligible to him. Indeed, such an assurance had no indefinite promise to serve as its object. Within Hadow's Covenant of Grace, membership in the group of "elect sinners" was necessary to give one an interest in Christ from the very start and thus Erskine's assurance of sense, which convinced the sinner that his faith was the faith of the elect, was the only proper assurance. Simply stated, from within Hadow's theology, Erskine's assurance of faith was a fabrication and his assurance of sense was, simply, "assurance."

Overall, in an analysis of Erskine's and Hadow's fierce disagreement on assurance, it is evident that both men were guided by the underlying federal structure of their theologies. Even after the points at issue had been debated and clarified extensively, Erskine could not shake the conviction that if men did not personally appropriate the promises of the gospel, they could not be saved; nor could Hadow dispel the certainty that an assurance essential to faith could be built only upon the scaffolding of an unlimited atonement. Both of these convictions, and the heated controversy that arose between them, were founded upon each man's distinctive continuation of Scottish federal thought.

Obscured Truth 5

In Erskine's fifth and final "obscured truth," one receives a paradigmatic view of the entire *Marrow* controversy. In Erskine's judgment, the Act 1720 had obscured the truth

> That there is a deed of gift or grant made by the Father to all the hearers of the gospel, affording warrant to ministers to offer Christ unto all, and a warrant unto all to receive him, which yet does not lead us into the Arminian camp.[286]

---

286. *Christian Magazine*, 377. Erskine's reference to Arminianism has in view the Arminian doctrine of an unlimited atonement.

According to Erskine, this truth had been impugned when the Assembly 1720 had condemned the passage from the *Marrow* that stated that

> The Father hath made a deed of gift and grant unto all mankind, that whosoever of them all shall believe in his Son shall not perish....[287]

As the opposition to this passage had focused largely upon the language of "deed of gift and grant," Erskine and his brethren stipulated that by that language,

> we understand no more, but the Revelation of the Divine Will in the Word, affording a Warrant, to offer Christ to all, and a Warrant unto all to receive him.[288]

Therefore, in condemning such language, the Assembly was condemning the Scriptural warrant for ministers to offer the gospel to all men. According to the Assembly 1722, however, the Act 1720 was not guilty of such an error. Rather, the Act 1720 had charged that the *Marrow* taught a universal redemption as to purchase and, to substantiate that claim, had adduced the passage in question along with several others. While the Brethren had ignored the other passages that had been cited, they had fixated upon this one in particular and had placed their own gloss upon the author's meaning. While the Assembly 1722 admitted that it fully agreed with the Brethren if their gloss was adopted as the meaning of the passage, they maintained that such was not the actual meaning of the *Marrow*. Rather, the *Marrow* actually did intend to teach a universal redemption as to purchase and the Brethren were simply avoiding the force of that teaching by neglecting the other passages that had been cited by the Act 1720.[289]

In the disagreement that gave rise to Erskine's fifth "obscured truth," then, one meets with a tension between two radically different readings of the same text. The question under debate did not concern a specific matter of doctrine; just as certainly as the Assembly did not argue that the gospel was not to be offered to all men, the Brethren did not argue for a universal redemption. Rather, the question under debate was what the *Marrow* meant when it spoke of a deed of gift and grant being made to all men in the gospel offer. When viewed from Erskine's federal paradigm, that language spoke simply of the full and free offer of the gospel. When viewed from within Hadow's system, it belied a universal redemption. In order to arrive

---

287. *AGA*, 535. See also *Representation*, 13.
288. *Representation*, 13–14. See also *Answers*, 73.
289. *AGA*, 552–53.

at an understanding of how these two men came to such starkly different interpretations of the same sentence, one must examine that proposition through their respective federal theologies.

In Erskine's understanding of the disputed expression, the deed of gift and grant in view was simply the gospel offer of salvation in Christ.[290] When the gospel was preached, Christ was "given" in that proclamation. While this "giving" of Christ in the gospel did not effectually bestow Christ and his saving benefits, it did present Christ so fully and sincerely that those who heard the proclamation had full warrant to accept the Christ who was given.[291] This insistence that Christ was a gift given in the gospel proclamation was intimately connected with Erskine's notion of the immediate graciousness of the Covenant of Grace. As God's grace in Christ was given immediately, nothing within the sinner could be rendered to procure it; grace was given as a gift, unsolicited and undeserved.

Insofar as Christ was "given" as a gift in the gospel proclamation, Erskine was adamant that he was to be "given" to all men. In this particular emphasis, Erskine almost invariably based his argumentation upon the indefinite nature of the Covenant of Grace. In the Council of Peace, Christ was entrusted with the "administration of the covenant," which Erskine defined as "The *intire management* of [the Covenant of Grace], whereby it may be rendered effectual to the end for which it was made."[292] Thus ordained to administer the Covenant of Grace to all men, Christ undertook that administration through one primary mean—the extension of the gospel offer to all men.[293] As all sinners came under Christ's administration of the covenant, they were all to hear the proclamation of Christ's testament.[294] In light of the particular sense in which Christ was "given" in the gospel, this proclamation of the covenant's testamentary promise to lost sinners did not unilaterally save them; rather, it offered salvation in Christ, the great promise of the covenant, to them as a gift to be either accepted or rejected.[295] As each individual sinner accepted or rejected the offered gift, Christ's

---

290. Isaiah 9:6; John 3:16; John 6:32; Acts 4:12; 1 John 5:11; and Revelation 22:17 were adduced as scriptural support for such language. See *ADG*, 23.

291. In the language of the Brethren, this was not a giving of possession, but a giving of offer. See, for example, *ADG*, 23; *Answers*, 74–75.

292. *Catechism*, 151 (20.91).

293. See *Catechism*, 151 (20.93).

294. See *Answers*, 52; *Catechism*, 151 (20.92), 153 (20.104); *ADG*, 21–24. As scriptural warrant for the demand that Christ be offered to all men, Erskine sometimes would cite Proverbs 8:4; Acts 13:47; and Mark 16:15 (*ADG*, 31), as well as John 3:14–15 (*Catechism*, 151 [20.92]).

295. Erskine argued that all the hearers of the gospel had a "right of *access*" to the

administration would produce the particularity that was the end of the Covenant of Grace—salvation for the elect and damnation for the reprobate.[296] While the saving internalization of the gospel would occur only in the elect, the external revelation of the gift of Christ in the gospel was to come to all men precisely because the Covenant of Grace had been indefinite in its formation.

While the universal offer of the gospel would thus effect a particular redemption, Erskine insisted that there was neither alteration nor insincerity in the promise of God as expressed in the gospel offer. Rather, Erskine posited that the one promise of God could be viewed in a "three-fold situation"—as it was in the heart of God, in the Word of God, and in the hand of faith.[297] Viewed as it was in the heart of God, the promise of salvation was particular only to the elect, taking into consideration the entirety of the divine purposes and the particularization of the Council of Peace. However, as this view of the promises was inscrutable and thus could never serve as the ground of faith, sinners were called to view the promise as it was in the Word of God, wherein that promise was extended to all men in common. When the promise was offered from this perspective, it was able to be grasped by the hand of faith, whereby it was taken into possession and applied for the actual salvation of the sinner in question. In this, the unity of the one saving promise of God was complete—offered indefinitely in the Word, it was apprehended as a gift by the hand of faith and thus realized the definiteness that it had in the heart of God. However, in its entirety, this process required that the gift of Christ in the gospel be offered to all men, just as it stood in the Word of God, for not even the elect could grasp the inscrutable promise of the heart of God with the hand of faith. Thus conceiving of the promise of the Covenant of Grace in its three-fold situation, Erskine was able sincerely to offer to all men a covenant that actually would save only the elect, and to do so in such a way that the inscrutable purposes of God were made accessible to faith.[298]

---

gospel promises, but only faith would impart a "right of *possession*." See *Catechism*, 150 (20.83–84).

296. E.g., *ADG*, 24.

297. See *Works*, 2:23. Such a threefold view of the promise of the covenant is also latent in places such as *ADG*, 23; *Answers*, 74–75.

298. In this, Erskine's notion of the threefold situation of the promise of God avoids the shortcomings of Boston's attempt to reconcile an unlimited offer with a limited application. To accommodate the universal offer of a promise that was specific to the elect in the heart of God, Boston allowed for the use of conditional phrases in the administration of the Covenant of Grace. In order to resolve the apparent tension that resulted between conditional phrases and an unconditional covenant, Boston stipulated that "the covenant itself is a different thing from the form of the external administration of

While Hadow agreed with Erskine that the gospel was to be offered to all men, he did not agree that this offering could be construed as the giving of a gift. As Hadow argued, Scripture never explicitly speaks of God "offering" anything to man.[299] Rather, Scripture only speaks of God declaring his intention to give certain things or promising those things. Therefore, whatsoever God "offered" to man in the gospel, he must be understood as promising to man.[300] However, this gospel promise was not an absolute promise, wherein one promises to give a thing without regard to conditions or other circumstances; rather, it was a conditional promise, wherein one promises to give a thing upon the meeting of certain conditions.[301] As God dispensed his mediate grace through divinely-enabled obedience to the Gospel Commands, the conditional nature of the gospel promise was perfectly logical—if an individual manifested the means of repentance and faith, God would infallibly and faithfully bestow the promised blessing of salvation. While Hadow held that the gospel offered salvation to all who heard it, that offer was a conditional promise, not a gift.[302]

In addition to his view of a mediate graciousness, Hadow's understanding of the milieu into which the gospel was preached was also formative for his conception of the gospel promises coming as a conditional promise rather than as a gift. At all points, Hadow was insistent that the application of the gospel promise should be exactly co-extensive with the offer of that promise. If the promise was extended to even one individual in whose life it failed to do as it promised, the veracity and faithfulness of God would be impugned.[303] As the gospel promise was proclaimed to a mixed multitude of elect sinners and reprobate sinners, this consideration led Hadow

---

it." Boston, *Works*, 8:556. See Boston, *Works*, 8:555–56. Such a resolution to the problem, however, has two chief difficulties. First, it implies an insincerity in the gospel offer, for the Covenant of Grace is not offered precisely *as it is* in itself. Secondly, this disingenuity actually makes the substance of the Covenant of Grace inaccessible to faith. If there is such an important dissonance between how the Covenant of Grace is described and what the Covenant of Grace is in its being, there seems to be an epistemological barrier to comprehending that covenant. Overcoming these weaknesses, Erskine's system maintained both the sincerity of the gospel offer, as being the same promise as that which lay in the heart of God, and the continuity of that promise with the very substance of the Covenant of Grace itself.

299. See "Letters," 81–82. Hadow's reasoning here comes under particular derision from Lachman. See Lachman, *Marrow*, 172–75. However, Hadow's reasoning is much sounder and fairer than Lachman wants to concede.

300. See "Letters," 83–84.

301. See ibid., 82–83, for Hadow's distinction between absolute and conditional promises.

302. Ibid., 85.

303. See ibid., 87–90, 98–102.

to view the gospel, in actuality, as two separate promises. The promise that reached all men in the preaching of the gospel was a conditional promise, declaring that God would save all those who had faith in him. By framing this general promise in a conditional manner, the preacher would not engage either the power or the faithfulness of God to apply salvation to all who heard the promise; the divine omnipotence would be engaged only to save those who met the condition of faith. However, preceding this general conditional promise, there was another vital absolute promise, wherein God promised to give faith and repentance unilaterally to the elect without any regard to condition or qualification on their part.[304] In this, God promised absolutely to bestow the condition which, in the general conditional promise, he promised to reward with salvation. By thus construing the gospel promise as two distinct promises,

> the elect are gathered out of the multitude, and the rest left inexcuseable, unto whom the conditional promise was proposed, and the benefits therein contained offered, as well as to the elect.[305]

In this, Hadow's system was able to assert both the efficacy of the gospel in saving the elect and the uniformity of its offer.[306]

Importantly, Hadow's double gospel promise was a microcosm of God's redemptive purposes and work within Hadow's federal theology.[307] In that tri-covenantal system, God first promised to save the elect in the Covenant of Redemption and then, in the Covenant of Grace, promised to save those who repented and believed. In the Covenant of Redemption, God had made an absolute promise whose application was dependent wholly upon his sovereign will; in the Covenant of Grace, he had made a conditional promise whose application was already determined by one's membership in one of the two groups created by the prior absolute promise. From all of eternity, then, God's redemptive work had been marked by precisely the double promise that Hadow articulated.

In light of their respective views of the gospel offer, one is able to see how Erskine and Hadow would have viewed the *Marrow*'s teaching that the gospel offer is a deed of gift and grant of Christ to all men. For Erskine, such a teaching was a faithful representation of how the gospel confronted sinners. That gospel told the sinner of his bankruptcy and demanded that

---

304. "Letters," 68–71, 86.
305. "Letters," 76.
306. See "Letters," 67–68, 75–76.
307. See, for example, *AD*, 131–132. There, the Tri-Covenantal structure of Hadow's system is seen to shape even his understanding of the Great Commission.

Christ be accepted without payment, as a gift. As the revelation of this promise in the Word gradually gained the clarity of that same promise in God's heart, it would distinguish between those who would accept it savingly and those who would reject it damningly; a differentiation that would be impossible if the promise were not extended to each and every individual sinner. For Hadow, the *Marrow*'s teaching belied a nascent universal redemption. If Christ was presented as a gift in the gospel promise, than all notions of conditionality were excised from that promise. Therefore, the covenant promise became an absolute promise and thus the very character of God demanded that the promised gift be given efficaciously to all to whom it was offered. If this absolute promise were extended to all men indiscriminately, then all men would necessarily be saved. In order for a minister to be able to offer Christ, as a gift, to all the hearers of the gospel, Christ would have had to have died for all men. A universal offer thus framed required a universal redemption.

In the debate encapsulated by Erskine's fifth "obscured truth," one sees once more the centrality of Erskine's and Hadow's differing federal structures. In Erskine's conception of an indefinite Covenant of Grace wherein God immediately communicated his grace to sinners, the Assembly's condemnation of the "deed of gift and grant" passage from the *Marrow* was undoubtedly destructive of the grace of the gospel. However, while Hadow certainly did posit the necessity of a conditional offer of salvation, that conditionality was necessitated by both the mediate manner in which God communicated his grace and the admixture of elect sinners and reprobate sinners among the gospel audience, not by a demand that man earn or merit his salvation. Indeed, within Hadow's concept of a definite Covenant of Grace wherein God communicated his grace to man via means, the *Marrow*'s condemned expression required a universal redemption for its validity. Underlying Erskine's fifth "obscured truth," then, was a fundamental dissonance rooted in Erskine's and Hadow's particular formulations of a shared Scottish federalism; formulations that led the two men, upon reading the same sentence, to come to starkly different conclusions about what it taught.

'OBSCURED TRUTHS' AND JUDICIAL ADMONISHMENT

In each of the five disparate "obscured truths" which compelled Erskine to involvement in the *Marrow* controversy, there resides a commonality. Underlying both Erskine's conviction that truth was being obscured and the Assembly's persuasion of Erskine's error were the specific refinements of Scottish federal theology entertained by Erskine and Hadow. In each instance, Erskine's and Hadow's dissension was not caused by either man's break with Scottish Westminster federalism, whether that break be conceived of as Hadow's flight to Neonomianism or Erskine's reversion to earlier, overshadowed emphases. Rather, the cause lay in each man's distinctive synthesis of areas of Scottish federalism that had yet to be formalized definitively. In his evangelical federalism, one sees Erskine's apprehension of an encroaching legalism within the Kirk leading him, in the consideration of his federal theology occasioned by the Simson controversy, to adopt emphases from within Scottish Westminster federalism that stressed the graciousness and immediacy of the gospel. In Hadow's federal structure, one likewise glimpses Hadow, endeavoring a Simson-inspired refinement from within a St Mary's faculty that included a reputedly Arminian, lay episcopal Professor of Divinity, insisting upon elements of the same federal tradition that emphasized the precision of the *ordo salutis* and was deeply suspicious of any indications of affinity for an unlimited atonement. The result of such concurrent refinement was two importantly different federal systems.

It is to this federally-grounded disjunction between Erskine's and Hadow's theology that the Assembly's ultimate disciplining of the Representers is attributable. Although the re-publication of the *Marrow* had attracted notice almost immediately, it is uncertain how many ministers within the Kirk had read or digested the book when the matter came before the Assembly 1720.[308] Due to unfamiliarity with the work itself and the complexity of the matters under debate, many ministers would have placed great weight upon the judgment of Hadow, Principal of one of Scotland's four schools of divinity and a man known throughout the Kirk for doctrinal fidelity.[309] When such a reputable minister first denounced the *Marrow* in 1719 and then assailed its defenders in 1721, all the while presenting the *Marrow*'s errors through a federal paradigm countenanced by contemporary Scottish Westminster federalism, it is not surprising that the preponderance of ministers accepted Hadow's judgment and joined in his opposition to the *Marrow* and its defenders. While it would be difficult to argue that the particulars of Hadow's federal theology were representative of the majority of individual ministers within the Kirk, the majority of ministers in the Assembly were willing to trust Hadow's judgment and thus his doctrine became the representative of the Assembly's. Viewed from within that federal structure, the *Marrow* truly was tainted by antinomianism and other heretical doctrine, and thus Erskine's support of it understandably brought the same charges

---

308. See, for example, Lachman, *Marrow*, 485, 487–88; MacInnes, *Evangelical Movement*, 177.

309. Wodrow, *Analecta*, 3:485–86.

upon him.[310] As Hadow's interpretation of the *Marrow* was imbibed by many throughout the Kirk, the *Marrow* and its defenders fell afoul of the church judicatories for the simple reason that, in the *de facto* federalism of the Assembly, they were guilty of the errors alleged against them.

Confessionalism, Legalism, and the Marrow

Since the days of the controversy itself, much attention has focused on the relative conformity to the Westminster Confession of both the *Marrow*'s defenders and its opponents.[311] When the necessary task of appreciating the particular construction of Erskine's own federal paradigm is undertaken, it is clear that, from within that evangelical federalism, Erskine's promulgation of *Marrow* doctrine was in positive conformity to the Westminster Confession. Formed from a group of theological positions in full continuity with the Confession, Erskine's evangelical federalism was decisive in shaping his apprehension that certain truths were obscured by the Act 1720 and then in guiding the entirety of his position in the *Marrow* controversy. Erskine's "*Marrow* doctrine," then, was Westminster doctrine.

Vital to a realization of Erskine's Confessionalism is this appreciation of his federal system. This necessity of theological nuancing is apparent in the reflections upon the *Marrow* controversy, and particularly the differing notions of assurance articulated therein, that occurred in the mid-nineteenth century within the newly-formed Free Church of Scotland. In that communion, zeal for Confessional adherence reasserted itself, assuming a prominence that it lacked at other periods in the history of the Kirk. In such an environment, William Cunningham, in failing to address the Representers' federally-rooted distinction between an assurance of faith and an assurance

---

310. See Bozeman, *Precisianist Strain*, 32–39, for intimations of the connection between Hadow's mediate graciousness and antinomian suspicion.

311. Philip indicates both the context and the abiding relevance of this debate. See Philip, "Marrow." The most sustained attack on Erskine's adherence to Westminster orthodoxy was mounted in the immediate aftermath of the controversy and stemmed from a procedural irregularity that had prevented Erskine from physically signing the Confession at both his licensure and his ordination. When this oversight emerged, Erskine physically subscribed the Confession, in accordance with the Formula 1711, before the Portmoak Kirk Session on 4 March 1723. Furthermore, in an action overlooked in both the primary and secondary literature, Erskine had physically signed a formula from the Synod of Fife owning the Confession as the confession of his own faith on 8 April 1703, only five days after his ordination. For the controversy over Erskine's failure to sign the Confession, see Erskine, *Remnant*, vi, x–xx; *Presbytery of Kirkcaldie 1693–1704*, 342–43, 357–58; *Marrow-Chicaning*, 16–19, 22–23. For the synodical formula that Erskine signed, see *Presbytery of Kirkcaldie 1693–1704*, 358–59.

of sense, condemned their doctrine of assurance as un-Confessional; while James Buchanan, in nuancing the Representers' more complex notion of assurance, was able to commend it as fully harmonious with the Confession.[312] For two renowned theologians of the same era and from the same stridently Confessional context, two very different conclusions regarding the Confessional status of an Erskinite assurance were possible, and that difference was directly connected to their respective willingness to understand some of the federal nuances of the Representers' doctrine. When Buchanan's more cautious and patient approach is taken, the full Confessional status of Erskine's doctrine can be affirmed.

Even as Erskine's evangelical federalism is seen to enjoy the countenancing of the Westminster Confession, a careful examination of Hadow's doctrine also shows his system to have been built upon positions defensible from the Confession. Currently, much of the secondary literature is unstintingly critical of Hadow, accusing him of a doctrine of conditional grace that is foreign to his actual theology.[313] In that theological system, taken on its own terms, Hadow undeniably did forward peculiar developments of the Westminster system—such as necessary penal sanctions within the Law of Nature and his view of the post-Fall status of the Covenant of Works—yet Hadow's notion of mediate grace, firmly connected to an insistence upon the absolute divine monergism in all salvation, asserted a truly gracious notion of the Covenant of Grace.[314] If Hadow did tend to construe the Confession's *ordo salutis*-shaped description of redemption as sequential requirements for redemption, his assertion of the divine provision of those requirements clears him of the effective semi-Pelagianism or Neonomianism that is often alleged against him.[315]

While Hadow's doctrine is not an abject legalism, it actually represents a much more nefarious threat to an evangelical presence within the Kirk. From first principles defensible within Scottish federalism, Hadow amalgamated a doctrinal system susceptible to legalistic emphases and abuses, yet subtle enough to avoid offending all but twelve of the Kirk's ministers. The predicament that this system caused for evangelicals is well-illustrated by John Willison. As late as 1744, Willison was able to lament the legalism

---

312. Cunningham, *Reformers*, 118, 122–27; Buchanan, *Justification*, 184–86. For a modern "Buchananist" interpretation of the doctrine, see Philip, "Marrow," 33–35.

313. See, for example, Philip, "Marrow," 27, 31–33, 35; J. B. Torrance, Introduction to *The Nature of the Atonement*, 12.

314. See Buchanan, *Justification*, 184; Cunningham, *Reformers*, 281–82.

315. See, for example, *AD*, 162–64. For the prominence of the *ordo salutis* in the Confession, see Barth, *Confessions*, 67–68, 139–45. See also T. F. Torrance, *The School of Faith*, xviii–xix. Hereafter, *School*.

that pervaded much Scottish preaching, yet defend the condemnation of the *Marrow*, a condemnation that proceeded from pseudo-legalistic emphases and did much to solidify a more legalistic approach to doctrinal questions in the General Assembly.[316] Like Willison, there were many other evangelical ministers within the Kirk whose doctrinal systems were, at the very least, unable to discern Hadow's more legalistic emphases; an inability evidenced in their willingness to accept Hadow's reading of *Marrow* doctrine. In contrast, Erskine's evangelical federalism was able to articulate, from within the Westminster tradition, a theology whose very structure so emphasized the graciousness of the gospel that Hadow's more legalizing emphases were irreconcilable with it. Erskine's evangelical federalism, then, represented a structural bulwark against the legalistic undertones festering in the early eighteenth-century Kirk.

THE CONTROVERSY'S AFTERMATH

While Erskine's evangelical federalism guarded against legalistic emphases, it also proved to be a barrier to true reconciliation with the Assembly. Although the Act 1722 had formally concluded the *Marrow* controversy, it did nothing either to reveal the federal underpinnings of the controversy or to reconcile the opposing parties. As a result, both the Representers and the Assembly remained convinced of the heterodoxy of the opposite party and a deep suspicion lingered on both sides of the dispute.[317] From the Assembly, this suspicion animated a protracted series of judicial proceedings evidently intended to harass Erskine for his unrepented *Marrow* sympathies and prevent his relocation from obscure Portmoak to a charge from whence he could more widely disseminate his admonished views.[318] The most prominent of these processes, precipitated by the attempt to translate Erskine to Kirkcaldy in 1724, was founded upon specious charges, thus both indicating the depth of estrangement and suspicion that persisted between Erskine and the courts of the Kirk and solidifying Erskine's conviction that he was being judicially persecuted by the Established Church because of his support for *Marrow* doctrine.[319]

316. *FIT*, 79–85; 43–44, 127–28, respectively.

317. Harper, *Memoir*, 43–44.

318. Ibid., 48. Boston perceived a similar treatment from the church judicatories. See Boston, *A GENERAL ACCOUNT OF MY LIFE*, 229. For an account of the controversy's denouement not specific to Erskine, see Lachman, *Marrow*, 418–76.

319. Erskine discusses the process concerning Kirkcaldy in Erskine, *Remnant*, iii–xxxii. This important preface appears only in the 1725 edition of the sermon. For an official account, see *Synod of Fife 1719-1738*, 186–210. For a succinct secondary

While legitimate blame often is placed upon the church courts for their pursuit of Erskine, Erskine himself was not without blame for the poor state of his relationship with the Assembly. While Erskine's efforts in the early days of the controversy display a willingness to engage in forthright and thorough theological discourse, his later actions seemed intent on simply antagonizing his opponents. A clear example of this tendency can be found in a sermon preached by Erskine on 10 May 1724. Then, in exhorting his hearers to come to Christ, Erskine proclaimed, in reference to Christ,

> Consider that his heart and his arms are open and ready to embrace all that are willing to be embraced by him. . . . I tell you good news, he is more willing to embrace you by far, than you are to be embraced by him.[320]

Here, Erskine seems to imply that there are some whom Christ wants to embrace who will never embrace him, thus giving intimation of an unlimited atonement that has made salvation possible for all yet effectual for none. In the larger context of his sermon, Erskine proceeds to qualify his statements in such a way that he remains clear of an unlimited atonement. However, while Erskine's words were thus harmonious with Reformed orthodoxy, they were also irresponsible; by skirting the very edges of orthodoxy with such provocative language, Erskine seemed to be making a calculated attempt to provoke his opponents. Indeed, if Erskine's opponents were to hear these words, they would have judged their fears about Erskine to be confirmed—while not brazenly teaching doctrinal error, he was subtly committed to such deviation and thus was using evidently sound language to forward heterodox, or even heretical, notions. While the church courts did display an uncharitable suspicion of Erskine's theology, such language by Erskine likewise manifests an antagonism that is culpable in fostering the doctrinal alienation that plagued his relationship with the wider Kirk.

As months and then years passed following the *Marrow* controversy, the church courts seemed unwilling to believe Erskine's continued protestations of orthodoxy, even as Erskine seemed unwilling to conduct himself in a manner that would help the judicatories invest such trust in him. Unearthed, yet both unrealized and unresolved, the variance between Erskine's evangelical federalism and the Assembly's federal structure continued to

---

account, see Lachman, *Marrow*, 421–26. Erskine also judged that the increased harassment he faced was due to the death of fellow Representer James Bathgate on 30 March 1724. Prior to his death, Bathgate had received a great deal of the judicatories' ire that, after his demise, became re-focused upon Erskine. See Brown, *Gospel Truth*, 110–11. See also Harper, 48–51.

320. *Works*, 1:169.

exacerbate a doctrinal and judicial estrangement between Erskine and the church judicatories.[321] Although Erskine's relationship with the Established Church thus seemed to reach a nadir late in 1725, matters improved noticeably in the following years.[322] Ironically, a good measure of this amelioration stemmed from the second process against John Simson, beginning in 1726 and concluding with Simson's suspension from teaching responsibilities, yet retention on the Glasgow faculty, in 1729.[323] Although Erskine was distressed and outraged at the lenity again shown to Simson, this was a sentiment that he shared with a larger, "evangelical" party within the Kirk; as Erskine's assessment of Simson's errors did not touch upon the nuances of his evangelical federalism that had figured in the *Marrow* controversy, he was able to find common cause with a large contingent of the Kirk and the strain of isolation seemed in abeyance even though an abiding suspicion lay only barely beneath the surface.[324]

SUMMARY

Erskine's involvement in the *Marrow* controversy is attributable to the profound differences that existed between his emerging evangelical federalism and the federal theology of James Hadow. While Scottish federalism had been formally consolidated in the Westminster Confession, that federal structure contained ambivalence of statement on certain particulars of federalism and thus within an overriding uniformity of federal thought, there was still important room for variation on certain matters. As Erskine and Hadow both operated within this common inheritance, they adopted different understandings of these less formalized areas of Scottish federalism and for each man these particular understandings coalesced into federal

---

321. Compare Erskine's characterization of the controversy in 1721 with his representation thereof in 1724 and 1725. See *Christian Magazine*, 377, 380–81; *Works*, 1:143; and Erskine, *Remnant*, viii, respectively. Also, compare Erskine's references to the controversy in *Works*, 1:89–90, 120–22 with those of *Remnant*, viii–ix; and Erskine, *Christ in the Believer's Arms*, 3–4. The first two references are from sermons preached in 1720 and 1721, respectively, while the latter two are from works authored in 1725. As one moves to the later works, Erskine's foremost desire noticeably shifts from reconciliation to vindication.

322. Wodrow judges that, by late 1725, most of the tension surrounding the controversy had dissipated. Wodrow, *Analecta*, 3:235–36.

323. Simson had received a one year suspension by both the 1727 and 1728 Assemblies, yet the suspension was not made indefinite until the Assembly 1729. The fullest treatment of the second process against Simson is, again, Skoczylas, *Simson*.

324. For examples of Erskine's contemporary assessment of Simson's errors, see *Works*, 1:506; 2:32, 72, 83.

structures with their own peculiarities and emphases. When these federal structures were subjected to the exigencies of the early eighteenth-century Kirk, they precipitated a fierce doctrinal disagreement. As the underpinnings of that disagreement remained undetected, and thus the disagreement remained unresolved, deep suspicion lingered. Doctrinally and judicially ostracized within the Kirk, Erskine became increasingly defensive of his evangelical federal paradigm even as that defensiveness made him suspect in the eyes of many ministers who were themselves proponents of a Westminster federalism. While direct confrontation dissipated after 1725, an abiding suspicion remained between Erskine and the generality of the Kirk.

In many senses, the *Marrow* controversy is thus paradigmatic of the nexus between Erskine as a man and Erskine as a theologian. In his defense of *Marrow* doctrine, Erskine's evangelical zeal burned, both in his writings and in the free gospel offer of his preaching. In that same defense, Erskine's tendentiousness also crept to the surface as Erskine antagonized rather than seeking reconciliation. In both components, one recognizes the Erskine of much extant literature. However, as the present account has shown, it was Erskine's underlying theological commitment to an evangelical federalism that dictated his course in the *Marrow* controversy. It was that evangelical federalism that caused Erskine to adhere to the *Marrow* cause even while other, equally earnest evangelicals joined in condemning the work, and it was the suspicion engendered by the failure to realize the controversy's federal underpinnings that fuelled Erskine's belligerent defense of his doctrine. Thus growing out of his evangelical federalism, the *Marrow* controversy would reverberate through Erskine's ministry for years to come.

Chapter III

The Secession Crisis

IF THE AFTERMATH OF the *Marrow* controversy had unearthed an estrangement between Erskine and many others within the Kirk, that estrangement seemed to explode in the Secession Crisis. Although much had occurred in Erskine's life prior to 1733, virtually every account thereof affords a position of interpretive prominence to the Secession of that year; a location that has had two deleterious effects upon an accurate understanding of Erskine's theology. First, it is an accepted truism that Erskine seceded over the Act Anent the Planting of Vacant Churches of 1732, a supposition that places patronage as the center of Erskine's thought and the chief determinant of his actions. Second, while interpreters have differed on exactly why patronage sparked Erskine's Secession, their varying analyses all implicitly portray Erskine and his "secessionist tendencies" as so discontinuous with the body of Scottish Covenantal dissent in the 1730s that Erskine determined to seek a new home outwith the judicatories of the Established Church.[1] Jointly, these two characteristics of most interpretations of the Secession present Erskine as a man driven to such excessively intractable opposition to patronage by the peculiarities of his own disposition that he was unable to maintain common cause with other ministers who were equally opposed to an increasingly-noxious patronage. However, when Erskine's course within

---

1. In the literature emerging from the Secession Crisis, the phrase "church judicatories" is ubiquitous, being used to refer to the Established Church envisioned as the conglomeration of its various individual judicatories, although the lowest judicatory of the individual Kirk Session is normally minimized in this phrase's referent. In the present work, a similar use of the phrase will be employed, although more precise reference to individual judicatories will be used where appropriate.

the Secession Crisis is examined on its own terms, Erskine displays a steady continuity of doctrinal emphasis and impetus. While the Secession changed much about the course of Erskine's ministry, it was not precipitated by any polemical or theological change within Erskine.

To move beyond the common notion of Erskine's Secession as a patronage-centered, innovative movement within Kirk dissent, one must ask a two-fold question: why did Erskine secede, and why was his Secession limited to only four ministers rather than drawing in the larger body of Covenantally-committed evangelical ministers in the Kirk?[2] When this more expansive question is explored, one realizes that Erskine's extrusion from the Established Church stemmed from a procedural irregularity rather than from either pertinent theological differences with other Covenantally-committed ministers or a personal desire for secession, thus creating not a marginalized dissenting body, but rather the ecclesial embodiment of decades of mainstream Scottish Covenantal dissent.

To arrive at an understanding of both the origins and the limitation of Erskine's Secession, it is first necessary to locate the Secession Crisis in its larger political and ecclesiastical context, as well as the specific context of Erskine's own ministry in the early 1730s. After establishing this context and acquiring an overview of the Secession Crisis, brief consideration will be given to a recent attempt to interpret the Secession. Then, the Secession will be viewed through a comparison of Erskine's actions and the critique offered contemporaneously by John Willison of Dundee, an evangelical of noted piety and eirenity who was prominent in the efforts to draw the Seceders back into the church judicatories in the 1730s and who went on to become one of the leaders of the Popular Party in the 1740s until his death in 1750.[3] By means of this comparison, the central question at hand will be addressed—why did Erskine secede when Willison, a renowned evangelical and strident Covenantal opponent of patronage, did not?

SCOTTISH POLITICS IN THE 1720S

Since the Union of Parliaments in 1707, many Scots had resented what they judged to be an overly-intrusive London government. This resentment came to a head in 1725 when the United Parliament sought to impose the Malt Tax on Scotland in violation of the express language of the Treaty of Union. Enraged by this latest transgression of what were supposed to be

---

2. The secondary literature recently has realized the need for this expanded question. See, for example, McIntosh, "Lessons," 7.

3. See *Fasti*, 5.320–22; Jinkins, "Willison, John."

guaranteed protections, many Scots erupted in protest and the country reached the "pinnacle of post-union disorder."[4] This disorder was particularly acute in Glasgow, resulting in the famous Shawfield Riots, in which an irate mob burned down the home of Daniel Campbell of Shawfield, the MP for the Glasgow burghs. In August 1725, the British government sent Archibald Campbell, the first Earl of Ilay, to make an investigation of the causes of the riots and of the government's ineffective response to them.[5] In the wake of this investigation, the Duke of Roxburghe was dismissed from his position as Scottish Secretary, with no one being appointed in his stead.[6] Rather than being vested in a concrete secretaryship, ruling power in Scotland came to be concentrated in Lord Ilay himself. In the years following 1725, Scotland was governed by a new arrangement—in return for bringing stability to Scotland and delivering the bulk of her Parliamentary votes to Robert Walpole's government, Ilay would receive control over government patronage and influence, both civil and ecclesiastical, in Scotland.[7] Using these resources and acting through Andrew Fletcher, Lord Milton, his agent in Edinburgh, Ilay came to exert such a firm and stable control over Scottish affairs that London was able to withdraw almost completely from direct involvement in Scotland, leaving Ilay to rule as "King of Scotland."[8] In those years, much of Scottish politics operated on a simple equation—a peaceful Scotland under Ilay meant a Scotland free from London interference.[9] Of course, such an equation worked to the advantage of both parties. For Scotland, it ensured a certain amount of freedom from London control; for London, it helped extinguish the flames of anti-Union sentiment in Scotland by removing the most grievous evidences of the Union itself.

Unfortunately for the Kirk, a vital component of Ilay's management was his use of ecclesiastical patronage.[10] In the years following the passage

4. Whatley, *Scots and the Union*, 345.

5. Upon his brother's death in 1743, Ilay would become the third Duke of Argyll, although he is most distinctively referred to as Ilay, sometimes modernized as "Islay." See Murdoch, "Campbell, Archibald, third duke of Argyll"; Whatley, *Scots and the Union* 265.

6. See Ferguson, *Scotland*, 143.

7. Whatley, *Scots and the Union*, 365; Allan, *Scotland in the Eighteenth Century*, 24.

8. Ferguson, *Scotland*, 143. See also Allan, *Scotland in the Eighteenth Century*, 22; Whatley, *Scots and the Union*, 328, 365; Devine, *Scottish Nation*, 22–24. Fletcher was the nephew of the famous Andrew Fletcher of the Union debates.

9. See Devine, *Scottish Nation*, 22; Whatley, *Scots and the Union*, 328.

10. On the importance of ecclesiastical patronage in eighteenth-century Scotland, see, for example, Devine, *Scottish Nation*, 84–102; Brown, *Religion and Society in Scotland Since 1707*, 68–76. Hereafter, *Religion*. Ilay pursued his agenda primarily via the General Assembly, which was run by his chosen leaders and filled with a

of the Patronage Act in 1712, the Kirk's opposition to the law evidently had convinced both the Crown and many English MPs to repeal the Patronage Act, yet the demands of Ilay and his brother, the Duke of Argyll, had kept the institution in place. So central were Ilay and Argyll to the continuation of patronage that Robert Wodrow judged that "the continouance of this burden upon us may justly lye at their dore."[11] In Ilay's estimation, the General Assembly existed only because of Parliamentary grant and thus the Kirk had no authority to question the State to whom she owed her very existence, particularly in regard to patronage, which Ilay deemed "a civil right, and a point of property, which he would never give up."[12] Prior to Ilay's ascendance, those holding control over the Crown's powers of patronage tended to exercise that patronage with at least some regard to the opinion of the congregations effected, yet in the years following 1725, the use of Crown patronage in Scotland became markedly more severe.[13] In this, Ilay stood as a problematic figure for the Scottish Church. His effective control of Scottish affairs kept London interference in Scotland to a minimum, thus helping the Kirk avoid the dreaded powers of episcopacy, yet the price the Kirk had to pay to ensure this effective control was submission to Ilay's extreme and determined use of the powers of ecclesiastical patronage.[14]

ERSKINE IN STIRLING

While the Kirk was experiencing these changes in its relationship to the State, Erskine personally experienced a remarkable change, as well. In 1731, after serving as minister at Portmoak for the entire twenty-eight years of his ordained ministry, Erskine was translated to a newly-created third charge in Stirling. While the process that would terminate in that translation occurred rapidly, it stemmed from some of the historical peculiarities of the town and parish of Stirling. In the tensions resulting from the Public Resolutions controversy, the large church building in Stirling had been split into two separate "churches," and congregations, by the addition of a wall in 1656.[15]

---

disproportionate number of Edinburgh lawyers. See G. Rosse, Edinburgh, to Andrew Fletcher, Lord Milton, 6 May 1732, 1; Macleod, *Theology*, 171–72; McIntosh, *Theology*, 11–13; Sefton, "Lord Ilay and Patrick Cuming," 205–6, 215–16. Hereafter, "Ilay."

    11. Wodrow, *Analecta*, 4:246. See also *Analecta*, 2:391, 3:490–92, 4:245–46; Sefton, "Ilay," 203–4.

    12. Wodrow, *Analecta*, 4:246. See also *Analecta*, 4:73; Sefton, "Ilay," 204–5.

    13. See Sefton, "Ilay," 204, 207; Drummond and Bulloch, *Scottish Church*, 39–40.

    14. See Wodrow, *Analecta*, 4:73 for an example of this latent tension.

    15. Simpson, *The Church of the Holy Rude: Stirling*, 23; Fulton, "The Managed Career of the Reverend Charles Moore of Stirling," 244. Hereafter, "Managed."

By the late 1720s, only the east half of the building was in use, with the ministry therein being the responsibility of Alexander Hamilton, in the first charge, and Charles Moore in the second charge. While this arrangement had remained unchanged, the continued growth of Stirling meant that, on 7 November 1730, the Guildry, Trades, and Tolerated Communities of Stirling were forced to petition the Town Council "complaining of their want of accomodatione in the church for hearing the gospell preached."[16]

The first remedy attempted by the Council was to arrange for Hamilton and Moore to share preaching duties in both halves of the church in exchange for an increase in stipend.[17] However, after considering this proposal, the two ministers rejected it at the Town Council's meeting on 14 December 1730. In addition to a popular desire for a third minister that was recognized by both of the existing ministers, Hamilton was already "ane old and infirm man," and thus they recommended that the Council await guidance from the Presbytery of Stirling and, upon receiving approval, proceed to calling an additional minister to a newly-created third charge.[18] Taking Hamilton and Moore's guidance in part, the Council began making preparations to have a third charge created in the West Kirk and, once that work was well-progressed, sought the "approbation" of the Presbytery.[19] By the end of January 1731, the Council had decided that the new minister would receive a salary of 12,000 merks Scots annually from the converted multure of the burgh and had confirmed from the advice of workmen that the newly-created charge would be better accommodated in a re-opened West Kirk than in an expanded East Kirk.[20] By late April, the magistrates, Town Council, elders, and congregation of Stirling had unanimously called Erskine to this new charge; on 27 May 1731, the Presbytery of Kirkcaldy

16. Renwick, ed., *Extracts From the Records of the Royal Burgh of Stirling. A.D. 1667-1752. With Appendix, A.D. 1471-1752*, 210. Hereafter, *Extracts*. See also Muirhead, "Religion, Politics and Society in Stirling During the Ministry of Ebenezer Erskine 1731-1754," 2-3. Hereafter, "Religion."

17. *Extracts*, 211-12.

18. *Extracts*, 212. The Town Council had held the patronage of the first charge since 1677, and since 1681 the minister of the second charge had been called by the Council in conjunction with the Guildry, Trades, Tolerated Communities, and heritors. That the Town Council was the active agent in the matter of a new third charge was thus unexceptional. See Muirhead, "Religion," 3. For more on the structure of burgh churches, see Campbell, "The Burgh Churches of Scotland," 185-94.

19. *Extracts*, 212-16.

20. *Extracts*, 213-14, 215-16. The scheme for paying the third minister was similar to that for paying the second minister. See Muirhead, "Religion," 3. This would seem to defuse the potential implications of Fulton's discussion of Colonel Blackadder's legacy for the support of a third minister. See Fulton, "Managed," 245; Wodrow, *Analecta*, 4:198, 226.

was presented with a formal call from the burgh to Erskine; and on 8 July 1731, the Presbytery of Stirling met to admit Erskine as the third minister at Stirling.[21] In a span of only five months, starting from Hamilton and Moore's rejection of the Council's offer that they undertake new duties, Stirling had created a third charge, provided both stipend and accommodation for that charge, unanimously chosen Erskine as the most suitable candidate for the charge, and extended a formal call to him. Stirling very much wanted a third minister and, from the very outset, it was evident that they wanted Erskine specifically.[22]

While the Council and people of Stirling were enthusiastic about Erskine's potential translation, the Presbytery of Stirling was much more reticent; as late as April 1731, Wodrow wrote that the "Presbytery [of Stirling] are against him, as being one of the Representers."[23] Reminiscent of the 1724 controversy over the attempt to translate Erskine to Kirkcaldy, it appears that Erskine's support of the *Marrow* made his movement an unwelcome prospect for the Presbytery of Stirling; a presbytery that, within the Synod of Perth and Stirling, was part of a synod free of any *Marrow* Representers.[24] For those within the Presbytery of Stirling prone to be suspicious of Erskine's lingering *Marrow* sympathies, the colleagues whom he would be joining in Stirling would have only added to their uneasiness. In 1720, Alexander

---

21. *Records of the Presbyterie of Kirkcaldie from April 23 1724 to July 22 1742. Volume 5th*, 149–150; *Records of the Presbytery of Stirling*, CH2/722/12, 98–99, 107–8. Hereafter, *Presbytery of Kirkcaldie 1724–1742* and *Presbytery of Stirling*, CH2/722/12, respectively. The date of Erskine's induction sometimes is given erroneously as 6 September. See Muirhead, "Religion," 3; Small, *History of the Congregations of the United Presbyterian Church 1733–1900*, 2:663.

22. Muirhead, "Religion," 3–4.

23. Wodrow, *Analecta*, 4:226. See 4:198 for another instance of resistance to Erskine's translation because of his *Marrow* sympathies. Erskine's willingness to move is also surprising. Although four congregations had formally sought Erskine's translation in the past—Burntisland in 1712, Tulliallan in 1713, Kirkcaldy in 1724, and Kinross in 1728—Erskine had always expressed a desire to stay in Portmoak. While the secondary literature contains some speculation on the factors leading to Erskine's acquiescence with Stirling's call, Erskine gave no indication of his motivation and thus all speculation remains unconvincing and unnecessary. Although Erskine was having difficulty with Sir John Bruce, patron of Kinross, at the time of his translation, that difficulty stemmed from Bruce's insolvency rather than a deeper antagonism that might have driven Erskine away. See Wodrow, *Analecta*, 4:215. For the suggestion of a further, aborted desire to translate Erskine to Dunfermline in 1724, see Wodrow, *Analecta*, 3:164. For Erskine's prior resistance to translation, see Erskine, *Remnant*, vii–xxi; *Fasti*, 4.328; Lachman, *Marrow*, 472. For some examples of the leading speculation concerning Erskine's motivations, see *Life*, 330; Muirhead, "Religion," 4–5; MacEwen, 40–41.

24. In 1731, of the eleven living Representers, five were in Erskine's old Synod of Fife, yet none were in the Synod of Perth and Stirling.

Hamilton had been brought before the Committee for Purity of Doctrine for theological positions largely synonymous with *Marrow* doctrine and, while he had been cleared of official suspicion by the Committee, he had remained a noted and popular evangelical.[25] Charles Moore, the minister of Stirling's second charge, did little to improve the scenario. While Moore is classed rightly as a proto-Moderate within the Kirk and was clearly under the influence of the house of Argyll, his nascent Moderate sensibilities had led him to cast the sole dissenting vote when the *Marrow* Brethren were censured by the Commission in 1722.[26] While this "support" for the *Marrow* cause certainly was rooted in the desire for calm rather than in sympathy for the Representers' system of doctrine, Moore was still suspected of *Marrow* tendencies and his record would have made him a doubtful monitor and counterbalance to the team of Hamilton and Erskine.[27]

Despite this hesitance to accept Erskine into the presbytery, when the Portmoak minister's proposed translation came before the Presbytery of Stirling, no formal opposition was registered.[28] Simply stated, it seems that the Presbytery of Stirling had Erskine forced upon them.[29] Before the matter was brought formally before the presbytery, the Stirling Town Council had decided upon their course of action and had fixed their eyes upon Erskine.[30] When the Presbytery of Stirling first had a chance to stop the translation, then, to have done so would have threatened a heated controversy. In calling Erskine, the Stirling Council was exercising its independence, and thus to thwart their efforts would have brought considerable ire, a prospect made all the less appealing due to the support that the Council likely would enjoy from James Erskine, Lord Grange, a Lord of Session and elder for the burgh of Stirling to the General Assembly who was known as an evangelically-minded opponent of overriding popular desires in the calling of pastors.[31]

25. In 1720, Hamilton had been minister at Airth and was translated to Stirling in 1726. Even earlier, Hamilton had achieved renown when, as a student in Edinburgh, he had climbed the Netherbow Port to remove James Guthrie's severed head. See *Fasti*, 1:204; 4:290, 319, 321.

26. See Fulton, "Managed," 231–34, 236, 240–41. Moore had been a member of the Commission in both 1721 and 1722, working against the Assembly's censure of the Representers the entire time. See *Fasti*, 4.325; Muirhead, "Religion," 5–6.

27. Wodrow, *Analecta*, 4:198; Fulton, "Managed," 243.

28. See *Presbytery of Stirling*, CH2/722/12, 98–100, 106–8. Similarly, there was no opposition from the Presbytery of Kirkcaldy when the call from Stirling was formally presented and accepted. See *Presbytery of Kirkcaldie 1724–1742*, 149–50.

29. See Wodrow, *Analecta*, 4:198; Fulton, "Managed," 245.

30. See Wodrow, *Analecta*, 4:226 for an indication of resentment at the Council's overbearing course.

31. For the Council's sense of independence, see Muirhead, "Religion," 56–57.

While it is impossible to determine precisely the presbytery's motivation in allowing Erskine's translation to Stirling, it is most likely that, faced with the veritable certainty of controversy if the translation was contested, and knowing that there were other contentious issues on the horizon, the presbytery simply let the translation happen, doubtlessly taking comfort that at least Erskine's synodical isolation from his Representing brethren would make him less troublesome and more manageable. In the recently-concluded Assembly, there had been an Overture that certainly would cause controversy enough.

PATRONAGE ON THE EVE OF THE SECESSION

As Erskine settled into Stirling, important changes were afoot in the wider Kirk. Following the imposition of the Patronage Act in 1712, certain abuses of the system of patronage had led to an Act of Parliament in 1719 that sought to clarify the procedure for filling a vacant charge. Under the terms of this Act, when a charge became empty, a patron had a fixed period of six months in which to fill that charge. Over the course of those six months, the patron could put forth a presentee for the vacant charge and, so long as that candidate was qualified, the presbytery in question was to accept him. However, many ministers and probationers within Scotland were averse to accepting presentations from secular patrons, and thus the six month period allotted to fill a charge often would expire without a patron even being able to find a man to accept his presentation. Even when such a presentee was found, he would often face opposition from the presbytery on the grounds that he was not "qualified." To patrons, this was tantamount to presbyteries robbing them of their powers of presentation. As the 1720s bore on, with Ilay exerting greater authority over Crown patronage and patrons seeking to exert similar authority over private patronage, this practice became highly problematic.[32] As a temporary remedy to the problem, "Riding Committees" were appointed and employed with greater frequency starting in 1729. In this practice, the Commission of the General Assembly would appoint committees that would travel around Scotland to ordain and install presentees to charges where the local presbytery refused to cooperate.[33] In 1731, motivated by Ilay's demands for uniformity, an Overture anent the Planting of Vacant Churches came before the Assembly as a more formal alleviation

---

On Grange, see Woodrow, *Correspondence*, 3:197–204; Muirhead, "Religion," 16; *Mar and Kelly Papers*, 1:286–87; Whatley, *Scots and the Union*, 265–66.

32. Sefton, "Ilay," 207.

33. See Sefton, "Ilay," 207–8, 216, for a balanced view of Riding Committees.

of this problem.³⁴ By the terms of this Overture, if the six month period allotted to a patron to fill a vacancy expired without the vacancy being filled, the power to fill the charge devolved upon a joint meeting of heritors and elders. At that meeting, attended by a representative from the presbytery, "a well qualified Gospel minister" was to be "elected and called by the heritors and elders in a conjunct meeting."³⁵

To some within the Scottish Church, this Overture 1731 was an acceptable resolution of a serious problem. Faced with intensifying demands from Ilay and others, the Kirk had to do something to introduce uniformity to the process of filling vacant charges, and this uniformity had to take some steps to protect the right of patronage. Given these criteria, the Overture 1731 was not overly onerous, for it did not give patrons an unchecked power to fill vacant charges and it even included a role for the elders of the congregation in question.³⁶ To others, however, two considerations made the Overture wholly unacceptable. First, the Overture gave power to all Protestant heritors with property in the parish, even those who were not members of the presbyterian Church. Second, the Overture granted to the joint meeting of heritors and elders not merely the power to present a candidate to a particular congregation, but rather it gave them the positive power to elect a man to fill the charge, thus obviating any role for congregational consent in the process.³⁷ By the terms of the Overture, it was entirely possible that an episcopalian heritor could have more control over the filling of a vacant presbyterian charge than did the members of that congregation. The Overture 1731, then, was a crystallization of the tension in which the Church of Scotland found itself, for it represented, in one Overture, the growing demands that the Kirk quietly concede a measure of its power in order to palliate Lord Ilay and thus maintain the degree of autonomy that Scotland had achieved.

---

34. For Ilay's involvement in the eventual passage of the Act 1732, see Rosse. See also Ferguson, 122.

35. *AGA*, 621. See *AGA*, 620–21 for the Overture in its final form. See also Mitchell, "Ebenezer Erskine," 159–61.

36. Even John Willison was of this opinion before seeing the exact details of the Overture. *CDMD*, xi–xv.

37. See Currie, *THE OVERTURE considered*, 51–53; *A PUBLICK TESTIMONY*, 12. Hereafter, *Overture* and *Public Testimony*, respectively.

THE SECESSION CRISIS

The historical progression of the Secession Crisis is both intricate and uncontested in the secondary literature. While a detailed narrative is thus foregone at present, the briefest of historical outlines is necessary to establish a chronological framework for the following analysis of those uniformly-agreed events.[38] At the Assembly 1732, the Overture 1731 was passed into an Act and, in accordance with an Act of the Assembly 1730 forbidding the recording of reasons of dissent from the decisions of church judicatories, two significant dissenting representations were refused and dissenting speeches by Ebenezer Erskine and others were not recorded.[39] On 10 October, in his capacity as outgoing moderator of the Synod of Perth and Stirling, Erskine preached a sermon before the synod that some ministers present found offensive and thus the synod voted to censure Erskine for his sermonic dissent; doing so without citing specific Scriptural passages or truths that Erskine had violated.[40]

When the Assembly 1733 upheld Erskine's censure, he submitted a written protestation to which three other ministers from the Synod of Perth and Stirling—William Wilson of Perth, Alexander Moncrieff of Abernethy, and James Fisher of Kinclaven—adhered. When the four ministers refused to retract their protestation, an Act and Sentence passed by the Assembly ordered them to appear before the Commission in August to retract the

---

38. For primary presentations of the controversy, see especially *TSP*; *N&S*; and *RN&S*. These works represent the efforts of the Seceding Brethren, a Committee of the Commission of the Assembly, and the Seceding Brethren, respectively. Indeed, Erskine seems to have been responsible personally for *RN&S*. See Ebenezer Erskine to James Erskine, Lord Grange, 23 January 1734 [1733], 2. Hereafter, "Erskine to Grange January 1734."

39. For the Act 1730, see *AGA*, 612. For the two representations, see *Public Testimony*; Struthers, THE HISTORY OF SCOTLAND, 1:599–610. For Erskine's dissenting speech, see *Life*, 358–60. On the Act's genesis, see Sefton, "The Early Development of Moderatism in the Church of Scotland," 39–41. Hereafter, "Moderatism."

40. For the text of Erskine's sermon, see *Works*, 1:483–507. For an account of the proceedings, see *The Fifth Synod Book of Perth and Stirling Since the Revolution Commencing Eighth Day of October 1728*, 123–38. Hereafter, *Synod of Perth and Stirling*. The phrase "sermonic dissent" has been chosen to avoid a superfluous debate. Even at the time of the Secession Crisis, there was disagreement over whether Erskine was censured for the *content* of his sermon, or only for certain harsh *expressions* therein. See, for example, *TSP*, 20–26. However, such a debate wrongly divides what was a unified dissent. Just as Erskine had chosen the content of his sermon, so had he chosen the exact expressions through which to convey it; the expression was as central to Erskine's dissent as was the content, and thus to censure either one was to rebuke Erskine's dissent, which was itself specific content given intentional expression.

protestation and express sorrow for their conduct.[41] Instead, the four Dissenting Brethren, as they came to be called, submitted to the Commission in August two representations in which they delineated their reasons for not retracting their protestation.[42] Unsatisfied, the Commission suspended the Brethren from their charges and ordered them to appear again before the Commission in November. At that meeting, the Commission found that the Brethren had ignored their suspension and continued to refuse retracting their protestation and thus, on 16 November 1733, the Commission voted to loose the four Brethren from their charges.[43]

In December 1733, the four ministers met at Gairney Bridge and, on 6 December, formed themselves into the Associate Presbytery, with Erskine being elected the first Moderator of the new presbytery.[44] In thus forming themselves into a presbytery, the Brethren were very explicit that they had not separated from the Church of Scotland, but rather had merely seceded from the "prevailing party" that had come to have control over the church judicatories.[45] As evidence of both this tenuous association with the Established Church and the apparent hope of an eventual return to the church judicatories, the Brethren declined to exercise the keys of government and discipline, believing that such an exercise would indicate a level of separation from the Established Church that was not their desire.[46] In 1734, the General Assembly took certain steps to pacify the Brethren and remove the grounds of their Secession. Most notably, the Assembly repealed both the Act 1730 and the Act 1732, and invited the four Brethren to return to their charges.[47] However, these efforts were to no avail. Shortly after forming themselves into a presbytery, the Brethren had published a *Testimony to the Doctrine, Worship, Government and Discipline of the Church of Scotland*, a document which outlined their principles and their reasons for seceding from the judicatories of the Established Church, and they remained con-

41. For the Assembly's Act and Sentence, see *AGA*, 624–26.

42. See *RTC*.

43. See *N&S*, 39–42.

44. *THE TESTIMONY AND CONTENDINGS Of the Reverend Mr. ALEXANDER HAMILTON, One of the Ministers of the Gospel at Stirling; Against the violent settlement of Mr. JAMES MACKIE, in the Parish of St. Ninians*, 71. Hereafter, *Contendings*. The meeting at Gairney Bridge was also attended by Ralph Erskine of Dunfermline and Thomas Mair of Orwell. Both of these ministers remained in the Established Church until February 1737.

45. See *TD*, 27–28.

46. *ADT*, v–vii.

47. The Presbytery of Stirling even invited Erskine to serve as Moderator; an offer that was formally extended by Moore and Henry Lindsay of Bothkennar, yet declined by Erskine. See *Contendings*, 79–80.

vinced that none of the central issues raised in that document had been addressed.[48] However, because of the efforts of the Assembly 1734 to address the Brethren's concerns, the members of the Associate Presbytery came under increasing pressure to accede to the Established Church, and thus issued a further pamphlet, *Reasons Why They Have Not Acceded to the Judicatories of the Established Church*, to explain their continued Secession.[49]

For several years following the Secession, Erskine exercised his pastoral office without significant impairment, enjoying his full stipend and use of the manse even after 1733.[50] However, in 1737, opposition began to coalesce around two events—the ongoing contention over the intrusion of James Mackie in the neighboring parish of St Ninians in 1734 and the observance of the first communion season in Stirling since Erskine had been loosed from his charge.[51] Furth of Stirling, the Secession Crisis was revived by the publication of John Currie's *Essay on Separation*.[52] In this treatise, which was to become the *de facto* official statement of the Established Church on the matter of the Seceded Brethren, Currie forcefully argued that the members of the Associate Presbytery had no excuse for remaining outwith the Established Church.[53] With the Secession Crisis rekindled, the Seceders, who by this date numbered eight ministers, were summoned to appear before the Assembly 1739 to answer for a libel brought against them concerning their exercise of the full judicial functions of government and discipline.[54] When the Seceders appeared, they did so as a constitute presbytery, reading their

---

48. See *TD*.

49. See *Reasons*. The pamphlet was published immediately before the sitting of the General Assembly 1735.

50. *Extracts*, 226–29; *RTC*, 1–10, 63–64; *TSP*, 60–64; *Life*, 408–9.

51. The most complete account of the controversy concerning Mackie is *Contendings*. Of particular note, this collection of papers relating to the Mackie affair contains both a prefatory letter from Erskine and a copy of the letter that Erskine had written to the Presbytery of Stirling in January 1735 declining their offer of the Moderator's chair. While the overall account provided by the papers is undeniably partisan, it is still the most thorough treatment of an otherwise overlooked, although vitally important, affair. See *Contendings*, 3–4.

52. John Currie, *AN ESSAY ON SEPARATION*. Hereafter, *Separation*.

53. See Currie, *Separation*, 1; MacEwen, *Erskines*, 104.

54. See *COPY OF A LIBEL AGAINST Messrs. Ebenezer Erskine and Others, Ministers, who have seceded from the Church of Scotland*. There were many within the Assembly who objected to libeling the Brethren, even at this late stage. See *FIT*, 91; Mitchell, 176–77; Morren, *ANNALS OF THE GENERAL ASSEMBLY OF THE CHURCH OF SCOTLAND*, 1–4. The original four Seceders had been joined by Ralph Erskine of Dunfermline and Thomas Mair of Orwell in February 1737, Thomas Nairn of Abbotshall in September 1737, and James Thomson of Burntisland in June 1738. See M'Kerrow, *History of the Secession Church*, 1:174.

Declinature, in which they declined the authority of the church judicatories over themselves and their congregations.[55] After giving the Seceders one more year to relent, the Assembly 1740 voted to depose the Seceded Brethren from "the office of the holy ministry," completely removing them from the communion of the Established Church.[56]

On Sunday, 18 May 1740, when Erskine and his parishioners arrived at the West Kirk for worship, they found the doors locked; Erskine had been removed from the West Kirk.[57] While the Stirling congregation held their worship in the fields that day, they quickly began efforts to construct a building for public worship.[58] John Gibb, a prominent citizen of Stirling, donated a large tract of land just down the castle hill from the West Kirk and, by 1742, volunteer laborers from Stirling and the surrounding areas had completed the new house of worship.[59] With Gibb's further provision of a "manse" for Erskine and the appointment of Trustees to provide legal security to a body outwith the Established Church, the Secession congregation of Stirling thus progressed from a dispossessed congregation in 1740 to a stabilized and prominent institution in the burgh, in addition to being the largest congregation within a growing Secession Church.[60]

Throughout Scotland, the Secession Church represented a sizeable contingent of presbyterians. As early as the summer of 1736, two Secession ministers had gone on a preaching tour of western Scotland and, by 1740, the original four Secession congregations had grown to thirty-six such congregations, supplied by the Secession's eight ministers.[61] While the exact membership totals of these congregations, either individually or corporately, is methodologically difficult to ascertain, Erskine's congregation in

---

55. See *Declinature*.

56. *AGA*, 655. See *AGA*, 653–55; *FIT*, 91–93. The vote was 140 in favor of deposition, 30 opposed. See Morren, *Annals*, 16–17.

57. Small, *History of the Congregations*, 2:663; Scott, *Ebenezer Erskine, The Secession of 1733, and the Churches of Stirling*, 9. Hereafter, *Erskine*. The third charge in Stirling would remain vacant until 1817 and the West Kirk was employed for secular uses. See Simpson, *Church of the Holy Rude*, 24.

58. Foreseeing the possibility of such a situation, some preparations had begun in 1739. See Scott, *Erskine*, 9.

59. Muirhead, "Religion," 77; Scott, *Erskine*, 10; Small, *History of the Congregations*, 2:664.

60. By the beginning of 1741, Thomas Turner, formerly of Tulliallan, and Daniel McQueen, formerly of Dalziell, were serving the two charges vacated by Hamilton and Moore, who had died in 1738 and 1736, respectively. See *Fasti*, 4:321, 325; Muirhead, "Religion," 67, 70–71. See also Scott, *Erskine*, 10; Small, *History of the Congregations*, 2:664.

61. Drummond and Bulloch, *Scottish Church*, 50–51.

Stirling provides a paradigmatic image of a popular and expanding Church body.[62] In 1737, when the Stirling Kirk Session had been preparing for their contentious communion season, they had ordered 3,000 communion tokens to be made for the event; when the new Secession church building was completed in 1742, it was capable of holding 3,000 people and included a preaching green behind the building to facilitate even larger crowds on special occasions.[63] Erskine's Secession congregation, then, was a large congregation that had experienced no attrition through either the vicissitudes of Erskine's deposition or the hardships of constructing a new building and providing for its minister.[64] While such figures cannot establish the size of the Secession Church conclusively, they do illustrate that by the early 1740s, the number of Scottish Presbyterians who adhered to the cause of the original Seceded Brethren had grown to a considerable minority within the nation; the Secession that had emerged from years of judicial contention was no marginalized affair.[65]

INTERPRETING THE SECESSION

The importance of the Secession for the history and theology of the Kirk has engendered many explanations for its origins.[66] While most such explanations have focused upon the role of Erskine's opposition to patronage in severing him from the Established Church, an important new analysis has been popularized by Callum Brown. In this interpretation, the Secession is held to have been an appeal to the lower orders of Scottish society, har-

---

62. Callum Brown highlights the limited usefulness of church attendance records for any attempt to establish the size of dissenting congregations in early to mid eighteenth-century Scotland. See Brown, *Religion*, 42–45. These difficulties are epitomized in Erskine's own congregation. Although his parishioners supported him resolutely and maintained their submission to him throughout the Secession Crisis, no group actually adhered formally to the Secession until 1738. For five years, then, Stirling had been without a statistically verifiable Secession congregation. That such irregular practices continued after 1740 seems certain. See Muirhead, "Religion," 62–63. The combined effect of all these complicating factors is to make any straightforward statement of the membership of the Secession Church tenuous at best and almost unavoidably misleading. Far more helpful is a simple statement of the number of Secession congregations.

63. *Records of the Holy Rude Kirk Session Stirling*, CH2/1026/6, 194. Hereafter, *Holy Rude Kirk Session* CH2/1026/6. See also Muirhead, "Religion," 77.

64. Muirhead, "Religion," 96.

65. The widespread popularity of the Secession Church was one of the reasons urged against libeling the Seceders in 1739. See Morren, *Annals*, 6.

66. See McIntosh, *Theology*, 93; McIntosh, "Lessons," 6, for indications of this significance.

nessing their discontent with increasing economic change, unsettlement, and inequality. Since the Established Church both catered to and furthered class hierarchy and the interests of its governing aristocracy, such socio-economic unrest easily translated into an ecclesiastical Secession.[67] In this interpretation, the Secession is seen as an essentially socio-economic movement employing the language and aspirations of religion as its vocabulary and as its catalyst.[68] That the resulting Secession Church was comprised of the less privileged ranks of Scottish society is seen as proof of this economic impetus for the Secession.

While the socio-economic interpretation of the Secession contains valuable insights into the phenomenology of the Secession Crisis and the later Secession Church, it is an incomplete explanation of the Secession's origins.[69] By reducing the Secession to economic concerns, Brown's analysis fails to account for the pre-occupation with ecclesiastical and doctrinal issues—among both ministers and parishioners—in what was a self-consciously ecclesial Secession.[70] Among the laity—living on the margins of an early 1730s Scotland still recovering from the famines and near economic collapse of the 1690s—there is much evidence that it was a distaste for newer, moderating tendencies in doctrine and an affinity for an experientially-preached gospel that compelled them to make the economically-unwise decision to move from the Established Church, wherein their religious life was financially subsidized by landowners, to the self-supporting Secession Church, wherein ministers' stipends, building construction and maintenance, and all other fiscal concerns would devolve upon the Seceders themselves.[71] While the socio-economic interpretation has much to offer Erskine

67. See also Drummond and Bulloch, *Scottish Church*, 43; Smout, *A History of the Scottish People: 1560–1830*, 218. An interesting permutation of this interpretation sees the Act 1732 as a rebellion by the general landed class against the smaller and wealthier class of patrons. See Sher and Murdoch, "Patronage and Party in the Church of Scotland, 1750–1800," 207–8.

68. See, for example, Brown, *Religion*, 77–80. Brown also detects this trend elsewhere. See ibid., 15–16.

69. For cautions about its phenomenological value, see Muirhead, "Religion," 7–8, 78–79, 96; Scott, *Erskine*, 10; Allan, *Scotland in the Eighteenth Century*, 74–75.

70. Erskine and his brethren often explicitly rejected the applicability of temporal considerations. See Erskine's speech to the Assembly 1732 in *Life*, 358–60. See also *Works*, 2:160, 165, 167, 169; *Reasons*, 42; *ADT*, 100. In this, Brown's interpretation succumbs to the trend detected in McIntosh, *Theology*, 30.

71. For an example of the prevalence of theological concerns for laymen, see *A LETTER TO THE Reverend Mr. MICHAEL POTTER Minister of the Gospel at* Kippen. Hereafter, *Letter to Potter*. See also *Public Testimony*; Menzies Fergusson, *Logie: A Parish History*, 1:164–68. Hereafter, *Logie*. See also Muirhead, "A Secession Congregation in its Community: The Stirling Congregation of the Rev. Ebenezer Erskine, 1731–1754,"

scholarship, a complete understanding of the Secession Crisis requires attention to the ecclesiastical and doctrinal issues that, by their own accounting, drove both Erskine and others into the Secession Church.

The pertinent, and crucial, ecclesiastical and doctrinal issues are brought into the clearest relief by a consideration of John Willison's critique of Erskine and the Secession that he led; a critique articulated most clearly in two works by the Dundee minister. First, one must consider *The Church's Danger and Ministers' Duty*, the sermon that Willison preached as the retiring Moderator of the Synod of Angus and Mearns when that Synod met on 16 October 1733. In that sermon, Willison considers the general problem of patronage, the specific matter of the Act 1732, and the looming issue of Erskine and his brethren. Even more importantly, one must examine Willison's monumental *A Fair and Impartial Testimony*, his 1744 work in which he mounted a robust, Covenantal critique of the state of Scottish Christianity in his day, including a wide-ranging rejection of the Secession.[72] In Willison's critique, one receives the clearest light that can be cast upon Erskine's Secession—the distillation of evangelical, anti-patronage, anti-Secession Covenantal thought.[73] What forced Erskine into secession, yet left Willison in the Established Church?

To arrive at the answer to this question, one must divide the Secession Crisis into three distinct phases, comparing the relevant portions of Willison's critique with Erskine's thought and actions in each successive phase. First, one must consider the period of Erskine's dissent, which chiefly comprises his opposition to patronage and his synod sermon. Secondly, one must examine the period of Erskine's protest, which begins with the Synod of Perth and Stirling's censure of Erskine and concludes with the Commission's vote to loose the Brethren from their charges in November 1733. Thirdly, one must evaluate the period of Erskine's Secession, which commences with the meeting at Gairney Bridge in December 1733 and concludes with the Associate Presbytery's adoption of the *Declinature* in 1739. In each of these

---

224, hereafter, "Congregation"; Muirhead, "Religion," 80–81; Devine, *Scottish Nation*, 88–90; McIntosh, *Theology*, 30; Robert Rainy, THREE LECTURES ON THE CHURCH OF SCOTLAND, 141; Woodside, *The Soul of a Scottish Church*, 31–34. On the economic hardships of the 1690s, see Whatley, *Scots and the Union*, 139–75; Cullen, Whatley, and Young, "King William's Ill Years," 250–76.

72. On the importance of *FIT*, see McIntosh, *Theology*, 32–33.

73. In subsequent years, the general esteem afforded Willison caused his view of Erskine and his brethren to become the standard interpretation of the Secession. At times, indebtedness to Willison is explicit; at other times, much more implicit. For an example of the former, see Morren, *Annals*, iv–v, 7; for an example of the latter, see Hetherington, *History of the Church of Scotland*, 639–49. The most recent treatment of the Secession explicitly adopts Willison's critique thereof. See McIntosh, "Lessons," 6–9.

phases, the focus of Erskine's thought and action was different and only when this progression is appreciated and compared with Willison's writings is one able to understand the true origins and implications of the Secession.

ANALYSIS OF THE SECESSION CRISIS

Erskine in Dissent: Until his Synod Sermon

Erskine's Position

When Erskine assumed the pulpit at St John's Kirk in Perth on 10 October 1732 to preach his outgoing sermon as moderator of the Synod of Perth and Stirling, he felt himself under a double obligation. In the first instance, as the messenger of God's Word to the synod, he was obliged to speak faithfully and without compromise to the assembled presbyters as Christ would speak to them if he were physically present.[74] In the second instance, Erskine felt constrained by recent actions of the General Assembly to exonerate his own conscience. As the Assembly had closed all judicial avenues for expressing dissent from perceived defections within the Church, Erskine judged that he could indemnify himself from complicity in those errors only in the press or from the pulpit.[75] With this double demand for fidelity and exoneration, Erskine sought, through his sermon, "to cast in the small mite of his testimony against what, to him, appears an injury done, either to Christ personal or mystical."[76]

The sermon that resulted from Erskine's efforts was a comprehensive, Covenantal critique of the state of the Kirk, including a thorough denunciation of patronage from within a traditional Covenantal paradigm. Looking back to the Patronage Act of 1712, Erskine lamented patronage as an affront to Christ's authority within the Church, for by that practice

> power is given to a malignant lord or laird, to present a man to take the charge of precious souls, who has perhaps no more concern about their salvation than the Great Turk.[77]

---

74. See *Works*, 1:504.

75. See *Works*, 1:483–84, 503. Critics have disagreed, arguing that Erskine had other, more proper, avenues of dissent open to him. See *N&S*, 7–8, 49–50; Mitchell, "Ebenezer Erskine," 164–65. However, an avenue of dissent that Erskine had not tried prior to his synod sermon is never cited.

76. *Works*, 1:484.

77. *Works*, 1:503.

Thus construed, patronage is seen as an irreparable institution both in its embrace of "malignants"—which, in the Covenanting idiom, spoke of those who were enemies to Scotland's Covenant engagements—and its diminution of the salvific, spiritual concerns of the ministry; concerns that were addressed by honoring the external call of the Christian people.[78] For Erskine, the institution of patronage was unacceptable most fundamentally because it allocated a role in the calling of pastors to men whose rejection of Scotland's Covenants manifested their opposition to the biblical commitments enshrined therein, thus taking initiative away from the Christians who comprised individual congregations.[79]

Given this principled opposition to patronage, there is little surprise that Erskine's sermon also denounced the newly-passed Act 1732. As Scripture nowhere provided for ministers to be called by the world's powerful men rather than by Church members, the Act 1732 was patently opposite to the Scriptures and thereby devoid of legitimate Christian authority.[80] Sadly, Erskine judged that this impotent Act was not an anomaly in the Kirk. Rather, the Act 1732 was symptomatic of an endemic confusion within the church judicatories that saw the Church as an earthly kingdom whose prosperity was to be pursued by collusion with powerful men, rather than seeing the Church rightly as a spiritual kingdom whose benefit was to be sought by faithfulness to the Covenantal and biblical obligations that rested upon her.[81] In renouncing the Covenantal embodiment of her biblical obligations at the Revolution, the Kirk had begun a descent into infidelity that had to be stopped by faithful ministers.[82]

In its entirety, Erskine's synod sermon fit within the general tenor of his doctrine and preaching for decades prior to its delivery. Upon its passage in 1712, Erskine had viewed the Patronage Act as an attack upon "the fundamental constitution of the Church of Scotland," and thereafter he maintained a public, Covenantal opposition to the practice.[83] Furthermore,

---

78. See *Works*, 1:488. In the 1730s, many patrons and heritors were still episcopalian, thus making their "malignancy" obvious. See McIntosh, *Theology*, 10. For Erskine on the external call, see *Works*, 1:490–91. See also *Works*, 1:493, 501. For similar concerns among other opponents of patronage, see *Public Testimony*, 10.

79. See Erskine's Assembly speech in *Life*, 359; *Works*, 1:504.

80. See *Works*, 1:504. Such a view of authority within the Church was not novel. See, for example, Guthrie, *PROTESTERS no Subverters*, 95–97, 109–10. Hereafter, *Protesters*.

81. See *Works*, 1:496–97.

82. *Works*, 1:502–4.

83. Letter dated 13 April 1712, printed in *Life*, 164. See *Works*, 1:92; *Life*, 163–64. For an account of Erskine's leading role in opposing an intrusion in the parish of Ballingry in 1717, see Harper, *Memoir*, 37–38. For concerns similar to Erskine's, see *Public Testimony*, 10.

when the Assembly 1732 had passed the Overture 1731, Erskine had delivered a dissenting speech that shared the same emphases, and even much of the same language, as his synod sermon.[84] In his synod sermon, Erskine was not proclaiming anything new, nor did he evidence any affinity for more drastic courses of dissent than he had followed previously.[85] The defections that Erskine decried in his sermon had been present in the Kirk for many years, and Erskine always had been content to dissent and testify against those defections from within the communion of the Kirk. In the case of the Act 1732, Erskine even entertained heightened hopes that his dissent would bear concrete fruit. After giving attention to the errors of that Act, Erskine registered his hope that

> I have good reason to believe, that this act is far from being the mind of the generality of presbyteries through this national church; and therefore would gladly hope a seasonable stand shall yet be made against it in order to prevent its pernicious consequences.[86]

In this expression of hope, one glimpses the true nature of Erskine's synod sermon. In that sermon, Erskine did not expound novel positions in an effort either to reclaim or to denounce benighted brethren in the synod. In his sermon, Erskine proclaimed the same positions that he had preached for years and, in so doing, thought that he was voicing a commonly-held dissent, rooted in Scotland's Covenant engagements, to which the faithful ministers within the synod would rally.[87] Erskine did not conceive that he was preaching against his fellow presbyters as if they were malignants, but that he was preaching on their behalf as the opponents of such malignants.[88]

---

84. For the text of Erskine's speech, see *Life*, 358–60.

85. Erskine even had preached against the Act 1732 prior to 10 October, indicating his opposition to that Act in a sermon preached on 4 June 1732. The connection between this earlier sermon and Erskine's synod sermon was so close that later in 1732, Erskine had them both printed and bound together to explicate his position in the gathering controversy. See Erskine, The STONE rejected by the Builders, exalted as the Head-Stone of the Corner. *A SERMON PREACH'D At the Opening of the Synod of* Perth *and* Stirling, *At* Perth, *October 10. 1732. To which is subjoin'd A SERMON preach'd* June 4th 1732, *on the Sabbath Evening after the Sacrament, from* Isa. ix. 6. — The Government shall be upon his Shoulder. Hereafter, *Stone Rejected* and *Government*, respectively (pagination is separate for the two sermons). For the text of this sermon in Erskine's collected works, see *Works*, 2:1–17.

86. *Works*, 1:504–5.

87. For the potential reprisals that Erskine did envision resulting from his sermon, see *Works*, 1:498, 503–4.

88. A similar theme can be detected in Erskine's June sermon.

Willison's Corroboration

When one considers the published version of Willison's sermon before the Synod of Angus and Mearns in Montrose in 1733, it becomes evident that not only was Erskine's synod sermon consonant with his previous stances, but it also was consistent with the preaching and writing of other ministers who viewed, and rejected, patronage from a Covenantal perspective. Just as did Erskine, Willison felt the dual weight of ministerial obligation and personal conscience when he stood from the moderator's chair to preach his retiring sermon in 1733.[89] In the Kirk of the early 1730s, this weight was especially pressing, for the Assembly's recent refusal to heed protestations that were brought before it had left dissenting ministers no other way to bear faithful witness to the truth and exonerate their own consciences.[90] Thus obliged to register his dissent from the Kirk's defections in order to avoid sinful complicity therein, Willison proceeded to offer a thorough critique of patronage, which he perceived to be "the main Spring of all our present Distress."[91] Indeed, Willison judged that patronage, with its denial of individual Christians' "unquestionable Right and privilege to have a *Judgment of Discretion*" in the selection of their pastor, was a certain sign that a church had been given up to reproach.[92] Focusing specifically on the Act 1732, Willison called upon the synod to address the ensuing General Assembly in an effort to rectify the errors that had been forwarded.[93]

Given Willison's reputation as an opponent of patronage, it is not surprising that he should thus array himself against the practice and its distillation in the Act 1732. What is perhaps surprising, however, is that in his published sermon, Willison denounced not only patronage and the Act 1732, but also the supporters of patronage, in notably "harsh" terms. As patronage brought such havoc upon the Church, those ministers who supported it did so out of "selfish Principles"; they were to blame for the present miseries of the Kirk; and they had proven to be the Church's "*Oppressors*."[94] Indeed, even for a minister to remain silent in the face of such wicked courses was for him to be numbered among the "*dumb Dogs*" whom Isaiah condemned.[95] In terms neither less certain nor more pacific

89. *CDMD*, iii–iv.
90. *CDMD*, x.
91. *CDMD*, vi.
92. *CDMD*, 60. See also *CDMD*, 24–29.
93. *CDMD*, 60–62. Willison enumerated these errors in *CDMD*, xi–xv.
94. *CDMD*, vi, viii, 56, respectively. See also *CDMD*, v–vi.
95. *CDMD*, iv–v. Erskine had used the same language in his synod sermon. See *Works*, 1:495, 507.

than those employed by Erskine, Willison thus exonerated his conscience before the Synod of Angus and Mearns in the hope that the lifting up of such a testimony would be used to work reformation in the Kirk.[96]

Observations

Upon an examination of Erskine's synod sermon and a comparison thereof with Willison's synod sermon of 1733, several salient points emerge. First, in his critique of patronage, Erskine forwarded nothing that was dissimilar from the criticisms advanced by Willison. While the two men obviously did not deliver identical sermons, each denounced both the institution of patronage and the Act 1732 based upon the same Covenantal considerations and in terms similarly severe. In the sermon that elicited his censure, Erskine showed no appreciable difference from Willison's example of contemporary Covenantal dissent. Second, in this attack upon patronage, Erskine did not evidence any grievances or objections that he had not consistently expressed from within the communion of the Established Church for twenty years. Third, both Erskine and Willison, in their respective sermons, sought to consolidate proponents of reformation. Each man conceived of himself as speaking both within, and to, a larger community of Covenantal dissidents. Fourth, if Erskine's sermon was to evoke censure and Willison's was to avoid the same fate, that variation must be attributable to factors external to each man's critique of patronage and the Act 1732, for in regard to those critiques, Erskine and Willison are virtually indistinguishable. If the Presbytery of Stirling was at all representative of the larger Synod of Perth and Stirling, one legitimately can surmise that Erskine was still viewed with suspicion concerning his *Marrow* advocacy, that his recent translation was accepted only begrudgingly, and that his censure represented an attempt to discourage radicalism and antagonism in his new synod home.[97] It was that factor alone—his new home in the Synod of Perth and Stirling—that

---

96. The severity of speech evidenced by both Erskine and Willison was not uncommon among opponents of patronage. See, for example, *Public Testimony*, 10–11.

97. The drive to censure Erskine was led by James Mercer of Clevage, minister of Aberdalgie in the Presbytery of Perth, of whom not much is known, and James Mackie, minister at Forteviot in the Presbytery of Perth, whose proto-moderate sensibilities would have found both the doctrine and the manner of Erskine's sermon distasteful. When Erskine said in Perth what Willison said in Montrose, it fell on the ears of these men, who were then able to conjure enough support to censure Erskine by a narrow majority in order to tame a known firebrand in his new synod home. See *Fasti*, 4:194 for Mercer; 1:102, 4:212, 314, for Mackie, the same minister who later would cause the controversy at St Ninians. See also *TSP*, 70–80. For indications of suspicion of Erskine within the Presbytery of Stirling, see Wodrow, *Analecta*, 4:226.

distinguished Erskine's Covenantally critical sermon both from his previous doctrine and preaching and from the preaching of Willison.

Erskine in Protest: Synod Censure to Commission Vote

A Critical Shift: Freedom to Dissent

After Erskine delivered his synod sermon, the Secession Crisis entered a second distinct phase; a phase in which Erskine's attention and concern shifted from the issues of patronage and Covenantal defection to the central issue of the freedom of ministerial dissent. Beginning almost immediately following his sermon, it became clear that in order to avoid censure, Erskine would have to retract his sermon and agree to forego like dissent in the future.[98] This demand for silence which formed the foundation for the synod's initial action against Erskine continued throughout the whole of this second phase of the Secession Crisis, culminating in the Act and Sentence 1733 that, in Erskine's judgment, made ministerial silence regarding the decisions of church judicatories a term of communion, even if those decisions were judged to be wrong. While some within the Assembly, as well as many subsequent commentators, urged that the synod sentence upheld by the Assembly censured only the harsh expressions that Erskine had used and not the substance of his dissent, the Brethren argued pointedly in their *Representations* that

> it is not simply the *Manner of Expression*, but *Some Truths of God seasonably delivered*, that we judge to be condemned, first by the Synod, and then by the General Assembly.[99]

By censuring Erskine, the church judicatories were not reprimanding ungracious expressions; they were limiting the freedom of ministers to preach seasonably against the sins of the day.[100] From Erskine's perspective, ministers' consciences were being bound not by the Word of God, but by the decisions of men.[101]

---

98. See *Synod of Perth and Stirling*, 127.

99. *RTC*, 42. This quotation is from Wilson and Moncrieff's Representation, to which Erskine and Fisher adhered. Erskine long had judged that those who objected to "offensive speech" most often were actually driven by doctrinal opposition. See Erskine's letter to John Currie in Currie, *PHARISAICAL Righteousness insufficient*, iii–v.

100. See *TD*, 59.

101. *Reasons*, 20–21; *TD*, 81–84. See also *N&S*, 3–4; *RN&S*, 58–59; *RTC*, 8. For similar concerns among the laity, see *Public Testimony*, 10–11.

From the first to the last, then, this second phase of the Secession Crisis is crucially different from the first phase thereof. While Erskine's synod sermon had comprised a Covenantal critique of the state of the Kirk, from the moment that the Synod of Perth and Stirling censured Erskine, the central issue of the Secession Crisis became the ministerial freedom to dissent from the decisions and actions of church judicatories.[102] It is that issue that alone bears the weight of the protest that Erskine tendered to the Assembly 1733 after its decision to uphold the synod's censure, and it is that concern that is chiefly addressed in the Brethren's *Representations*.[103] Insofar as patronage, doctrinal purity, or any other of the components of Erskine's initial sermon featured in the Secession Crisis in this second phase, they did so only as a function of the larger concern over ministerial freedom.[104] Demanding the freedom to denounce defection in the Kirk, the Brethren would continue to denounce the sins of patronage and doctrinal error, yet "*Restraint of Ministerial Freedom* is the first and more immediate Point upon which our Secession turned."[105] In Erskine's estimation, dissenting from and protesting against wrong actions of church judicatories was not only a right, but a positive duty.[106] By dissenting, a minister was able to exonerate his own conscience from complicity in prevailing sin, to prick the consciences of any who might have gone astray, and to emit a witness to truth to subsequent generations.[107] Once the censure of the Synod of Perth and Stirling was fixed upon Erskine, however, this freedom of dissent was denied to him. At each subsequent point of the Secession Crisis, regardless of concessions that might have been made, the underlying sentence of the Synod of Perth and Stirling was upheld, and thus each proffered judicial remedy required that Erskine renounce the positions taken in his sermon. Because of his inability to honor the underlying synod censure's demand that he retract his sermonic dissent, Erskine consistently asserted that his continued defiance of the church courts was dictated not by his opposition to patronage or to the Act 1732, but by his insistence that he be allowed to testify against

---

102. See *TD*, 85–87.

103. For a transcript of Erskine's Protest, see *RTC*, 8. In the entire Protest, there is not a single reference to patronage. The Protestation tendered by the Brethren to the Commission in November 1733 is also notably devoid of explicit references to either patronage or the Act 1732. See *TD*, 27–28. See also the Brethren's description of their Secession, *TD*, 45–46.

104. See *RTC*, 15–19; *TD*, 27–28.

105. *Reasons*, 19. See also *TD*, 46–47; *Contendings*, 70–71.

106. See *Works*, 2:161–63.

107. See *RTC*, 15; *Life*, 359–60.

the errors of those practices and of all like defections.[108] For Erskine, in the second phase of the Secession Crisis, the reasons why he had been censured had become extraneous; what mattered was the fact of that censure.

History of Freedom to Dissent

In this insistence upon the importance of the freedom to dissent, Erskine was firmly within the stream of Scottish presbyterian divines. While the freedom to dissent had been prominent throughout the Kirk's history, it had assumed heightened importance in the years following the Revolution Settlement.[109] Over the twenty-eight years of intense persecution that presbyterians had suffered under the Second Episcopate, various ministers had followed differing courses in response to episcopal uniformity and proffered royal Indulgences. Often, those who rejected such overtures from the civil magistrate judged that the acceptance of them by other ministers was sinful and had tainted those ministers with a guilt that remained even when presbytery was on the cusp of re-establishment. The problem posed by this situation was felt most acutely by Alexander Shields, Thomas Linning, and William Boyd, the three remaining Cameronian ministers who acceded to the Revolution Church in 1689. How could a minister enter into Church communion with others whom he judged to be unrepentant for past sins? As some of the Cameronian laity judged that such communion inevitably would taint faithful ministers with the guilt of sinful ministers, Alexander Shields sought to assure them that such communion could be had in purity if done properly. As Shields clarified,

> The Question is not, whether we shall join in Communion with Ministers. . .upon Terms obliging us to Justifie these Defections and Complyances, or to Condemn our Testimonies against them, or to surcease from, or leave off testifying against them: That is not imposed or required; And if it were, I should be yet as much for Separation as ever. But the Question is, Whether we shall join in Union and Communion with these Ministers, that albeit they will not confess them to be Defections or sinful Complyances, yet do allow us to keep our Opinion, and to Protest against them?[110]

---

108. E.g., *Reasons*, 9, 18–19; *TD*, 23–24, 102, 107–8.

109. See Donaldson, "The Emergence of Schism in Seventeenth-Century Scotland," 279. Hereafter, "Schism."

110. Shields, *Church-Communion ENQUIRED INTO*, 28.

From the very foundation of the Revolution Church, the right to testify against sin, even within the Church, had been the crucial consideration that allowed ministers of varying opinions to remain within one Church communion. As Shields urged his followers, membership in the Established Church did not require the surrender of past stances for truth or remove one's right to witness against the errors of the Established Church; if it did, the Revolution Church would have been drastically different, with a remnant of Covenanting ministers unable to acquiesce to its terms.[111] In the freedom to dissent, the Revolution Church found the adhesive that alone could hold disparate contingents together, and for the decades that separated the Revolution from the Secession Crisis, it was that same freedom that had continued to allow ministers with Covenantal commitments to abide within the Established Church.[112]

Summary of Erskine's Position

When the Synod of Perth and Stirling first censured Erskine, the course of the entirety of Erskine's protest was set. In bowing to that censure, Erskine would have been complicit in the denial of his freedom to dissent, and in each subsequent stage of the escalating Crisis, this fundamental barricade to Erskine's acquiescence remained. At each subsequent point, the central issue was the same for Erskine; either he lay down his testimony without being shown its error, or he resist the sentence of the church judicatories. As the sentences against such resistance became increasingly severe, Erskine's conviction that he had no option but to abide by his dissent remained. As Erskine expressed the ultimate result of this process in a letter in 1734, he and his brethren "were shut out before we made a Secession from the Established Church."[113] Rather than choosing Secession over the issue of patronage, Erskine and his brethren were cast out of the Established Church "for no other Reason, but because they could not find Freedom in their

---

111. See ibid., 39–40. While some of the Cameronian laity remained outwith the Revolution Church, none of their ministers did.

112. See, for example, [Linning and Webster], *A LETTER From a Friend to Mr.* John Mackmillan, 1–2, 17; Boston, *The EVIL and DANGER of SCHISM*, 17–18. Even the Committee of the Commission responsible for authoring *N&S* showed, from its argumentation, that it saw the importance of dissent. See *N&S*, 30–34.

113. Ebenezer Erskine, Stirling, to James Erskine, Lord Grange, 19 February 1734, 3. Hereafter, "Erskine to Grange February 1734." See also *Contendings*, 73; *TD*, 96–97; Guthrie, *A CRY From the Dead*, vi–vii. Hereafter, *Cry*. For this reason, Erskine would often refer to the Seceders as "the ejected brethren." See *Contendings*, 70. This passive element to Erskine's Secession often is missed. See Carson, "The Doctrine of the Church in the Secession," 11, 187.

Conscience to retract the Testimony they had been helped to emit against some prevailing Defections."[114]

Willison's Assessment

While the first phase of the Secession Crisis found marked congruity of sentiment between Erskine and Willison, the second phase of that Crisis evidences an important divergence. Theoretically, Willison had much in common with Erskine's central contention in this second phase of the Secession. Willison was convinced of the Church's obligation to testify against sin and he personally availed himself of a freedom to dissent from Church defections in order to exonerate his own conscience of implicit guilt.[115] Even more to the point, Willison continued to agree with Erskine's doctrinal position, especially as he perceived it to be an assault upon the system of patronage that he loathed.[116] However, upon the counsel of "many of the leading Men in Judicatories," Willison concluded that the harsh manner of Erskine's expression, and not the actual substance of his critique, "was the only Thing they quarrelled in his Sermon."[117] As the foundation of Erskine's censure was thus uncharitable speech and not a restriction of the freedom of ministerial dissent, Willison judged that Erskine ought to have submitted to the discipline of the church judicatories even if they were acting arbitrarily, as Willison conceded that they were.[118] Rather than complying with arbitrary discipline for the sake of peace, however, Erskine and his brethren had acted obstinately, and thus although Willison continued to agree with Erskine's doctrinal position, he condemned his precipitous and prideful defiance.[119]

---

114. *Contendings*, 71. See also *TD*, 27–28; *Reasons*, 9, 18–19. Some commentators have observed that if Erskine had been allowed to exonerate his conscience before the Synod of Perth and Stirling without censure, the differences that existed over patronage would not have been sufficient to cause the Secession. See, for example, Mitchell, "Ebenezer Erskine," 163; Sefton, "Rev. Robert Wallace: An Early Moderate," 3–4. Hereafter, "Wallace."

115. See *CDMD*, iii–iv, ix; *FIT*, xi–xiv, 18, 30–34, 65, 128.

116. *FIT*, 74.

117. *FIT*, 74. See also *CDMD*, xvi. In *FIT*, Willison writes that the reports of "some leading Men" also had induced him to support the Overture 1731 initially. However, upon discovering the particulars of that proposal for himself, Willison became decidedly opposed thereto. While this experience seems to have caused Willison some disillusionment with such "leading Men," he evidently did not apply the learned skepticism to the leading men's description of Erskine's case. See *FIT*, xi–xii.

118. *FIT*, 73–74.

119. *FIT*, 74–76.

In his construction of the Secession Crisis, it is clear that Willison fundamentally misunderstands Erskine's reasons for the course that he pursued in the second phase of that Crisis. When Willison wrote glibly that Erskine was initially censured because of his harsh expressions and that the Act 1732 was "the great Occasion of their protesting and seceding," he evidences a profound ignorance of the Brethren's repeated contentions that Erskine's censure concerned the substance of his sermon and not the simple expression thereof, and that their protest was sparked by the freedom to dissent and not by the Act 1732.[120] Certainly, Willison does not have to agree with Erskine on these contentious positions; yet in his writings on the Secession, Willison does not even allude to the Brethren's positions or to the arguments with which they defended those positions. Simply stated, Willison seems almost wholly unacquainted with the writing and the argumentation of the Brethren.[121] While it does appear that Willison has some familiarity with the *Act, Declaration, and Testimony* and the *Testimony to the Doctrine*, he does not seem to have any awareness of the remainder of the Brethren's writings; a situation that is particularly problematic since it is in their *Representations* and their *Reasons* that the Brethren give the most detailed attention to their own situation, while their *Act, Declaration, and Testimony* and their *Testimony to the Doctrine* are more concerned with the general state of the Church of Scotland.[122] Being unfamiliar with their arguments, Willison is unable to interact with those arguments on any convincing level and the superficial characterization that he gives of the Seceders, although it has enjoyed vast influence, is regrettably simplistic.[123] Writing his *Testimony* in 1744, Willison had the opportunity therein to offer a thoroughly-considered evaluation of the Secession and the reasons offered for it; that he offered the caricature that he did indicates that even at the height of the Secession Crisis, Willison was unfamiliar with the case that Erskine made for the course that he was pursuing.

---

120. *FIT*, 94. See, for example, *RN&S*, 6–9.

121. Lachman incorrectly accuses Willison of a similar, and culpable, unfamiliarity with the literature to emerge from the *Marrow* controversy. See Lachman, *Marrow*, 193–98; *FIT*, 127.

122. See *FIT*, 91, 96–97.

123. For other examples of Willison's misunderstanding of Erskine's position, see *FIT*, 74–75, 93.

Summary

This second phase of the Secession is the crucial phase for understanding the limitation of that Secession. In the first instance, the second phase of the Secession set the foundation for all demands that would be placed upon the Brethren in subsequent years: in order to end the judicial process against them, Erskine would have to renounce his synod sermon, and all four of the Brethren would have to renounce their Protest before the Assembly 1733. In this, submission to the judicatories required that Erskine emit a judicial testimony that what he preached in his synod sermon had been unlawful and that his protest before the Assembly 1733 had been insubstantial; his critique of the Church and his testimony against arbitrary Church power would have to be surrendered. As each following year of the Crisis showed, this was a surrender that Erskine's sensibilities would not allow him to make. Conversely, the considerable number of ministers who supported the Brethren were able, at every turn, to register their dissent from the arbitrary course followed by church judicatories.[124] Willison himself is exemplary of this ability. Willison was able to preach against the defections of the Church before the Synod of Angus and Mearns in 1733, he was able to enter a dissent against sisting the Brethren with a libel in 1739, and he was able to criticize the church judicatories in his *Testimony* in 1744.[125] In each instance, Willison and others were able to register their dissent from the judicatories and they never were required to surrender past dissents. For Erskine and the other Brethren, the case was different. The arbitrary censure imposed by the Synod of Perth and Stirling abided and thus it remained the barricade to the conclusion of the process against Erskine. The limitation of the Secession by this synod action has led some commentators to suppose that the Secession initially was a localized reaction to patronage; in actuality, the Secession was geographically localized in its earliest stages because the one restriction on the ministerial freedom to dissent that had been imposed, and that was never removed, had been imposed on the synod level.[126] While the four Brethren thus were bound over into Secession, ministers from every other synod were given no reason to enter Secession; while the Brethren had to separate from the church judicatories in order to exonerate their conscience in relation to the defections of the Church, men from every other synod

---

124. See, for example, *TD*, 26–27.

125. Morren, *Annals*, 7.

126. For an example of a critique of the Secession as a localized phenomenon, see McIntosh, "Lessons," 7. While Fisher, Wilson, and Moncrieff had not been censured by the Synod of Perth and Stirling, they joined with Erskine, and thus came under the Assembly's censure, because of their synodical association with his earlier sentence.

were allowed to exonerate their consciences from within the communion of the Church.

On the surface, the situation that resulted seems mildly incredible. How could the balance of ministers in the Kirk miss the fact that Erskine and his brethren were being disciplined for exercising a freedom that they themselves cherished?[127] In John Willison, one receives an answer. Although a prominent man in the larger Church, Willison does not appear to have read the Brethren's earlier writings, and thus he is unaware of their arguments and reasons for their actions. In some respects, this ignorance is understandable. By the time the Brethren's earlier writings were printed and circulated, most ministers already would have heard of the decision of the Commission in November and likely would have formed unfavorable opinions of Erskine's course, particularly in light of his past difficulties with church judicatories. Furthermore, John McIntosh notes that

> the eighteenth-century Church was much more locally orientated than historians have consistently assumed, and that what happened at the Assembly was much less important than has been supposed to have been the case.[128]

Simply stated, many ministers likely were similar to Willison, taking their impression of church judicatories' proceedings from anecdotal reports and without either immediate access to the more detailed arguments of the Brethren or primary concern with such "distant" events. As a result, Willison and others sympathetic to the Brethren exerted every effort to voice their dissent from the judicatories' arbitrary treatment of the Brethren without realizing that the root of the Brethren's plight was the judicatories' suppression of their right to that same freedom of dissent. In this, the critical rupture within the evangelical wing of the Church was introduced into the Secession Crisis; the Brethren, bound by the censures that rested upon them, were unable to submit to the judicatories, and Willison and their other ostensible allies, free to dissent at every turn and unacquainted with the Brethren's chief concerns, were unable to understand why the Brethren were behaving so incorrigibly.

---

127. Some, of course, realized the root of the Brethren's discipline, yet were unsympathetic to their cause for other reasons. See Sefton, "Moderatism," 82–85.

128. McIntosh, *Theology*, 26.

Erskine in Secession: Gairney Bridge to the Declinature

In the third and final phase of the Secession Crisis, the focus of Erskine's attention shifted once more. In the years following their formal Secession from the church judicatories, Erskine and his brethren became consumed not with issues of dissent, but with one central question—was the Church of Scotland still a true, reforming Church of Christ?[129] In answering this question, the events of 1734–1739 would be decisive.

General Assembly 1734

Five months after Erskine and his brethren formed the Associate Presbytery at Gairney Bridge, the General Assembly of the Church of Scotland convened in Edinburgh for a meeting that would be vital in the unfolding of this third phase of the Secession Crisis. As Erskine conceded, the Assembly 1734 had been populated by "the Flower and Strength of the sound Part of the Ministers of the Established Church" and had made remarkable steps toward reformation, most particularly in relation to patronage and the Act 1732.[130] However, the Brethren remained concerned that while the Assembly 1734 had removed several obnoxious effects of the judicatories' defection, they had not touched the underlying causes of it.[131] Although the Acts 1730 and 1732 had been repealed, that repeal had been based upon the trouble they had caused rather than upon their unlawfulness, and thus the abuses enshrined in them were still left available to judicatories, making "*the Repeal rather a mocking of the Church of Christ than a relieving her.*"[132] Furthermore, the Act and Sentence 1733—that Act 'upon which our *Secession* was principally laid'—still stood unrepealed.[133] While the actions of the Assembly undid the effects of that Act, the failure to repeal it formally meant that if Erskine re-entered the judicatories in such a situation, he would be admitting to the justice of that sentence and would stand under constant danger of its limitations upon ministerial freedom being re-imposed in the future.[134] Additionally, the corrupt party that ostensibly had been overcome

---

129. See, for example, *Works*, 2:160–61.
130. *Contendings*, 75. See *Reasons*, 8–9.
131. *Contendings*, 3, 77.
132. Ibid., 4. See also ibid., 75–76.
133. *Reasons*, 5.
134. See *Contendings*, 76–77; *Reasons*, 21, 23–26. The Brethren detected the same abiding danger of future abuse in other areas. See, for example, *Reasons*, 31–34. See also Guthrie, *Protesters*, 76–77, 81–82, 92.

at the Assembly 1734 had shown no repentance, had not been censured, and remained as powerful and as prominent in the church judicatories as they always had been.[135] In Erskine's estimation, the Assembly 1734 had made many positive advances, yet the grounds for the Brethren's Secession had not been fully removed, and thus they were left with no option but to remain in Secession, awaiting "other Steps taken toward Reformation" within the judicatories.[136] Erskine entertained hopes that progress begun by the Assembly 1734 would continue in the future through the labors of the faithful ministers who remained in the Assembly, yet he insisted that professions of reformation at the Assembly 1734 must be coupled with tangible proof of that reform before he could accede to the judicatories with confidence.[137] In Erskine's estimation,

> there is a great Difference betwixt a positive Reformation, and a Stop or Sist given to Deformation. I am far from derogating from the Stand made by the worthy Members at the last Assembly against the Career of the corrupt Party. But allow me to say, that, to me, any Thing done appears rather a Check or Restraint upon these Men for a Time, than any real cleanly Reformation.[138]

In Willison's estimation, the Assembly 1734 had gone much further on the road to reformation. Speaking of that Assembly as God's providential gathering of his pious remnant from around the Kirk, Willison judged that the ongoing work of its members had gotten "the Door opened, Stumblingblocks removed, and the Way paved for the Return of their four Brethren to Communion with them as before."[139] This optimism of Willison's centered upon the Assembly 1734's repeal of the Act 1732; judging that it was the aggravating cause of the Secession, Willison felt that its removal cleared all

---

135. *Contendings*, 74–75.

136. Ibid., 70. See also *Reasons*, 5. The Brethren enumerated six reforms that were needed before they could accede. See *Reasons*, 41–43. Woodside classes these six reforms as the blueprint for a proto-Disruption. Woodside, *Soul of a Scottish Church*, 11–14.

137. For instances of Erskine's hopefulness, see *Contendings*, 3, 74; *Reasons*, 18, 20; *ADT*, vii; *TD*, 45–46. Erskine's hopes were dimmed by the Assemblies 1735 and 1736. See *ADT*, vii.

138. *Contendings*, 74. See also ibid., 75.

139. *FIT*, 75–78, 94. Willison recognized that there were still extant grounds for the Brethren's Secession, yet he judged that the chief grounds had been removed and that what remained was surpassingly minor. See, for example, *FIT*, 92–93. See also *Reasons*, 27–28.

obstacles that would prevent the Brethren's return.[140] When the Assembly's actions failed to entice the Brethren back, Willison became impatient with the Brethren and what he felt to be their unreasonable demands and their uncharitable judgments of the motivations of their sympathizers within the judicatories. In Willison's judgment, such a course eventually so discouraged many like-minded, godly ministers that they stopped attending General Assemblies and thus, ultimately, Erskine's recalcitrance had "put a Stop to a begun National Reformation."[141]

In their disagreement over the merits of the Assembly 1734, one sees both Erskine and Willison impeding the Brethren's return to the judicatories. In the first instance, Erskine's expectations for the degree and the level of reformation that were to be accomplished by the Assembly 1734 were almost impossibly high. While Erskine's insistence that the Act and Sentence 1733 be repealed is understandable, his expectation that all objectionable Acts would be repealed and condemned was certainly higher than a single General Assembly could attain.[142] In the second instance, Willison manifests an inability even to grasp the expectations and objections that Erskine had. Once more, this ignorance of Erskine's true concerns and grievances seems to stem from Willison's unfamiliarity with the early writings of the Seceders. Although the Brethren had declared explicitly in their *Representations* that the primary cause for their protest was not the Act 1732, but rather the Act 1733, Willison judged that in repealing the Act 1732, the Assembly 1734 had removed the irritating cause of the Secession and he gave no attention to the failure to repeal the Act and Sentence 1733. As with Willison's unfamiliarity with the Brethren's concerns in the second phase of the Secession, the difficulty with Willison's critique of the Secession is not that he disagrees with the Brethren's negative assessment of the Assembly 1734; the difficulty is that he seems wholly unaware of their reasons for it.

In addition to his lack of acquaintance with their writings, Willison's misapprehension of the Brethren's actions in this third phase of the Secession Crisis was exacerbated by two further factors. First, Willison repeatedly makes accusations against Erskine and his brethren that are factually wrong. For example, Willison faults the Seceders for not conferring with

140. See *FIT*, 78, 94.

141. *FIT*, 94. See also *FIT*, 75–76, 78. This weighty charge, that the Secession eviscerated the evangelical wing of the Kirk and thus paved the way for the ascendance of the Moderate Party, resurfaces often in the secondary literature. However, the chief support for such a supposition seems to be Willison's reflections to that effect. See, for example, Morren, iv–v; Smout, 218; Skoczylas, "Regulation," 174, 193–95.

142. This stringent expectation remained in the years following 1734. See, for example, *Cry*, vii.

any non-Seceders before their meeting at Gairney Bridge, even though there were two ministers at the Gairney Bridge meeting itself who did not secede with Erskine and his three brethren[143]; Willison chastises the Seceders for withdrawing from any communion with non-Seceders following the Gairney Bridge meeting, ignoring that Erskine continued to labor admiringly alongside Alexander Hamilton, a non-Seceder, in Stirling until the latter's death in 1738[144]; Willison charges that the Brethren used any possible pretense or occasion to win adherents, yet the Brethren are known to have turned away applicants to their cause who were unable to understand fully the true foundations of that cause[145]; and Willison rebukes Erskine and his brethren for immediately "constituting themselves into a distinct judicatory for licensing Preachers and ordaining Ministers," yet the Brethren explicitly avoided such "Acts of Jurisdiction" until 1737 for the avowed reason that they wanted to avoid precisely the stigma that Willison later attached to them.[146] In these and other instances, one realizes that Willison extrapolated a great deal concerning the motivations and tempers of the Seceders

---

143. See, for example, *FIT*, 93. The other two ministers, Ralph Erskine and Thomas Mair, both seceded later, in 1737. For the documents relating to their accession to the Associate Presbytery, see *ADT*, 103–19. However, their later identity as "Seceders" does not alter the fact that, at Gairney Bridge, they were "non-Seceders," and thus would have offered to Erskine and the other three "Seceders" a perspective that eschewed Secession—precisely the perspective that Willison claims was culpably absent at Gairney Bridge.

144. See, for example, *FIT*, 75–76, 94–95. For corroboration of this critique, as well as a polemical use of it, see, respectively, Grange to Erskine, 3; *A LETTER TO THE Valiant and Undaunted CHAMPION of our BROKEN COVENANTS, The Reverend and Renowned Mr. EBENEZER ERSKINE*. Hereafter, *Valiant Champion*. For Erskine's close relationship with Hamilton, see *Contendings*, 4; *Cry*, iii–v; Ebenezer Erskine to James Erskine, Lord Grange, 10 March 1737, 1. Hereafter, "Erskine to Grange 1737." For other instances of positive interaction between Seceders and non-Seceders in this phase of the Secession Crisis, see Scott, *Erskine*, 8. See also *TD*, 27. Erskine also maintained that there were worthy ministers in the Established Church in the 1730s with whom he had "Communion and Correspondence." *Contendings*, 70. Even toward those from whom he became estranged, such as Currie, Erskine continued to show charity and concern. See *Cry*, viii.

145. See *FIT*, 91, 96; Erskine to Grange February 1734, 1–2.

146. *FIT*, 75. See *FIT*, 93; *ADT*, v–viii. The Brethren maintained that they had had the right to exercise the Keys of Doctrine, Discipline, and Government throughout the Secession Crisis, yet had purposefully refrained from using the latter two. See *TD*, 111–15. See also "VINDICATION OF THE FIRST SECEDERS FOR NOT RETURNING TO THE ESTABLISHED CHURCH IN 1734," 482. Hereafter, "Vindication." For the ordination questions framed by Erskine and his brethren in 1737, see Gib, *THE PRESENT TRUTH: A DISPLAY OF THE SECESSION-TESTIMONY*, 1:ix–xv. Hereafter, *Display*. For an account of the first Secession probationer, see Tait, *Two Centuries of Border Church Life*, 82–101.

from inaccurate reports of their actions; reports that were refuted explicitly in the Seceders' writings to which Willison did not have access. Secondly, as Willison was not exposed to the Brethren's explanations for their cause, he seems simply to have placed his own motivations upon them. Throughout his treatments of the Secession, and particularly in his *Testimony*, Willison clearly is consumed with the issue of patronage, judging that, second only to ingratitude for the gospel, patronage is the fount from which all defection in the Kirk has flowed.[147] As patronage was foremost in Willison's mind and concerns, he seems to have imputed that prominence to the concerns of the Brethren, as well. Supposing that the Brethren were motivated primarily by opposition to patronage, Willison judged that the repeal of the Act 1732 ought to have drawn them back into the judicatories; in speaking of ways in which the faithful ministers who remained in the Assembly had gotten "the Door opened, Stumbling-blocks removed, and the Way paved" for the Brethren's return, the only specific example of such efforts that Willison adduces is the annual sending of ministers to London "to solicit the King and Parliament for Relief from Patronages."[148] Simply stated, whenever Willison spoke of addressing the Brethren's concerns and the causes of the Secession, he spoke of patronage. Imputing his own priorities to the Brethren rather than allowing them to speak for themselves, Willison was both ill-equipped to address the concerns that the Brethren did have and inclined to attribute their actions to petulance and excessive zeal rather than to reasoned concerns and objections.[149] In the stalemate that followed the Assembly 1734, both Erskine and Willison are culpable; Erskine for his failure to entertain realistic expectations of any church judicatory, and Willison for his failure to listen to the expectations that Erskine did have rather than ascribing to him his own.

---

147. See, for example, *FIT*, xvii, 43–44, 58–62, 87, 122.

148. *FIT*, 78. McIntosh suggests precisely the opposite; that Willison and others who remained within the Assembly "were mounting a much more comprehensive opposition to defections from truth within the Church than Erskine and the Seceders with their preoccupation with the one issue of patronage." McIntosh, "Lessons," 7. However, as has been indicated, Willison saw patronage as the root of these more "comprehensive" defections. Erskine, conversely, viewed patronage as one of the manifold evils that sprang from an underlying defection and since the Synod of Perth and Stirling's censure of him, Erskine's attention had been directed primarily at others of those defections.

149. The people of Stirling gave a much different portrayal of Erskine's character and disposition than that to which Willison was led by these incorrect suppositions. See *RTC*, 9–10.

The Kirk a True Church?

Following the rising of the Assembly 1734, Erskine held a very particular view of the status of the Established Church. As Erskine argued,

> there is a Difference to be put betwixt the established Church of *Scotland*, and the Church of Christ in *Scotland*; for I reckon that the last is in a great Measure driven into the Wilderness by the first; and since God in his adorable Providence has led us into the Wilderness with her, I judge it our Duty to tarry with her for a while there, and to prefer her Afflictions to all the Advantages of a legal Establishment in Communion with Judicatories, as they stand at present.[150]

While this difference between the Church of Scotland and the Church of Christ in Scotland did not place the two as mutually exclusive bodies in Erskine's conception, it did place them in a vital disjuncture. While there were still many laymen and ministers who were members of both bodies, there were also significant numbers of both laity and clergy who had been cast out of the Church of Scotland although they remained members of the Church of Christ in Scotland. By intruding ministers upon dissenting congregations and then refusing to allow dissenting parishioners to receive ordinances from any minister other than the intruded ones whom they denied to be lawful ministers, the church judicatories effectively had excommunicated a significant number of the Scots people; by his providential hand, God then had brought Erskine and his brethren out of the Established Church in order to minister to and serve this scattered and afflicted portion of his people in the land.[151] The resulting situation found some members of the Church of Christ in Scotland still in the Church of Scotland, with a body of faithful ministers there to serve them; and other members of the Church of Christ in Scotland outwith the Church of Scotland, with a body of ministers to serve them, as well.[152] In this situation, both bodies of ministers were to labor in their respective spheres, either within the Church of Scotland or without, in the hopes that the Lord might bring reform and allow all of the Church of Christ in Scotland to return to the Church of Scotland.[153] In the mid-1730s,

---

150. *Contendings*, 73.

151. Ibid., 71–72, 73–74, 78. Many laymen similarly considered themselves to be "virtually excommunicated." *Public Testimony*, 11. See also *Letter to Potter*, 13.

152. Erskine to Grange January 1734, 1; Erskine to Grange February 1734, 1. The laity outwith the Established Church even had expressed the intention to call and support ministers for themselves if the Established Church continued to keep them in effective excommunication. See *Public Testimony*, 11; *Contendings*, 7; Morren, *Annals*, 13–14.

153. For examples of the Brethren's call for faithful ministers within the Church

Erskine's view of the Church of Scotland thus was highly nuanced. While the Church of Scotland still harbored components of the Church of Christ in Scotland, it no longer contained the whole of that mystical body. The tension in such a situation could not abide forever.

In the years that intervened between the Assembly 1734 and the *Declinature* in 1739, the Kirk was consumed with controversy that would affect that tension. Among other issues, the Kirk was confronted with the perceived doctrinal errors of Archibald Campbell and William Wishart; the continued use of forced settlements to consolidate the powers of patronage; and the erastian-tinged components of the Porteous Act.[154] While it is not surprising that Erskine's position on such controversial issues was at odds with the course pursued by the Kirk in such matters, what perhaps is more surprising is that on each respective controversy, Erskine and Willison assumed commensurate positions. Willison was not willing to tolerate defections that Erskine lamented. Rather, both men denounced the lenity shown to Campbell and Wishart; both categorically criticized forced settlements; and both took umbrage at a perceived erastian arrogation in the Porteous Act.[155] If Willison was more willing to impute sincere motives to his opponents than was Erskine—Willison conceded that many who obeyed the Porteous Act did so out of the conviction that it did not contain erastian elements, for example—the former was no less strident in his opposition to the specific actions considered than was the latter. How, then, could Erskine have become convinced by 1739 that the Established Church was no longer a true Church of Christ while Willison remained convinced of the opposite?

---

of Scotland to join them in their cause, though not necessarily in their judicatory, see *Works*, 2:169; *Contendings*, 3–4; *TD*, 113–14; *ADT*, 24–25. Currie addresses these implicit calls in *Separation*, 150–51. Watt partly apprehends this dynamic. See Watt, "Erskine," 115–16.

While never endeavoring to argue this point, Lachman often alludes to a quotation from Erskine that would seem to refute this contention. See, for example, Lachman, "Erskine, Ebenezer," in *DSCHT*, 299; "Erskine, Ebenezer" in *DNB*, 529. However, read and understood in its larger context, Erskine's sentiment is a rejection of the proposal for immediate accession; it is not a call for the faithful ministers still in the Established Church to join the Brethren in the Associate Presbytery. For that quotation in context, see *Contendings*, 74–75.

154. Wishart had been appointed at Ilay's behest. For more on Wishart, see *Fasti*, 1.33; Stewart, "Wishart, William." For more on Campbell, see Batty, "Campbell, Archibald."

155. For doctrinal lenity in the judicatories, see *FIT*, 85–86, 89–91; *ADT*, vii, 88–89. For the occurrence of forced settlements, see *FIT*, 53–58; *ADT*, viii; *Reasons*, 27–28; *TD*, 56–58. For the Porteous Act, see *FIT*, 87–89; *Works*, 3:46, 52. For an example of how Willison's and Erskine's shared position on such controversies differed from that of the majority party, see Currie's defense of the Assembly's lenity with Campbell in *Separation*, 26–27, 113–24.

A Tradition of Kirk Evaluation

While the differing temperaments of each man undoubtedly played a role in their differing conclusions, a more material reason for Erskine's and Willison's divergence during the third phase of the Secession Crisis is embedded in the tumultuous history of Scottish theology. Given the vicissitudes of the Kirk's history, multiple generations of presbyterians had been forced to explain, and thus "excuse," the behavior of their forebears, even as they were required to justify their own courses. Through such apologetic needs, Scottish theology had developed a crucial distinction between a healthy, reforming Church, and a sickly, backsliding Church, and it was this distinction that underlay the division that occurred between Erskine and Willison in the 1730s.

A distinction between Churches in different conditions had been very important in the apologetic of the Protesters, as they sought to clarify why they pursued the course that they did.[156] As James Guthrie explained, one had to remember

> 1. That there is a difference betwixt a sound or a healthfull growing reforming, and an unsound sickly decaying declining state of a Church. 2. That there is a difference betwixt a troubled distempered, and a quiet peaceable state of a Church.[157]

Since Guthrie and his fellow Protesters judged that the Kirk of their day was in a "sickly, decaying, declining, troubled, distempered condition," they were compelled to pursue measures that, if the Church were in a reforming and pacific condition, they would have refused.[158] For Guthrie and his fellow Protesters, a Church in a path of reform was entitled to patience and tenderness, while a defecting Church required rigor.

---

156. Erskine was strongly influenced by the Protesting party of the mid-seventeenth century, especially in the person of James Guthrie, who had ministered in Stirling until his execution in Edinburgh in 1661. Perhaps most telling of Erskine's admiration for Guthrie was his publication, in 1738, of the final sermon that Guthrie preached in Stirling, along with several other previously published works by the Covenanting minister, to which Erskine attached an important prefatory letter. See *Cry*, 4: For instances of Erskine's indebtedness to Guthrie, and the Protesters more generally, see *Works*, 1:504–5; *Holy Rude Kirk Session* CH2/1026/6, 211; *ADT*, 14, 18–21; *TD*, 32–33; *RTC*, 10–12, 15, 23–26; *RN&S*, 64–65; *TSP*, 8–10; *Cry*, vi. Given Erskine's reverence for the Protesters, it is instructive to note that John Willison's view of the Protesters was more critical. See *FIT*, 10–11. Currie, too, was critical of the Protesters. See Currie, *Separation*, 69–71, 148.

157. Guthrie, *Protesters*, 32.

158. Ibid., 33.

This distinction that Guthrie articulated would become even more important in the days following the Revolution, as the remaining Cameronian ministers had to explain why, after refusing measures such as James VII's second Indulgence, they were willing to accede to a Revolution Church that lacked an explicit Covenantal foundation. In Alexander Shields' effort to explain precisely this situation, he traces several distinctions that the Covenanters had made during the times of persecution. Among such distinctions, Shields writes that

> We distinguished between a Church in a growing Case, coming forward out of Darkness, and advancing in Reformation, and a Church declining and going back again. In the former many things may be born with, which in the latter are noways to be yielded unto, as in the time of the former Prelacy many did hear Prelatical Men, &c. In times of Defection and Division the Church was declining and going back, and in that Case it was needful to be very peremptory in Tenaciousness: But now she is growing and coming forward out of Darkness, and advancing, tho weakly, in Reformation; And therefore now, sure it must be born with to hear Presbyterian Ministers, tho formerly guilty of Defections, as much as in former times to hear Prelatical Men.[159]

In Shields' formulation, Guthrie's distinction receives a further application—the state of a Church is determinative of whether certain errors are to be forborne or resisted. If a Church is even mildly reforming, certain errors and imperfections can be overlooked in order to aid further reformation. However, if a Church is in a course of defection, the exact same errors and imperfections must be resisted rigorously in order to stop the Church from sliding further into corruption. In this, the trajectory of the Church is a vital consideration in determining how that Church is to be handled.[160]

When this distinction, as refined in Covenanting thought, is brought into the Kirk of the 1730s, the implications for Erskine's and Willison's differing evaluations of the state of that Kirk are profound. From Erskine's perspective, the Church was in a state of decline and increasing defection. While Erskine remained remarkably silent on the *Marrow* affair throughout the course of the Secession, events in the early 1740s would show that his perception of the Church's doctrinal error in that earlier controversy

---

159. Shields, *Church-Communion*, 24.

160. See also James Renwick and Alexander Shields, *AN INFORMATORY VINDICATION OF A Poor, wasted, misrepresented Remnant of the suffering, Anti-popish, Anti-prelatick, Anti-erastian, Anti-sectarian, true Presbyterian Church of CHRIST in Scotland*, 27–28.

provided the foundation for his conviction of the Kirk's defection.[161] Having receded from doctrinal truth in the *Marrow* affair, the Church added judicial abuse to the course of its defection in the aftermath of that controversy and in the Secession Crisis. Time and again—in the *Marrow* controversy, in the Brethren's protest against the actions of the Assembly 1733, and many other times—a testimony to truth had been lifted up only to be ignored. The Church had continued on a course of defection and thus the errors of the 1730s were to be the more sharply resisted and denounced.[162] From a backsliding Church, they were manifestations of "further and higher Steps of Defection."[163]

From Willison's perspective, the Church of the 1730s was still in a state of hopeful reformation. The prominence and importance of this reforming direction of the Church in Willison's argumentation is brought into stark relief when compared with John Currie's presentation of the majority party's position. While Currie founds the Kirk's claim to be a true Church upon the static considerations of Word, Sacraments, and Discipline, Willison goes beyond these considerations to defend church judicatories because of their perceived momentum toward reform.[164] While the *Marrow* affair served as the bedrock of Erskine's conviction of the Kirk's defection, Willison judged that the Assembly 1722's conclusion of the matter "did Justice to Truth," even as he ignored the judicial harassment faced by the *Marrow* Representers throughout the 1720s and judged the claimant evil underlying the Secession—the Act 1732—to have been definitively repealed.[165] Indeed, in Willison's estimation, the period of the Kirk's history since the Revolution was the most wonderful that it had known since the Reformation; a period crowned by the reforming and courageous Assembly of 1734.[166] With the

---

161. The limited attention that Erskine does give to the *Marrow* controversy in the midst of the Secession Crisis deals mostly with the conduct of the judicatories and their abuse of the Representers rather than with the doctrinal defections that would receive Erskine's renewed attention in the 1740s. See, for example, *ADT*, 83–84. Of course, Erskine's previous support of the *Marrow* was used in attacks against him in spite of his clear attempts to disavow the errors imputed to that earlier stand. See *Valiant Champion*, 9–10; Gib, *Display*, 1:ix–x, respectively.

162. In large part, the Brethren attributed this continued decline to the presence of so many ministers within the Assembly who had been intruded into their charges. See, for example, *TD*, 43, 93–95. Erskine had perceived this danger firsthand in the Mackie case. *Contendings*, 78–79.

163. *Cry*, vii.

164. See Currie, *Separation*, 1–2, 15, 22. See also Carson, "Doctrine of the Church," 266–67.

165. *FIT*, 44.

166. *CDMD*, 22; *FIT*, 18–19, 75–78.

Kirk on this trajectory of reformation, Willison was much more patient with the errors of the 1730s and more willing to work alongside men of differing principles. Within a Church making sincere strivings toward reformation, such errors and differences were simply regrettable reminders that even reforming Churches still inhabit a sinful world.[167] In this crucial distinction between a defecting and a reforming Church, one sees how Erskine and Willison were able to have the same principles, to criticize the same defections for the same reasons, and yet come to starkly different conclusions as to what such defections meant for the state of the Church.

The Declinature

The differing conclusions that Erskine and Willison were reaching concerning the state of the Kirk came to a head in 1739, when the eight ministers who then comprised the Associate Presbytery were libeled by the General Assembly and summoned to appear before her bar. For some time, Erskine had become pessimistic about the state of the Kirk. In 1738, Erskine had written

> WHEN the Reformation of Corruptions, and the purging out of evident Scandals is the only Condition demanded, what can be the Reason that it is not granted? One of the two it must needs be, *viz*. either because the Judicatories will not; or else because they cannot reform. If it be because they will not, they are to be withdrawn from as Wicked. If it be because they cannot, or want Power, it says, The Keys of Discipline is taken ftom [from] them, and that they are not Christ's Officers and Stewards.[168]

Faced with renewed calls for judicial submission to the Established Church, Erskine and his brethren took the final step of formally declaring that the judicatories of that Church were no longer true courts of Christ and calling for all faithful ministers to come out of those judicatories lest they involve themselves in the sin thereof.[169] After years of an ambiguous relationship,

---

167. See *FIT*, 79–87.

168. *Cry*, vii–viii. Provocatively, Erskine asserted that this one consideration undid the whole of Currie's argumentation in *Separation*. See *Cry*, viii. Such a pessimism had become clear since 1737, the same year the Associate Presbytery began exercising acts of jurisdiction. See, for example, *Works*, 2:443, 467; 3:145–46.

169. Both at the time of the Secession Crisis and in the secondary literature, one finds suspicion that Erskine and his brethren withdrew from the Established Church because of issues pertaining to the *purity* of the Church. See, for example, *N&S*, 54; Mitchell, "Ebenezer Erskine," 177–78. However, it was because Erskine and his brethren judged that the Church of Scotland was no longer a *true* church of Christ that they

the Church of Scotland and the Church of Christ in Scotland had been severed. In the three considerations that the Seceders adduced for their pronouncement of the Established Church's apostasy—that her judicatories were filled with men who did not have the call of Christ to the ministry, that she had failed to defend doctrinal truth, and that she had allowed the State to usurp Christ's sole Headship over the Church—one sees the climax of the divergence introduced between Erskine's and Willison's perception of the Kirk by the inheritance of Covenanting theology. Willison agreed that the Kirk of the 1730s contained men who were not properly called; that it had allowed doctrinal error within its pale; and that it had sinfully submitted to the erastian pretensions of the British State, yet he in no manner agreed that such errors established the foundation for the Brethren's pronouncement. In this crucial disparity, one sees the difference between rigor with a defecting Church and patience with a Church moving haltingly toward reform.

SUMMARY OF THE CRISIS

Having viewed the Secession in its three distinct phases, one is able to understand both the origin and the limitation of the Secession. The Secession had its origins in the Synod of Perth and Stirling's attempt to repress Ebenezer Erskine's freedom to dissent from the actions of church judicatories. In all of the judicial proceedings and polemical vitriol that ensued, that one central factor never changed; in order to conclude the judicial process against him, Erskine had to renounce, either explicitly or implicitly, sentiments that he judged to be a witness to truth. Thus faced, at every turn, with the demand that he renounce his previous testimony, Erskine eventually was extruded from the Established Church. In prior disagreements with the course of church judicatories, Erskine had been content with witnessing against those courses and had given no indication of a desire for secession.

---

called for the remnant of faithful ministers to withdraw therefrom; this call was not based upon a declaration that the Kirk was not a *pure* church of Christ. As Erskine wrote to the Presbytery of Stirling, "I never expect to see a Church upon Earth free of Imperfections, but it is desireable [to] see a Church wrestling after it, and holding fast that whereunto she has attained, especially when obliged thereunto by solemn Covenant Engagements." *Contendings*, 79. Erskine did not demand a pure Church, only a Church striving after purity. See also *Works*, 1:488; 2:152–70; *TD*, 99.

Carson bases a large portion of his evaluation of the Seceders on the supposition that they seceded over issues of purity. However, he bases this analysis almost wholly on the writings of William Wilson, thus detailing, and widely imputing, a view that Erskine explicitly rejected, both in word and action. See Carson, 11, 183–91, 309–10.

In the Secession Crisis, however, this freedom to dissent was denied him and he therefore was cast out of the Church before he seceded.[170]

In John Willison, one finds the key to the other vital component of the Secession; namely, its limitation. Although Willison agreed with the particulars of the synodical critique of the Kirk that brought Erskine under censure and jealously cherished his own freedom to dissent from the actions of church judicatories in order to exonerate his conscience, he soundly condemned Erskine's Secession. From an examination of Willison's critique of the movement, it appears that this anomaly stemmed from Willison's ignorance of the true grounds of the Secession. In his *Testimony*, Willison at times provides detailed discussion of the exact semantics of the Assembly's decisions in the Secession Crisis, yet he never enters into any sustained consideration or refutation of the Brethren's assertion that the judicatories were repressing their freedom of dissent and that the only options thus opened to them were either sinful subjection to silence or continued defiance.[171] Willison never discusses these arguments; he does not even refer to them and say that they are wrong. Rather, he ignores them altogether, leaving one to conclude that he is unaware of them. Had Willison ever engaged the substantial arguments of the Brethren, even in a way of refutation, matters would be quite different. As matters stand, it appears that Willison rejected the Secession because he misunderstood the Secession, judging it to center upon patronage rather than upon the freedom of ministerial dissent.

As Willison was a well-respected, well-connected minister within the larger Kirk, one is left to imagine that his ignorance of the true cause of Erskine and the other Seceders was not unique. Rather, in the vital second phase of the Secession Crisis, when the issue was not patronage, but rather the Brethren's ability to continue in full communion with the Kirk without having to renounce what they considered to be a witness to truth, the majority of ministers thought that the issue under contention was Erskine's harsh expressions, the Act 1732, or some other related issue.[172] When the commendable efforts of the Assembly 1734, repealing the Act 1732 and removing the concrete effects of the Act and Sentence 1733, failed to win the Brethren back to the church judicatories, this unfamiliarity made many see not the need to address the deeper reasons for the Secession, but rather only a manifestation of the schismatic spirit that they suspected to lay within Erskine all along. From the time of the Commission's decision in November

170. See *Reasons*, 9.

171. *FIT*, 91–92.

172. For an example of the resulting sympathy for Erskine, yet ignorance of his cause, see MacInnes, 84.

1733 to loose the Brethren from their charges, then, the final rupture of 1739 and 1740 was unavoidable. Unable to acquiesce to the terms of the judicatories' sentence, the Brethren were forced into Secession; unaware of the reasons for the Brethren's action, those who were their allies focused their reforming efforts on patronage rather than on the specific restriction upon ministerial freedom that hung over the Brethren. This dissonance between the complaint that the Brethren offered and the remedy that their allies sought to provide only served to convince the Seceders that the Assembly was unwilling to reform and the Seceders' erstwhile allies that they were schismatics whose severity placed them beyond reclamation.

A Willisonian Historiography?

In addition to elucidating the nature of the Secession itself, a comparison between Erskine's actions and Willison's critique also presents, in microcosm, the fallacies of the later Secession historiography's use of the Secession Crisis. While later Seceders loathed Willison, they unwittingly adopted Willison's central characterization of the Secession—that of a patronage-driven dispute that split the evangelical presence in the Kirk between two communions.[173] As has been demonstrated, however, that characterization contains a double error. In the first instance, while Erskine's objection to patronage had a role to play in the Secession, the Secession itself was precipitated by Erskine's censure and the restriction of his freedom to dissent involved therein. In the second instance, by 1739, Erskine was convinced that there could no longer be a legitimate evangelical presence in the Assembly; indeed, the governing premise of the Seceders' *Declinature* was the apostasy of the Established Church. While Willison maintained notions of a pan-presbyterian evangelical presence until his death, Erskine did not. When the Seceders of the mid-nineteenth century attempted a posthumous reconciliation between Erskine and a larger pan-presbyterian evangelical party, and then sought to portray this party as prescient opponents of a pro-patronage Moderate Party, they thus over-emphasized the centrality of Erskine's objection to patronage, even if not the strength of that objection, and they obscured the extent of the rupture between Erskine and the Established Church.

Ironically, while the attempt thus made to present Erskine as foreseeing the later patronage abuses of Robertson's Moderates is fallacious, there does appear to have been an even more profound way in which Erskine issued

---

173. See, for example, "Vindication."

an unheeded warning about the coming abuses of the Moderates.[174] In his central demand for the ministerial freedom to dissent and his concern that that right was under assault from increasingly overbearing church courts, Erskine penetrated to the core of the coming, new Moderate regime's strict subordination of all Church courts to the radical court of the Assembly and its demand that all dissent from below be suppressed.[175] That one of the leaders in securing Erskine's censure before the Synod of Perth and Stirling, James Mackie, would later become Moderator of the Assembly during the years of Moderate consolidation only makes such a suggestion more tantalizing; on the synodical level, Erskine confronted the judicial repression of dissent that later would permeate the entire Kirk.[176]

IMPLICATIONS OF THE SECESSION

As has been seen, throughout the Secession Crisis, Erskine continued to evidence the modified Covenantalism that he had refined in the earlier Abjuration Oath controversy.[177] While Erskine's articulation of this Covenantal dissent showed no development from its expression twenty years previously, the Secession Crisis precipitated two crucial developments relative to that Covenantal dissent; developments that constitute the central implications of that Crisis.

First, while the exigencies of the Oath controversy had brought Erskine's modified Covenantalism into harmony with a Constitutionalist perspective on Church-State matters, the particularities of the Secession Crisis manifested the principial tension between these two paradigms; a tension evident in John Currie's enunciation of the majority party's Constitutionalist perspective. In his critique of Erskine's position, with the prominence that it lent to the Covenants and Covenantal obligations, Currie expounded a Constitutionalism that reverenced Scotland's Covenants as noble documents for the Kirk, yet afforded them no role in discussions of the present establishment.[178] When the contours of establishment were discussed, the majority view had primary reference to the Revolution Settlement, Acts of

---

174. I am indebted to conversation with Professor S. J. Brown on this point. See also Brown, "William Robertson (1721-1793) and the Scottish Enlightenment," 13-15.

175. See Sefton, "Moderatism," 168-77, 214-18 on this "new" Moderatism.

176. Mackie was elected moderator of the General Assembly on 9 May 1751. In 1753, he was translated from St. Ninians to St. Cuthbert's in Edinburgh. See *Fasti*, 1:102, 4:314.

177. The prominence of the Covenants in Erskine's position exposed him to ridicule by some of his opponents. See *Valiant Champion*.

178. For examples of such reverence, see Currie, *Separation*, 1-2, 44, 103.

Parliament, and Acts of the General Assembly; the Covenants remained conspicuously silent.[179] When the possibility of a Covenantal renaissance was broached by Currie's majority position, it was held that societal Covenantal renewal could occur only if the Covenants were amended to preclude forcing the juror to consent to the truths of Scripture, thus allowing both Christians and non-Christians to swear them in good conscience.[180] The contrary, Covenantal notion that the State should use its power to pursue reformation and religious uniformity was "tyrannical."[181] Unlike the Oath controversy, the Secession Crisis revealed the Covenantal and Constitutional perspectives not as slightly different voices of a common dissent, but as profoundly dissonant notions of the foundation of Kirk establishment and the purpose of Kirk engagement with the State.[182]

In addition to accentuating the divergence between the Covenantal and Constitutionalist paradigms, the Secession Crisis also transformed the Covenantal perspective, for Erskine, from a dissenting principle into an active principle. Since the Revolution, ministers of the Covenantal persuasion had existed as a dissenting minority within the Established Church, and thus they had never had the opportunity to enact the substance of their agenda—the re-establishment of the Kirk upon strictly Covenantal foundations.[183] Beginning with the accession of Shields, Linning, and Boyd, the freedom to dissent from Church courses had kept Covenantally-committed

---

179. In the entirety of *N&S*'s treatment of the Secession Crisis, the Covenants are not addressed once. Given the prominence that the Brethren had given to the Covenants throughout the controversy, this absence is noteworthy. Such a Constitutionalist position had marked Currie's earlier writings against patronage, as well. See, for example, Currie, *Jus populi divinum*, 79–96; Currie, *A FULL VINDICATION OF THE People's Right to Elect their own PASTORS*.

180. See Currie, *Separation*, 109–13.

181. Currie, *Separation*, 96. From this position, Currie denounced the persecution of Roman Catholics that had occurred during the Second Reformation. See Currie, *Separation*, 93–96. See also Currie, *Separation*, 145–47. Kidd suggests that the Secession had pushed Currie to some of these positions by co-opting the Covenants and the days of the Second Reformation, thus making them "unusable" to polemicists within the Established Church. See Kidd, *Subverting*, 185. However, Currie's earlier reticence to pursue his position with Covenantal arguments suggests that his later position was not so novel.

182. In Muirhead's assessment, Erskine "wanted a return to the seventeenth-century theocracy." Muirhead, "Religion," 79. However, such a stark categorization is inaccurate. See, for example, *RTC*, 3; *TD*, 100.

183. The Seceders' rejection of the present basis for establishment was made plain in the Formula of Questions required of probationers and ministers that they adopted in 1737. In the third question, which addresses the establishment of presbytery in Scotland, there is no mention of the Revolution Settlement. See Gib, *Display*, 1:x; Hamilton, *Erosion*, 9–10.

ministers within the Established Church by allowing them to exonerate their consciences while still holding communion with ministers of differing persuasions.[184] Indeed, precisely such a situation had persisted throughout the first thirty years of Erskine's ministry. Although Erskine strongly dissented from the Kirk's actions in the Abjuration Oath controversy, the *Marrow* controversy, both Simson processes, the Act 1732, and a host of other instances, his freedom to declare his dissent from those courses had kept him in the establishment without any thought of secession. It was only in the anomalous actions of the church judicatories over the Secession Crisis, actions which extruded Erskine from the Established Church by removing his freedom to dissent, that Erskine's attachment to the judicatories was severed. In this severance, a vital difference was introduced between the modified Covenantalism of Erskine and the virtually identical Covenantal commitments of Willison and others.[185] While an abiding freedom to dissent had kept the latter as minority dissenting voices within the Kirk, the restriction of that freedom in the former had led to Erskine's modified Covenantalism becoming the majority voice of the Secession and thus the foundations and commitments of Covenantally-committed presbyterians became no longer the basis for dissent, but rather the basis for action.[186]

If Erskine's ability to act upon his Covenantal commitments distinguished his modified Covenantalism from the views of Willison and other evangelicals within the Established Church, such a paradigm also sharply distinguished him from the other dissenting religious movements of his day. Since the founding of the Revolution Church, a remnant of Cameronian

---

184. For the same trend in an earlier age, see Donaldson, "Schism," 277–82.

185. See, for example, *CDMD*, 35–36; *FIT*, 30–33. Watt judges that Willison's *Testimony* was itself a distinct brand of Covenant renewal. See Hugh Watt, *Recalling the Scottish Covenants*, 70–91. Hereafter, *Recalling*.

186. That such a dissenting Covenantal party remained in the Established Church is seen in ministers' varying responses to the Porteous Act, which Kidd intimates can be used to gauge one's adherence to a Covenantal perspective. Although contemporary observers noted a host of difficulties in ascertaining obedience or disobedience to the Porteous Act, it is estimated that about one-third of the Kirk's ministers refused to acquiesce with the Act's demands. While this is clearly a minority, it is a sizeable enough contingent that one government advisor could class the resulting disaffection as "greater than was either in the years 1713, 1714, or 1715." Paton, ed., *Report on the Manuscripts of the Right Honourable Lord Polwarth*, 141. Hereafter, *Polwarth Papers*. Clearly, there was still a dissenting Covenantal party in the Kirk, although Kidd suggests that the Brethren's "appropriation of the Covenants" may have pushed some more moderate ministers further into the Constitutionalist camp. See Kidd, *Subverting*, 185. For an account of Erskine's "obedience" to the Porteous Act—in which he read the Act from his pulpit in Stirling, pausing after each paragraph to denounce the unlawfulness and error contained therein—see *Polwarth Papers*, 142. See also Kidd, *Subverting*, 187.

praying societies had existed within Scotland and, since 1706, had coalesced under the ministry of John Macmillan. However, the Macmillanites' Covenantal views were devoid of any "modified" sensibilities and their resulting rejection of the civil magistrate relegated them to the radical fringe both of the wider Scottish Church and of political discourse, if not of popular imagination.[187] As the early days of the Secession indicate, while there were important affinities between the Seceders and the Macmillanites, the Macmillanites saw the modification of the Seceders' Covenantalism to be the "Gordian Knott" that had to be severed before full communion could be had between the two groups.[188] On the other ideological extreme, the decade preceding the Secession Crisis had witnessed the rise of the Glasite movement, the most popular incarnation of an Independency that had middling influence in Scotland.[189] While the Glasites were sympathetic to certain aspects of Erskine's views of establishment, their categorical rejection of the Covenants placed them outwith historical Scottish theology and contrary to the ideology of the Covenantally-committed members of the Established Church, even if not contrary to the *de facto* praxis of the Revolution Kirk.[190] In opposition to both such trends, Erskine's modified Covenantalism represented neither a rejection of the actual setting of the contemporary Kirk nor a renunciation of her Covenanted past, but rather Covenantal commitments contextualized for post-Union Scotland.

In Erskine's modified Covenantalism and its enshrinement in the emergent Secession Church, one sees the formation of a Covenantal Revolution Church. Since the Revolution, both Covenantal and Constitutionalist paradigms had coexisted in the Established Church, with the former being subsumed within the latter. In Erskine and his Secession, the Covenantal dissent that had echoed through the Revolution Church became

187. See, for example, Kidd, "Conditional," 1161–62.

188. Erskine to Grange February 1734, 1–2.

189. For more on the Glasite movement, see Hornsby, "The Case of Mr John Glas," 115–137; Hornsby, "John Glas: His Later Life and Work," 94–113; Murray, "The Influence of John Glas," 45–56.

190. Both before and during the Secession Crisis, John Glas and his followers attempted to co-opt Erskine's more "modified" statements, including those in his synod sermon, to support their views of the Church and of establishment. However, such attempts invariably take Erskine's words, and even a letter that Erskine wrote to Glas, out of context and distort his position by neglecting the Covenantalism that was so prominent in his system. See, for example, Glas, REMARKS UPON THE MEMORIAL OF THE Synod of ANGUS against Mr. Glas, AND THE Sentence of the Commission deposing him from the Ministry, 9–12; A SUPPLEMENT TO Mr. EBENEZER ERSKINE'S SYNODICAL SERMON. As the Relief Presbytery was founded after Erskine's death, it falls outwith the purview of the present account. However, similar observations concerning views of the Covenants would apply to that popular dissenting movement.

ecclesialized, thus obtaining the opportunity to show that its vision was the proper way forward for a Kirk still bound by Covenantal commitments, yet situated in a radically new post-Union, post-toleration Scotland. The material difference between Erskine and the previous forty years of Covenantal dissidents, including those who remained in the Established Church, was not his theological commitment, but rather his situation outwith the Kirk judicatories, free to pursue what they had been free only to advocate.

SUMMARY

The Secession of 1733 resulted from the procedural irregularity of Ebenezer Erskine's censure at the hands of the Synod of Perth and Stirling in 1732. Once that censure was imposed, a series of judicial confrontations was begun which eventually extruded Erskine from the Established Church even though he had neither pertinent theological differences with other Covenantally-committed ministers nor a prior interest in secession. Thus Erskine was afforded a theological and historical anomaly—the opportunity to construct a national Church on a contemporary Covenantal foundation in post-Revolution Scotland. For Erskine, this foundation was embodied in a modified Covenantalism that was neither a historical relic nor the result of personal and circumstantial phenomena; rather, it was a response to the exigencies of post-Union Scotland that issued from the tradition of Covenantal dissent that had been present in the Revolution Church since its founding. While much had changed for Erskine through the Secession Crisis, it appears that nothing had changed about Erskine or about the doctrinal commitments that always had guided his ministry and that would now guide a Covenantal Revolution Church as it sought to make its way in the unfamiliar territory of leadership rather than dissent.

Chapter IV

Erskine in the 1740s

A TRIAL FOR THE COVENANTAL REVOLUTION CHURCH

As ERSKINE SHIFTED, IN the 1740s, from a dissident to an ecclesiastical leader, one glimpses the final coalescence of his theology. In the Abjuration controversy, Erskine had established himself as a proponent of a robust modified Covenantalism; in the *Marrow* controversy, he had honed his evangelical federalism; in the Secession Crisis, Erskine, with both pillars of his doctrinal system intact, had been extruded from the Established Church. In the years following that extrusion, Erskine would chart an ecclesiastical program that would be unfalteringly guided by the convergence of these two doctrinal commitments even in the midst of pronounced temperamental vacillations. Propelling the Secession Church forward was Erskine the theologian.

When Erskine and his fellow Seceders began their course of transforming decades of Covenantal dissent into an actual Covenantal Revolution Church, they quickly encountered both auspicious growth and troubling controversy. In 1740, when the General Assembly had formally deposed the Seceders, the Associate Presbytery had been comprised of eight ministers and thirty-six congregations. By 1745, the Associate Presbytery had grown to twenty-six ministers and forty-three congregations, a size that, for logistical reasons, demanded that the Associate Presbytery be recast as one Associate Synod comprised of three presbyteries.[1] Despite such

---

1. Many of the new Secession congregations had formerly been prayer societies.

marked and rapid growth, however, the Associate Church was troubled by numerous controversies throughout the 1740s and, by the end of that decade, the fledgling Secession Church had split into two rival Synods. In the secondary literature, the troubles of the 1740s assume prominence and are held to reveal such fundamental difficulties that they cast a pall over the entirety of Erskine's theological system; in John Carson's analysis of the Secession's ecclesiology, the "failures" of the 1740s prove that the underlying theological structure provided by Erskine was "an inadequate foundation for the doctrine of the Church."[2] In the 1740s, then, Erskine's model faced an immediate and severe test—was Erskine's articulation of a Covenantal Revolution Church viable as a model for a national Church in post-Union Scotland?

In order to consider such a potentially subjective question, the present account first will establish the Secession Church in the context of 1740s Scotland and then will focus upon three of the great challenges confronting Erskine's Secession Church—how would the Secession Church interact with other communions, how would it interact with the civil magistrate, and how would it handle interaction within its own communion when differences arose? In considering these three areas of Church interaction, one must have recourse to the range of controversies that confronted the Secession in the 1740s, for, as commentators long have sensed, it is in those controversies that Erskine's theory showed its true fruit. Conveniently, the controversial course of the 1740s divides itself roughly into these three areas. In considering the Secession's interaction with other communions, primary attention will be given to the dispute that arose between Erskine and George Whitefield in 1741. As that affair was nearing its conclusion, three events occurred that elucidate the Secession's interaction with the civil magistrate—the Seceders' renewal of Scotland's Covenants in 1743, a controversy within the Associate Presbytery precipitated by that renewal, and Erskine's conduct in the 1745 Jacobite Rising. Finally, the implications of Erskine's Covenantal

---

For a representative account of the process by which these prayer societies became Secession congregations, see Lee, *Greyfriars Glasgow: The Mother Church of the Secession in the West*, 23-28. The "Disjunction" of the Associate Church was approved on 11 October 1744, with the Associate Synod holding its first meeting in March 1745, at Stirling. The three new presbyteries were the Presbyteries of Dunfermline, of Edinburgh, and of Glasgow. Erskine and his Stirling congregation were included in the Presbytery of Glasgow. See *Minutes of the Proceedings of the Associate Presbytery and Associate Synod, Commencing January 7. 1741*, 863, 877-80. Hereafter, *Minutes of AP and AS from 1741*. See also M'Kerrow, 1:254-56. Interestingly, the first meeting of the Associate Synod was opened with a sermon preached by Erskine. The text was Psalm 118:22-23. *Minutes of AP and AS from 1741*, 880-81.

2. Carson, "Doctrine of the Church," 258.

Revolution Church for intra-communion interaction are disclosed by the Burgess Oath controversy and the resulting Breach of 1747. When the primary events of the 1740s are thus grouped and considered in turn, a surprising picture emerges. While Erskine's Covenantal Revolution Church revealed several problematic weaknesses in the 1740s, it nonetheless proved to be what Erskine held it to be—a viable and stridently distinct national Church alternative to the Established Church in post-Union Scotland.

SCOTLAND IN THE 1740S

A Changed and Changing Society

When Erskine and his fellow Seceders began their efforts to construct a Covenantal Revolution Church, they did so in a Scotland profoundly different than the nation which had rejected a Covenantal foundation for the national Church after the Revolution; a nation whose appearance had been altered most radically by more than three decades of life under the Treaty of Union. At the time of that Union, Scotland had remained what it long had been—a largely agrarian society that, while far from insular, had most external influences mediated through repatriated countrymen who brought back with them ideas and philosophies that they had imbibed elsewhere.[3] By the 1740s, Scotland was in the throes of reconfiguration. With access to Britain's overseas colonies opened under the Union, thus providing both ample raw materials and ready markets, Scotland's economy was lurching forward under the tutelage of the linen and tobacco industries.[4] While Scotland's greatest economic growth would not come until later, the 1740s already manifested surprising movement from stagnation to prosperity.[5]

Along with this gathering economic expansion, Scotland was experiencing a philosophical broadening. With exposure to both English and Continental thought extended through the Union, Scottish philosophers and theologians increasingly were led to consider how faith—from its foundation in Scripture, to its focus upon the biblical God, to its outworking in love—was

---

3. Devine, *Scottish Nation*, 26–27.

4. See ibid., 58–59; Smout, *History*, 226–27; Allan, 92–93; Lynch, *Scotland: A New History*, 380–81; Mitchison, *Lordship to Patronage: Scotland 1603–1745*, 168–69, 173. What innovation there was in the agricultural sector was largely confined to isolated improvement efforts. See especially Smout, *History*, 272–74; Mitchison, *Lordship to Patronage*, 173–74; Lynch, *Scotland*, 343. The one traditional enterprise that did see widespread growth was the cattle trade.

5. See Smout, *History* 226; Saville, "Impasse and Potential in the pre-1707 Economy."

to be understood in light of an emerging "Reason."[6] The important changes that this influx of English and Continental thought was precipitating were embodied in the person of Francis Hutcheson, professor of Moral Philosophy at Glasgow from 1729 to 1746.[7] By his revolutionary practice of lecturing in English rather than in Latin and his innovation of the moral sense theory, by which the construction of morality was divorced from all metaphysical considerations, Hutcheson portended a new mode of Scottish thought that was both modernized and willing to alter traditional assumptions about such crucial issues as morality, divine revelation, and faith.[8]

The cumulative effect of these landmark changes was the creation of a growing divide within Scottish society. On the one hand, there was a segment of the population increasingly committed to Scotland's place within Great Britain. This "polite" class of Scots drew great political influence from its London connections, it made considerable sums of money from markets attributable to Scotland's membership in Great Britain, and it increasingly educated its young at English schools.[9] For Scots thus finally benefiting from Scotland's place within the Union, any challenge to the current, amicable settlement of the Established Church was unappealing, especially when that challenge came from men who, like Erskine, publicly denounced both Scotland's pre-occupation with worldly prosperity and the means by which that wealth was obtained.[10] On the other hand, the changes within Scottish life and society had also engendered a sentiment among some that the economic reconfiguration of the preceding decades was not a positive change and that Scotland under the Union had not become more "modernized," but rather more "pagan."[11] While this sentiment did not demand Erskine's drive

---

6. See Fergusson, ed., *Scottish Philosophical Theology 1700–2000*, 3–5. For a discussion of the Continental context that was influencing Scotland, see Barth, *From Rousseau to Ritschl*, 11–57. Hereafter, *Rousseau*. Orr suggests that the prevalence of federalism fuelled the ascendance of rationalism. Orr, *The Progress of Dogma*, 303–4.

7. As a student, Hutcheson had been deeply influenced by the teaching of John Simson, yet he was also indebted to a wider spectrum of English and Continental philosophers and theologians. See Allan, *Scotland*, 137–38; Devine, *Scottish Nation*, 73–74; Smout, *History*, 215–16, 448–52; McIntosh, *Theology*, 9; Ferguson, *Scotland*, 210–11. On Hutcheson's role in exposing Scotland to English and Continental thought, see especially Smout, *History*, 451.

8. See Allan, *Scotland*, 137–38; Barth, *Rousseau*, 35–36; Cameron, "Theological Controversy: A Factor in the Origins of the Scottish Enlightenment," especially page 128; Ferguson, *Scotland*, 209–10.

9. See Smout, *History*, 265–71, 461–62; Devine, *Scottish Nation*, 27–28; Ferguson, *Scotland*, 203–4; Barth, *Rousseau*, 35. Devine offers Archibald Campbell, Earl of Ilay, as a prototype of this new kind of Scot. See Devine, *Scottish Nation*, 25.

10. See, for example, Allan, *Scotland*, 99; *Works*, 2:282–83, 329, 3:45; *AFR*, 109.

11. On economic concern in the period, see Smout, *History*, 223–27; Lenman, *The*

for a Covenantal Revolution Church, it was not immediately hostile thereto. The Scotland in which Erskine sought to found his Covenantal Revolution Church, then, was neither wholly resistant nor entirely amenable to such an experiment.[12] The viability of that experiment would depend ultimately not upon considerations inherent to the milieu in which it was attempted, but rather upon the ability of that Covenantal Revolution Church to function as a legitimate national Church in that post-Union milieu.

Political Vicissitudes

While the overall trajectory of Scottish society was somewhat ambivalent to the success or failure of Erskine's Covenantal Revolution Church, there was one factor that was decidedly auspicious for that endeavor—the political situation created by Edinburgh's Porteous riot of February 1736 and the resulting Porteous Act 1737.[13] With the passage of the Porteous Act, Walpole's government suffered a great loss of popularity in Scotland; when Walpole hesitatingly declared war on Spain in 1739, Scottish approval of the government suffered only more.[14] The great benefit that this burgeoning disapproval held for the Secession Church was that it loosened the Earl of Ilay's grip upon Scotland; with Walpole's position becoming more precarious, Ilay was forced to focus his energies upon simply retaining the reigns of power rather than upon fully exploiting them. Furthermore, Walpole's call for strict punitive measures to be taken against Edinburgh following the Porteous riots and his advocacy of the Porteous Act had created an open split between Walpole and the Duke of Argyll. While Ilay remained loyal to Walpole, the Argathelian party within Scotland was split and thus Ilay no longer knew the vast control in Scotland that he had once enjoyed. This slip

---

Jacobite Risings in Britain: 1689-1746, 231-32. On the widespread fear that Scotland was becoming more pagan, see Allan, *Scotland*, 97; Ferguson, *Scotland*, 225; Allan, 131-132; *Scotland*, Mitchison, *Lordship to Patronage*, 175-76; Smout, *History*, 265-71.

12. Brown posits that tensions caused by changes in agriculture were creating an agrarian uneasiness that was being channeled into denominational fights rather than violent uprisings. See Brown, *Religion*, 78-80, 83. Smout, on the other hand, leaves little room for Brown's proposal, asserting that the dissenting presbyterian movements of the 1740s were inimical to radicalism. See Smout, *History*, 307-9. For an interesting alternative to Brown, see Mitchison, *Lordship to Patronage*, 170-71. At the very least, it seems that Brown's pronouncements concerning agrarian radicalism are overly severe for the Scotland of the 1740s, regardless of their possible merit for later eighteenth-century Scotland. See Smout, *History*, 223-27, 304; Lynch, *Scotland*, 379.

13. On the Porteous riot and the Porteous Act, see Ferguson, *Scotland*, 144-46; Smout, *History*, 210-11; Devine, *Scottish Nation*, 23.

14. See Ferguson, *Scotland*, 144-46.

in Ilay's control over Scotland was clearly signaled in the elections of 1741, when he failed to deliver a pro-Walpole majority among Scottish Members of Parliament.[15] In 1742, Walpole's poor performance in the 1741 elections forced him to resign and Ilay saw his power pass to the newly reconstituted office of Secretary of Scotland, then filled by the fourth Marquis of Tweeddale.[16] It was not until 1746, in the wave of recriminations that followed the defeat of the Jacobite Rising of 1745, that Tweeddale was removed from this office and Ilay resumed the control that he had previously exercised.[17] However, by that date, the unrest in Scottish politics had achieved its beneficial end for the Secession Church—in the years of the Associate Presbytery's final rupture with the General Assembly and of its early development and growth, its most powerful opponent was first gravely distracted and then divested of a large measure of his power, thus enabling the Secession Church to separate fully from the General Assembly and then begin to establish itself with remarkably little governmental interference.[18] Once more, one sees that the success or failure of Erskine's attempt to found a Covenantal Revolution Church would not be unduly influenced by external considerations. The true test would be the viability of that ecclesial vision itself.

INTERACTION WITH OTHER COMMUNIONS

Erskine's Controversy with George Whitefield

As the 1740s unfolded, the first test that awaited Erskine and his version of a Covenantal Revolution Church was the test of how that Church would interact with other communions within post-Union, post-toleration Scotland.

---

15. Prior to the 1741 elections, thirty of Scotland's forty-five MPs were pro-Walpole; after the elections, only nineteen had been retained. In neglecting the Porteous fallout and the Argathelian split, Lynch seems to misdiagnose the reasons for Walpole's Scottish embarrassment. See Lynch, *Scotland*, 325–26.

16. See Ferguson, *Scotland*, 144–46; Devine, *Scottish Nation*, 23; Lynch, *Scotland*, 325–26.

17. See Mitchison, *Lordship to Patronage*, 163; Ferguson, *Scotland*, 146–47.

18. Even the General Assembly managed to remain remarkably free from governmental interference in these years. See McIntosh, *Theology*, 7. One concrete alteration within the General Assembly that did accompany the shifts in national government came in the alternation of two men as the government's manager within the Assembly. After 1736, Ilay had sought to control events within the Assembly through the orchestrated management of Patrick Cumming. When Tweeddale assumed the Secretaryship, that power within the Assembly passed to Robert Wallace, only to be reappropriated by Cumming upon Ilay's resumption of power in 1746. See Sefton, "Wallace"; Drummond, 62–63; Skoczylas, "Regulation," 171.

The distillation of this test came in Erskine and the Associate Presbytery's controversy with George Whitefield upon the latter's evangelistic tour of Scotland in 1741. On the surface, this test appears to have been an abject failure for Erskine.[19] In the Associate Presbytery's public opposition to Whitefield, they seemed unwilling to countenance the ministry, or even the presence, of any non-seceding ministers. However, upon closer examination, the root of Erskine's controversy with Whitefield appears to be rather different than is commonly understood and the controversy itself is seen to disclose a flawed, yet hopeful, ability within Erskine to prioritize doctrinal concerns in such a way that allows joint labor with those of other communions.

The course that the controversy between the Associate Presbytery and Whitefield followed is straightforward. On 18 May 1739, a twenty-four-year-old Whitefield first recorded his receipt of a letter from Ralph Erskine, minister in the Associate Presbytery and Ebenezer's younger brother.[20] What followed was an intensifying exchange of letters between Whitefield and both of the Erskine brothers that eventually led to the Associate Presbytery inviting Whitefield to come to Scotland for an evangelistic tour.[21] Eventually, Whitefield accepted this invitation and, after returning from his well-received visit to America, Whitefield came to Scotland in 1741.[22] When Whitefield disembarked at Leith on 30 July 1741, he immediately stepped into the midst of the simmering dispute between the Associate Presbytery and the Established Church. Whitefield was welcomed at the port by both Ralph Erskine from the Secession and Alexander Webster from the Church of Scotland, each of whom was eager to procure Whitefield's assurance that he would preach in the pulpits of their respective churches.[23] As Whitefield had come on the invitation of the Erskine brothers and the Associate Presbytery, he insisted that that body had the first claim on his labors and thus he preached his first sermon on Scottish soil at Ralph Erskine's church in Dunfermline the following Sunday.[24]

The amiable relationship thus begun between Whitefield and the Associate Presbytery was not to last long. On 5 August, the Associate Presbytery convened for the purpose of conversing with Whitefield about matters of

19. E.g., "Doctrine of the Church," Carson, 208.

20. Butler, *John Wesley and George Whitefield in Scotland*, 4, 11–12.

21. Butler attributes the increasing Calvinism of Whitefield's views during the late 1730s to his exchange with the Erskines. See ibid., 13–14.

22. See ibid., 20–22.

23. MacEwen, *Erskines*, 117–18.

24. Drummond and Bulloch, *Scottish Church*, 52.

Church government, the obligations of the Solemn League and Covenant, and the limitation of Whitefield's preaching to only Secession pulpits. While this meeting was intended to bring about agreement between the Associate Presbytery and Whitefield on all of these matters, it actually produced only increasing discord and ultimately a rift between the two parties.[25] As a result of this rift, the Associate Presbytery began openly to oppose Whitefield's preaching and Whitefield began to fill any Church of Scotland pulpits that would allow him to preach. Over time, the Secession's opposition to Whitefield became sharper and Whitefield's success in Scotland became more pronounced. The fervor that Whitefield created in Scotland reached its pinnacle in the famous Cambuslang Work of 1742 in which tens of thousands of Scots travelled great distances to hear evangelistic preaching and to celebrate communion.[26] The mass conversions that accompanied this revival were of a decidedly dramatic nature, convincing the Work's supporters of God's agency in the conversions and the Work's opponents of their delusional quality. In the midst of the uproar caused by Cambuslang, the Associate Presbytery called for a day of fasting and humiliation on 4 August 1742, thus evidencing their strong opposition to the Work that was occurring.[27] In the months that followed, the zeal that had marked Cambuslang slowly faded, yet reflection upon the rupture between Whitefield and the Associate Presbytery and what that rupture implied about the state of the Secession in its earliest days, did not.

25. For more on the meeting itself, see M'Kerrow, *History of the Secession Church*, 1:203–7; Fraser, *The Life and Diary of the Reverend Ralph Erskine, A.M. of Dunfermline, one of the Founders of the Secession Church*, 333–35, hereafter, *Ralph Erskine*; *Works*, 3:68. The chief problem with most accounts of the presbytery's meeting with Whitefield is that they are largely anecdotal. As neither the final nor the scroll minutes of the Associate Presbytery record the meeting's contents, it is difficult to know precisely what transpired at that meeting. See *Minutes of the Associate Presbytery and Synod, 1741–1744*, 33, hereafter, *Minutes of AP&S 1741–1744*; *Scroll Minutes for Associate Presbytery, 17 February 1741—3 December 1741*, 164–65. Given this uncertainty, it is better to base one's analysis of the break between Erskine and Whitefield upon the course of their correspondence prior to that meeting and their words thereafter rather than upon anecdotal accounts of the meeting.

26. On the Cambuslang Work, see Fawcett, *The Cambuslang Revival*. The revival at Cambuslang actually began under the preaching of William Macculloch, the parish minister, on 18 February; Whitefield did not preach his first sermon at Cambuslang until 11 July. See M'Kerrow, *History of the Secession Church*, 1:210; Ferguson, *Scotland*, 125. However, the Seceders saw the Cambuslang Work as the continuation of the fervor that Whitefield had evoked and thus viewed Whitefield's earlier ministry in Scotland and the Cambuslang Work as causally related. See, for example, *Works*, 3:52; *AFR*, 109–10.

27. *Minutes of AP&S 1741–1744*, 99–105; Associate Presbytery, ACT OF THE ASSOCIATE PRESBYTERY ANENT A PUBLICK FAST. Hereafter, *Fast*.

Traditional Interpretation of the Controversy: Erskine versus Episcopacy

The interpretation that Secession historians have offered of the Associate Presbytery's break with Whitefield and their subsequent opposition to the Cambuslang Work traditionally has had two chief characteristics, both of which implicate Erskine in a failure to embrace other communions. First, the Secession historiography has insisted that the root of the Associate Presbytery's break with Whitefield lay in matters of Church polity. According to this interpretation, the split between the Seceders and Whitefield was due almost entirely to Whitefield's refusal to adopt presbyterianism and to recognize the obligations of the Solemn League and Covenant. Typically, this genre of analysis proceeds to point out that there were also many ministers within the Established Church who opposed Whitefield's presence in Scotland because of his episcopal ecclesiology.[28] The tendency of this interpretation is to indicate that there was opposition to Whitefield throughout Scottish presbyterianism and if the Seceders were more prominent in their opposition, it was only because their unanimity allowed them to pass presbyterial Acts against Whitefield and his work, whereas opponents of Whitefield within the Church of Scotland were intermixed with many who supported his labors and thus prevented judicial action. Secondly, the Secession historiography almost invariably retreats into offering apologies for the conduct of the Erskine brothers and the rest of the Associate Presbytery, at once blaming such "narrow" stances on the spirit of the age and stipulating that this episode shows the Erskines at their worst.[29] Combined, these two emphases portray the Associate Presbytery's break with Whitefield as a controversy based almost solely upon matters of polity that became overly, and regrettably, vitriolic.[30]

There undoubtedly is much truth in such a presentation of the controversy, particularly in its emphasis upon the sharp ecclesiological differences that existed between Erskine and Whitefield. Throughout his ministry, Erskine repeatedly had articulated a *ius divinum* view of presbytery, viewing the rejection of presbyterianism as a fundamental rebellion against Christ as King of his Church and a denial of the clear plan for church government

---

28. E.g., M'Kerrow, *History of the Secession Church*, 1:205–6, 219, 222; Fraser, *Ralph Erskine*, 339–40, 346–47.

29. E.g., MacEwen, *Erskines*, 123–24; M'Kerrow, *History of the Secession Church*, 1:206, 215. Of course, non-Secession interpreters adopt this critique, as well. See, for example, Stanley, LECTURES ON THE HISTORY OF THE CHURCH OF SCOTLAND, 75–79

30. For a compact example, see M'Kerrow, *History of the Secession Church*, 1:219.

that Christ had laid down in his Word.[31] In opposition to such a stand, Whitefield maintained that no form of church government could claim exclusive divine sanction and thus pled for toleration on matters of polity.[32] Certainly, then, the traditional interpretation of the controversy is correct to indicate the severity of the difference that existed between Erskine and Whitefield in such matters.

Towards a More Accurate Interpretation: Erskine versus the Established Church

While such an ecclesiological divide did exist, the traditional interpretation of the rupture that occurred between Erskine and Whitefield is wrong to insist that that rupture had its foundation therein. Indeed, to posit that differing ecclesiologies were the cause of Erskine's estrangement from Whitefield ignores the simple fact that Erskine knew of Whitefield's episcopal views before he ever invited him to come to Scotland. In a letter to Whitefield of June 1741, Erskine wrote

> It would be very unreasonable to propose or urge that you should incorporate as a member of our Presbytery, and wholly embark in every branch of our reformation, unless the Father of lights were clearing your way thereunto; which we pray he may enlighten in his time, so as you and we may see eye to eye.[33]

Here, Erskine makes the somewhat surprising statement that he does not expect Whitefield to "wholly embark in every branch of our reformation"; in other words, Erskine did not expect Whitefield to renounce episcopacy in favor of presbytery. Given that, in the same letter, Erskine proceeded to urge Whitefield to come to Scotland and preach the gospel, it is quite clear that while Erskine did not find Whitefield's episcopacy to be ideal, he was nonetheless willing to work with Whitefield in spite of it.

Evidently, Erskine's reasons for wanting Whitefield to come to Scotland outweighed his objections to Whitefield's views on polity. The reasons that were thus decisive for Erskine are also made clear in his letter to Whitefield of June 1741. In urging Whitefield to come preach in Scotland, Erskine made clear that he desired Whitefield's presence and ministry in Scotland for one reason—to strengthen the hand of the Associate Presbytery in their

---

31. E.g., *Works*, 1:491; 2:344, 347, 441, 457; 3:47.

32. See Drummond and Bulloch, *Scottish Church*, 52–53; Fawcett, *Cambuslang Revival*, 186; Butler, *John Wesley and George Whitefield in Scotland*, 16–17.

33. *Life*, 426.

struggle against the Established Church.³⁴ Erskine wanted Whitefield to come to Scotland to preach to Scots who could find no true preaching from Established Church pulpits and, in this preaching, Erskine was certain that Whitefield would aide the cause of the true Church in Scotland—the Secession Church—in its struggle against the false church in Scotland—the Established Church. If Whitefield was willing to come and do this, Erskine was willing to forebear even with his denial of presbyterianism and his rejection of the Solemn League and Covenant; the larger evangelistic mission of the Church was injecting a measure of catholicity into Erskine's theological system.

When one thus considers the contents of Erskine's letter to Whitefield of June 1741, the outcome of the ill-fated meeting of the Associate Presbytery on 5 August must be viewed quite differently. The break in fellowship that occurred as a result of that meeting could not have resulted from Whitefield's episcopacy, his stance on the Solemn League and Covenant, or any other such consideration. Whitefield already had made all of these stances very clear to both of the Erskine brothers and thus to the entire Presbytery, and Ebenezer Erskine had remained willing to work with Whitefield in spite of them.³⁵ The real cause of the break between Erskine and Whitefield was the disintegration of the one consideration that had made Erskine willing to work with Whitefield in spite of their variance in so many other areas. The controversy that followed the 5 August meeting was the result of Whitefield's refusal to confine himself to Secession pulpits.³⁶ At that meeting of the Associate Presbytery, Whitefield had declared that he was willing to preach in any pulpit that was opened to him, even those of the Church of Scotland.³⁷ For Erskine, such a stance was unacceptable. As he had told Whitefield in his June 1741 letter, the Established Church had scattered and offended God's flock, and if Whitefield were to come and preach in the pulpits of that Church, he would only help the cause of a body that was working to destroy the cause of truth in Scotland. Based upon Whitefield's refusal to renounce such cooperation, Erskine discontinued all fellowship with Whitefield and changed from Whitefield's host to his antagonist. The sole deciding factor in Erskine's opposition to Whitefield was Erskine's opposition to the Established Church. In the controversy that followed, Erskine

34. See *Life*, 425.

35. For an account of the extensive, two-year-long correspondence that occurred between Whitefield and several members of the Associate Presbytery up until the 5 August Presbytery meeting, see Fraser, *Ralph Erskine*, 286–329.

36. Rainy approaches this position, yet retains elements of the traditional interpretation. See Rainy, *Three Lectures*, 137–41.

37. See, for example, Drummond and Bulloch, *Scottish Church*, 52–53.

was certain to cite all of Whitefield's errors, both in his theology and in his methodology, but the fact remains that none of these objections had been substantial enough in Erskine's consideration to preclude cooperation with Whitefield if he had consented to preach only in Secession pulpits.

That Erskine's opposition to Whitefield resulted from his opposition to the Established Church is clear when one considers Erskine's sermonic denunciations of Whitefield's ministrations and the Cambuslang Work that they spawned. In a sermon preached in December 1743, Erskine used some of his most condemnatory language in reference to Cambuslang, speaking of the Work there as an "awful delusion" and a "delusive influence."[38] Continuing to speak of the spirit that marked Cambuslang, Erskine declared his judgment

> that instead of being a sprit of truth and love, it is a spirit of malignancy and enmity against the truth, and covenanted cause of God in this land, and that it inspires the convicts and subjects of it with an inveterate prejudice against those who bear up the testimony of Jesus, and do not strike sail unto the corrupt established church, and the course of defection she is carrying on in opposition to solemn covenants for reformation.[39]

In seeking to prove that Cambuslang was a work of delusion, Erskine pointed simply to the fact that it created and exacerbated both enmity against the Secession and affinity with the Established Church. Erskine was opposed to Whitefield's ministry, and to the embodiment of that ministry at Cambuslang, because it led people to reject the Secession and embrace the Church of Scotland.[40] Animating Erskine's opposition to Whitefield was his opposition to the Established Church.

The Erskinite priority upon opposition to the Established Church is also seen in the Associate Presbytery's *Act of the Associate Presbytery anent a Publick Fast*, uniformly portrayed as representing the depths of the Presbytery's hostility to Whitefield.[41] Despite such a characterization, the Act

---

38. *Works*, 3:68.

39. Ibid., 3:68–69.

40. See also ibid., 3:91. There, in a later sermon, the animating force of Cambuslang is "a subtle devil" because it attached to "judicatories that deny the obligation of solemn covenants, and at the same time inspire men with enmity against a testimony for covenanted reformation, and all that own it."

41. Currie, *A NEW TESTIMONY UNTO, AND FURTHER VINDICATION OF THE Extraordinary Work of GOD at* Cambuslang, Kilsyth, *and other Places in the West of* Scotland, 10. Hereafter, *Testimony*. See also MacEwen, *Erskines*, 121–22; Drummond and Bulloch, *Scottish Church*, 55–56; M'Kerrow, *Scottish Church*, 1:215; Mitchell, "Ebenezer Erskine," 183.

itself shows that the central concern of the Presbytery was not the ministry of Whitefield, either at Cambuslang or otherwise, but rather the doctrinal defection of the Established Church.[42] While Erskine and his brethren undeniably take a negative view of Whitefield and his ministry, those evils are seen, most fundamentally, not as sins, but rather as judgments upon the Established Church's previous sins of rejecting the Seceders' testimony, deposing the Associate Presbytery, and subjecting the Scottish people to preaching devoid of gospel truth.[43] In Whitefield, God was giving the Established Church "an open Discovery of their Apostasy from him."[44] Indeed, even when Whitefield's sins are addressed, they are used not to condemn Whitefield, but to incriminate the Established Church that was countenancing the ministry of a man who believed and taught such errors.[45] The foundation of the Associate Presbytery's opposition to Whitefield and the Cambuslang Work, which was epitomized in their call for a day of fasting and humiliation, was their opposition to the sin of the Established Church.

Allies Within the Established Church?

If the tension that existed between the Seceders and the Church of Scotland was the cause of Erskine's opposition to Whitefield, the literature produced over the course of the controversy makes it clear that a large measure of the support that Whitefield received from the Established Church sprang from the same source. By the early 1740s, the ministers of the Associate Presbytery, with their advocacy of *Marrow* doctrine, their opposition to patronage, and their recognized gifts for preaching, had become known throughout Scotland as the evangelical face of the Kirk.[46] In welcoming Whitefield to their pulpits and extolling the successes of his ministry from those pulpits, many within the Established Church sought to counteract this image and to reassert the Assembly's evangelical identity. In the words of one minister within the Assembly who opposed Whitefield's presence in Scotland, many Church of Scotland ministers welcomed Whitefield purely out of a desire to "break the Seceders."[47] If Whitefield would come into Established Church

42. See Associate Presbytery, *Fast*, 1–4.
43. See ibid., 4. Elsewhere, the Associate Presbytery refers to Whitefield as "an Instrument of the Lord's Wrath unto this Generation." *AFR*, 123.
44. Associate Presbytery, *Fast*, 4.
45. See ibid., 4–5. See also *Works*, 3:68–69.
46. See, for example, MacEwen, *Erskines*, 123–24.
47. Bisset, *A LETTER TO A Gentleman in* Edinburgh, *CONTAINING REMARKS Upon a late* APOLOGY *for the Presbyterians in Scotland, who keep Communion in the*

pulpits and win many converts, he would show that the Associate Presbytery did not have a monopoly on conversions and evangelical zeal and perhaps the Secession would disappear. In short, many Church of Scotland ministers sought to use the success of Whitefield's evangelistic tour of Scotland in 1741 and of the Cambuslang Work in 1742 as propaganda against the Secession Church.[48]

The polemical use of Whitefield's success is seen perhaps most strikingly in the personal journal of the conversions at Cambuslang that was kept by William Macculloch, the parish minister of Cambuslang at the time of the Work. In an effort to chronicle the fruits of the revival, Macculloch recounted the conversion narratives and experiences of one hundred and six converts of Cambuslang in two large volumes. In the first of these two volumes, there is also the record of a purported dialogue between two supporters of Cambuslang and Ebenezer Erskine and James Fisher of the Associate Presbytery.[49] Macculloch's record claims that the interview was the result of the two Cambuslang supporters travelling to see the two Secession ministers to question them about their public opposition to the Cambuslang Work. In particular, the two Cambuslang supporters desire to discourse with the Seceders about "that wherein the life of Religion consists."[50] However, the dialogue that is recorded quickly shows itself to be little more than an attack upon Erskine and Fisher personally and the entire Secession cause generally. When the conversation turns to the substance of religion, which the Seceders' interlocutors claimed was the topic that they most wanted to discuss, the record of the conversation is blank, claiming only that the words spoken by the Seceders "are not distinctly remembered."[51] In one instance, such a conspicuous omission of what was supposed to be the substance of the interview is followed immediately by a sustained monologue by one of the interlocutors in which the foundation and the principles of the Secession Church are attacked and posited to be contrary to Scripture.[52] Eventually, the recorded interview draws to a close with the two interlocutors proposing to Erskine and Fisher that they come back into the Established Church

---

Ordinances of the Gospel, with Mr. George Whitefield, a PRIEST of the Church of England, 5.

48. E.g. Currie, *Testimony*. Erskine was aware of this polemical use of conversions. See, for example, *Works*, 3:53–54, 68–69; Associate Presbytery, *Fast*, 4–5.

49. See Macculloch, *Examinations of persons Under Spiritual Concern at Cambuslang, during the Revival, in 17-41-42*, 1:154–68. The authenticity of this account is dubious. See *Works*, 3:56.

50. Macculloch, *Examinations*, 1:157.

51. Ibid., 1:163. Similarly, see ibid., 1:159, 162–63.

52. See ibid., 1:163–64.

and, from that position, work for the good of Christ's Church in Scotland.[53] That such a clear polemic against the Secession Church and her ministers is found in the heart of what purports to be an account of the conversions of men and women at Cambuslang is very instructive. Without doubt, Macculloch was a devoted minister who long had desired to see precisely the sort of revival that came under Whitefield and his influence.[54] However, even in Macculloch's presentation of the fruits of the Cambuslang Work, an attack upon Erskine and the other Secession ministers is evident. While a sincere evangelical desire to see revival in Scotland certainly animated a good deal of the support that Whitefield received from many quarters within the Church of Scotland, so too did a more polemical desire to "break the Seceders."

The picture that emerges from these considerations is one of overriding, elemental animus between the Associate Presbytery and the Church of Scotland. However, it is precisely this dissension that the traditional Erskine historiography tends to obscure, particularly with its suggestion of a polity-driven, pan-presbyterian opposition to Whitefield that, in drawing both the Associate Presbytery and certain members of the Established Church under the same banner, offered the possibility of a degree of reconciliation between those two groups in the first few years after the Seceders' deposition.[55] When one considers the writings that were issued during the controversy, it is evident that such a united opposition to Whitefield simply did not exist. As has been seen, Erskine was opposed to Whitefield's Scottish ministrations because they were done in association with the Established Church; thus, opposition to Whitefield that came from within the Established Church actually partook of the same guilt with Whitefield in Erskine's estimation, for that opposition was affiliated with the General Assembly. Furthermore, even those ministers within the Established Church who opposed Whitefield remained decidedly opposed to Erskine and the other Seceders. Even when such ministers found freedom to commend the Seceders' opposition to Whitefield, mild passages of praise were mixed with charges that the Seceders were inexcusable for their secession from the Established Church and were hypocritical for first inviting Whitefield to Scotland and then blaming the General Assembly for entertaining him.[56] While Erskine and

53. Ibid., 1:168.

54. Virtually without exception, the secondary literature speaks very favorably of Macculloch, both as a man and as a minister. See, for example, M'Kerrow, *Scottish Church*, 1:209–10.

55. For an interesting variation on this interpretation, see Rainy, *Three Lectures*, 140–41.

56. See, for example, Bisset, *A Letter*, 5–9.

his brethren were becoming increasingly convinced of the apostasy of all wings of the Established Church, the members of the Assembly, both those who supported Whitefield and those who opposed him, were becoming increasingly convinced that the Seceders were narrow-minded men whose secession had shown them to be enemies of the Church.[57] Quite simply, neither the Seceders nor Whitefield's opponents within the Established Church perceived the unified opposition to Whitefield that later Secession historians have imagined.

The Whitefield Controversy: A Positive Trajectory on an Uneven Road

When one realizes the true basis of Erskine's dispute with Whitefield, it becomes clear that that affair presents a complicated, yet optimistic, picture of Erskine's ability to embrace Christians of other communions within his Covenantal Revolution Church. Most vitally, in the earliest stages of his communication with Whitefield, Erskine demonstrated an ability to prioritize different areas of theological concern and, as long as there was agreement on the more important doctrines, to allow a degree of latitude on those of secondary importance. The relevance of this doctrinal prioritization to Erskine's dealings with Whitefield is seen in the introduction to the Associate Presbytery's *Act Concerning the Doctrine of Grace*, which Erskine co-authored with Alexander Moncrieff in 1742. In that introduction, as Erskine and Moncrieff chronicle the varying attacks that have been made against the doctrines of grace through the generations, it becomes apparent that Erskine's opposition to episcopacy was founded upon the general episcopalian embrace of Arminian soteriology.[58] Erskine's secondary opposition to episcopacy grew out of his primary opposition to Arminianism. In Whitefield, however, Erskine had met an embodied anomaly, for Whitefield was an avowed Calvinistic episcopalian and thus held a soteriology that was essentially synonymous with Erskine's. As a result, Erskine was able to accept Whitefield because he was a Calvinist and was not forced to reject him because he was an episcopalian; Whitefield's Calvinist soteriology had removed the central problem with his episcopacy. Indeed, it is significant that such doctrinal prioritization is evident in the *Act Concerning the Doctrine*

---

57. For further instances of Erskine's assessment to this effect, see *Works*, 3:41, 45, 60–61. Of course, Erskine and his fellow Seceders did believe that there were still sincere Christians among the laity of the Church of Scotland. See Associate Presbytery, *Fast*, 4–5.

58. See *ADG*, vi–vii, x. Similarly, see *AFR*, 100.

of Grace, a document self-consciously modelled as a defense of *Marrow* doctrine. Through the experience of the *Marrow* controversy and the lingering doctrinal suspicion that resulted from it, Erskine had spent much time striving to defend his evangelical federalism and thus soteriological matters had assumed a decided pre-eminence in his theological system. Years of attention and a concern to defend his doctrine had led Erskine to see all things through the lens of soteriology and soteriological impact; the foundation gradually had been established to cooperate with men of differing opinions in some areas as long as the core of "*Marrow* doctrine" was held.

While Erskine's willingness to prioritize doctrinal commitments offered promise for his ability to interact with other communions, his controversy with Whitefield also highlighted several problems in this same area. First, the growing catholicity that Erskine manifested was a time-sensitive catholicity. When Erskine spoke of his willingness to labor alongside Whitefield and his episcopalian views, he always made it clear that he would undertake such labor while Whitefield awaited light on matters of polity. As Erskine's cooperation envisioned not only joint gospel labor, but also Whitefield's own eventual conversion to the presbyterian fold, one is left to wonder how long Erskine would have continued in such cooperation if Whitefield persisted in his episcopalian sentiments. If Whitefield had agreed to absent himself from Church of Scotland pulpits, yet had remained an episcopalian throughout his life, would Erskine have been willing to work with him in 1750? The answer is far from certain. When projected onto Scotland generally, one is left to wonder if Erskine's budding catholicity would have facilitated long-term fellowship with other communions who, rather than moving toward presbytery, were entrenched by toleration.

Even more problematic than Erskine's time-bound catholicity was his behavior once the prospects of cooperation with Whitefield had disintegrated. As indicated previously, Erskine's commitment to the rigors of Covenanting holiness meant that, once Whitefield had shown himself a friend to the "false church" of the General Assembly, Erskine joined the other Seceders in offering a detailed denunciation of every error that the evangelist had committed; in Erskine's case, such a denunciation extended even to questioning the legitimacy of Whitefield's conversion.[59] In this detailed criticism of Whitefield, Erskine eviscerated all of the legitimate movement that he had made toward a prioritized catholicity. While Erskine was willing to cover over many things personally, he demanded that all be denounced publicly and, in so doing, Erskine failed to impart to others the catholicity that he was developing personally. Although the implications of Erskine's

---

59. See *Works*, 3:43, 52, 60, 68.

evangelical federalism were providing the foundations for greater catholicity, his commitment to certain practices of the Covenanting heritage were undercutting those same foundations. While the image of Erskine as a rigid man incapable of any compromise that emerges from his controversy with Whitefield is both regrettable and inaccurate, it is an image for which Erskine himself must bear much of the blame.

Lying behind these areas of concern is perhaps the central complication for Erskine's ability to embrace other communions—his abiding animus with the Church of Scotland. As has been seen, Erskine's controversy with Whitefield was an extension of his estrangement from the Established Church and, as that controversy shows, after Erskine's formal break with the Assembly in the Seceders' *Declinature*, Erskine entertained no hopes for reunion with the church judicatories. In this, Erskine categorically rejected communion with many Kirk ministers whose theological commitments and views were much more amenable to his than were Whitefield's. Erskine was most unwilling to entertain communion with those men with whom that communion ought to have been most obvious, and the implications of this, both for Erskine's ability to interact with other communions and for the spirit that he helped to instil in the Secession Church, cannot be overlooked. While the trauma of the Secession Crisis and Erskine's legitimate sense that he had been wronged in that process explain his alienation from the Kirk, they cannot justify his anathematizing otherwise like-minded men because of their affiliation with the Established Church.[60] Practically speaking, such a stance would provoke a future of unending "Whitefield controversies"; communion with other bodies would always be contingent upon their rejection of the Established Church and, if that rejection were not forthcoming, any progress toward catholicity would be obscured.

Erskine's estrangement from the Assembly, then, has a tortured, multi-faceted function in the Whitefield controversy. In the first instance, that estrangement drove Erskine to a catholic willingness to embrace the episcopalian Whitefield in joint labor; outwith the specific ecclesiological situation in which Erskine found himself, it is doubtful he would have evidenced the willingness to work with Whitefield that he did. In the second instance, however, that estrangement threatened the catholic progress that Erskine had made. Indeed, as those within the Assembly who cooperated with Whitefield did so under the pretense of "Catholic love and communion," Erskine developed a deep skepticism about the very principle of doctrinal prioritization that had driven him to more catholic views of the

---

60. So Carson, "Doctrine of the Church," 345.

Church.[61] Taken in tandem, these dual effects of Erskine's estrangement from the Established Church involved him in a measure of hypocrisy, viewing the Established Church's willingness to countenance Whitefield's errors as evidence of her assumed defection even though, had Whitefield agreed to confine himself to Secession pulpits, Erskine would have been willing to countenance precisely the same errors himself.

As viewed through the paradigm of his controversy with Whitefield, Erskine's conception of a Covenantal Revolution Church required much progress in order to be able to embrace other communions, yet the comprehensive picture that emerges is optimistic. In his initial interaction with Whitefield, Erskine had shown an ability for doctrinal prioritization, a central component of any program of catholicity. While there was progress to be made, the trajectory of Erskine's thought was in the direction of that progress. As the Whitefield controversy made clear, the course that lay ahead was being navigated by Erskine's consistent theological commitments rather than by personal predilections that could vacillate from the evangelical warmth of Erskine's 1741 letter to Whitefield to the acerbity of Erskine's denunciations of his former correspondent only a few years later.

INTERACTION WITH THE CIVIL MAGISTRATE

If the Secession Church was, indeed, the realization of a Covenantal Revolution Church in post-Union Scotland, another of the most pressing issues to be confronted by that Church would be the question of how it would interact with the civil magistrate. Pointedly, how would a Covenantal Revolution Church interact with an uncovenanted civil magistrate? How could the Associate Presbytery simultaneously affirm the Covenants and avoid sectarian withdrawal within Hanoverian Scotland? To construct Erskine's position on such a matter, one must examine the complex of issues and controversies that arose surrounding the Associate Presbytery's infamous renewal of Scotland's Covenants, both National and Solemn League, in 1743. While the singularity of the Associate Presbytery's Covenant renewal easily is distorted into a picture of sectarianism and anachronism, a careful examination reveals an operative modified Covenantalism that produced a viability for Erskine's Covenantal Revolution Church.[62] By defining the Covenants evangelically and insisting upon the popular constitution of the civil magistrate, Erskine's modified Covenantal system proved capable of re-

61. *Works*, 3:52–54.

62. For examples of such dismissive interpretations, see Ferguson, *Scotland*, 125–26; MacEwen, *Erskines*, 113; T. F. Torrance, *Theology*, 247.

taining a Covenantal foundation, yet purposefully engaging the post-Union British State.

The Renewal of Scotland's Covenants

Erskine's articulation of his modified Covenantal views in the 1740s emerged in a very specific context. Following the Secession Crisis, Erskine quickly had begun working to see the Associate Presbytery formally renew Scotland's Covenants.[63] While the Presbytery was agreed that God had precipitated the Secession Crisis and led them out of the General Assembly specifically for the purpose of renewing the Covenants in opposition to decades of Covenant defection, deciding upon how that Covenant renewal was to transpire proved contentious.[64] After consideration, the Presbytery decided that, while they would reassert the whole of the Solemn League and Covenant, they would reassert only one-third of the 1638 National Covenant.[65] Omitting both the list of Parliamentary Acts establishing Protestantism and the Bond from the 1638 Covenant, the Presbytery retained only the explicitly-doctrinal first section of that earlier Covenant, which was itself a recapitulation of the King's Confession of 1580–1581.[66] To the Covenants in this form, the Associate Presbytery added their own Bond, by which renewal was made, and an acknowledgment of sins.[67]

As the Presbytery recently had been involved in a judicial process that saw them excommunicate one of their number for his support of a representation calling for armed insurrection against the government, the draft acknowledgement of sins submitted to the Presbytery for consideration

---

63. In 1741, Erskine oversaw the publication of a collection of sermons, speeches, and other documents from the seventeenth century addressing the obligations of the Covenants with the explicit hope that such a publication would serve as a catalyst for Covenant renewal. To this collection, Erskine added a prefatory letter. See *A COLLECTION Of several REMARKABLE and VALUABLE SERMONS, Speeches and Exhortations*, vi-vii. Hereafter, *Collection*. This important work receives only two peripheral references in the secondary literature and is never clearly cited. See *Life*, 434; United Associate Synod, "Historical Account of the Secession," 68. Hereafter, *Christian Monitor*.

64. For the importance of Covenant renewal to the Seceders' self-identity, see *Works*, 3:61–63, 71; *Collection*, v, viii; *AFR*, 81, 93, 115; *A&D*, 44, 46; *Christian Monitor*, 67–68. Erskine judged that this commitment to the Covenants marked the Associate Presbytery, rather than the Assembly, as the present embodiment of the historic Church of Scotland. See, for example, *Works*, 3:80; *Contendings*, 79.

65. For the text of both Covenants as reasserted by the Presbytery, see *AFR*, 84–90.

66. For the context of the King's Confession, see Lumsden, *The Covenants of Scotland*, 105–15; Torrance, *Theology*, 59–60.

67. For the text of the Bond, see *AFR*, 115–18. See also *Christian Monitor*, 68.

contained a denunciation of the refusal to render obedience to civil magistrates who did not meet certain religious qualifications.[68] Immediately, Thomas Nairn, minister at Linktoun, objected to the implicit position that Christians were obligated to render obedience to all lawful commands of the present civil magistrate. As the disagreement between Nairn and the Presbytery deepened, he further alleged that by excising the list of Parliamentary Acts and the Bond from the 1638 National Covenant, the Associate Presbytery was omitting the Covenants' civil components and, therefore, was swearing new and different Covenants rather than Scotland's historic Covenants.[69] Despite repeated attempts at reconciliation, Nairn and the Presbytery remained at odds and finally Nairn seceded from the Associate Presbytery, eventually finding his way to the Macmillanite communion.[70]

In order to clarify the issues that had been raised by Nairn's intricate objections, the Presbytery published their answers to Nairn's similarly-published reasons of dissent and secession, to which answers the Presbytery added a *Declaration Concerning the Present Civil Magistrate* drafted and published specifically to articulate the Presbytery's position concerning the magistrate in light of the controversy with Nairn.[71] Finally, on 28 December

---

68. *A&D*, iv, 17–19. The Seceders also denounced the use of offensive arms to propagate the gospel, which they carefully distinguished from the seventeenth-century Covenanters' use of defensive arms for self-defense. *A&D*, 54–55, 93–94. The Covenanting movement already had made the same distinction between offensive and defensive arms. See, for example, Renwick and Shields, *Informatory Vindication*, 20.

69. See *A&D*, 25–27. Interestingly, Nairn's position is used in a later attempt to rehabilitate the Seceders to nineteenth-century sensibilities. See *Christian Monitor*, 67–68, 71–76.

70. Due to other considerations, the paragraph that had caused Nairn's objection was eventually excised from the Confession of Sins, made into a separate Act, and passed unanimously. For a copy of the Presbytery's unanimously-passed Act, see Appendix IV. It was Nairn's joining with the long-isolated John Macmillan that allowed for the formation of the Reformed Presbytery in 1743. However, in 1745, Nairn seceded from the Reformed Presbytery and, in 1751, he formally re-entered the Established Church. See *Life*, 433–34; M'Kerrow, 1:241; Needham, "Thomas Nairn," 618.

71. The entire document was approved on 29 September 1743. See *A&D*, vi–viii; *Minutes of AP and AS from 1741*, 773. In the Seceders' estimation, their *Declaration* was the substance of their civil testimony, thus constituting the counterpart to their ecclesiastical testimony contained in earlier documents such as the *ADT* and the *TD*. See *A&D*, 44–45. Given the importance of this document, it is surprisingly obscure in the secondary literature, scarcely being mentioned and never receiving even the most superficial analysis. See, for example, *Life*, 432–37; MacEwen, *Erskines*, 112–14. In both, the Seceders' Covenant renewal is treated without any reference being made to the *Declaration*.

For Nairn's position, see Nairn, *A SHORT ACCOUNT Of Mr. THOMAS NAIRN*. In the Associate Presbytery's response, they reproduce *verbatim* the relevant portions of Nairn's work and thus, for ease of reference, most subsequent citations will be to the

1743, the Associate Presbytery solemnly renewed the Covenants at a service in Stirling.[72] On 14 February 1744, the Presbytery approved an Act making the renewal of the Covenants, by means of the Presbytery's Bond, a term of both ministerial and Christian communion within the Secession Church.[73] It was in the course of this protracted process that Erskine's view of a Covenantally-delineated Church alongside a popularly-constituted magistracy was clarified.

The Identity of the Covenants

In three important respects, Erskine's view of Scotland's Covenants and their appropriate role in the post-Union world was epitomized in 1744, when Covenant renewal was made a term of ministerial and Christian communion within the Secession Church.[74] First, Erskine viewed the Covenants as codifications of biblical truth and obligations; a view dating to the earliest days of his ministry. Even more precisely, as the Covenants were Scotland's Covenants, they represented the height that biblical faith had attained in that nation; namely, Erskine conceived of the Covenants as a comprehensive, definitive confession of Westminster presbyterian faith as that tradition had been embodied in the official standards of the Scottish Kirk.[75] Second, as distillations of presbyterian doctrine, the Covenants required to

---

Presbytery's work. For a friendly secondary treatment of Nairn's objections, see *Christian Monitor*, 72–76.

72. See M'Kerrow, *Scottish Church*, 1:244–48.

73. The text of the Act is printed in *AFR*, 118–19. Due to the upheaval that soon erupted within the Secession Church over the Burgess Oath controversy, the actual implementation of Covenant renewal as a term of Christian communion was extremely sporadic. Much more indicative of the actual desires of the Presbytery was the rigorous enforcement of Covenant renewal as a term of ministerial communion. See M'Kerrow, *Scottish Church*, 1:249; *Life*, 434.

74. This action modifies one of Carson's most pervasive critiques of the Seceders' ecclesiology. Throughout his work, Carson alleges that the Seceders equated the Scottish nation with the church visible because of Scotland's *national* Covenant obligations; an equation productive of much error and confusion. See, for example, Carson, "Doctrine of the Church," 9, 65, 148–61, 180–83. While Erskine and his brethren did judge that all Scots rested under an obligation to renew the Covenants, their Act 1744 explicitly identifies Covenant *subscription*, rather than Covenantal *obligation*, as constituting the church visible. It was only when an individual personally renewed the Covenants that he entered the communion of the church visible; an act of renewal that Erskine insisted must be voluntary. See Glas, *Remarks*, 11.

75. *Works*, 3:68; M'Kerrow, *Scottish Church*, 1:248–49; Carson, "Doctrine of the Church," 239.

be experientially appropriated—or, renewed—by individual Scots. By personally swearing the Covenants' articulation of presbyterian doctrine, one would

> return to the Lord, by taking hold of his *Covenant of Grace*, which stands fast with Christ our glorious New Covenant-Head; and, in the Faith of this his Covenant, and the Grace and Strength therein promised, casting away all our Transgressions and Idols, devoting ourselves unto the Lord in a *Covenant of Duty*, and swearing unto him . . . .[76]

As the Covenants were symbols of Scottish Westminster faith, personal renewal of them was synonymous with the divinely-mandated profession of faith in Christ that, in the economy of the Covenant of Grace, brought duty in the wake of privilege.[77] Thirdly, while the Covenants clearly were of foundational importance for the Church, they did not directly impinge upon matters pertaining to the magistracy; a fact evidenced by the Seceders' Bond. While in 1638, both ecclesiastical and civil entities had adhered to the Covenants and thus the 1638 Bond had been able to speak to overtly civil concerns, only the Church was affirming the Covenants in 1743 and thus the Bond was limited to those matters over which the Church had authority.[78] If the Covenants were to impact the magistracy, that impact would come only indirectly as reformation spread from individual Christians to the society that they inhabited.[79] Simply stated, the Covenants were a distillation of the

76. *AFR*, 93. Witsius speaks of the Sinaitic Covenant as a "covenant of sincere piety" in a manner that closely mirrors Erskine's "covenant of duty." See Witsius, 2:186. For more on the connection between the Seceders' Covenant renewal and the Covenant of Grace, see *AFR*, 115–16; *Minutes of AP and AS from 1741*, 597, 649; *Works*, 3:71, 90; *AFR*, 93–95. Also, note the Presbytery's requirement that *ADG* be passed, purging the doctrines of grace of accumulated defection, before *AFR* could be undertaken and their subsequent joint issuance of both Acts. See *Minutes of AP and AS from 1741*, 649–50; *A&D*, iii; M'Kerrow, *Scottish Church*, 1:238; both the Ruddimans and the Duncan 1744 joint publications of both Acts.

77. Erskine equated the duty of covenanting with the public profession of Christ required in Romans 10:10. See *Works*, 3:90. See also *Works*, 3:143; *Collection*, vii; *AFR*, 93–95, 115–16; *Contendings*, 79. In this, the call for national Covenant renewal was not a call for men to act as if they were in the Covenant of Grace, but rather a call for them to enter the Covenant of Grace. See Carson, "Doctrine of the Church," 180–83.

78. *A&D*, 39, 41. On the connection between doctrinal truth and civil application in the Covenanting tradition, see T. F. Torrance, *Theology*, 152; Greaves, "John Knox and the Covenant Tradition," 23–32; Burrell, "The Covenant Idea as a Revolutionary Symbol," especially pages 338, 342–43, 348.

79. See *A&D*, 49, 96; *Works*, 3:328; *AFR*, 81. The inexorable movement of Covenanted Reformation from Church to State can also be detected in Erskine's arrangement of the twenty-eight entries in *Collection*. See *Collection*, x–xii. Erskine envisioned

truth around which the Church gathered and by which it was defined.[80] In a Scotland whose materialism was being fed by economic expansion, whose intellect had been infiltrated by a newly-indigenous rationalism, and whose insipid latitudinarianism had been unmasked by the reception afforded to Whitefield, the personal appropriation of these confessional Covenants was a term of communion befitting a true Church.[81]

The Foundation of the Civil Magistrate

Erskine's ability to conceive of the Covenants as Kirk-delineating documents without necessitating an infringement upon the civil magistrate rested upon his modified Covenantalism's categorical distinction between the Church and the magistracy. In Erskine's opinion, while the Church was a spiritual kingdom graciously constituted by Christ's mediatorial work, the magistracy was a physical kingdom naturally constituted by God's essential law. In this understanding of a naturally-constituted civil magistrate, Erskine and his fellow Seceders were indebted to Samuel Rutherford's refinement of Scottish political theory. By melding John Knox's recourse to almost exclusively biblical norms with George Buchanan's appeal to the dictates of natural reason, Rutherford had created a political philosophy that mediated the divine ordination of, and purposes for, government through the

---

this national reformation then spreading to England and Ireland. See *Works*, 3:61–63; *AFR*, 117.

80. *A&D*, 16.

81. See *Works*, 3:52–54, 68–69; *AFR*, 108–10, 118. Erskine's intentional use of Covenant renewal as a weapon against a proto-ecumenism is neglected by most commentators, who imply that the resulting hindrance to ecumenical effort was an unintended consequence of the Act 1744. See, for example, *Life*, 435–36; M'Kerrow, *Scottish Church*, 1:252–54; MacEwen, *Erskines*, 113; T. F. Torrance, *Theology*, 247; Ferguson, *Scotland*, 125–26. Implicit in this interpretation is the supposition of a pan-presbyterian evangelical "party" whose potential for reunion was dampened by the Act. See, for example, *Life*, 449.

The Secession always had required, as a term of ministerial communion, both a subscription of the Westminster Standards that exceeded the rigor even of the Formula 1711 and an adherence to Secession documents considered to be contemporary applications of that Westminsterian truth. See Erskine to Grange February 1734, 1; Gib, *Display*, 1:ix, xi. See also *Christian Monitor*, 65; Hamilton, *Erosion*, 9–10; McCrie, *Statement of the Difference Between the Profession of the Reformed Church in Scotland, as Adopted by Seceders, and the Profession Contained in the New Testimony and Other Acts, Lately Adopted by the General Associate Synod*, 39–48. In this, the first generation of Seceders pre-dated the trend noticed in Fergusson, "The Confession in the Life of the Church of Scotland," 201–3.

similarly divine rights of the populace.[82] In Erskine and his fellow Seceders, this amalgam of divine purpose and popular will is starkly evident in their assertion that

> the *Remainder* of natural Light, in the moral Dictates of right Reason, is the *natural* and *eternal Law of God*. Now, this *Divine Law*, not only endues Men, in their present Estate, with a *natural Inclination* to Civil Society and Government, but it prescribes unto them an *indispensable Necessity* of erecting and maintaining the same in some Form, as a *moral Duty*, the Obligation and *Benefit* whereof no Wickedness in them can *loose* or *forfeit*. And, therefore, *wherever* they voluntarily constitute or consent unto *any* Form of Civil Government, under the Rule of *any* particular Persons, whatever Sin be in the *Circumstances* of this their Deed, with respect to the *Government* or *Governors* which they constitute or consent unto; yet the *Deed itself*, or the *Substance* of the Deed, is *always* in Consequence of, and agreeable *to God's Law*; wherefore, their Governors, *as such* and in the *Substance* of the Matter, are *ordained of God*, according to that Law; and this is that *Divine Ordination* which the Apostle ascribes to *all* Magistrates, *as such*, and, particularly, unto *these* of his Day in the *Roman* Empire; while, whatever distinguishing *Qualifications* or *Approbation* God may bestow upon *some*, yet *no* Civil Magistrates in the World can have any other *Sort* of *Divine Ordination*.[83]

In popularly choosing a magistrate, the nation actualized the divine compulsion toward government; popular consent was the defining essence of the divinely-mandated magistracy.[84]

This primacy of popular consent had many important implications, one of which was the distinction between divine ordination and divine

---

82. See Fergusson, "Church," 117–18; G. D. Henderson, "Idea of Covenant," 9–10. See also, for example, Buchanan, *De Jure Regni apud Scotus*, 242–43. Hereafter, *De Jure*. For a succinct view of Rutherford's amalgam, see Samuel Rutherford, *LEX REX*, 9. There, Rutherford discusses how God's unilateral choice of David to assume the throne of Israel is not actualized until David is chosen by the people.

83. *A&D*, 70.

84. See especially *A&D*, 54. While the Presbytery did recognize a distinction between a *"Providential Dispensation"* and a *"preceptive Institution,"* they deemed that distinction inapplicable to the question of the civil magistrate. *A&D*, 70. The magistrate who ruled with the consent of the governed ruled not only in accordance with providence, but also in accordance with God's law, and thus "all *providential* Magistrates are also *perceptive*." *A&D*, 87. See *A&D*, 87–88. The Seceders, however, did not proceed to the extreme that Carson supposes. See Carson, "Doctrine of the Church," 173.

approbation that it introduced.[85] When Erskine and his brethren applied the principle of the divine ordination being mediated through popular consent to their present situation, they were led to insist that no Scriptural or Covenantal qualifications impinged upon magisterial legitimacy. While there were certain Scriptural or Covenantal qualities that were desirable in a magistrate and that would win the divine approbation, the absence of those qualities could divest the magistrate of the divine ordination only as a function of the popular will.[86] If religious considerations turned the people, as a political body, against a particular magistrate, then they would be justified in rescinding their contractual agreement with him.[87] However, if the political nation supported a religiously-unqualified magistrate, individuals had no right to refuse his authority, for it was not those religious qualities that were essential to the magistrate's legitimacy, but only the people's acceptance of his religious credentials.[88] This position is given its sharpest point in the Presbytery's assertion, in reference to the fact that God called his people in the Old Testament to be obedient even to wicked kings in lawful commands, that

> while the *Primores Regni*, and *better Part* of the Nation, acknowledged *such* as *their* Kings, *consenting* to their regal Authority; the *Office* and *Authority* of these Kings did, *therefore*, still continue *valid*, so as the *particular Subjects* were bound in Conscience to *submit* unto, and *obey* their *lawful* Commands; because that *Civil Authority*, having its *Rise*, in the *Consent* of the *People* according to the *indispensible Law of Nature*, it could not be *subverted* by their *Defection* and *Apostasy*, or by their Kings, in Consequence thereof, *wanting* scriptural Qualifications.[89]

According to Erskine and his fellow presbyters, popular consent constitutes the magistrate even if he lacks Scriptural qualifications and even if the consenting majority is apostate.[90] Without final regard to any other consideration, it was the consent of the governed that made a man a right magistrate.[91]

---

85. Similarly, see *A&D*, 80.

86. See *A&D*, 5, 16, 46, 55, 79–80.

87. *A&D*, 17.

88. *A&D*, 16–17. The Seceders cautioned that if legitimating religious qualifications were pushed too far in the present, sinful world, it would terminate in anarchy. See *A&D*, 80.

89. *A&D*, 58.

90. *A&D*, 89.

91. *A&D*, 70, 74–77, 87, 91–92.

A Divergence from the Covenanting Past?

In this rejection of religious qualifications for the magistrate, Erskine's view appears to differ from the developed Covenanting tradition. Indeed, Nairn was of such an opinion, charging that Scotland's Covenants had made Covenantal qualifications essential to the magistracy.[92] However, the body of Covenanting political theory is not so monochromatic. In the National Covenant of 1638, Scotland saw the embodiment of Knox's ideal that the magistrate of a reformed land should be held to more rigorous standards than the magistrates of heathen nations.[93] However, neither Knox nor the Second Reformation generation explicitly gave these more stringent standards legitimating authority independent of being criteria of popular consent.[94] Indeed, Rutherford explicitly held that popular consent alone could invest a magistrate with the divinely-ordained magisterial office.[95] Whatever their role in determining the desirability of a magistrate might be, religious considerations were irrelevant to the foundation of magistracy. The generation of the Second Reformation, then, judged that even Covenanted Scotland came under the prescription of the *Confession of Faith* 23.4 that

> Infidelity, or difference in religion, doth not make void the magistrates' just and legal authority, nor free the people from their due obedience to them....[96]

As Scotland endured decades of revived Stuart persecution, the Covenanting view of the magistrate understandably became more nuanced.[97] The complex and problematic approach that resulted can be seen in the

---

92. Erskine and his brethren responded that although the Covenants had involved the true religion being "*secured* by the fundamental Constitution of the Civil Government," the true religion had not been made a "*Part* of our *Civil Constitution*," which could lead to erastianism. *A&D*, 15. See also *A&D*, 12, 15–16, 55, 60–61, 88–89; Nairn, 19.

93. See Knox, "A Letter to the Lords and Others Professing the Truth in Scotland," in *Selected Writings*, 365. See also John Knox, *Appellation to the Nobility*, in Mason, ed., *John Knox on Rebellion*, 104; and ibid., xx, xxii–xxiv.

94. See Knox, *Summary of the Proposed Second Blast of the Trumpet*, in *Selected Writings*, 435. For Buchanan's concurrence, see Buchanan, *De Jure*, 245–46.

95. See Rutherford, *Lex Rex*, 6–9, 16–22, 45–50. Similarly, see Gillespie, AARON'S ROD BLOSSOMING, 107, 113–14. Hereafter, *Aaron's Rod*.

96. The exact interpretation of *WCF* 23.4 was contested between Nairn and the Presbytery. Nairn asserted that the cited injunction applied only to uncovenanted lands, while Erskine and the Seceders held it to apply to both uncovenanted and Covenanted lands. See Nairn, *Short Account*, 19, 23–25, 56; *A&D*, 14–15, 91–93.

97. The Presbytery recognized that, from the time of Charles II, matters became confused in this area. *A&D*, 93–94.

thought of James Renwick and Alexander Shields. Marking the apogee of pre-Revolution Covenanting political theory, Renwick's and Shields' system contained two different emphases pertaining to the interface between religious qualifications and popular consent in determining magisterial legitimacy. In some instances, Renwick and Shields saw the legitimating power of religious qualifications as limited to their adoption as expressions of the popular will. In such reasoning, James VII's uncovenanted Roman Catholicism invalidated his magistracy specifically because that uncovenanted Roman Catholicism violated the popular will as expressed in Acts of Parliament.[98] In other instances, Renwick and Shields held the legitimating power of religious qualifications to be independent of, and superior to, the consideration of popular consent. Taking this emphasis to its most radical conclusion, Renwick and Shields asserted that in times of national apostasy, a faithful remnant may dissolve the relationship binding them to the magistrate.[99] According to such a position, the popular consent of an apostate nation was insufficient to invest the magistrate with legitimacy.

Viewed holistically, one sees that the historical particularities of the later Covenanters facilitated an imprecision in their articulation of the roots of magisterial legitimacy. As the "Glorious Revolution" of 1688 showed, Renwick, Shields, and their contemporaries lived under a magistrate who was both uncovenanted and unpopular.[100] Writing in such a situation, Renwick and Shields understandably denounced James both as lacking Covenantal qualifications and as lacking popular approval, yet they did so without explicitly stating the relationship between the two considerations or between either consideration and ultimate magisterial legitimacy.[101] While effective in their situation, such argumentation did not address the legitimacy of a magistrate who lacks Scriptural or Covenantal qualifications, yet retains the consent of the populace. Indeed, such argumentation contained some emphases that support such a magistrate's legitimacy and some emphases that reject it. While Nairn's demand for a Covenantally-qualified magistrate was consonant with the contours of Covenanting political thought, Erskine's insistence that the only ultimately relevant magisterial qualification was popular consent was equally continuous with Covenanting theory. The fullness of Covenanting thought in the extreme conditions of Stuart perse-

---

98. See especially Renwick and Shields, *Informatory Vindication*, 25–27. Furthermore, see ibid., 3–8, 13, 22–23.

99. Ibid., 23–24.

100. The Presbytery recognizes this complexity of the later Covenanters' position, yet they do not explore its role in their disagreement with Nairn. *A&D*, 93–94.

101. For a representatively unclear line of argument, see Renwick and Shields, *Informatory Vindication*, 20.

cution could not be imported seamlessly into the vagaries of Hanoverian Scotland.[102] Contextual application of that witness would prove crucial.

Modified Covenantalism: A Viable Paradigm?

As articulated during the Secession's protracted drive to renew Scotland's Covenants, Erskine's modified Covenantalism seemed to provide a foundation for interaction between a Covenanted Revolution Church and an uncovenanted Hanoverian State. Emerging from the extremities of Stuart persecution, Scottish Covenanting political theory had become complex and often problematic in regard to the foundations of magisterial legitimacy. Faced with such an inheritance, Erskine consistently adopted those emphases that would legitimate the Hanoverian State and place the Secession Church on a footing to engage with that State rather than rejecting it.[103] The importance and the viability of the position that resulted are clear in the disparity between Erskine's view and the Macmillanite view espoused by Thomas Nairn. While Nairn's recognition of Scotland's historic Covenants forced him into isolating sectarianism, Erskine was able to extol the Covenants, and even use them as the foundation for profound criticism of the Union, yet also interact with the present civil magistrate in the hopes that God ultimately would bring further reform through such efforts.[104] In

102. This perhaps is best illustrated by Renwick's and Shields's contention that Stuart tyranny had dissolved the magistracy and returned the Covenanters to their "native and radical liberty." Ibid., 35.

103. Often, Erskine seemed driven to these hermeneutical decisions by his conviction that for truth to have meaning, it must have *present* meaning. See *Works*, 3:90–91; *A&D*, 27–34, 40–41, 67–68; *AFR*, 95–96. Interestingly, Erskine and his brethren also distinctively used old emphases to legitimize the popular State. For example, the distinction between the person of the magistrate and the office of the magistracy had been used by both Knox and the later Covenanters to countenance rebellion against the magistrate because of his violation of the magistracy. See Renwick and Shields, *Informatory Vindication*, 22–24; Mason, ed., *John Knox on Rebellion*, xviii–xix; Greaves, "John Knox," 27–28. The Seceders, however, used the distinction to allow Christians to render obedience to the present magistrate in spite of any transgressions of the magisterial office. See *A&D*, 70, 72–74, 80. In many ways, a complex tradition was tailored to countenance the realities of post-Union Scotland.

104. *A&D*, 80–81. For the Seceders, the Union was a "*Gravestone*" upon the Covenanted Reformation in Scotland. *A&D*, 51. See also *AFR*, 102–103, 108–109; *A&D*, 50–51. Provocatively, Erskine cited Nehemiah 9:38 as one of the two foremost Scriptural precedents for the Presbytery's renewal of the Covenants. See *Works*, 3:71. In its context, especially that of verses 36–37, Nehemiah 9:38 is a call for Israel to renew their Covenant engagements with God specifically because they find themselves servants in the land given to their fathers, enslaved by a foreign king who has been placed in authority over them because of their sin.

that interaction, the divinely-instituted distinction between a Covenanted Church and the State dictated that the Church would extricate herself from civil entanglements, the State would remain clear of religious interference, and both would work concurrently for greater societal reformation.[105] In the years following the Seceders' Covenant renewal, Erskine would be offered an important opportunity to show that this theoretical position was able to produce concrete action that was loyal both to the Covenants and to the uncovenanted British State; when Prince Charles Edward Stuart landed at Glenfinnan on 19 August 1745, the matter of Covenantal loyalty to an uncovenanted civil government became a crucial issue.[106]

Modified Covenantalism Tested: The Jacobite Rising of 1745

While the prospect of a Roman Catholic Stuart monarch won few presbyterian supporters to the 1745 Jacobite Rising, Erskine's zeal for the Hanoverian cause distinguished him during those times of rebellion.[107] Being lobbied directly by the Earl of Hume for assistance, Erskine took an active role in recruiting citizens of Stirling to join the government militias that were being raised to repel the advancing Jacobites as 1745 entered its waning months.[108] As a result of Erskine's efforts, by the end of 1745, his congregation in Stirling had raised two companies of militia that later would prove singularly valorous, and Erskine's own son, David, stood as the elected Captain of the newer of those two companies.[109]

---

105. For the Church's role and limitation, see *A&D*, 13–14, 16, 41; *AFR*, 115. For the State's role and limitations, see *Works*, 3:80; *A&D*, 16, 53, 71, 87–88; *AFR*, 92, 106–9, 115; Glas, *Remarks*, 11. For the interaction between the two entities, see Glas, *Remarks*, 10–11; *A&D*, 16, 39, 46, 51–52; *AFR*, 82–83, 108–9. The result of such a position is that even in a Covenanted land, the church and the magistrate exercise different authorities within different realms. Gillespie spoke of this situation as the church and the magistrate exercising a "divided execution." Gillespie, *Aaron's Rod*, 89. While neither Gillespie nor Erskine made the application, Gillespie's description of the distinction that Erskine shared with his forebear actually creates the ideological and theological space for a later Hanoverian religious toleration. See Gillespie, *Aaron's Rod*, 89–90.

106. See Ferguson, *Scotland*, 150.

107. Lenman, *Jacobite Risings*, 254, 257; Ferguson, *Scotland*, 151. Lenman maintains that it is inaccurate to conceive of the Jacobite party as a Roman Catholic party. However, for Erskine and his brethren, it was the Roman Catholicism of the House of Stuart that most decisively colored the Rising. See M'Kerrow, *Scottish Church*, 1:258–60. For a brief account of Hanoverian support by the Seceders in Edinburgh and Glasgow, see M'Kerrow, *Scottish Church*, 1:260–63.

108. See Ebenezer Erskine, Stirling, to the Earl of Hume, Edinburgh, 27 December 1745. Hereafter, "Erskine to Hume."

109. See Erskine to Hume. On the Seceders' valor, see *Extracts*, 278.

While Erskine and others were committed to defending Stirling, many on the Town Council were not and Stirling surrendered to the Jacobite forces on 8 January 1746. From that date, the Jacobites occupied the town and commenced an unsuccessful siege of the castle.[110] When the Jacobites thus took control of Stirling, Erskine was forced to leave the town, partly due to his prior activity in rallying support against the Jacobites and partly out of a desire to avoid any appearance of countenancing the Stuart government.[111] In this time of self-termed "exile," Erskine continued to preach from Tillibody, just north of Stirling, while the Jacobite forces occupying Stirling converted the Secession Church building into a magazine for military supplies.[112] Fortunately, the Secession Church building survived the occupation, and, with Stirling rid of occupying forces on 1 February due to the advance of the Duke of Cumberland, Erskine returned to the town and resumed his ministry there.[113]

Principles Proven

What emerges from Erskine's personal correspondence during the uncertain days of 1745–1746 is a picture of a man very committed to the Hanoverian cause. Erskine labored to recruit men to the militia, he gave his own son to the defense of the Hanoverian succession, he collected and conveyed military intelligence to government forces, and well-attested anecdotal evidence suggests that the sixty-five year old Erskine took up arms himself to defend the town of Stirling.[114] For the prominence of his efforts on behalf of the government, Erskine even received the personal gratitude of the Duke of Cumberland.[115] Indeed, from Erskine's correspondence, it is evident that his most prominent service to the government was rendered at a time when the prospects of the Hanoverian forces were still in doubt. In the final days

---

110. On 30 January 1746, the *St. James's Evening Post* reported that the surrender of Stirling had been resisted fiercely by Erskine and Walter Stevenson, the convener of the trades for Stirling, and that this protest was joined by the majority of the townspeople. The Town Council took exception to the *Evening Post*'s account and published their own narrative of events which presents the surrender as both judicious and, upon later reflection by initial opponents, popular. For the text of the *Evening Post*'s account, as well as the Council's rejoinder, see *Extracts*, 274–82. See also Ferguson, *Scotland*, 152; Muirhead, "Religion," 86–87.

111. *Life*, 443.
112. Ibid., 440, 444–45.
113. *Extracts*, 276; *Life*, 440–41.
114. See Erskine to Hume; *Life*, 438–39, 444.
115. *Life*, 444.

of 1745, when Erskine's labors were at their height, half of his congregation had been cut off by the advancing Jacobites, the new additions to the militia were receiving arms and earnestly commencing training to prepare for battle, and Erskine feared that the provisions for Stirling's defenses were about to be exhausted.[116] When considering Erskine's allegiance to the Hanoverian succession, then, one must not see such allegiance as a veiled attempt to curry favor with obvious victors; rather, one must see Erskine's allegiance as clear evidence of his loyalty to the reigning, uncovenanted civil magistrate.

While Erskine thus showed active support for the government, he did not do so without condition. In his correspondence with the nobility who were seeking to use his influence to recruit men for the militia, Erskine was insistent that certain criteria be met for any regiment of Seceders that he gathered. In addition to criteria not specific to Seceder scruples, Erskine insisted that each Seceder regiment have the power of choosing a minister to accompany it and dispense gospel ordinances to it, and that all Seceders joining the militia be excused from taking the oath normally administered to individuals entering military service.[117] In this, Erskine guarded Seceder militiamen against both the defection of submitting to a minister in the Established Church and the perjury that Seceders saw to be involved in the pertinent government oath. In this conditional service to the government, what previously had been a theoretical position of Erskine's was given practical exercise—submissive service was to be given to the uncovenanted civil magistrate, yet it was to be rendered in a way that protected the spiritual rights of a Covenanted Kirk and her members. In this, the '45 Rising actually provided a beneficial opportunity for Erskine and his fellow Seceders, for it afforded them the chance to prove that their Secession from the Established Church and their continual lamentation of the sins of the State did not imply disloyalty to that State.[118] The Secession simultaneously could serve and testify against the State, even as a Seceder militiaman could fight and die for a government whose oath of loyalty his conscience forbid him to swear, and a government regiment could receive religious ordinances from a minister who rejected the Established Church. In action, Erskine bore out the promise of modified Covenantalism—full civil cooperation was given to the magistrate, even though uncovenanted, yet it was given in such a way that the spiritual prerogatives of the Church were protected, and all

---

116. Erskine to Hume.

117. For Erskine's most explicit enumeration of these criteria, see *Life*, 442. In other instances, Erskine obliquely would refer to "The Terms of their engageing." Erskine to Hume. For more on the Seceders' views of certain governmental oaths, see *ADT*, 30–33.

118. See *Life*, 441; M'Kerrow, *Scottish Church*, 1:258.

was done in an effort to consolidate present reform in the hope that further reform would ensue.

Modified Covenantalism: Theologically Coherent?

While Erskine's actions in the '45 showed his modified Covenantalism to be viable in practice, some have found the system to be theologically untenable. In his assessment of the Seceders' ecclesiology, John Carson argues that when the Seceders imported, from the Scottish federalist tradition, the distinction between the mediatory kingdom of Christ—in which, by the merits of his mediatorial work, Christ governs his elect and the Church they comprise—and the essential kingdom of Christ—in which, because of his essential deity, Christ exercises divine omnipotence in all of Creation—their doctrine of the State was fatally compromised.[119] In Carson's estimation, by declaring that the magistracy was under Christ's essential kingdom and then insisting that that kingdom was ruled for the benefit of Christ's mediatorial kingdom, the Seceders involved themselves in a two-fold error.[120] In the first instance, Erskine and his brethren succumbed to the logical error of positing that a universal and essential dominion was exercised subservient to a limited and mediatorial dominion. In the second instance, Erskine and his brethren slid into a pseudo-Nestorian Christology by necessarily dividing both the Person and Work of Christ between those two kingdoms; a situation that, in Carson's view, requires two different "christs" working simultaneously in two different ways in two different kingdoms.

The intimation of a resolution to Carson's concerns rests in Erskine's expansive, indefinite Covenant of Grace.[121] As the Covenant of Grace, in its first making, began with the universal body of mankind considered indefinitely and moved, through the Council of Peace, to a salvific and eternal definiteness, it established a basis for Christ's universal and essential sovereignty to be employed in his limited and mediatorial work on behalf of

---

119. For examples of such a distinction in the Presbytery's Covenant renewal, see A&D, 87–89; AFR, 115. See also Gillespie, Aaron's Rod, 86, 90–96, 113–14; Rutherford, Lex Rex, 123, 211; Renwick and Shields, Informatory Vindication, 22–23.

120. See Carson, "Doctrine of the Church," 37–42, 168–69, 175–77, 339.

121. That Carson misses such a resolution is not surprising, as he strongly, and inexplicably, implies that Erskine held a tri-covenantal view of federal theology, even though Erskine maintained his bi-covenantal views until the end of his life. See Carson, "Doctrine of the Church," 30–31. Herein lies one of the greatest weaknesses of Carson's thesis for Erskine studies. Carson presumes to assess the impact of the Seceders' federal theology upon their ecclesiology, yet the federal scheme he uses for this critique is one explicitly rejected by Erskine.

the elect. In that one Covenant, in whose work the Son eternally has been employed and which takes all men under its purview in some capacity, Christ exercises dominion both essentially, prior to the Council of Peace, and mediatorially, through and subsequent to that Council. In Erskine's lengthy treatments of the Covenant of Grace, there is never any indication that, because of his mediatory undertaking in the Council of Peace, Christ is divested of the essential dominion that he possessed at the Covenant's outset. In this, Erskine's federal scheme creates the theological space to see Christ, in the one Covenant of Grace, simultaneously working both essentially in all Creation and mediatorially in and for the Church; a space more difficult to discern in the competing tri-covenantal scheme, in which a restricted Covenant of Grace considers Christ only in relation to his limited, mediatorial work. Unlike the tri-covenantal arrangement, Erskine's federal system did not make Christ's "pre-mediatorial" essential reign Covenantally distinct from his present mediatorial dominion and thus was not susceptible to the potential error of obscuring the unity between the essential and mediatory dominions of Christ.

When this grid is expanded from salvific matters to those concerning the divine government of human affairs through which salvific purposes are realized, the same Christological unity remains; Christ simultaneously can act both essentially in the State and mediatorially in the Church without requiring a division in either his Covenantal work or his essential Person. While Erskine never afforded specific attention to such matters, he did identify the Council of Peace as the bridge between Christ's essential and mediatory kingdoms, thus subsuming both kingdoms under the one Covenant of Grace.[122] Had concerns such as Carson's been raised in Erskine's day, it therefore is possible that Erskine could have articulated a paradigm in which a Christ unified in Covenantal work and essential Person channeled his essential dominion into his mediatory reign.

Summary

As seen in the complex of issues arising from the Associate Presbytery's Covenant renewal, Erskine's modified Covenantalism proves itself capable of meeting the challenge of simultaneously affirming Scotland's Covenants and rendering responsible submission to the uncovenanted Hanoverian State. By demarcating the Church Covenantally, Erskine and his brethren were able to adhere to the Covenants, and even to use them as definite terms of communion in an age of perceived latitudinarianism, yet were able to

---

122. *Works*, 3:90.

avoid encroachment into the natural sphere of the civil magistrate, whose ordination was rooted in '*natural Principles*' rather than in such doctrinal matters.[123] While the course of the 1740s may have revealed weaknesses in other areas of Erskine's modified Covenantalism, that same decade, particularly in the 1745 Rising, showed Erskine's system to be a viable way for a Covenanted Revolution Church to function both faithfully and submissively in a post-Union Scottish milieu.

INTERACTION WITHIN OWN COMMUNION

While the events surrounding the Seceders' Covenant renewal may validate the stance of Erskine's Covenantal Revolution Church in relation to an uncovenanted civil magistrate, the years following that Covenant renewal appear to make the entire matter irrelevant. As epitomized in the Breach of 1747, the Secession Church appeared incapable of internal cohesion, casting fundamental doubt upon the ability of Erskine's system to facilitate interaction within one's own communion. Indeed, such an assessment marks the common interpretation of the Breach; an interpretation that sees the Breach as manifesting both the failure of Erskine's ecclesiology and a theological change within Erskine himself. According to this traditional view, when Erskine's rigorous ecclesiology imploded in the Breach, he became so saddened by the destruction of the Secession Church that he was unable even to enter into the controversy that was tearing his Synod apart. While such an interpretation of the Breach is unchallenged in the extant literature, it does not prove to be the most faithful interpretation thereof. In actuality, the Breach shows Erskine developing the doctrinal prioritization evidenced in the earlier controversy with George Whitefield into a definite distinction between the essentials and the non-essentials of the faith and evidencing a willingness to accept those of different positions on the latter. In the course that Erskine followed through the Breach, he showed that he was able to act as the leader of an accepting majority, and that his Covenantal Revolution Church was capable of functioning as a diverse Church body.

The Controversy

In 1744, the Associate Synod began considering whether the Burgess Oath that was required of those individuals becoming Burgesses in several Scottish burghs involved an unlawful recognition of the current Established

123. *A&D*, 71.

Church or only an approbation of the Protestant, presbyterian settlement of the Kirk; in April 1747, the effects of that question precipitated a rupture of the Associate Synod into two competing judicatories—the Burgher Synod, comprised of those who were willing to accept the Burgess Oath, and the anti-Burgher Synod, comprised of those who were opposed to the Oath.[124] Given the impassioned and labyrinthine nature of the debates that filled those years of controversy, perhaps the greatest challenge to situating the Burgess Oath controversy and the resulting Breach, as the split of 1747 is known, within the context of Erskine's theology and ministry is maintaining Erskine's perspective on the tumultuous debates. In order to maintain that perspective, one must both examine Erskine's writings on the controversy and rightly understand his notable silence as the Synod that he had helped found disintegrated.

In examining Erskine's written contributions to the Burgess Oath controversy and Breach, one must have chief recourse to two documents. First, one must consider Erskine's *The True State of the Question, Upon Which a Breach Followed in the Associate Synod, at Edinburgh, Thursday April 9, 1747*, written shortly after the Breach, in which Erskine addressed the controversy that had ruptured the Associate Synod.[125] Secondly, one must evaluate a letter that Erskine, acting as moderator of the Burgher Synod, wrote to the anti-Burgher Synod on 19 June 1747 requesting an informal meeting for prayer and conference in the hopes of reconciling the freshly-constituted rupture.[126] While both of these Erskinite contributions are significant, most interpretive weight traditionally has fallen upon what followed Erskine's production of them—silence. Following Erskine's letter to the anti-Burgher

---

124. The first consideration of the Burgess Oath occurred while the Secession Church was still the "Associate Presbytery." However, as the bulk of the controversy would occur after the Associate Presbytery had been formed into a Synod, it is referred to as the Associate Synod here. For a full statement of the Burgher position, see Hall, *AN IMPARTIAL SURVEY Of the religious Clause in some BURGESS-OATHS*, especially pages 1–39. See also M'Kerrow, *Scottish Church*, 1:280–81. For a full statement of the anti-Burgher position, see Gib, *Display*, 2:1–111, esp. 1–29. The troublesome oaths were those of Edinburgh, Glasgow, and Perth. The Oath used in Stirling contained no reference to religion. See Muirhead, "Religion," 88–89.

125. See Erskine, *THE TRUE STATE OF THE QUESTION, UPON WHICH A BREACH followed IN THE ASSOCIATE SYNOD*. Hereafter, *Question*. Very soon after Erskine's pamphlet was published, a response, composed chiefly of excerpts from the proceedings of the anti-Burgher Synod, was published. See Some Seceders in and about Glasgow, *A SHORT VINDICATION OF THE ASSOCIAT SYNOD, FROM THE CHARGE of SCHISM, PERJURY*, &c. Hereafter, *Short Vindication*.

126. For a full transcript of the letter, see Erskine, *A NARRATIVE OF THE SEPARATION OF THE MAJORITY of MEMBERS FROM THE ASSOCIATE PRESBYTERY OF DUNFERMLINE*, 50–52.

Synod, he virtually disappeared from the still-raging debate and that disappearance has unfailingly been seen to indicate a sorrowful disassociation from the entire affair.[127] However, the more likely cause of Erskine's absence from the debate was his declining health and his increasing age. As early as 1744, Erskine's congregation in Stirling had approached the Presbytery about obtaining assistance for their aging pastor and by January 1752, Erskine's condition had reached such an extremity that his congregation was forced to call James Erskine as a full assistant.[128] Quite clearly, Erskine's health and strength were declining just as the alienation between the Burghers and the anti-Burghers was escalating. As a result, one must resist the temptation to interpret Erskine's silence as an indication of sorrowful disbelief; the factors of growing age and declining health certainly preclude such a simplistic assessment. Rather, one must examine the writings that Erskine did leave and the actions that he did take, drawing from them Erskine's view of the Breach and the issues surrounding it before his declining health obviated prominence in the debate. When Erskine's writings, rather than his silence, are given interpretive prominence, three issues emerge at the center of Erskine's concern—the Burgess Oath itself; the Sentence 1746, in which a poorly-attended meeting of the Synod voted 13–9 to declare the Oath unlawful; and the Sentence 1747, in which the Synod voted unanimously, although with nearly two-thirds of those present abstaining, to remand the Sentence 1746 to the presbyteries for consideration, thus immediately precipitating the Breach.[129]

Erskine's Position on the Central Issues of the Breach

Erskine's writings are remarkably terse on the issue of the Burgess Oath itself. Strikingly, Erskine's only written reference to the Oath's lawfulness was an observation that when that precise question had arisen in 1737, as he and the other three initial Seceders had been drafting their *Act and Testimony*,

---

127. Some accounts give the impression that Erskine never entered the controversy at all, neglecting even to mention or cite his *Question*. See, for example, MacEwen, *Erskines*, 128, 132.

128. *Minutes of AP and AS from 1741*, 847. See also *Minutes of AP and AS from 1741*, 888; Ebenezer Erskine, Stirling, to Alison Scott, Gateshall, 13 August 1751. James Erskine, the third son of Ebenezer's brother Ralph, later was called as Ebenezer's successor in Stirling. See *Life*, 455. James Erskine, although related to Donald Fraser, is not a lineal ancestor. See Scott, *Genealogy*, 46–47.

129. For the text of the Burgess Oath, see Erskine, *Question*, 3. For the text and passage of the Sentence 1746, see *Minutes of AP and AS from 1741*, 931–35. For the text of the Sentence 1747, see Erskine, *Question*, 4–5.

they had refrained from addressing it in the document.[130] Clearly, Erskine's implication was that nothing had changed in the intervening decade; the Burgess Oath still did not demand judicial action.

As Erskine was willing to countenance the Burgess Oath, it is not surprising that he was opposed to the Sentence 1746 which denounced that Oath as necessarily sinful. Being absent from the April synod meeting at which the Sentence was passed, Erskine immediately registered his formal protest against the synod's actions at the next meeting of the synod, in September 1746.[131] From this first act of formal opposition to the Sentence 1746, it was clear that Erskine's dissatisfaction therewith was rooted not in his view of the Burgess Oath, but in his view of the Sentence 1746 itself.[132] In the first instance, Erskine was opposed to the manner in which the Sentence had been passed. In his estimation, it was unacceptable that such a contentious Sentence had been passed by a slim majority at a poorly attended meeting.[133] Furthermore, Erskine was very dissatisfied with the novelty of the Sentence. Erskine strongly felt the Sentence 1746 to be an innovation, for

> that Decision, *April* 1746. declaring the first Clause of some Burgess Oaths sinful, was never any Part of the Testimony of the Church of *Scotland*, or yet of any of the Lord's Witnesses since our Reformation from Popery: But rather that first Clause itself seems to have been a Part of it; and therefore ought not to have been condemned . . . .[134]

In the best case, the Sentence 1746 was an innovation with no previous precedent; in the worst case, it was a positive overturning of the previous witness of the Scottish reformers.

---

130. Erskine, *Question*, 8. Of the original four Seceders, William Wilson did not live to see the Breach, dying in 1741; Erskine and James Fisher both became Burghers; and Alexander Moncrieff became an anti-Burgher. For some of the oaths and bonds that the Seceders did denounce, see *ADT*, 30–33.

131. For the text of Erskine's dissent, see *Minutes of AP and AS from 1741*, 952. See also M'Kerrow, 1:282–83.

132. See *Minutes of AP and AS from 1741*, 952.

133. Erskine, *Question*, 3, 11. Erskine is biased, however, in his handling of the passage of both the Sentence 1746 and the Sentence 1747. While Erskine pointedly notes that the Sentence 1746 was passed at a poorly-attended meeting, he says simply that the Sentence 1747 "carried by Twenty Votes," neglecting to mention that only 20 of the 55 of the voting members present cast a vote. Ibid., 11, 5.

134. Ibid., 7. The exact year in which the Burgess Oath was first instituted was a matter of some debate between the Burghers and the anti-Burghers. However, Erskine clearly felt it to be a product of the Reformation. MacEwen dates the Oath to 1591. See MacEwen, *Erskines*, 126.

While Erskine thus made his opposition to the Sentence 1746 very evident, the majority of his efforts in the controversy were devoted to explicating his position on what he held to be the more important Sentence—the Sentence 1747. In Erskine's judgment, that Sentence simply represented the concrete implementation of the Barrier Acts of 1639, 1640, and 1641.[135] In the spirit of those Acts, the Sentence 1747 would refer the question of the sinfulness of the Burgess Oath to the presbyteries and Kirk-Sessions of the Secession Church before such an important measure was enforced within the Synod. Even more important than this procedural aspect of the Sentence 1747, however, were its implications for the future course of the Associate Synod. As Erskine argued, rejection of the Sentence 1747 would have been a material deposition of all those Seceders who did not share in the scruples of the Oath's opponents, precipitating a series of Church censures that ultimately would have torn the Synod apart.[136] In contrast, the approval of the Sentence declared a willingness to remain in communion across lines of division on the Oath as resolution of the dispute was sought.[137] Support for the Sentence 1747 was support for an expansive communion within the Associate Synod; rejection of that Sentence rejected any such attempts at catholicity. In this, Erskine saw his support for the Sentence 1747 not in terms of his opposition to the Sentence 1746, but rather in terms of his desire for mutual forbearance within the Synod on the matter of the Oath.

Foundational to Erskine's call for mutual forbearance was his distinction between the heart of the Secession witness and other, peripheral matters. In Erskine's letter to the anti-Burghers of 19 June 1747, he freely recognized that the anti-Burghers professed to maintain 'the Testimony for the covenanted Reformation' as much as did the Burghers.[138] Indeed, Erskine argued that it was that shared profession that made an immediate resolution of the Breach so necessary, for a public rupture between two bodies that held to the same testimony only damaged the name of Christ among men. What separated the Burghers and the anti-Burghers was not a difference as to the essentials of the faith; rather, it was merely a difference as to the *adiaphora*. Indeed, the matters that divided the two groups were so peripheral to the heart of the Secession testimony, and to the gospel, that Erskine judged that "the Godly through the Land might differ in their Judgments, as to the Lawfulness or Sinfulness of the first Clause of some *Burgess*

---

135. See Erskine, *Question*, 5.
136. See ibid., 11–12, 15.
137. Ibid., 12–13.
138. Ralph Erskine, *Narrative*, 51.

Oaths."[139] Since the issue was a matter of personal judgment and not of fidelity to the Secession witness, both parties within the Associate Synod were to continue in communion with each other. As Erskine pled,

> Sound Divines of great Name differ in their Judgment anent many controverted Points, and about the meaning of several Texts of Scripture, and yet live in Union and Communion one with another; and might not we much more live in Love and Unity, notwithstanding of different Sentiments anent the Meaning of two or three Words in some *Burgess Oaths*? If every one should make his Mind a Law, and a Term of Communion to others, in Matters of this Sort, there could be no such Thing as Church-Communion and Fellowship upon Earth; for, while *we know in part*, we cannot shun to differ in Judgment about many Things.[140]

If the Seceders were to entertain any ideals of Church communion in a fallen world, they must exercise mutual forbearance with each other on matters as non-essential as the Burgess Oath.

Within this context of mutual forbearance, Erskine wanted the Seceders to work toward a unity founded upon complete reconciliation. In his letter to the anti-Burghers, Erskine recognized that such reconciliation required effort by both parties to the dispute and expressed a willingness to work personally to restore the unity that had been shattered.[141] At the very height of the Breach, Erskine longed for both sides in that dispute to expend real effort to effect reconciliation within a context of mutual forbearance on issues that were peripheral to the heart of the Secession testimony.[142] Erskine was insistent that such unity could be obtained and he was willing to labor in order to realize it.

Themes of Erskine's Position

When one considers Erskine's plea for both mutual forbearance on the question of the Burgess Oath and reconciliation of the Breach, several key themes emerge from that plea. Perhaps most prominently, one sees Erskine's

---

139. Erskine, *Question*, 14.
140. Ibid., 13.
141. See Fraser, *Ralph Erskine*, 51.
142. The exact date of Erskine's *Question* is not known. However, it was evidently published sometime between the Breach, on 9 April 1747, and 18 May 1747, when the anti-Burgher response to it was completed. Erskine's letter to Mair and Gib was written on 19 June 1747. See *Short Vindication*, 15; Ralph Erskine, *Narrative*, 52.

continued insistence upon continuity between the historic Church of Scotland and the contemporary Secession Church; a continuity determinative of the course that must be followed, both procedurally and philosophically. Procedurally, Erskine judged that the Secession's continuity with the Scottish Kirk demanded that the terms of the Sentence 1746 be remitted to the inferior judicatories for consideration in accordance with the Barrier Acts of the Second Reformation.[143] In this, Erskine argued that the actions and procedures of the Associate Synod were controlled by century-old Acts of the Church of Scotland.[144] As a result, while Erskine did not rebuke the anti-Burghers for their opposition to the Burgess Oath, he did insist that their opposition to the Sentence 1747 was a rejection of Church law.[145] Philosophically, the Associate Synod's continuity with the historic Church of Scotland had even broader implications for the course that the Seceders must follow. As the Secession Church was the present embodiment of the National Church, the Secession had to act like a truly national Church and not like a sect. Just as it was incumbent upon a National Church to maintain unity despite differences on minor issues, Erskine insisted the Associate Synod was to maintain unity despite disagreements over the Burgess Oath; the Seceders could not claim the sectarians' prerogative of absolutizing non-essentials.[146]

In addition to this undercurrent of assumed continuity with the historic Church of Scotland, Erskine's position is marked by his characteristic demand for liberty of conscience. In Erskine's estimation, the great error of the anti-Burghers' course was that it made the personal scruples of a few individuals into a law that would bind all Christians.[147] However, as Erskine had maintained throughout his ministry, the conscience of the individual Christian could be bound only by Scripture and never by the dictates of

---

143. Erskine, *Question*, 8–9. For the same emphasis within the Burgher Synod as a whole, see Associate Synod (Burgher), *ACT OF THE ASSOCIATE SYNOD, Met at Stirling, the twenty-ninth Day of October, One thousand seven hundred and forty-seven, DECLARING THE NULLITY OF THE Pretended Synod, That FIRST met in Mr. GIB's House in Bristo, near Edinburgh, April 10th 1747*, 21–22, 30–32. Hereafter, *Nullity*. The anti-Burghers' rejection of the Barrier Acts' applicability was based upon procedural, rather than philosophical, considerations. See *Short Vindication*, 10–12.

144. See Erskine, *Question*, 9–11. For similar emphases by the Burgher Synod as a whole, see, for example, Associate Synod (Burgher), *Nullity*, 3–4, 14–16, 30–32, 33–34. Indeed, the overall structure of the Burghers' *Nullity* is self-consciously modelled after the General Assembly 1638's nullification of certain previous Assemblies, even quoting directly from that Act at points. See *AGA*, 5–8.

145. Erskine, *Question*, 15.

146. Ibid., 12–13.

147. Ibid., 13.

man.[148] As the matter at the heart of the Sentence 1746 fell into the latter category, the Seceders were obligated to practice mutual forbearance until a resolution had been reached that did not do violence to anyone's conscience. To do otherwise was to exercise "a Lordly Dominion over the Faith and Practice of the Lord's Heritage" and thus to require the sort of implicit faith and blind obedience that were expressly denounced in the Westminster Confession of Faith 20.2.[149] The absence of a binding Scriptural mandate necessitated mutual forbearance.

The third central theme of Erskine's argumentation regarding the Breach is far less prominent in his earlier writings than are the previous two themes. Throughout his writing on the Breach, Erskine argues for an expansive communion within the Church. Interestingly, this apparently newer theme emerges as a function of the two previous, and much more familiar, themes of Erskine's argument. In addressing the Sentence 1747 and its allowance of mutual forbearance on the matter of the Oath, Erskine wrote that he supported such a measure

> Because it is the express Command of God, *Eph.* 4. 1, 2, 3. and *Phil.* 3.15, 16. that in Things not yet attained, or determined in the Church, we should with all Lowliness, Meekness and Long-suffering, forbear one another in Love, *endeavouring to keep the Unity of the Spirit in the Bond of Peace*. And if in any Thing we be otherwise minded, or of a different Judgment, God in due Time shall reveal even this unto us, and so we shall in his Light come to see Eye to Eye: Nevertheless, *whereunto we have attained already, let us walk by the same Rule, let us mind the same Thing*; that is, Let us join Hand in Hand in maintaining the Testimony for Truth wherein we are all agreed.[150]

Here, Erskine advocates a united witness on the essentials of the faith, alongside a willingness to maintain communion with others in spite of disagreement on peripheral matters. The consideration which Erskine proposes as the foundation of this distinction between essentials and *adiaphora* is the inherited determination of the Church. Mutual forbearance is to be exercised in "Things not yet attained, or determined in the Church," while uniformity of practice is to be required in matters "wherein we are all agreed."[151] If the historic Kirk has attained to consensus—whether that consensus is founded upon the clear teachings of Scripture or the correct

---

148. Ibid., 9–10.
149. Ibid., 9. Similarly, see Associate Synod (Burgher), *Nullity*, 29.
150. Erskine, *Question*, 7–8.
151. Ibid.

deliberation of Church bodies—the standard thus agreed must be insisted upon, while if that historic Kirk has not reached such uniformity of opinion, mutual forbearance must prevail as the Church waits for God to give light. Simply stated, the past consensus of the Church binds the conscience of Christians, while matters on which the Church has not reached agreement still allow liberty of conscience and demand mutual forbearance. In this, Erskine's assertion of the Secession's wholesale inheritance of the Church of Scotland's heritage and his insistence upon the liberty of the individual's conscience coalesce to form the framework of an expansive communion befitting a National Church. In the Scottish Kirk's heritage that he claims, Erskine finds the concrete parameters that cohesion demands, while in the liberty of conscience that he maintains, Erskine finds the charity that large-scale unity requires. By holding both principles together, Erskine is able to chart a course that would preclude the Secession from becoming either an impotent association of essentially independent congregations or an exclusivist sect; Erskine's Covenantal Revolution Church appears a valid structure for a National Church.

The Distinctiveness of the Breach Within Erskine's Ministry

The distinctiveness of the Breach within the complex of controversies that marked Erskine's ministry, and thus the unique contribution that it offers to an understanding of Erskine's theology, lies in the nature of the issues at stake. Quite simply, the issues under debate in the Burgess Oath controversy and Breach are unique among all of the issues that Erskine debated throughout his ministry in their being numbered among the *adiaphora*, among those issues on which the historic Kirk had not reached conscience-binding consensus. In all of the other controversies in which Erskine played a role, he was convinced that the Church was receding from attained Reformation standards, whether in doctrine or practice; in the Breach, Erskine was persuaded that the Church was treading on new ground, and thus her decretive powers were severely limited.

An example of this vital distinction emerges even within the literature surrounding the Breach. In seeking to belittle Erskine's appeal to the precedent of the Barrier Acts, the anti-Burgher response to his *True State* observed that Erskine never had claimed that the Act 1744 making Covenant renewal a term of communion should be referred to the inferior judicatories.[152] Given this inconsistent standard, the anti-Burgher pamphlet argued, Erskine's appeal to the Barrier Acts in the Breach controversy was cer-

152. See *Short Vindication*, 13.

tainly disingenuous. In such a line of argument, however, the anti-Burgher pamphlet misses the importance of Erskine's heritage-driven distinction. In renewing the Covenants, Erskine was convinced that the Seceders were reasserting something that had been determined many generations before; they were reaffirming the biblical, theological consensus of the Kirk and thus were obliged to bind the consciences of all Seceders by those theological standards, an obligation formalized in the making of Covenant renewal to be a term of communion. In the Breach, there was no such inherited consensus.[153] As Erskine pointed out, such a consensus as to the sinfulness of the Burgess Oath was noticeably absent from the inheritance of the Reformation and from the continuation of that inheritance in the early days of the Secession.[154] As a result, mutual forbearance was required and Erskine was able to concede freely that although his opponents differed from him on the current question, they still held to the central truths of the Secession witness and were to be numbered among the godly persons of Scotland.[155] The Breach, then, provides not a contradiction of Erskine's stance in the matter of Covenant renewal and other earlier controversies; rather, it provides a depth to what previously had been a decidedly one-dimensional theological portrait of Erskine. To the image of Erskine as a polemicist acting in relation to essential matters, it adds a glimpse of Erskine as a Churchman acting in relation to non-essential matters. If Erskine had been rigorous and unwilling to compromise in the former instances, he showed surprising charity and forbearance in the latter.

An Opportunity for Evangelical Union?

Alongside this novelty of subject matter within the Burgess Oath controversy, there ran an abiding emphasis of Erskine's that, in light of a propensity within the secondary literature, must be noted. At no point during the Breach did Erskine entertain notions of reunion, or even rapprochement, with the Established Church. Indeed, as Erskine's insistence upon the Associate Synod's continuity with the historic Church of Scotland implies, the Established Church remained, in his view, an illegitimate ecclesiastical body. In most extant accounts of the Breach, however, this abiding animus is replaced with a supposition that the Breach actually opened the door to

---

153. Similarly, see Associate Synod (Burgher), *ACT OF THE* Associate Synod, *DE-CLARING THE GROUNDS* Upon which Supplies *were granted to these Congregations of the* Separating Brethren, *who applied for the same*, 44. Hereafter, *Supply*.

154. See Erskine, *Question*, 7–8.

155. See Ralph Erskine, *Narrative*, 51; Erskine, *Question*, 14.

reconciliation between Erskine and an evangelical party within the Assembly. As is so often the case, this historiography has its roots in the work of Donald Fraser. After writing of the grief and emotional turmoil that Erskine supposedly suffered because of the Breach, Fraser writes that

> Some time after the breach, he received a letter from the Rev. Mr. BISSET of Aberdeen, sympathizing, in the kindest manner, with him and his brother Ralph on this trying occasion; and intimating, that, if they would return to their old terms of church-fellowship, (meaning, we suppose, if they would cease to require the swearing of the Bond,) he and several clergymen in the north would join them.[156]

However, Fraser continues, Erskine found solace during the Breach not in human consolations, but only in looking to Christ, a statement that Fraser supports by means of a quotation from Erskine himself.

While Fraser's scenario seems to indicate the possibility of an evangelical merger, such a construction collapses under the least scrutiny. First, the quotation that Fraser evinces to show Erskine's sorrow over the division of the Breach actually is taken from a sermon that Erskine preached in December 1743, fully three-and-one-half years before the Breach.[157] Furthermore, even the supposed sentiments of Bisset are of questionable authenticity. During the Whitefield controversy, Bisset had written a pamphlet critical of Whitefield, yet he also therein was harshly critical of the Seceders and of the grounds of their Secession from the Established Church.[158] That Bisset's position would change from one of denunciation of the Secession's foundations to one of desired accession to the Seceders in such a short period of time is very dubious. Most likely, the "return to their old terms of church-fellowship" that Bisset had in mind was a change in the Erskines' stance toward the Established Church, a change which Bisset evidently felt would win support from some within the Assembly for welcoming the Erskines back. While the precise implications of such a letter are not immediately germane, one thing is apparent—Fraser has misappropriated and under-interpreted evidence in an effort to support his historiographical interest in an imagined pan-presbyterian evangelical unity. As Fraser's account serves as the headwaters for all subsequent Erskine scholarship, this interpretation has marked the majority of that scholarship. In MacEwen's account of the Breach, Fraser's misappropriated quotation is even transformed into Erskine's response to Bisset's letter in the next instalment of their ongoing

156. *Life*, 449.
157. For the quotation in context, see *Works*, 3:98.
158. See Bisset, 5–9.

correspondence that, in fact, seems never actually to have happened.[159] Contrary to the desires of the secondary literature, not even the ecclesial trauma of the Breach elicited from Erskine the least indication of any desire for reconciliation with an evangelical party within the Established Church; a party that, in Erskine's judgment, remained illusory.

The Breach's Verdict

Virtually without exception, the Breach is seen as the great failure of Erskine's ministry. In some instances, it is presented as a failure so fundamental that it casts a disparaging shadow over all of Erskine's life and thought.[160] However, the actual nature of Erskine's position within the Breach demands a more nuanced assessment of that controversy. In the first instance, it must be conceded that the position that Erskine articulated within the Breach evidenced the theoretical viability of Erskine's Covenantal Revolution Church. As Erskine's own writings make clear, he never concentrated his argument on an attempt to prove either the lawfulness of the Burgess Oath or the error of the Sentence 1746. Rather, Erskine's efforts were fundamentally directed toward vindicating the Sentence 1747 and its call for mutual forbearance concerning the Oath until consensus could be reached in the Church at large. When dissension arose, Erskine never argued that the anti-Burghers should be cast out of the Associate Synod; rather, once they had withdrawn, he pled with them to return and to share communion with the Burghers. To facilitate that communion, Erskine outlined a vision of expansive Church communion that both would guarantee fidelity on the essential matters of the faith that had won the Church's consensus over the ages, and would protect diversity of opinion on the *adiaphora* upon which the Church was still patiently waiting for light. Taken on its own merits, Erskine's vision of a Covenantal Revolution Church, as Erskine sought to implement it during the Breach, showed itself both able to maintain doctrinal precision and fidelity in essentials, and willing to accommodate variety and disagreement in non-essentials. In the Breach, Erskine's Covenantal Revolution Church showed itself capable of facilitating intra-communion diversity.

While his actions in the Breach showed Erskine's Covenantal Revolution Church to be ecclesiologically legitimate in post-Union Scotland, that controversy also indicated some of the weaknesses inherent in Erskine's system; weaknesses that, in large part, were embedded in the very foundation of the Secession Church. Most importantly, while Erskine called for

159. See MacEwen, *Erskines*, 133–34.
160. See, for example, ibid., 128.

a distinction between the essentials of the Secession witness and the *adiaphora*, along with mutual forbearance on the latter, that spirit of catholicity was evidenced far too late in Erskine's ministry. As already evidenced and discussed in relation to his controversy with Whitefield, Erskine long had judged himself bound to denounce every minute defection or error of his opponents once fellowship had been broken. In previous controversies, this had meant that once communion was lost because of disagreement on the essentials of the faith, Erskine detailed all of the erroneous views of his opponents, even on the *adiaphora*. As manifested in his disagreement with Whitefield, this tendency saw Erskine publicly condemning positions with which he was willing to forbear privately as long as the essentials were agreed. In the Breach, this impulse to catalogue rigorously every difference with one's opponents and the tendency to offer no distinction between differences on the essentials and on the *adiaphora* appeared to bear its fruit in the anti-Burgher position; a position that made the "core" of the Secession witness as expansive as Erskine had made his previous denunciations of opponents. While Erskine's call for mutual forbearance on the *adiaphora* in the Breach was commendable, that call was undermined by Erskine's previous demand that even errors in the non-essentials be denounced alongside errors concerning the central truths of Christianity. Erskine long had held such a distinction, yet he never had expressed or evidenced it publicly and thus never had encouraged such differentiation within the Secession Church. Erskine's methodology had helped foster a rigorous spirit in the Secession and that rigor proved unable to assimilate itself to Erskine's later calls for charity.

In addition to the rigor of the Secession Church, the very fact of that Church's existence militated against the long-term cohesion of Erskine's Covenantal Revolution Church. By the time of the Breach, toleration had reigned in Scotland for thirty-five years and, as the Secession itself had shown, this meant that there were no external constraints upon the founding of new ecclesiastical groups. With separation and re-formation a possibility, co-existence with those of differing opinions became less appealing. The radical ecclesiastical change ushered in by toleration is seen by a simple comparison of the issues underlying the Burgess Oath controversy with those at the heart of the Covenantal opposition in the earlier Abjuration Oath controversy. While there were important differences between the anti-Burgher position and the Covenantal non-juror position, those differences underlay a common ultimate grievance—swearing the oath in question, whether Burgess or Abjuration, would involve the juror in defection from Covenantal obligations. In the Abjuration Oath controversy, with the bonds of Church unity still strong, Erskine and the other non-jurors were willing to retain communion with the Established Church while personally refusing the objected oath. In the later Burgess Oath controversy, with the notion of Church unity altered by decades of toleration and the Secession itself, the anti-Burghers deemed it more desirable to found a different communion than to maintain personal opposition while abiding with those with whom they differed. While the dissenters' position in each circumstance did not differ, the options open to them for action did. In its very success, the Secession seems to have undercut its potential to succeed.

The effects of this removal of external constraints upon fragmentation were exacerbated by the final Secession weakness uncovered by the Breach. Despite being characterized as a sect, the Secession Church was a diverse ecclesiastical body. As the events surrounding the Seceders' Covenant renewal had revealed, there were some within the Secession with strong Macmillanite sympathies, and the Burgess Oath controversy unearthed further differences pertaining to views on Church purity, intra-communion diversity, and other related issues. This diversity should not be surprising. In the 1740s, the Secession Church was the only legitimate body of presbyterian dissent in Scotland. The Macmillanites, while presbyterian, placed themselves on the radical fringe with their rejection of the civil magistrate; the growing Glasite movement had distanced itself from presbytery; and the Relief Church, which also would prove a viable body of presbyterian dissent, was yet to be founded. Due to the lack of other dissenting bodies, ministers had come into the Secession for varying reasons and had brought with them divergent views on various issues. As this disparate body of ministers addressed issues other than their shared opposition to the Established Church, they uncovered their diversity while simultaneously realizing that all previous external impediments to further fragmentation had been removed. That the rupture of the Breach—which was followed by further ruptures within both the Burgher and the anti-Burgher Synods—occurred as this composite group further grouped itself into like-minded factions perhaps is not surprising. The Secession, as the only legitimate presbyterian alternative to the Established Church, had assumed the diversity of a national Church, yet in post-toleration, post-Secession Scotland, it was divested of all external compulsion for cohesion in the face of intra-communion diversity.

Overall, the Breach offers a mixed verdict on the viability of Erskine's Covenantal Revolution Church within post-Union Scotland. Theologically and theoretically, Erskine's system was tenable, offering both a standard around which the Church could cohere and sufficient space for diversity on non-essential matters. However, the exigencies of post-toleration, post-Secession Scotland ensured that maintaining cohesion within that Church would not be easy. As a diverse ecclesiastical body in a post-toleration society, the Secession faced great incentives to further fragmentation, and into this fragile situation Erskine's past conduct had injected the potential poison of an exacting rigor not only in the essentials of the faith, but also in non-essential matters. While the events of the Breach demonstrated the weaknesses of this situation, the potential of Erskine's Covenantal Revolution Church must not be obscured. In Erskine's call for mutual forbearance on the Burgess Oath as a matter not previously determined by the Church, one sees a coherent plan for protecting and countenancing diversity on the *adiaphora* within a broad communion, while in his urgings for reconciliation of the Breach, there is a glimpse of the possibility of overcoming the potentially destructive example that he had set for the Secession Church. While the way forward for Erskine's Covenantal Revolution Church would be difficult, that Church was able to facilitate intra-communion diversity on non-essentials and thus remained a viable option, both theologically and practically.

IMPLICATIONS OF THE 1740S

Doubtlessly, the 1740s were a difficult and trying decade for Erskine and his Covenantal Revolution Church. No sooner was that Church fully distinguished from the Established Church than it began a series of controversies that would profoundly test its claims to be the true Church of Scotland. However, in that tumultuous decade, two crucial considerations emerged. First, in spite of severe tests and pronounced weaknesses, Erskine's Covenantal Revolution Church proved itself ecclesiologically coherent in post-Union Scotland. In his controversy with George Whitefield, Erskine evidenced a doctrinal prioritization capable of facilitating cooperation with other communions, even if that catholicity proved notably weak at certain points. Through the complex of issues arising from the Seceders' Covenant renewal, Erskine maintained a possibility proven in the Jacobite Rising of 1745—a Church faithful in its Covenantal foundations, yet civilly submissive to the uncovenanted British State. In the midst of the acrimony surrounding the Burgess Oath controversy and resulting Breach, Erskine articulated a distinction between the essentials and non-essentials of the faith, coupled with a willingness to show mutual forbearance on the latter, that would allow a burgeoning Associate Synod to accommodate significant intra-communion diversity on the *adiaphora*. In each thematic grouping of controversies, the overarching picture that emerges is that of a viable national Church.

Secondly, throughout the 1740s, one sees no development in Erskine's attitude toward the Established Church, a fact that runs contrary to the desires of the Secession historiography. That influential historiography presents Erskine as sharing common cause with an evangelical wing of the Established Church in the Whitefield controversy, then regrettably alienating that party with his Covenant renewal, only to enter a period of withdrawn mourning upon seeing the excesses of his ways in the trauma of the Breach. However, the actual course of the 1740s presents a sharply dissonant picture of Erskine being driven by the implicit assumption that the Established Church had apostatized and the Secession Church stood as the only legitimate embodiment of the Church of Christ in Scotland. In his controversy with Whitefield, Erskine's estrangement from his former correspondent proceeded upon the sole consideration that, in refusing to absent himself from Established Church pulpits, Whitefield was willing to aide the work of a false church while damaging the progress of the true Church in Scotland, the Secession Church. In the controversies surrounding the Secession's Covenant renewal, Erskine enunciated an idea of the true Church of Scotland being demarcated by its ownership of Scotland's Covenants; Covenants which he labored to see the Secession renew and which he excoriated the Established Church for renouncing. In the Burgess Oath controversy and resulting Breach, Erskine simply assumed that the Associate Synod must function in conformity to the Barrier Acts of the Second Reformation and must define its categories of essentials and non-essentials of the faith by the consensus, or lack thereof, of the Kirk in previous generations. In both instances, Erskine assumed that the Secession Church was the Kirk, a position patently implying his rejection of the Established Church. In 1739, with the Seceders' *Declinature*, Erskine had assumed the starkest of positions toward the Established Church—its courts were no longer right courts of Christ and thus the Established Church was a false church. Throughout the 1740s, Erskine did not relent from this position; indeed, he showed no change at all. For Erskine, the Established Church remained a false church with whom judicial cooperation was not only undesirable, but impossible.

While Erskine's Covenantal Revolution Church was thus proving its legitimacy and asserting its identity with the historic Kirk, it was doing so in an ever-changing Scotland. With the initial glimmerings of economic growth, the "expanding" of the national mind, and the ascendance of an increasingly "polite" society, Scots were asking new questions from within new paradigms. Throughout the 1740s, Erskine and his brethren were crafting their response to a society rife with latitudinarianism and decades-long defection from perpetually-binding Covenants. As the trends within the Established Church that Erskine and his brethren had been denouncing since their extrusion from the church judicatories continued, theirs was a response that came to resonate with many of their countrymen, a fact indicated by the Secession Church's growth in the first half of the decade and resilience and continued growth in the second half thereof.[161] In Erskine's Covenantal Revolution Church, the doctrinal foundation that had marked the Kirk since the Reformation was brought into the 1740s and contextually applied in such a way that it granted the Secession Church both a claim and an ability to be the *National* Church of Scotland as it engaged with the uncovenanted British State not with the intention of co-existence, but of conjoint reform. While Erskine's Covenantal Revolution Church was itself in need of reformation in certain areas, it nonetheless constituted a legitimate, tenable, and stark alternative to the Established Church as the Kirk continued to seek a way forward in the new realities of post-Union Scotland.

Insofar as the Secession Church successfully charted that uncertain way forward, it did so as a result of the guiding theological commitments that Erskine had brought to it. Indeed, the 1740s reveal Erskine in his final maturity, blending his evangelical federalism with his modified Covenantalism to create a theological system capable of guiding a church that would both cling to essential truth and recognize the realities of post-Union, post-toleration Scotland. Tragically, that theologically-driven system that Erskine had brought to his Covenantal Revolution Church seemed undercut by, among other factors, the zeal with which Erskine's more austere tendencies had attached to the rigorous criteria of Covenanting holiness in previous years. While Erskine's personal excesses had thus made the task before his Covenantal Revolution Church more difficult, his doctrinal system had likewise made that task possible.

---

161. See, for example, Woodside, *Soul of a Scottish Church*, 34–38.

Conclusion

ERSKINE'S FINAL YEARS

While Erskine's declining health had precluded an extensive involvement in the Breach, the closing years of Erskine's life did contain important productivity for the aging minister. Prior to the Breach, Alexander Moncrieff had served as the Professor of Divinity for the Associate Synod, and his departure with the anti-Burghers necessitated his replacement. James Fisher was the Burghers' choice to fill the vacant position, yet as he first considered and then prepared for the additional responsibilities, Erskine was asked to "take under his inspection the students of Divinity" for the Synod, a request that Erskine honored for two years, finally resigning in 1749 due to his health and Fisher's willingness to assume the duties.[1] Following his resignation from the Divinity position, Erskine worked alongside Fisher and Ralph Erskine in composing the Synod's *Catechism*. As previously discussed, in this last labor, Erskine made one of his most significant contributions to the body of Scottish theology; a contribution that likewise is invaluable in grasping the theological commitments that had guided Erskine's life. While Erskine clearly was capable of these more reclusive pursuits, the public exertions of the ministry became increasingly difficult for him, leading first to extensive

---

1. *Minutes of the Proceedings of the Associate Synod Commencing on the Sixteenth day of June, One thousand seven hundred, and forty seven years*, 979. Hereafter, *Minutes of AS*. See also *Minutes of AS*, 1033. Most likely due to his age and the spontaneous nature of his appointment, Erskine never delivered formal lectures to his students, choosing rather to read and comment upon Francis Turretin, the generally recognized and recommended text for Secession divinity students for some time before his tenure. Overall, it would appear that Erskine, advanced in age and aware that he would be filling the theological chair only temporarily, simply read from the accepted text rather than generating his own lectures or devising his own curriculum. See M'Kerrow, *Scottish Church*, 3rd ed., 780, 786; *Life*, 451–52.

provision of supply from the presbytery and synod and ultimately, in 1752, the calling of a full assistant to Erskine's Stirling congregation. Finally, on 2 June 1754, Erskine passed quietly from this life, his body being buried beneath the pulpit in the Stirling church by a congregation still firmly attached to a man whom they knew not as a polemicist, but as their pastor.

ERSKINE'S LIFE AND THEOLOGY IN REVIEW

As the preceding account has argued, the pastor thus laid to rest was a man driven by his dual commitment to both an evangelical federalism and a modified Covenantalism. In each of these systems, Erskine was seeking neither to reclaim a forsaken theology nor usher the Kirk into an era of new principles. Rather, Erskine was attempting to bring the common inheritance of Scottish theology, obscured and complicated by the Second Episcopate, into a radically different post-Union Scotland in such a way that that theology would address the spiritual and practical needs of contemporary Scots. In perhaps the more central of the two systems within Erskine's thought—his evangelical federalism—this process is clearly seen. After formally adopting the federalism of the Westminster Confession, the Kirk had little respite before it was plunged into the internecine disputes of the Commonwealth and often brutal persecution of the Second Episcopate. Finally emerging from such troubles at the Revolution, the Kirk was concerned with consolidating its establishment against a never-absent episcopalian threat and then, when John Simson came before the General Assembly for teachings that effectively undermined the entire federalist substructure, the Kirk found itself with a federal tradition, "formalized" in fields rather than in assembly halls, that contained differing emphases and developments in "minor" areas of federalism that were not conclusively established in the Westminster Confession. When Erskine drew from this uniformly-imbibed federalist tradition to craft his defense of the gospel against Simson's errors and the incipient rationalism that it portended, he self-consciously chose emphases, and even terminology, that in his view most powerfully brought a gracious gospel to bear upon a Kirk sliding toward at least a toleration of legalistic emphases. Sharing the guiding concerns of his forebears, Erskine adopted some of their formulations in the areas of Confessional silence, yet also rejected some of the structures they had developed within those silent quarters as they had sought to combat error in their own generations. Erskine's resulting evangelical federalist structure was a robust presentation of a free and gracious gospel that was firmly within the parameters of Westminster federalism and resistant to the legalizing emphases of others in his day. Erskine did not reclaim and he did not innovate; rather, he spoke, from within the tradition of Westminster federalism, to what he perceived were the needs of his generation.

While its emergence within his system is more diffuse, both temporally and controversially, Erskine's modified Covenantalism was no less the contextual application of the inheritance of Scottish theology than was his evangelical federalism. From the earliest days of presbytery's reestablishment in 1690, a voice of Covenantal dissent had echoed through the Revolution Church. While Linning, Shields, and Boyd might have been the most obvious tokens of this dissent, they were joined by many other ministers who likewise held Scotland's Covenants, neglected in the Kirk's constitutional establishment, as the true foundation of the Church of Scotland and thus both a grid from which to critique the post-Revolution world and a model for which the Kirk was to aim in her reforms. While this Covenantal impulse mourned the Covenants' absence from the Revolution Settlement, a commitment to Church unity held these dissidents within the Established Church under the implied, and principled, understanding that, as they were expected to tolerate what they perceived as the Kirk's defections, so the Kirk was expected to allow them the freedom to dissent from those defections in order that their consciences not be defiled. The exercise of this freedom over the years showed the abiding presence of their Covenantal dissent; a dissent to which Erskine joined his own voice in the Abjuration Oath controversy in 1712. In that controversy, Erskine clearly aligned himself with the nebulous dissenting party who held the Covenants, rather than a civil establishment, as normative for the Kirk and determinative of her actions, yet without requiring antagonism toward the uncovenanted Hanoverian State. The modified Covenantalism thus glimpsed in Erskine abided for twenty years more until, in 1732, Erskine's attempt to exercise a right of dissent that had been vital to mollifying Covenantal dissidents for decades resulted in his censure by the Synod of Perth and Stirling. When the course thus began terminated in 1739–1740, with Erskine formally extruded from the Established Church, he began a process of transforming a modified Covenantal dissent into an operative ecclesiological program. The modified Covenantalism that Erskine enunciated in the coming years of the Secession Church was synonymous with that expressed earlier in his ministry; synonymous with that which had guided Covenantal dissidents since 1690. In this, Erskine's modified Covenantalism, and the Covenantal Revolution Church that it animated, was the contextual application of the tradition of Scottish Covenantal dissent to Erskine's own situation—extruded from the Established Church in a post-Union, post-toleration Scotland. Erskine's only novelty was that he would be afforded the opportunity to implement what others had only described.

In and through his development of these two doctrinal systems, one glimpses an ever-clearer picture of Ebenezer Erskine. Often, Erskine is reduced to personality, defined by either his zeal or his tendentiousness. As the preceding study has shown, Erskine undeniably was both, at turns evangelically fervent and irresponsibly antagonistic. However, Erskine was always more than either of these things. At every point in his ministry, Erskine was driven by his theological commitments; commitments that both grew out of his own life and identity and catered to the dispositions of his personality. If Erskine's evangelical federalism shaped the message that allowed his zeal to draw thousands to the preaching green behind his Stirling church, so too did the Covenantalism that he sought to modify provide the rigorous standards of holiness to which his implacability attached. However, in both instances, it was Erskine's theology that was primary and that must anchor any coherent understanding of him. Indeed, through that theology—a theology that sought to apply Scotland's theological heritage to a radically new nation—one arrives at Erskine's core, for one glimpses the heart of a pastor, buried beneath the pulpit of his church, who, while remaining faithful to the inheritance given him, sought to press the gospel upon his countrymen with immediacy. Erskine could be rapturous. Erskine could be contentious. But, animating Erskine's ministry was his theology, and animating his theology was an evangelical federalism and a modified Covenantalism that Erskine was convinced represented the only faithful way forward for the Kirk in its new post-Union, post-toleration milieu.

IMPLICATIONS: PERSONAL, THEOLOGICAL, AND HISTORICAL

When Erskine is thus understood as a man driven by a dual commitment to both his evangelical federalism and his modified Covenantalism, each of which emanated from firmly within an inherited Scottish theology, a host of implications emerge. Simply stated, Erskine needs to be examined anew. Quite often, Erskine is placed on lists of ministers who have profoundly impacted the Kirk, yet he seldom is understood. His ecclesiastical descendants revere him, yet they have little appreciation for what was truly remarkable about his theology or for the difficulties into which he led his co-laborers. While the specific implications of the present study to these ends cannot be enumerated in full at present, four core observations require to be made in conclusion.

First, the preceding study demands that Erskine be seen as a robust, committed Westminster federalist. In the extant literature, Erskine is given no such consideration. For many interpreters, Erskine was animated by an evangelical fervor that was uninterested in the finer nuances of doctrinal systems.[2] While Erskine did not depart from orthodoxy, so the interpretation goes, he was not overly attentive to the implications of its rigorous application. Another group of interpreters is typified by Charles Bell, who argues that Erskine attempted to correct perceived problems within federalism, yet ultimately failed because of his imbibed commitments to the same Scottish Westminster federalism that he was seeking to amend.[3] In both such assessments, as well as many others like them, Erskine stands as a man departing from the rigors of a self-conscious Scottish Westminster federalism. However, particularly as seen in the *Marrow* controversy, Erskine was precisely the opposite. With the first process against John Simson as his catalyst, Erskine began, around 1714 or 1715, a process of considered theological refinement that, by the time of the *Marrow* controversy, had produced an evangelical federalism that was an intentional adoption of Scottish federalism against perceived errors rather than a flight from that federalism inspired by either indifference or disagreement. Furthermore, it was this evangelical federalism and Erskine's commitment to it that prepared the ground for the synod censure that precipitated the Secession Crisis; that injected a growing catholicity and doctrinal prioritization into Erskine's theological system; that shaped the Secession Church's first doctrinal statements; and that provided coherence to his doctrine of the State. At the center of Erskine's thought and the forefront of his actions lay his self-consciously Westminsterian evangelical federalism and to obscure either this federalism itself, or its roots in Scottish Westminster federalism, is to miss the theological structure that drove Erskine's ministry.

In the evangelical nature of Erskine's federalism, there emerges a second implication of the preceding evaluation. Led by T. F. Torrance, a school of Scottish theologians and historians have identified a paradigmatic shift within Scottish theology from the earnest, evangelical warmth of the Scots Confession to the formulaic, "logico-causal" precision of the Westminster Confession.[4] In Torrance's judgment, this shift created a tension between missionary, evangelical zeal and strident Westminster federalism that

---

2. E.g., Mechie, "Theological Climate," 268; Harper, *Memoir*, 84.

3. Bell, *Calvin and Scottish Theology*, 161–68.

4. T. F. Torrance, *Theology*, 4–45, 125–53; *School*, xviii–xxi. See also Barth, *Confessions*, 133.

conflicted Erskine and some of his contemporaries.[5] In Erskine's evangelical federalism, however, one confronts a theological system that was warmly evangelical not in spite of its Westminster federalist structure, but *because of* that structure.[6] Particularly through his expansive Covenant of Grace and his insistence upon the immediacy of grace, Erskine articulated a federalism that was both firmly within the confines of Westminster thought and structurally incompatible with legalistic emphases. Indeed, it was his federal theology that undergirded two of the most pronounced evangelical components of Erskine's thought—his free offer of the gospel to all mankind and his doctrine of assurance. Throughout his ministry, Erskine was led to some of his most warmly evangelical positions because of his Westminster federal theology, and thus the relationship between evangelical warmth and federalist dogma needs re-examination. Indeed, that relationship needs re-examination even from those who would eschew Torrance's dichotomy. In the present day, many within the Reformed, evangelical community are displaying a resurgence of interest in, and commitment to, federal theological structures, yet that federal renaissance is notably void of some of the central features of Erskine's evangelical federalism. Perhaps most notably, the bi-covenantal paradigm that had such prodigious influence on Erskine's evangelical federalism receives little advocacy in the present literature.[7] In such a day, from both those in agreement with Torrance and those not, Erskine's evangelical federalism—self-consciously founded upon Scriptural argumentation and structurally productive of evangelical views—warrants attention.

In addition to considerations regarding federal theology, the present evaluation of Erskine necessitates a revision of the traditional understanding of the Secession that he led; a Secession that represented the ecclesializing of the tradition of Covenantal dissent that had reverberated through the Established Church since the Revolution. Most importantly, the organic

---

5. See T. F. Torrance, *Theology*, 242–43. Note especially ibid., 246–47, where Torrance is addressing questions in *Catechism* authored by Erskine, although not thus attributed by Torrance.

6. McGowan argues a similar point in relation to Boston's federalism, yet focuses on matters other than federal structure. McGowan, "Federal Theology as a Theology of Grace," 41–51.

7. E.g., Horton, *God of Promise*, especially 78–82; Golding, *Covenant Theology*, especially 138–42; Macleod, "Covenant Theology." For a notable exception, see Robertson, *The Christ of the Covenants*, 53–54. The articulation of such a federal structure, with its requirement that the Covenant of Grace be seen as a progressively-revealed intra-Trinitarian Covenant, also offers the potential of addressing some concerns being raised regarding federalism's resurgence. See, for example, Niehaus, "An Argument Against Theologically Constructed Covenants," especially 259–62, 270–73.

continuity between the tradition of Covenantal dissent and Erskine's Secession Church, coupled with the foundation of the Secession in a procedural anomaly rather than an unprecedented wilful withdrawal, locates the Secession within the lineal development of Scottish theology and removes any suppositions of novelty. In the very earliest years of his ministry, Erskine had articulated a Covenantal critique of the Abjuration Oath that was not at all dissimilar from the like critique of other Covenantally-committed ministers. Decades later, Erskine voiced the same dissenting paradigm, yet with one crucial change. Unlike other Covenantally-committed ministers, Erskine had been extruded from the Established Church and thus, required to chart his own ecclesiastical course rather than dissent from someone else's, Erskine's Covenantal dissent had generated a fully-developed modified Covenantalism. In this, the Secession Church to which Erskine's name will ever be connected must be understood not as a temporally-localized response to patronage abuses, but rather as the judicative embodiment of a tradition of Scottish dissent that had never been absent from the Revolution Church, thus offering both theologians and historians not a new phenomenon to study, but rather the opportunity to study, in full flower, a dissenting tradition that had been subtly shaping disputes within the Kirk for decades. In the Secession Church, that dissenting tradition moves from the shadows to the microscope. Furthermore, in that movement, the Secession most likely also compelled Covenantally-committed ministers still in the Established Church to distance themselves from a commonly-inherited tradition, thus facilitating a development—perhaps, even, a divergence—within a dying Covenantal dissent.

Finally, the modified Covenantal system by which Erskine brought Scotland's Covenants to bear upon his post-Union, post-toleration milieu demands that Erskine's Covenantal Revolution Church be seen as a legitimate ecclesiastical program for the Kirk. Contrary to popular perception, the Covenants did not have to become either a superseded artefact or an instrument of self-inflicted anachronism in post-Revolution Scotland. In Erskine's modified Covenantalism, he presented a third possibility—that the Covenants be used as the ground upon which the Kirk stood as it reached out to a disorientingly different world. While the exacting rigor that Erskine imported into the Secession Church tarnished the promise of Erskine's theological system, that weakness must not obscure the fact that Erskine's Covenantal Revolution Church represented a viable ecclesiastical option within post-Union Scotland; a fact that expands one's understanding of the capabilities of Scottish Covenantal thought, illuminates the desires of early eighteenth-century Scots, and intimates a faithful way forward for present-day Churches in an increasingly post-confessional age.

What, then, of the juxtaposed assessments of Erskine's significance cited at the opening of the present treatment—that of Erskine as an instigator of both the Kirk's missionary spirit and her factionalism? In the first instance, it does appear legitimate to describe Erskine as an important transitional figure—along with others, to be certain—who helped move the Kirk from the more inwardly-focused age of the late seventeenth and early eighteenth centuries to the evangelical, missionary spirit of the later eighteenth century and beyond by enunciating an earnestly evangelical doctrinal system intelligible within its Westminster federalist tradition, James Hadow's suspicions notwithstanding. In the second instance, Erskine's status as a prophet of faction appears more complex. Undeniably, Erskine's rigorous covenanting holiness proved problematic for the Secession Church, yet the existence of that Secession seems to be the result not of Erskine's, but of the Synod of Perth and Stirling's, transgression of the Revolution Kirk's balance of coexistence and freedom to dissent. While Erskine thus can be criticized for injecting a certain intolerance into the Secession, he cannot justly be blamed for a factionalism that spawned that Secession.

In Erskine's life, he acquired many opponents. Through the trauma of the Breach, one of the bitterest of them became Adam Gib. Following Erskine's death, Gib enquired of Robert Campbell, himself a sought after preacher, if he had ever heard Erskine preach. When Campbell replied that he had not, Gib informed him, "Well then, Sir, you never heard the Gospel in its majesty."[8] While over two hundred and fifty years—and all of the reflections upon Erskine that have filled those years—separate Erskine from the present day, perhaps nothing has exceeded the profundity of Gib's words. In the eyes of a man who had become as estranged from Erskine as any other man had ever been, there resided something in Erskine's proclamation and ministry that superseded his varyingly contentious personality and transcended his ubiquitous controversial engagements. There, the gospel was majestic. In Erskine's federal theology, the graciousness of that gospel shone unhindered; in his modified Covenantalism, the doctrinal truth of that gospel anchored and defined the Church as it sought to reform society. In Erskine, one sees a man, for all of the difficulties that he injected into that effort, taking the gospel believed upon by his fathers and bringing it into a Scotland that they never would have recognized. When Erskine scholarship is able to replicate Gib's feat—to see behind Erskine's personality and his evident penchant for controversy to the doctrinal system that drove that personality in those controversies—perhaps the majesty of the gospel that

---

8. *Life*, 482. On Campbell, who would succeed James Erskine as minister of Ebenezer Erskine's congregation, see Small, *History of the Congregations*, 2:665–67.

Erskine preached will once more be glimpsed and the great goal of Erskine's ministry will be realized afresh as received truth pierces contextual distractions and becomes not only truth received, but also truth appropriated and lived.

Appendix I

Text of 1712 Oath of Abjuration[1]

I, A.B., Do TRULY and sincerely Acknowledge, profess, Testify and Declare in my Conscience, before GOD and the World, That Our Sovereign Lady Queen ANNE, is Lawful and Rightful Queen of this Realm, and of all other Her Majesty's Dominions and Countries thereunto belonging. And I do solemnly and sincerely Declare, That I do believe in my Conscience, the Person pretended to be *Prince of Wales*, during the Life of the late *King James*, and since his Decease pretending to be, and taking upon himself the Stile and Title of *King of England*, by the Name of *James the Third*, or of *Scotland*, by the Name of *James the Eight*, or the Stile and Title of *King of Great Britain*, hath not any Right or Title whatsoever to the Crown of this Realm, or any other the Dominions thereunto belonging: And I do Renounce, Refuse and Abjure, any Allegiance or Obedience to him. And I do Swear, That I will bear Faith and true Allegiance to her Majesty *Queen Anne*, and Her will defend to the utmost of my Power against all Traiterous Conspiracies and Attempts whatsoever, which shall be made against Her Person, Crown or Dignity: And I will do my utmost Endeavour, to disclose and make known to Her Majesty and Her Successors, all Treasons and Traiterous Conspiracies, which I shall know to be against Her, or any of them. And I do faithfully Promise, to the utmost of my Power, to Support, Maintain and Defend the Succession of the Crown against him the said *James*, and all other Persons whatsoever, **as** the same is, and stands settled by an Act, Instituted, *An Act declaring the Right and Liberties of the Subject, and settling the Succession of the Crown*

---

1 Taken from *The Oath of Abjuration Displayed, In its sinful nature and Tendency, in its Inconsistency with Presbyterian Principles and Covenants; the Security it affords to the Church of England*, 2–3.

to Her Present Majesty, and the Heirs of Her Body, being Protestants; and as the same by another Act, Instituted, *An Act for the further Limitation of the Crown, and better securing the Rights and Liberties of the Subject,* is, and stands settled and entailed after the Decease of Her Majesty, and for Default of Issue of Her Majesty, to the *Princess* Sophia, *Electress and Dutchess* Dowager *of* Hannover, *and the Heirs of her Body, being* Protestants. And all these things I do plainly and sincerely Acknowledge and Swear, according to these express Words by me spoken, and according to the plain and common Sense and Understanding of the same Words, without any Equivocation, Mental Evasion, or secret Reservation whatsoever. And I do make this Recognition, Acknowledgement, Abjuration, Renunciation and Promise, Heartily, Willingly and Truly, upon the true Faith of a Christian. *So Help me, GOD.*

Appendix II

Problematic Sections

PROBLEMATIC SECTION OF THE LIMITATIONS

That whosoever shall hereafter come to the Possession of this Crown, shall joyn in Communion with the Church of *England*, as by Law established.

That every King or Queen of this Realm, who shall come to, and succeed in the Imperial Crown of this Kingdom, by Vertue of this Act, shall have the Coronation Oath administered to Him, Her, or Them at their Respective Coronations.

PROBLEMATIC SECTION OF THE CORONATION OATH

The Arch-Bishop, of Bishop shall say,
Will you preserve unto the Bishops and Clergy of this Realm, and to the Churches committed to their Charge, all such Rights and Privileges as by Law do, or shall appertain unto them, or any of them?

King and Queen shall say,
All this I promise to do . . . . *So Help me GOD.*[2]

---

2. Taken from *The Oath of Abjuration Displayed, In its sinful nature and Tendency, in its Inconsistency with Presbyterian Principles and Covenants; the Security it affords to the Church of England*, 3.

Appendix III

Text of 1715 Oath of Abjuration[3]

"I A.B. DO TRULY and sincerely acknowledge, profess, testify, and declare, in my Conscience, before God and the World, that our Sovereign Lord King *George*, is Lawful and Rightful King of this Realm, and all other his Majesty's Dominions and Countries thereunto belonging: And I do solemnly and sincerely declare, that I do believe in my Conscience, that the Person pretended to be the Prince of *Wales*, during the Life of the late King *James*, and since his Decease pretending to be, and taking upon himself the Stile and Title of King of *England*, by the Name of *James* the Third, or of *Scotland*, by the Name of *James* the Eighth, or the Stile or Title of King of *Great Britain*, hath not any Right or Title whatsoever to the Crown of this Realm, or any of the Dominions thereto belonging. And I do renounce, refuse, and abjure any Allegiance or Obedience to him: And I do swear, that I will bear Faith and true Allegiance to his Majesty King *George*, and him will defend to the utmost of my Power, against all Traitorous Conspiracies and Attempts whatsoever, which shall be made against his Person, Crown, or Dignity; and I will do my utmost Endeavour to disclose and make known to his Majesty and his Successors, all Treasons and Traitorous Conspiracies, which I shall know to be against him, or any of them. And I do faithfully promise, to the utmost of my Power, to support, maintain, and defend the Succession of the Crown, against him the said *James*, and all other Persons whatsoever; which Succession, by an Act, intituled, *An Act for further Limitation of the Crown, and better securing the Rights and Liberties of the Subjects*, is and stands limited to the Princess *Sophia*, Electress and Dutchess Dowager of

3. Taken from PLAIN TRUTHS; OR, A COLLECTION Of SCARCE and VALUABLE TRACTS, 65–66.

Hanover, and the Heirs of her Body being Protestants. And all these Things I do plainly and sincerely acknowledge and swear, according to these express Words by me spoken, and according to the plain and common Sense and Understanding of the same Words, without any Equivocation, Mental Evasion, or Secret Reservation whatsoever; and I do make this Recognition, Acknowledgement, Abjuration, Renunciation, and Promise, heartily, willingly, and truly, upon the true Faith of a Christian. *So help me God.*"

Appendix IV

Full Text of the Act of the Associate Presbytery

AT EDINBURGH, THE THIRD *Day of* February, *One thousand seven hundred and forty three Years.* THE Presbytery are of Opinion, that, in regard they had *formerly* agreed, That it was not suitable to their present Circumstances, to blend *Civil* and *Ecclesiastick* Matters in the Oath of God, in renewing the Covenants; because that the Cognizance of *Civil* Affairs belongs not properly to them as a *Church Judicatory*; and some Members being of the Mind, that the *Reduplication* of the Oath upon that Clause of the Confession of Sins, which was the Occasion of the *Dissent*, would, upon the Matter, amount to the foresaid Blending; that therefore the said Clause shall be *left out*. Yet, that none may misconstruct the Principles of the Presbytery, on the Head of the *Civil Magistrate*; although the *National Apostasy*, under which the Lord's Remnant through the Land have been groaning, while our *Rulers* have not only *neglected*, but *contradicted* their Duty, of espousing and supporting the covenanted *Principles* and *Reformation* of this Church, whereby they have greatly provoked the Lord to Anger, be Ground of Humiliation before the Lord: Yet the Presbytery do hereby *condemn* the *dangerous Extreme* that some have gone into, of *impugning* the present Civil Authority over these Nations, and Subjection thereunto in *lawful* Commands, on account of the Want of these Qualifications, which Magistrates ought to have by the Word of God and our Covenants; even though they allow us in the free Exercise of our Religion, and are not manifestly unhinging the Liberties of the Kingdom; an Opinion and Practice *contrary* to the plain Tenor of Scripture, and to the known Principles of this Church, in her Confession and Covenants, and of all other reformed Churches: And that *some few* others carry their Zeal against the Defections and Evils of the Times, to the *dangerous Extreme* of espousing Principles in favours of propagating Religion by *offensive* Arms; quite *contrary* to that Disposition, which ought to be in all the professed Followers of Christ, who came not to destroy Men's Lives, but to save them. And likeways the Presbytery agree, That, unless the Reverend Mr. *Nairn retract* the Principles contained in the said *Dissent*, that tend to overthrow Civil Magistracy, they will *proceed* against him according to the Rules of this Church.[4]

4. Transcribed in *AFR*, 82–83.

Bibliography

I. ECCLESIASTICAL RECORDS

Acts of the General Assembly of the Church of Scotland, M.DC.XXXVIII.–M.DCCC.XLII. Edinburgh: Edinburgh Printing, 1843.

"Case of Ebenezer Erskine and others. 1733–9." General Assembly Papers. National Archives of Scotland, Edinburgh, CH1/5/12, 13.

COPY OF A LIBEL AGAINST Messrs. Ebenezer Erskine *and Others, Ministers, who have seceded from the Church of* Scotland. *Edinburgh the fifteenth Day of March, One thousand seven hundred and thirty nine Years.* 1739.

The Fifth Synod Book of Perth and Stirling since the Revolution Commencing Eighth Day of October 1728. National Archives of Scotland, Edinburgh, CH2/449/8.

General Assembly of the Church of Scotland. *Unto the QUEENS Most Excellent Majesty, The Humble Address and Representation of the Commission of the General Assembly of the Church of Scotland, mett by Appointment of the said Assembly at Edinburgh the 5th of March, One Thousand seven Hundered and Twelve Years.* 1712.

Minutes of the Associate Presbytery and Synod, 1741–1744, Volume II. National Archives of Scotland, Edinburgh, CH3/27/3.

The minutes of the Associate Session of Stirling. 2d Book. National Archives of Scotland, Edinburgh, CH3/559/1.

Minutes of the Proceedings of the Associate Presbytery and Associate Synod, Commencing January 7. 1741, Volume II. National Archives of Scotland, Edinburgh, CH3/28/1.

Minutes of the Proceedings of the Associate Synod Commencing on the Sixteenth day of June, One thousand seven hundred, and forty seven years. National Archives of Scotland, Edinburgh, CH3/28/2.

A Narrative and State of the PROCEEDINGS of the JUDICATORIES of the Church of Scotland, Against Masters Ebenezer Erskine, William Wilson, Alexander Moncrieff, *and* James Fisher, *late Ministers thereof. WHEREIN The said PROCEEDINGS are fairly stated and fully vindicated, from the Aspersions cast upon them by these Men, and their Adherents.* Edinburgh: Davidson and Fleming, 1734.

Records of the Holy Rude Kirk Session Stirling. National Archives of Scotland, Edinburgh, CH2/1026/6.

Records of the Holy Rude Kirk Session Stirling. National Archives of Scotland, Edinburgh, CH2/1026/8.

Records of the Presbytery of Kirkcaldie from October 11, 1693-April 13, 1704, Vol. 2d. National Archives of Scotland, Edinburgh, CH2/224/3.

Records of The Presbytery of Kirkcaldie from April 13 1704 to Oct 1 1713. Volume 3. National Archives of Scotland, Edinburgh, CH2/224/4.

Records of the Presbyterie of Kirkcaldie from April 23 1724 to July 22 1742. Volume 5th. National Archives of Scotland, Edinburgh, CH2/224/6.

Records of the Presbytery of Stirling. National Archives of Scotland, Edinburgh, CH2/722/12.

Records of the Presbytery of Stirling. National Archives of Scotland, Edinburgh, CH2/722/13.

The Records of the Synod of Fife: 1696–1705. National Archives of Scotland, Edinburgh, CH2/154/5.

Records of the Synod of Fife: 1719–1738. National Archives of Scotland, Edinburgh, CH2/154/7.

Register of Baptisms begune at Stirling the 20th day of March 1739 years By order of Mr Erskine & his Session, being the Register of the Associate Congregation of Stirling keept by Wm Stevenson Presenter & Session Clerk. 1739 years the Era of the Secession. National Archives of Scotland, Edinburgh, CH3/559/17.

Scroll Minutes for Associate Presbytery, 17 February 1741—3 December 1741. National Archives of Scotland, Edinburgh, CH3/27/4.

The Session Book of Portmoak, Commencing from the year of our Saviour 1703. 1703–1735. National Archives of Scotland, Edinburgh, CH2/304/1.

II. UNPUBLISHED LETTERS

Alexander, James, Stirling, to James Erskine, Lord Grange, Edinburgh, 1 September 1736. National Archives of Scotland, Edinburgh, GD124/15/1460/1.

Erskine, Ebenezer, Portmoak, to Mr. Hackstoun, Laird of Kinnestoun, Cullross, 2 November 1726. Special Collections, New College Library, Edinburgh, ERS E1.

———, Stirling, to Alison Scott, Gateshall, 13 August 1751. Special Collections, New College Library, Edinburgh, Box 8.3.1.

———, Stirling, to Alison Scott, Gateshall, undated. Special Collections, New College Library, Box 8.3.3. [Dates to late 1751–early 1752]

———, Stirling, to the Earl of Hume, Edinburgh, 27 December 1745. Special Collections, New College Library, Edinburgh, Box 8.3.8.

———, Stirling, to James Erskine, Lord Grange, 19 February 1734. National Archives of Scotland, Edinburgh, GD124/15/1425/2.

———, to James Erskine, Lord Grange, 23 January 1734 [1733]. National Archives of Scotland, Edinburgh, GD124/15/1425/1.

———, to James Erskine, Lord Grange, 10 March 1737. National Archives of Scotland, Edinburgh, GD124/15/1470.

———, to James Fisher, Kinclaven, 21 August 1733. Special Collections, New College Library, Box 24.6.6. [Spurious letter; not actually authored by Erskine]

Erskine, James, Lord Grange, Edinburgh, to Ebenezer Erskine, 24 December 1737. National Archives of Scotland, Edinburgh, GD124/15/1484.

Fletcher, Andrew, Lord Milton, to Archibald Campbell, Lord Ilay, March 1735. Transcript in the hand of Andrew Fletcher. Saltoun Papers, National Library of Scotland, Edinburgh, 16559/102.

Rosse, G., Edinburgh, to Andrew Fletcher, Lord Milton, 6 May 1732. Saltoun Papers, National Library of Scotland, Edinburgh, 16551/61.

III. SECESSION PUBLICATIONS

Associate Presbytery. *ACT, Declaration* and *Testimony for the DOCTRINE, WORSHIP, DISCIPLINE, and GOVERNMENT of the Church of SCOTLAND; Agreeable to The Word of God, the Confession of Faith, the National Covenant of Scotland, and the Solemn League and Covenant of the Three Nations: And against Several Steps of Defection from the same, both in former and present Times.* Edinburgh: Lumisden and Robertson, 1737.

———. *ACT OF THE ASSOCIATE PRESBYTERY ANENT A PUBLICK FAST At Dunfermline, the fifteenth Day of July, One thousand seven hundred and forty two Years.* 1742.

———. *ACT OF THE Associate Presbytery, CONCERNING THE Doctrine of GRACE: Wherein the said DOCTRINE, As revealed in the Holy Scriptures, and, agreeably thereto, set forth in our Confession of Faith and Catechisms, Is ASSERTED, and VINDICATED From the Errors vented and published in some Acts of the Assemblies of this Church, passed in Prejudice of the same. WITH AN INTRODUCTION, Discovering the Rise and Progress of the Opposition to the DOCTRINE OF GRACE, and the Reason of passing and publishing this Act, in Vindication of the same.* Edinburgh: Duncan, 1744.

———. *ACT OF THE Associate Presbytery, For RENEWING the NATIONAL COVENANT of Scotland, and the SOLEMN LEAGUE and COVENANT of the three Nations, IN A WAY and MANNER agreeable to our present SITUATION, and CIRCUMSTANCES in this Period.* T. W. and T. Ruddimans, 1744.

———. *ACTS AND PROCEEDINGS OF THE MINISTERS AND ELDERS ASSOCIATE TOGETHER For the EXERCISE of CHURCH-GOVERNMENT and DISCIPLINE in a PRESBYTERIAL CAPACITY, met at Edinburgh, May 16th, 1739. Containing their DECLINATURE. Read in presence of the General Assembly, and given in to the Moderator thereof, May 17, 1739.* Glasgow: Bryce and Paterson, 1758.

———. *ANSWERS BY THE Associate Presbytery, TO Reasons of Dissent, given in to the said Presbytery, at Stirling, December 23, 1742; as also, the Representation and Petition dictated to their Clerk, and Reasons of Dissent and Secession, given in to them at Edinburgh, February 3, 1743; by the Reverend Mr. Thomas Nairn, Minister of the Gospel at Abbotshall. Together with A Declaration and Defence Of the ASSOCIATE PRESBYTERY's Principles anent the present Civil Government.* Edinburgh: T. W. and T. Ruddimans, 1744.

———. *Bond of the Covenant SWORN BY THE MINISTERS OF THE ASSOCIATE PRESBYTERY 28 DEC. 1743.* Edinburgh: Schenck, n.d.

———. *REASONS by Mr. EBENEZER ERSKINE Minister at Stirling, Mr. WILLIAM WILSON Minster at Perth, Mr. ALEXANDER MONCRIEFF Minister at Abernethy, and Mr. JAMES FISHER Minister at Kinclaven, Why they have not ACCEDED to the Judicatories of the Established Church.* Edinburgh: Lumisden and Robertson, 1735.

———. *The Representations of Masters Ebenezer Erskine and James Fisher and of Masters William Wilson and Alexander Moncrieff to the Commission of the late General Assembly.* Edinburgh: Lumisden and Robertson, 1733.

———. *A REVIEW of the NARRATIVE and STATE of the Proceedings of the Judicatories against Mr.* Ebenezer Erskine *Minister at* Stirling, *Mr.* William Wilson *Minister at* Perth, *Mr.* Alexander Moncrieff *Minister at* Abernethy, *and Mr.* James Fisher *Minister at* Kinclaven; *Emitted by a Committee of the Commission of the General Assembly.* WHEREIN *The Reasonings of the said* Narrative *are examined, and the Representation that is made of the Proceedings of the Judicatories enquired into.* Edinburgh: Lumisden and Robertson, 1734.

———. *A TESTIMONY TO THE DOCTRINE, WORSHIP, GOVERNMENT, and DISCIPLINE of the CHURCH of SCOTLAND: OR, REASONS by Mr.* Ebenezer Erskine *Minister at* Stirling, *Mr.* William Wilson *Minister at* Perth, *Mr.* Alexander Moncrieff, *Minister at* Abernethy, *and Mr.* James Fisher *Minister at* Kinclaven, *for their PROTESTATION entred before the Commission of the General Assembly,* November 1733, *upon the Intimation of a Sentence of the said Commission, loosing their Relation to the respective Parishes, &c.* Edinburgh: Lumisden and Robertson, 1734.

———. *THE TRUE State of the PROCESS AGAINST Mr.* Ebenezer Erskine *Minister of the Gospel at* Stirling: *SETTING FORTH The Proceedings of the Synod of* Perth *and* Stirling *against him, AND THE ACT of the late ASSEMBLY concerning him, and some other Ministers Adhering to his PROTEST. Together with a PREFACE and APPENDIX, CONTAINING Some REMARKS on the Preface to the two Acts of Assembly lately publish'd.* Edinburgh: Lumisden and Robertson, 1733.

Associate Synod (Burgher). *ACT OF THE* Associate Synod, *DECLARING THE GROUNDS* Upon which Supplies *were granted to these Congregations of the* Separating Brethren, *who applied for the same. AND GIVING THE REASONS Why they have not proceeded at present, in a Way of* ECCLESIASTICK CENSURE *against the said* Brethren. Edinburgh: Gray, 1749.

———. *ACT OF THE* ASSOCIATE SYNOD, *Met at* Stirling, *the twenty-ninth Day of* October, *One thousand seven hundred and forty-seven, DECLARING THE NULLITY OF THE* Pretended Synod, *That FIRST met in Mr.* GIB's *House in* Bristo, *near* Edinburgh, *April 10th 1747.* Glasgow: Newlands, 1747.

———. *THE ASSEMBLY'S SHORTER CATECHISM EXPLAINED, By Way of QUESTION and ANSWER. Wherein it is essayed, to bring forth the Truths of GOD, contained in that EXCELLENT COMPOSURE, more fully than has been attempted, in any one of the explicatory Catechisms hitherto published; and, at the same time, as compendiously as the Subject would allow. IN TWO PARTS. I. Of what MAN is to BELIEVE concerning GOD. II. Of the DUTY which GOD requires of MAN. By some MINISTERS of the GOSPEL. PART FIRST.* Glasgow: Urie, 1753.

IV. OTHER PRIMARY SOURCES

AN APOLOGY FOR THE PREBYTERIANS of Scotland *Who are HEARERS of The Reverend Mr.* George Whitefield, *SHEWING, That their keeping Communion* with him, in the Ordinances of the GOSPEL, stands justified by the Principles and Practice of the CHURCH of SCOTLAND from the REFORMATION to this Day, especially by the Westminster CONFESSION of FAITH, and Solemn League and Covenant. Edinburgh: Lumisden and Robertson, 1742.

Bisset, John. *A LETTER TO A Gentleman in Edinburgh, CONTAINING REMARKS Upon a late APOLOGY for the Presbyterians in Scotland, who keep Communion in the Ordinances of the Gospel, with Mr. George Whitefield, a PRIEST of the Church of England; and shewing that such a Practice is not justifiable by the Principles and Practice of the Church of Scotland, from the Reformation to this Day, nor by the Westminster Confession of Faith, Solemn League and Covenant. In which LETTER, Mr. Whitefield's Religion, Orthodoxy, and Moral Character, are set in a proper Light, by Collections from his own printed Performances.* 1742.

Boston, Thomas. *The Complete Works of the Late Rev. Thomas Boston, Ettrick: Including His Memoirs, Written by Himself.* 12 vols. Edited by Samuel M'Millan. London: Tegg, 1853. Reprint, Stoke-on-Trent: Tentmaker, 2002.

———. *The EVIL and DANGER of SCHISM. A SERMON PREACHED BY The late LEARNED and PIOUS Mr. THOMAS BOSTON, Minister of the Gospel at Etterick. The Second Edition, compared with the Original Copy, and Corrected. With, A PREFACE.* Edinburgh: Lumisden, 1753.

———. *A GENERAL ACCOUNT OF MY LIFE BY THOMAS BOSTON, A.M. MINISTER AT SIMPRIN, 1699–1707 AND AT ETTRICK, 1707–1732. PRINTED FOR THE FIRST TIME FROM THE ORIGINAL MANUSCRIPT. WITH INTRODUCTION, NOTES, AND BIBLIOGRAPHY BY THE REV. GEORGE D. LOW, M.A. EDINBURGH.* London: Hodder and Stoughton, 1908.

Buchanan, George. *De Jure Regni apud Scotus.* 1579. Reprint, Harrisonburg, VA: Sprinkle, 1982.

Calvin, John. *Institutes of the Christian Religion.* Translated by Ford Lewis Battles. Edited by John T. McNeill. 2 vols. LCC 20–21. Philadelphia: Westminster, 1960.

Cameron, James K., ed. *The First Book of Discipline.* Edinburgh: Saint Andrew, 1972.

The Case of the Church of Scotland, With Relation to the BILL for a TOLERATION to the Episcopal Dissenters, to set up Meeting-Houses, and use the English Service in SCOTLAND. 1712.

A COLLECTION Of several REMARKABLE and VALUABLE SERMONS, Speeches and Exhortations, At RENEWING and SUBSCRIBING the National Covenant of Scotland: And at ENTERING into and SUBSCRIBING the Solemn League and Covenant Of the THREE KINGDOMS of Scotland, England and Ireland. Wherein The Nature, Necessity and Excellency of the Duty of COVENANTING, with the Evil and Danger of Apostasy, are clearly and convincingly held forth from the Word of God. By several Reverend, Learned and Pious DIVINES of that Period. Published as very Seasonable and Necessary for these Times. Glasgow: Paton, 1741.

"A copie of the letters that passed between Mr James Hadow principal of the Colledge of St. Andrews & Mr Alexr Hamilton Minister of the Gospel at Airth. Transcribed from the Authenticke copies April 27th 1717." Special Collections, New College Library, Edinburgh.

Currie, John. *AN ESSAY ON SEPARATION: OR, A VINDICATION OF THE CHURCH OF SCOTLAND. IN WHICH the chief THINGS in the Testimonies of these Reverend Brethren who lately made a Secession from her are considered, and shown to be no Ground of Separation or Secession.* Edinburgh: T. Lumisden and J. Robertson, 1738.

———. *A FULL VINDICATION OF THE People's Right to Elect their own PASTORS. WHEREIN A DISCOVERY is made of the false Reasonings, Misrepresentations, Inconsistencies, &c. of the Author of two late Pamphlets; The one intituled,* A modest and humble Enquiry concerning the Right and Power of Electing and Calling Ministers to vacant Churches; *The other,* The publick Testimony made more publick. Edinburgh: Lumisden and Robertson, 1733.

———. *Jus populi divinum, Or, The People's Right to elect their PASTORS.* Edinburgh: Brown, 1727.

———. *THE OVERTURE considered; OR, QUERIES ANENT THE Assembly's Overture, Concerning the Method of planting vacant Churches, transmitted to Presbyteries for their Remarks,* May 14th, 1731; *IN A* LETTER *to a Member of the ensuing General Assembly*. Edinburgh: Lumisden and Robertson, 1732.

———. *A NEW TESTIMONY UNTO, AND FURTHER VINDICATION OF THE Extraordinary Work of GOD at Cambuslang, Kilsyth, and other Places in the West of Scotland. In which the Objections raised against that Work by sundry, particularly by the Seceding Brethren, in the Causes of their late publick Fast, and in Mr. Fisher's Review are considered.* Glasgow: Smith and Hutcheson, 1743.

———. *PHARISAICAL Righteousness insufficient, OR, The absolute Necessity of exceeding the Righteousness of Scribes and Pharisees, Shewn in a DISCOURSE From Matth. v. 20. Delivered at KIRKCALDY November 12. 1727.* Edinburgh: Duncan, 1728.

———. *THE Plain Perjury AND Great Iniquity OF THE SECEDING BRETHRENS New Covenant, DISCOVER'D: In a familiar DIALOGUE between a Seceder, and an Adherer to the Church of Scotland.* Edinburgh: Lumisden and Robertson, 1744. Special Collections, National Library of Scotland, Edinburgh.

Dickson, David. *TRUTH'S VICTORY OVER ERROR OR, An Abridgement of the Chief Controversies in Religion, which since the Apostles days to this time, have been, and are in agitation, between those of the Orthodox Faith, and all Adversaries whatsoever; a list of whose names are set down after the Epistle to the Reader.* Edinburgh: Reid, 1684.

Dickson, David and James Durham. *The Sum of Saving Knowledge: Or, A Brief Sum of Christian Doctrine, Contained in the Holy Scriptures, and Holden Forth in the Foresaid Confession of Faith and Catechisms; Together with The Practical Use thereof.* In Westminster Confession of Faith. Glasgow: Free Presbyterian, 1976.

Donaldson, Gordon, ed. *Scottish Historical Documents.* Glasgow: Wilson, 1974.

Dunlop, William. *A COLLECTION OF Confessions of Faith, CATECHISMS, DIRECTORIES, BOOKS of DISCIPLINE, &c. Of Public Authority in the Church of Scotland. Together with All the Acts of Assembly, which are STANDING RULES concerning the DOCTRINE, WORSHIP, GOVERNMENT and DISCIPLINE of the CHURCH of Scotland.* Vol. 1. Edinburgh: Watson, 1719.

Durham, James. *A COMMENTARIE Upon the BOOK of the REVELATION. WHEREIN The Text is explained, the Series of the several Prophecies contained in that Book, deduced according to their order and dependence upon each other; the periods and succession of times, at, or about which, these Prophesies, that are already fulfilled, began to be, and were more fully accomplished, fixed and applied according to History; And those that are yet to be fulfilled, modestly, and so far as is warrantable, enquired into.* Together with Some practical Observations, and several Digressions, (an INDEX whereof is prefixed) necessary for vindicating, clearing, and confirming many weighty and important Truths. *Delivered in several LECTURES, by that learned, laborious, and faithfull Servant of Jesus Christ, M. JAMES DURHAM, Late Minister of the Gospel in* Glasgow. *To which is affixed a brief Summary of the whole REVELATION, with an Alphabetical* INDEX *of the chief and principal purposes & words contained in this Commentarie*. Edinburgh: Higgins, 1658; Glasgow: Sanders, 1680.

[Erskine, Ebenezer]. *AN ESSAY UPON The Design, the Reference, the Penalty and Offence of the ABJURATION OATH, In a Letter to a Presbyterian Minister. From whence it will appear, that such of the Ministers of this Church, as have refused the ABJURATION, have not walked upon such insufficient Grounds, as are represented in some late Pamphlets.* 1713.

Erskine, Ebenezer. *The Backslider Characterized; OR, The Evil and Danger of Defection, described in a Sermon on John vi.66.* Edinburgh: Walker, 1726.

———. *The Believer Exalted in Imputed Righteousness; Being a Sermon Preached at the Celebration of the LORD's Supper, at Largo, Sabbath Morning, June 4th, 1721.* Edinburgh: Walker, 1728.

———. *Christ in the Believer's Arms; Being a Sermon Preached by Mr. Ebenezer Erskine, at Strathmiglo, May 10th, 1724.* Edinburgh: Walker, 1726.

———. *God's Little Remnant Keeping Their Garments Clean in an Evil Day.* 1725.

———. *The Humble Soul the Peculiar Favourite of HEAVEN; Being a SERMON preached at Orwell, July 27th, 1721.* Edinburgh: Lumisden and Robertson, 1728.

———. *Notebook.* Special Collections, New College Library, Edinburgh, ERS E3.

———. *Notebook.* Special Collections, New College Library, Edinburgh, ERS E4.

———. *Notebook, dated on cover 1694-6&7.* Special Collections, New College Library, Edinburgh, ERS E2.

———. *A SERIOUS ADDRESS TO THE Christian World: OR, THE Precious PROMISES of the Most High GOD, to Repenting Sinners. FOUND IN THE MANUSCRIPTS OF THAT Late Learned and Reverend Divine MR. EBENEZER ERSKINE, Minister of the Gospel at STIRLING.* Glasgow, 1789.

———. *Sermons and Discourses Upon the Most Important and Interesting Subjects; By the Late Reverend Ebenezer Erskine, Minister of the Gospel at Stirling.* Edinburgh: Gray and Alston, 1761.

———. Sermon Manuscripts. Special Collections, King's College, University of Aberdeen, MS 3245/3.

———. *Signed Fragments.* Special Collections, New College Library, Edinburgh, Box 8.3.4.

———. *The STONE rejected by the Builders, exalted as the Head-Stone of the Corner. A SERMON PREACH'D At the Opening of the Synod of Perth and Stirling, At Perth, October 10. 1732. To which is subjoin'd A SERMON preach'd June 4th 1732, on the Sabbath Evening after the Sacrament, from Isa. ix. 6. —- The Government shall be upon his Shoulder.* Edinburgh: Duncan, 1732.

———. *THE TRUE STATE OF THE QUESTION, UPON WHICH A BREACH followed IN THE ASSOCIATE SYNOD, At EDINBURGH, Thursday April 9. 1747.* Glasgow: Newlands, 1747.

———. *The true Substance and Strength of a Church and Nation. TWO SERMONS UPON ISAIAH vi. 13. So the holy Seed shall be the Substance thereof. PREACHED*

At the Administration of the Sacrament of the LORD's SUPPER, at Dunfermline, June *the 10th, and 11th, 1733.* Edinburgh: Alex. Alison, for John Brown, 1735.

———. *The Whole Works of the Late Rev. Ebenezer Erskine Minister of the Gospel at Stirling CONSISTING OF SERMONS AND DISCOURSES ON THE MOST IMPORTANT AND INTERESTING SUBJECTS.* Edinburgh: Ogle & Murray, 1871. Reprint, Glasgow: Free Presbyterian, 2001.

Erskine, Ralph. *A NARRATIVE OF THE SEPARATION OF THE MAJORITY of MEMBERS FROM THE ASSOCIATE PREBYTERY OF DUNFERMLINE, At PERTH, May 5th, 1747. TOGETHER WITH An EXACT DOUBLE of the MINUTES of the said SEPARATING MAJORITY on that Occasion, with OBSERVATIONS upon them. AS ALSO, A COPY of a LETTER sent by the MEMBERS of the ASSOCIATE SYNOD, which met at Stirling in June 1747, to their Separating Brethren, proposing a Meeting with them, for PRAYER and CONFERENCE, anent our present Differences; together with the ANSWERS of these Brethren, and REMARKS upon the same.* Glasgow: Newlands, 1747.

THE Fatal and Lamentable End OF Mr. EBENEZER's Artificial Tabernacle, IN ITS Perigrination to LOGIE: IN A LETTER FROM A COUNTRYMAN in Logie Parish TO HIS FRIEND at EDINBURGH. Edinburgh, 1739.

Gib, Adam. *THE PRESENT TRUTH: A DISPLAY OF THE SECESSION-TESTIMONY; IN THE THREE PERIODS OF THE RISE, STATE, AND MAINTENANCE of that TESTIMONY. IN TWO VOLUMES.* Edinburgh: Fleming and Neill, 1774.

Gillespie, George. *AARON'S ROD BLOSSOMING; OR, THE DIVINE ORDINANCE OF CHURCH GOVERNMENT VINDICATED; SO AS THE PRESENT ERASTIAN CONTROVERSY CONCERNING THE DISTINCTION OF CIVIL AND ECCLESIASTICAL GOVERNMENT, EXCOMMUNICATION AND SUSPENSION, IS FULLY DEBATED AND DISCUSSED, FROM THE HOLY SCRIPTURE, FROM THE JEWISH AND CHRISTIAN ANTIQUITIES, FROM THE CONSENT OF LATER WRITERS, FROM THE TRUE NATURE AND RIGHTS OF MAGISTRACY, AND FROM THE GROUNDLESSNESS OF THE CHIEF OBJECTIONS MADE AGAINST THE PRESBYTERIAL GOVERNMENT, IN POINT OF A DOMINEERING ARBITRARY UNLIMITED POWER.* London: E.G, 1646. Reprint, Harrisonburg, VA: Sprinkle, 1985.

Gillespie, Patrick. *The Ark of the Covenant Opened: Or, A TREATISE of the COVENANT of Redemption BETWEEN God and Christ, as the Foundation of the Covenant of Grace.* London: Parkhurst, 1677.

———. *THE ARK OF THE TESTAMENT OPENED, OR, The Secret of the Lords Covenant unsealed, IN A TREATISE OF THE COVENANT OF GRACE. Wherein an Essay is made for the promoting and increase of Knowledge, in the mysterie of the Gospel-covenant, which hath been hid from Ages and Generations, but now is made manifest to the Saints.* 2 vols. London: R. C., 1661.

Glas, John. *REMARKS UPON THE MEMORIAL OF THE Synod of ANGUS against Mr. Glas, AND THE Sentence of the Commission deposing him from the Ministry.* Edinburgh: Davidson, 1730.

Guthrie, James. *A CRY From the Dead; OR, THE GHOST OF THE Famous Mr. James Guthrie appearing. Being the last SERMON he preached in the Pulpit of Stirling, before his Martyrdom at Edinburgh, June 1661. TO which is added, His Last SPEECH upon the Scaffold. His Ten CONSIDERATIONS anent the Decay of Religion: With an Authentick PAPER sign'd and writ with his own Hand, with*

Relation to the Call of Mr. ROBERT RULE to Stirling. Which gives some Light into the infamous Action of his being stoned, for pushing Mr. RULE's Settlement in Stirling, in Opposition to the Publick Resolution Party, about five Years before his Execution. Glasgow: Duncan, 1738.

———. *PROTESTERS no Subverters, AND Presbyterie no Papacie; OR, A VINDICATION of the Protesting Brethren, and the Government of the Kirk of Scotland, from the Aspersions unjustly cast upon them, in a late Pamphlet of some of the Resolution-party, Entituled A DECLARATION &c. With a Discovery of the insufficiency, inequality and iniquity of the Things propounded in that Pamphlet, as Overtures of Union and Peace. Especially, Of the iniquity of that absolute and unlimited submission to the Sentences of Church-Judicatories that is holden forth therein, and most unjustly pleaded to belong to the Being and Essence of Presbyterial Government. By Some Witnesses to the way of the Protestation.* Edinburgh, 1658.

Hadow, James. *THE ANTINOMIANISM OF THE MARROW OF Modern Divinity DETECTED. Wherein the LETTER To a PRIVATE CHRISTIAN, about Believers receiving the Law, as the Law of Christ, is specially considered.* Edinburgh: Mosman, 1721.

———. *THE Doctrine and Practice OF THE CHURCH OF SCOTLAND, ANENT THE Sacrament of Baptism, VINDICATED From the Charge of Gross Error EXHIBITED In a Print called,* The Practice and Doctrine of the Presbyterian Preachers, about the Sacrament of Baptism, Examined. Part I. 1704.

———. *THE Doctrine and Practice OF THE CHURCH OF SCOTLAND, ABOUT THE Sacrament of Baptism, VINDICATED From the Charge of Gross Error EXHIBITED In a Print called,* The Practice and Doctrine of the Presbyterian Preachers, about the Sacrament of Baptism, Examined. Part II. Edinburgh: George Mosman, 1704.

———. *THE Record of God AND DUTY of FAITH Therein required. A SERMON On I JOHN v. ver. 11, 12. BEFORE The Synod of Fife At St. Andrew's April 7th, 1719.* Edinburgh: Mosman, 1719.

Hall, Archibald. *AN IMPARTIAL SURVEY Of the religious Clause in some BURGESS-OATHS; Of the CONSTITUTION of the ANTIBURGHER-JUDICATURES; and, Of the CENSURES they inflicted on their Brethren of the BURGHER DENOMINATION. IN THREE PARTS. With a PREFACE; WHEREIN The NATURE and SEASONS of public COVENANTING are explained upon Scripture-principles, in order to satisfy the SCRUPULOUS about the EXPEDIENCY of RENEWING OUR SOLEMN COVENANTS at present.* Edinburgh: Wilson, Robertson, & Tennent, 1771.

Henderson, G.D, ed. *Scots Confession, 1560.* Edinburgh: Church of Scotland Committee on Publications, 1937.

THE HISTORY AND ARGUMENT OF THE Scots Presbyterians That have Scruples in Relation to some Words contain'd in the Oath of Abjuration, As it now stands. In a LETTER from a Gentleman at Edinburgh to a MEMBER of Parliament. London: Popping, 1717.

Kirk, James, ed. *The Second Book of Discipline.* Edinburgh: Saint Andrew, 1980.

Knox, John. *Selected Writings of John Knox: Public Epistles, Treatises, and Expositions to the Year 1559.* Edited by Kevin Reed. Dallas: Presbyterian Heritage, 1995.

A LETTER TO THE Reverend Mr. MICHAEL POTTER Minister of the Gospel at Kippen; AS AN ANSWER of his Letter, lately sent by him to the Reverend Mr. EBENEZER ERSKINE Minister of the Gospel at Stirling, upon Occasion of that slanderous Reproach that doth go thro' this Land on his Name, that he doth yearly receive Money from Rome *to work unhappy Divisions in the Church of CHRIST in this Land.* Edinburgh, 1738.

A LETTER TO THE Valiant and Undaunted CHAMPION of our BROKEN COVENANTS, The Reverend and Renowned Mr. EBENEZER ERSKINE; *In relation to The* present Heresies, Backslidings, Defections, *and* Lukewarmness *of the TIMES, and his Apostolical Testimonies against them:* By a bold young Soldier under his Banner, *Euzelus Philalethes,* Author of *SHAFTSBURY'S Ghost conjur'd.* London, 1738.

[Linning, Thomas and James Webster]. *A LETTER From a Friend to Mr.* John Mackmillan, *wherein is Demonstrate the Contrariety of his Principles, and Practices, to the Scripture, our Covenants, Confession of Faith, and Practice of CHRIST, and the Primitive Christians, Containing also Remarks on his and Mr.* John Mackniely's *Printed Protestation, Declinature and Appeal, compared with what they gave in to the Commission of the late General Assemblie, upon the 29th day of* September *1708. the One Vastly differing from the Other.* 1709.

[Logan, Allan]. *The Oath of Abjuration Enquir'd into: In a Letter to a Friend.* 1712.

Macculloch, William. *Examinations of persons Under Spiritual Concern at Cambuslang, during the Revival, in 17-41-42.* Volume I. Special Collections, New College Library, Edinburgh.

Marrow-Chicaning DISPLAYED; IN A LETTER TO THE Reverend Mr. EBEN-EZER ERSKINE, Minister of the Gospel at Portmoak: *CONTAINING Some Observations upon the Preface to his Sermon, entituled,* God's little Remnant, *& c. To which are subjoined, Some Things concerning Assurance in the direct Act of justifying Faith, and the Tendency of the* Marrow, *and the Practices of its Favourites, to advance Gospel Holiness.* By a Lover of Peace and Truth in this Church. 1726.

M'Claren, John. *THE NEW SCHEME OF DOCTRINE Contained in the ANSWERS OF Mr. JOHN SIMSON, Professor of Divinity in the Colledge of* Glasgow; *to Mr. WEBSTER's Libel, considered and examined.* Edinburgh: Reid, 1717.

Nairn, Thomas. *A SHORT ACCOUNT OF Mr. THOMAS NAIRN, Minister of the Gospel in* Linktoun *of Arnot, formerly* Abbotshall, *his SECESSION from the ASSOCIATE PRESBYTERY; WITH THE* Grounds *and* Reasons *For his so doing.* 1743.

Norton, John. *The Orthodox Evangelist. Or A TREATISE Wherein many Great EVANGELICAL TRUTHS (Not a few whereof are much opposed and Eclipsed in the perillous hour of the Passion of the Gospel) Are briefly Discussed, cleared, and confirmed: As a further help, for the Begetting, and Establishing of the Faith which is in Jesus. As also the* State of the Blessed, Where; *Of the condition of their SOULS from the instant of their* Dissolution: *and of their Persons after their* Resurrection. London: Macok, 1657.

The Oath of Abjuration Considered, Both as to the Lawfulness and Expediency of its being taken by the Ministers of the Church of Scotland, In a Letter to a Friend. Edinburgh, 1712.

The Oath of Abjuration Displayed, In its sinful nature and Tendency, in its Inconsistency with Presbyterian Principles and Covenants; the Security it affords to the Church of England. Together with some REMARKS upon the Evasions and Explications offered thereupon, by the Ministers who took it, shewing them to be Contradictory to the Sense of the Oath, and Meaning of the Imposers. Being the Copy of a Letter sent to one of the Jurant-Ministers of the Presbytery of Dumblane. 1712.

Pascal, Blaise. *Pensées.* Translated and Introduced by A. J. Krailsheimer. London: Penguin, 1995.

Paton, Rev. Henry, ed. *Report on the Manuscripts of the Right Honourable Lord Polwarth* Vol. 5. Historical Manuscripts Commission 67. London: Her Majesty's Stationary Office, 1961.

PLAIN TRUTHS; OR, A COLLECTION Of SCARCE and VALUABLE TRACTS. CONTAINING, I. The several DECLARATIONS and DEPOSITIONS, made in Council, on Monday the 22d of October 1688. concerning the BIRTH of the PRINCE of Wales. II. Seasonable QUERIES, relating to the BIRTH and BIRTHRIGHT of a certain PERSON. III. A Petition of Witnesses for Examination of a certain FACT. IV. A Letter to a FRIEND, concerning the Imprisonment of the Seven Bishops, in the Reign of King James the Second. V. A Letter from a Nonjuring Clergyman, to a Clergyman of the Church of England. VI. Mr. Down's Letter to Lord SCUDAMORE, before his Entring into Parliament. To which is Added, The Form of the Abjuration OATH. 1714.

A PUBLICK TESTIMONY; BEING THE Representation and Petition OF A Considerable Number of CHRISTIAN PEOPLE within the Bounds of several Synods of this CHURCH, In their own Name, and in Name of all adhering thereunto, presented and given in to the GENERAL ASSEMBLY met at Edinburgh, May 4th 1732, ANENT GRIEVANCES. Edinburgh: Lumisden and Robertson, 1732.

Queries, Agreed unto by the Commission of the General Assembly; And put to these Ministers, who gave in a REPRESENTATION and PETITION against the 5th and 8th Acts of Assembly 1720. Together with the ANSWERS Given by these Ministers to The said QUERIES. 1722.

Renwick, James, and Alexander Shields. *AN INFORMATORY VINDICATION OF A Poor, wasted, misrepresented Remnant of the suffering, Anti-popish, Anti-prelatick, Anti-erastian, Anti-sectarian, true Presbyterian Church of CHRIST in Scotland. United together in a general Correspondence. By way of Reply to various Accusations, in Letter, Informations and Conferences given forth against them.* Edinburgh: Drummond, 1744.

Renwick, R., ed. *Extracts From the Records of the Royal Burgh of Stirling. A.D. 1667–1752. With Appendix, A.D. 1471–1752.* Glasgow: Glasgow Stirlingshire and Sons of the Rock Society, 1889.

Report On the Manuscripts of the Earl of Mar and Kellie Preserved at Alloa House, N.B. Historical Manuscripts Commission 60. London: His Majesty's Stationery Office, 1904.

The Representation and Petition of Several Ministers of the Gospel, to the General Assembly, Met at Edinburgh May 1721; With the 5th Act of Assembly May 1720, to which it relates. Edinburgh, 1721.

Rutherford, Samuel. *LEX REX, OR, THE LAW AND THE PRINCE; A DISPUTE FOR THE JUST PREROGATIVE OF KING AND PEOPLE.* 1644. Reprint, Harrisonburg, VA: Sprinkle, 1982.

———. *A SURVEY OF THE SPIRITUAL ANTICHRIST. OPENING The secrets of Familisme and Antinomianisme in the Antichristian Doctrine of John Saltmarsh, and Will. Del, the present Preachers of the Army now in England, and of Robert Town, Tob. Crisp, H. Denne, Eaton, and others. In which is revealed the rise and spring of Antinomians, Familists, Libertines, Swenck-feldians, Enthysiasts, & c. The minde of Luther a most professed opposer of Antinomianism, is cleared, and diverse considerable points of the Law and the Gospel, of the Spirit and Letter, of the two Covenants, of the nature of free grace, exercise under temptations, mortification, justification, sanctification, are discovered. In Two PARTS.* London: J. D. & R. I., 1648.

Shields, Alexander. *Church-Communion ENQUIRED INTO: OR A TREATISE AGAINST SEPARATION FROM This National Church of SCOTLAND. WHEREIN I. Some Truths confessed on all Hands, are held forth, which if Rightly considered would do much to End the present Controversie. II. Some Concessions are laid down, for clearing the present Debate. III. The Controversie is stated, and Truth vindicated. IV. The Objections are solidly and clearly answered.* Which was left in Manuscripts by the Reverend and Worthy Mr. *Alexander Shields*, Minister of the Gospel at St. Andrews, when he was sent by the Church of *Scotland* unto *Caledonia*. 1706.

Simson, John. *The Case of Mr. John Simson Professor of Divinity in the University of Glasgow: consisting of the original papers of the process carried on against him by Mr. James Webster.* Glasgow: Govan, 1715.

Some Reasons Humbly Offered, why the English Oath of Abjuration should not be imposed upon the subjects of North Britain, especially the Ministers of the Gospel there. 1712.

Some Seceders in and about Glasgow. *A SHORT VINDICATION OF THE ASSOCIAT SYNOD, FROM THE CHARGE of SCHISM, PERJURY, &c. Led against them In a late PAMPHLET, intitled, THE TRUE STATE of the QUESTION, upon which a BREACH followed in the ASSOCIAT SYNOD, at EDINBURGH, Thursday April 9. 1747.* Glasgow: Lundin, 1747.

Some Thoughts, and Questions Upon the OATH of ABJURATION, and Act tolerating the English Liturgy in SCOTLAND, in 1712. 1712.

A SUPPLEMENT TO Mr. EBENEZER ERSKINE'S SYNODICAL SERMON. Edinburgh: Printed for the author, 1732.

THE TESTIMONY AND CONTENDINGS Of the Reverend Mr. ALEXANDER HAMILTON, One of the Ministers of the Gospel at Stirling; Against the violent Settlement of Mr. JAMES MACKIE, in the Parish of St. Ninians. Where is also contained, A LETTER, directed to the Presbytery of Stirling, during the Dependence of the said Process, from Mr. Ebenezer Erskine, on the Occasion of his being invited to the Moderator's Chair. Edinburgh: Duncan, 1736.

Traill, Robert. *Justification Vindicated*. 1692. Reprint, Edinburgh: Banner of Truth, 2002.

Videte Apologiam nostram Contra WEBSTERUM, & c. OR, A LETTER FROM A PRIVATE CHRISTIAN, TO A Reverend Minister and Member of the present Commission Of the Late GENERAL ASSEMBLY; Pointing out several Articles of Reverend Professor *Simson*'s new Scheme of Divinity, which he is said to recommend to his Students in the above Latine Words, referring them to his Answer to the late Reverend Mr. *Webster*'s Libel against him, to be compared with the Passages of the *Marrow of Modern Divinity*, condemned as erroneous by the Fifth Act of the General Assembly 1720; or with the Representation given in by the Twelve Reverend Ministers to the last General Assembly 1721, in Defence of the *Marrow*, that it may be considered, whether the Reverend Professor *Simson*, or the Reverend Recommender and Vindicator of the *Marrow*, and the twelve Representing Ministers, be most liable to Censure. 1722.

A Vindication of the Ministers and Ruling Elders, in the Church of Scotland, Who have refused the OATH of ABJURATION. 1713.

THE VIPER Shaken off without Hurt into the Fire: BEING A short Answer to a Pamphlet lately published, INTITULED, Marrow Chicaning display'd, *&c. IN A LETTER To* the Reverend Mr. A. A ———-n *Minister of the Gospel at* ————-. Edinburgh: 1726.

[Webster, James]. *A Second Defence of the Lawful Prejudices, Containing a Vindication of the Obligation of the National Covenant and Solemn League, In answer to a Letter from the Country, & c. Written by the Minister of Humby.* Edinburgh, 1707.

Westminster Confession of Faith. Glasgow: Free Presbyterian, 1994.

Willison, John. *THE CHURCH's Danger AND THE MINISTER's Duty Declared, in a SERMON Preach'd at the Opening of the Synod of Angus and Mearns, At MONTROSE The 16th Day of October 1733. WITH A PREFACE and POSTSCRIPT TOUCHING Some more Evils of the present Time.* Glasgow: Duncan, 1733.

———. *A Fair and Impartial TESTIMONY, Essayed in Name of a Number of Ministers, Elders, and Christian People of the CHURCH of Scotland, UNTO The laudable Principles, Wrestlings and Attainments of that CHURCH; AND AGAINST The Backslidings, Corruptions, Divisions, and prevailing Evils, both of former and present Times. AND NAMELY, The Defections of the ESTABLISHED CHURCH, of the Nobility, Gentry, Commons, Seceders, Episcopalians, & c. CONTAINING A brief HISTORICAL DEDUCTION of the chief OCCURRENCES in this CHURCH from her Beginning to the Year 1744, with REMARKS; And HUMBLE PLEADINGS with our Mother, to exert herself to stop DEFECTION, and promote REFORMATION.* Edinburgh: Lumisden and Robertson, 1744.

Wilson. *A DEFENCE OF THE REFORMATION-PRINCIPLES OF THE Church of Scotland. WHEREIN The EXCEPTIONS that are laid against the Conduct of the ASSOCIATE PRESBYTERY, as also against their judicial Act and Testimony, by the Reverend Mr. Currie in his Essay on Separation, are examined; and the injurious Reflections cast upon our Reforming Period from 1638 to 1650, in the foresaid Essay, are discovered.* Edinburgh: Lumisden and Robertson, 1739.

Witsius, Herman. *The Economy of the Covenants Between God and Man: Comprehending A Complete Body of Divinity.* Translated by William Crookshank. London: Baynes, Maitland, Lochhead, and Nelson, 1822. Reprint, Kingsburg, CA: den Dulk Christian Foundation, 1990.

Wodrow, Robert. *ANALECTA: OR, MATERIALS FOR A HISTORY OF REMARKABLE PROVIDENCES; MOSTLY RELATING TO SCOTCH MINISTERS AND CHRISTIANS.* Edinburgh: Maitland Club, 1842.

———. *The Correspondence of the Rev. Robert Wodrow*. Edited by Rev. Thomas M'Crie. Edinburgh: Wodrow Society, 1843.

[Wodrow, Robert]. *The Oath of Abjuration Considered, In a Letter to a Friend.* 1712.

V. SECONDARY SOURCES

Allan, David. *Scotland in the Eighteenth Century.* Harlow, UK: Longman, 2002.

Barber, Sarah. "Scotland and Ireland under the Commonwealth: a question of loyalty." In *Conquest and Union: Fashioning a British State, 1485–1725*, edited by Steven G. Ellis and Sarah Barber, 195–221. London: Longman, 1995.

Barth, Karl. *Church Dogmatics.* Vol. 4/1, *The Doctrine of Reconciliation.* Edited by G. W. Bromiley and T. F. Torrance. Translated by G. W. Bromiley. Edinburgh: T. & T. Clark, 1956.

———. *From Rousseau to Ritschl, being the translation of eleven chapters of* Die Protestantische Theologie IM 19. Jahrhundert. Translated by Brian Cozens. Library of Philosophy and Theology. London: SCM, 1959.

———. *The Theology of the Reformed Confessions*. Translated by Darrell L. Guder and Judith J. Guder. Louisville: Westminster John Knox, 2002.

Batty, Margaret. "Campbell, Archibald." In *Oxford Dictionary of National Biography*, edited by H. C. G. Matthew and Brian Harrison, 9:733–34. Oxford: Oxford University Press, 2004.

Beaton, Donald. "The 'Marrow of Modern Divinity' and the Marrow Controversy." *Records of the Scottish Church History Society* 1 (1926) 112–34.

Bell, M. Charles. *Calvin and Scottish Theology: The Doctrine of Assurance*. Edinburgh: Handsel, 1985.

Bevan, Jonquil. "Seventeenth-Century Students and Their Books." In *Four Centuries: Edinburgh University Life 1583–1983*, edited by Gordon Donaldson, 16–27. Edinburgh: University of Edinburgh, 1983.

Bierma, Lyle D. *German Calvinism in the Confessional Age: The Covenant Theology of Caspar Olevianus*. Grand Rapids: Baker, 1996.

———. "The Role of Covenant Theology in Early Reformed Orthodoxy." *The Sixteenth Century Journal* 21 (1990) 453–62.

Bower, Alexander. *The History of the University of Edinburgh*. Edinburgh: Oliphant, Waugh and Innes, 1817.

Bozeman, Theodore Dwight. *The Precisianist Strain: Disciplinary Religion & Antinomian Backlash in Puritanism to 1638*. Chapel Hill: University of North Carolina Press, 2004.

Bradley, James E. "Toleration and Movements of Christian Reunion, 1660–1789." In *The Cambridge History of Christianity*, edited by Stewart J. Brown and Timothy Tackett, 7:348–370. Cambridge: Cambridge University Press, 2006.

Brown, Callum G. *Religion and Society in Scotland Since 1707*. Edinburgh: Edinburgh University Press, 1997.

Brown, John of Whitburn. *Gospel Truth Accurately Stated and Illustrated, by the Rev. Messrs James Hog, Thomas Boston, Ebenezer and Ralph Erskine, and others. Occassioned by the republication of the Marrow of Modern Divinity. collected BY THE REV. JOHN BROWN, WHITBURN. A NEW EDITION, GREAtlY ENLARGED AND IMPROVED.* Glasgow: Blackie, Fullarton, 1831.

Brown, Keith M. "Scottish Identity in the Seventeenth Century." In *British Consciousness and Identity: The Making of Britain, 1533–1707*, edited by Brendan Bradshaw and Peter Roberts, 236–58. Cambridge: Cambridge University Press, 1998.

Brown, Stewart J., and Timothy Tackett. "Introduction." In *The Cambridge History of Christianity*, edited by Stewart J. Brown and Timothy Tackett, 7:1–11. Cambridge: Cambridge University Press, 2006.

Brown, Stewart J. "William Robertson (1721–1793) and the Scottish Enlightenment." In *William Robertson and the Expansion of Empire*, edited by Stewart J. Brown, 7–35. Cambridge: Cambridge University Press, 1997.

Brown, Thomas. *Church and State in Scotland: A Narrative of the Struggle for Independence from 1560 to 1843*. Edinburgh: MacNiven & Wallace, 1891.

Bruggink, Donald Jay. "The Theology of Thomas Boston, 1676–1732." PhD diss., University of Edinburgh, 1956.

Buchanan, James. *THE DOCTRINE OF JUSTIFICATION: AN OUTLINE OF ITS HISTORY IN THE CHURCH, AND OF ITS EXPOSITION FROM SCRIPTURE. WITH SPECIAL REFERENCE TO RECENT ATTACKS ON THE THEOLOGY OF THE REFORMATION*. Edinburgh: T. & T. Clark, 1867.

Buckroyd, Julia. *Church and State in Scotland 1660-1681*. Edinburgh: Donald, 1980.

Burleigh, J. H. S. *A Church History of Scotland*. London: Oxford University Press, 1960.

Burrell, S.A. "The Apocalyptic Vision of the Early Covenanters." *Scottish Historical Review* 43 (1964) 1–24.

———. "The Covenant Idea as a Revolutionary Symbol: Scotland, 1596-1637." *Church History* 27 (1958) 338–50.

Butler, Dugald. *John Wesley and George Whitefield in Scotland, or, The Influence of the Oxford Methodists on Scottish Religion*. Edinburgh: Blackwood and Sons, 1898.

Calhoun, D. B. "Traill, Robert." In *Dictionary of Scottish Church History and Theology*, edited by Nigel M. de S. Cameron, 827. Downers Grove, IL: InterVarsity, 1993.

Cameron, James K. "Theological Controversy: A Factor in the Origins of the Scottish Enlightenment." In *The Origins and Nature of the Scottish Enlightenment*, edited by R. H. Campbell and Andrew S. Skinner, 116–30. Edinburgh: Donald, 1982.

Campbell, A. J. "The Burgh Churches of Scotland." *Records of the Scottish Church History Society* 4 (1932) 185–94.

Campbell, Rev. William M. "The Scottish Westminster Commissioners and Toleration." *Records of the Scottish Church History Society* 9 (1947) 1–18.

Carson, John L. "The Doctrine of the Church in the Secession." PhD diss., University of Aberdeen, 1987.

The Christian Magazine XIII (4 October 1819) 376–81.

Colley, Linda. *Britons: Forging the Nation 1707-1837*. 2nd ed. New Haven: Yale University Press, 2005.

Como, David R. *Blown by the Spirit: Puritanism and the Emergence of an Antinomian Underground in Pre-Civil-War England*. Stanford: Stanford University Press, 2004.

Cowan, Ian B. *The Scottish Covenanters 1660-1688*. London: Gollancz, 1976.

Cullen, Karen J., Christopher A. Whatley, and Mary Young. "King William's Ill Years: new evidence on the impact of scarcity and harvest failure during the crisis of the 1690s on Tayside." *Scottish Historical Review* 85 (2006) 250–76.

Cunningham. William. *HISTORICAL THEOLOGY: A REVIEW OF THE PRINCIPAL DOCTRINAL DISCUSSIONS IN THE CHRISTIAN CHURCH SINCE THE APOSTOLIC AGE*. Edinburgh: T. & T. Clark, 1863.

———. *The Reformers; and the Theology of the Reformation*. Edinburgh: T. & T. Clark, 1862.

Devine, T. M. *The Scottish Nation: 1700-2000*. London: Penguin, 1999.

Donaldson, Gordon. "The Emergence of Schism in Seventeenth-Century Scotland." In *Schism, Heresy and Religious Protest: Papers Read at the Tenth Summer Meeting and the Eleventh Winter Meeting of the Ecclesiastical History Society*, edited by Derek Baker, 277–94. Cambridge: Cambridge University Press, 1972.

———. *Scotland: Church and Nation Through Sixteen Centuries*, 2nd ed. Edinburgh: Scottish Academic, 1972.

———. *Scotland: James V–James VII*. Edinburgh History of Scotland 3. Edinburgh: Mercat, 1965.

Drummond, Andrew L., and James Bulloch. *The Scottish Church 1688-1843: The Age of the Moderates*. Edinburgh: Saint Andrew, 1973.

Du Toit, Alexander. "'Unionist Nationalism' in the Eighteenth Century: William Robertson and James Anderson (1662-1728)." *Scottish Historical Review* 85 (2006) 305-14.

Eijnatten, Joris Van. "Reaching audiences: Sermons and oratory in Europe." In *The Cambridge History of Christianity*, edited by Stewart J. Brown and Timothy Tackett, 7:128-46. Cambridge: Cambridge University Press, 2006.

Emerson, Everett H. "Calvin and Covenant Theology." *Church History* 25 (1956) 136-44.

Fawcett, Arthur. *The Cambuslang Revival: The Scottish Evangelical Revival of the Eighteenth Century*. Edinburgh: Banner of Truth, 1971.

Ferguson, William. *Scotland: 1689 to the Present*. Edinburgh History of Scotland 4. Edinburgh: Mercat, 1965.

Fergusson, David. *Church, State and Civil Society*. Cambridge: Cambridge University Press, 2004.

———. "Church, State, and Civil Society in the Reformed Tradition." In *Reformed Theology: Identity and Ecumenicity*, edited by Wallace M. Alston Jr. and Michael Welker, 111-26. Grand Rapids: Eerdmans, 2003.

———. "The Confession in the Life of the Church of Scotland." In *Reformed Theology in Contemporary Perspective. Westminster: Yesterday, Today—and Tomorrow?*, edited by Lynn Quigley, 201-14. Edinburgh: Rutherford House, 2006.

———. "Predestination: A Scottish Perspective." *Scottish Journal of Theology* 46 (1993) 457-78.

Fergusson, David, ed. *Scottish Philosophical Theology 1700-2000*. Library of Scottish Philosophy. Exeter, UK: Imprint Academic, 2007.

Fergusson, R. Menzies. *Logie: A Parish History*. Paisley, UK: Gardner, 1905.

Ferrier, Andrew. MEMOIRS OF THE REV. WILLIAM WILSON, A.M. MINISTER OF THE GOSPEL AT PERTH, ONE OF THE FOUR BRETHREN—THE FOUNDERS OF THE SECESSION CHURCH, AND PROFESSOR OF THEOLOGY TO THE ASSOCIATE PRESBYTERY: WITH BRIEF SKETCHES OF THE STATE OF RELIGION IN SCOTLAND, FOR FIFTY YEARS IMMEDIATELY POSTERIOR TO THE REVOLUTION; INCLUDING A Circumstantial Account of the Origin of the Secession. Glasgow: Robertson & Atkinson, 1830.

Finlay, Richard J. "Keeping the Covenant: Scottish National Identity." In *Eighteenth Century Scotland: New Perspectives*, edited by T. M. Devine and J. R. Young, 121-33. East Linton, UK: Tuckwell, 1999.

Fleming, J. R. *The Secession of 1733: A Bicentenary Tribute*. Edinburgh: Church of Scotland Committee on Publications, 1933.

Forbes, Eric. "Philosophy and Science Teaching in the Seventeenth Century." In *Four Centuries: Edinburgh University Life 1583-1983*, edited by Gordon Donaldson, 28-37. Edinburgh: University of Edinburgh, 1983.

Fraser, Donald. *The Life and Diary of the Reverend Ebenezer Erskine, A.M. of Stirling, Father of the Secession Church. To Which is Prefixed, a Memoir of His Father, The Rev. Henry Erskine, A.M. of Chirnside*. Edinburgh: Oliphant, 1831.

———. *The Life and Diary of the Reverend Ralph Erskine, A.M. of Dunfermline, one of the Founders of the Secession Church*. Edinburgh: Oliphant and Son, 1834.

Fulton, Henry L. "Moore (Muir), Charles." In *Dictionary of Scottish Church History and Theology*, edited by Nigel M. de S. Cameron, 606. Downers Grove, IL: InterVarsity, 1993.

———. "The Managed Career of the Reverend Charles Moore of Stirling." *Records of the Scottish Church History Society* 20 (1980) 231–47.
Glassey, Lionel K. J. "Introduction." In *The Reigns of Charles II and James VII & II*, edited by Lionel K. J. Glassey, 1–11. London: Macmillan, 1997.
———. "William II and the Settlement of Religion in Scotland, 1688–1690." *Records of the Scottish Church History Society* 23 (1989) 317–29.
Golding, Peter. *Covenant Theology: the Key of Theology in Reformed Thought and Tradition*. Geanies House, Ross-shire, UK: Christian Focus, 2004.
Grant, Alexander. *The Story of the University of Edinburgh During its First Three Hundred Years*. London: Longmans, Green, 1884.
Greaves, Richard L. "John Knox and the Covenant Tradition." *Journal of Ecclesiastical History* 24 (1973) 23–32.
Hamilton, Ian. "United Secession Church." In *Dictionary of Scottish Church History and Theology*, edited by Nigel M. de S. Cameron, 841. Downers Grove, IL: InterVarsity, 1993.
———. *The Erosion of Calvinist Orthodoxy: Seceders and Subscription in Scottish Presbyterianism*. Rutherford Studies in Historical Theology. Edinburgh: Rutherford House, 1990.
Harper, James. *MEMOIR OF THE REV. EBENEZER ERSKINE, A.M., FATHER OF THE SECESSION CHURCH*. In James Harper, John Eadie, and William Lindsay, *LIVES OF EBENEZER ERSKINE, WILLIAM WILSON, AND THOMAS GILLESPIE, FATHERS OF THE UNITED PRESBYTERIAN CHURCH*. Edinburgh: Fullarton, 1849.
Harten, P. H. van. *DE PREDIKING VAN EBENEZER EN RALPH ERSKINE*. Gravenhage: Boekencentrum, 1986.
Hazlett, Ian. "Ebbs and Flows of Theology in Glasgow 1451–1843." In *Traditions of Theology in Glasgow 1450–1990*, edited by William Ian P. Hazlett. Edinburgh: Scottish Academic, 1993.
———. "The Scots Confession 1560: Context, Complexion and Critique." *Archiv fur Reformationsgeschichte* 78 (1987) 287–320.
Helm, Paul. "Calvin and the Covenant: Unity and Continuity." *Evangelical Quarterly* LV (April 1983) 65–81.
———. "Calvin, English Calvinism and the Logic of Doctrinal Development." *Scottish Journal of Theology* 34 (1981) 179–185.
Henderson, G. D. "The Idea of the Covenant in Scotland." *The Evangelical Quarterly* 27 (1955) 2–14.
Henderson, Henry F. *The Religious Controversies of Scotland*. Edinburgh: T. & T. Clark, 1905.
Herron, Andrew. *Kirk By Divine Right*. Edinburgh: Saint Andrew, 1985.
Hetherington, W. M. *History of the Church of Scotland*. Edinburgh: Johnstone, 1842.
Hopfl, Harro, ed. *Luther and Calvin on Secular Authority*. Cambridge Texts in the History of Political Thought. Cambridge: Cambridge University Press, 1991.
Horn, D. B. *A Short History of the University of Edinburgh: 1556–1889*. Edinburgh: University Press, 1967.
Hornsby, J. T. "The Case of Mr John Glas." *Records of the Scottish Church History Society* 6 (1938) 115–37.
———. "John Glas: His Later Life and Work." *Records of the Scottish Church History Society* 7 (1941) 94–113.

Horton, Michael. *God of Promise: Introducing Covenant Theology*. Grand Rapids: Baker, 2006.

Isbell, Sherman. "Burgess Oath." In *Dictionary of Scottish Church History and Theology*, edited by Nigel M. de S. Cameron, 109-10. Downers Grove, IL: InterVarsity, 1993.

———. "Church and State (Theological Questions)." In *Dictionary of Scottish Church History and Theology*, edited by Nigel M. de S. Cameron, 180-82. Downers Grove, IL: InterVarsity, 1993.

Jinkins, Michael. "Willison, John." In *Oxford Dictionary of National Biography*, edited by H. C. G. Matthew and Brian Harrison, 59:397-98. Oxford: Oxford University Press, 2004.

Kenyon, J. P. *Revolution Principles: The Politics of Party 1689-1720*. Cambridge: Cambridge University Press, 1977.

Ker, John, and Jean L. Watson. *The Erskines: Ebenezer and Ralph*. Edinburgh: Gemmell, 1880.

Kidd, Colin. "Conditional Britons: The Scots Covenanting Tradition and the Eighteenth-century British State." *English Historical Review* 117 (2002) 1147-76.

———. "Constructing a civil religion: Scots Presbyterians and the eighteenth-century British state." In *The Scottish Churches and the Union Parliament 1707-1999*, edited by James Kirk, 1-21. Edinburgh: Scottish Church History Society, 2001.

———. "Protestantism, constitutionalism and British identity under the later Stuarts." In *British Consciousness and Identity: The Making of Britain, 1533-1707*, edited by Brendan Bradshaw and Peter Roberts, 321-42. Cambridge: Cambridge University Press, 1998.

———. "Religious Realignment Between the Restoration and Union." In *A Union for Empire: Political Thought and the British Union of 1707*, edited by John Robertson, 145-68. Cambridge: Cambridge University Press, 1995.

———. "Scotland's Invisible Enlightenment: Subscription and Heterodoxy in the Eighteenth-century Kirk." *Records of the Scottish Church History Society* 30 (2000) 28-59.

———. *Subverting Scotland's Past: Scottish Whig Historians and the Creation of an Anglo-British identity, 1689-c.1830*. Cambridge: Cambridge University Press, 1993.

Kirk, James. "'Melvillian' Reform in the Scottish Universities." In *The Renaissance in Scotland: Studies in Literature, Religion, History and Culture Offered to John Durkan*, edited by A. A. MacDonald, Michael Lynch, and Ian Cowan. Leiden: Brill, 1994.

———. *Patterns of Reform: Continuity and Change in the Reformation Kirk*. Edinburgh: T. & T. Clark, 1989.

Knox, R. Buick. "Establishment and Toleration during the Reigns of William, Mary and Anne." *Records of the Scottish Church History Society* XXIII (1989) 330-360.

Lachman, David C. "Erskine, Ebenezer." In *Oxford Dictionary of National Biography*, edited by H. C. G. Matthew and Brian Harrison, 18:527-30. Oxford: Oxford University Press, 2004.

———. "Erskine, Ebenezer." In *Dictionary of Scottish Church History and Theology*, edited by Nigel M. de S. Cameron, 299-300. Downers Grove, IL: InterVarsity, 1993.

———. *The Marrow Controversy 1718-1723: An Historical and Theological Analysis*. Rutherford Studies in Historical Theology. Edinburgh: Rutherford House, 1988.

———. "Marrow Controversy." In *Dictionary of Scottish Church History and Theology*, edited by Nigel M. de S. Cameron, 546-48. Downers Grove, IL: InterVarsity, 1993.

———. "Protesters." In *Dictionary of Scottish Church History and Theology*, edited by Nigel M. de S. Cameron, 681. Downers Grove, IL: InterVarsity, 1993.

———. "Resolutioners." In *Dictionary of Scottish Church History and Theology*, edited by Nigel M. de S. Cameron, 710. Downers Grove, IL: InterVarsity, 1993.

Lee, John R. *Greyfriars Glasgow: The Mother Church of the Secession in the West*. A Story of Two Hundred Years *1738-1938*. Glasgow: Maclehose, 1938.

Lenman, Bruce. *The Jacobite Risings In Britain: 1689-1746*. Dalkeith: Scottish Cultural, 1980.

Letham, Robert. "The *Foedus Operum*: Some Factors Accounting For Its Development." *Sixteenth Century Journal* XIV (1983) 457-467.

Lillback, Peter A. *The Binding of God: Calvin's Role in the Development of Covenant Theology*. Texts and Studies in Reformation and Post-Reformation Thought. Grand Rapids: Baker Academic, 2001.

Lumsden, John. *The Covenants of Scotland*. Paisley, UK: Gardner, 1914.

Lyall, Francis. "Church and State (Legal Questions)." In *Dictionary of Scottish Church History and Theology*, edited by Nigel M. de S. Cameron, 179-80. Downers Grove, IL: InterVarsity, 1993.

———. *Of Presbyters and Kings: Church and State in the Law of Scotland*. Aberdeen: Aberdeen University Press, 1980.

Lynch, Michael. *Scotland: A New History*. London: Pimlico, 1992.

MacEwen, A.R. *The Erskines*. Famous Scots Series. Edinburgh: Oliphant, Anderson, & Ferrier, 1900.

MacInnes, John. *The Evangelical Movement in the Highlands of Scotland, 1688 to 1800*. Aberdeen: Aberdeen University Press, 1951.

Macleod, Donald. "Covenant Theology." In *Dictionary of Scottish Church History and Theology*, edited by Nigel M. de S. Cameron, 214-218. Downers Grove, IL: InterVarsity, 1993.

———. "Faith as Assurance." *The Monthly Record of the Free Church of Scotland*, May 1988, 99-101.

Macleod, John. *Scottish Theology*. Edinburgh: John Knox, 1973. Reprint, Greenville, SC: Reformed Academic, 1995.

Macpherson, Hector. "The Political Ideals of the Covenanters, 1660-88." *Records of the Scottish Church History Society* I (1926) 224-32.

Makey, Walter. *The Church of the Covenant 1637-1651: Revolution and Social Change in Scotland*. Edinburgh: Donald, 1979.

Mason, Roger A, ed. *John Knox on Rebellion*. Cambridge Texts in the History of Political Thought. Cambridge: Cambridge University Press, 1994.

Maxwell, Thomas. "The Church Union Attempt at the General Assembly of 1692." In *Reformation and Revolution: Essays Presented to The Very Reverend Principal Emeritus Hugh Watt, D.D., D.LITT. on the Sixtieth Anniversary of His Ordination*, edited by Duncan Shaw, 237-57. Edinburgh: Saint Andrew, 1967.

———. "Presbyterian and Episcopalian in 1688." *Records of the Scottish Church History Society* 13 (1959) 25-37.

———. "William III and the Scots Presbyterians." *Records of the Scottish Church History Society* 15 (1966) 117-40 (Part I); 169-91 (Part II).

Maxwell, William D. *A History of Worship in the Church of Scotland*. London: Oxford University Press, 1955.

McCoy, Charles S. "Johannes Cocceius: Federal Theologian." *Scottish Journal of Theology* 16 (1963) 352–70.

McCrie, Thomas. *Statement of the Difference Between the Profession of the Reformed Church in Scotland, as Adopted by Seceders, and the Profession Contained in the New Testimony and Other Acts, Lately Adopted by the General Associate Synod.* Edinburgh: Paul, 1807.

McGiffert, Michael. "From Moses to Adam: The Making of the Covenant of Works." *Sixteenth Century Journal* 19 (1988) 131–55.

McGowan, A. T. B. "Federal Theology as a Theology of Grace." *Scottish Bulletin of Evangelical Theology* 2 (1984) 41–50.

———. *The Federal Theology of Thomas Boston*. Rutherford Studies in Historical Theology. Edinburgh: Rutherford House, 1997.

McGrath, Alister E. *Reformation Thought: An Introduction*. Oxford: Blackwell, 1988.

McIntosh, John R. *Church and Theology in Enlightenment Scotland: The Popular Party, 1740–1800*. Scottish Historical Review Monographs 5. East Linton, UK: Tuckwell, 1998.

———. "Lessons From the Secession (of 1733)." *The Monthly Record*, November 2006, 6–9.

McWilliams, David B. "The Covenant Theology of the Westminster Confession of Faith and Recent Criticism." *Westminster Theological Journal* 53 (1991) 109–24.

Mechie, Stewart. "The Theological Climate in Early Eighteenth Century Scotland." In *Reformation and Revolution: Essays Presented to the Very Reverend Principal Emeritus Hugh Watt, D.D., D.LITT. on the Sixtieth Anniversary of His Ordination*, edited by Duncan Shaw, 258–72. Edinburgh: Saint Andrew, 1967.

Mitchell, James. "Ebenezer Erskine." In *Scottish Divines: 1505–1872*, pp. 149–88. Edinburgh: MacNiven and Wallace, 1883.

Mitchison, Rosalind. *Lordship to Patronage: Scotland 1603–1745*. Edinburgh: Edinburgh University Press, 1983.

M'Kerrow, John. *History of the Secession Church*. Edinburgh: Oliphant and Son, 1839.

———. *History of the Secession Church*. 3rd ed. Edinburgh:Fullarton, n.d.

Morgan, Alexander. *Scottish University Studies*. London: Oxford University Press, 1933.

Morren, N. *ANNALS OF THE GENERAL ASSEMBLY OF THE CHURCH OF SCOTLAND, FROM THE FINAL SECESSION IN 1739, TO THE ORIGIN OF THE RELIEF IN 1752: WITH AN APPENDIX OF BIOGRAPHICAL SKETCHES, ILLUSTRATIVE DOCUMENTS, AND NOTES*. Edinburgh: Johnstone, 1838.

Morrison, N. Brysson. *They Need No Candle: The Men Who Built the Scottish Kirk*. London: Epworth, 1957.

Muirhead, Andrew T. N. "Religion, Politics and Society in Stirling During the Ministry of Ebenezer Erskine 1731–1754." MLitt diss., University of Stirling, 1983.

———. "A Secession Congregation in its Community: The Stirling Congregation of the Rev. Ebenezer Erskine, 1731–1754." *Records of the Scottish Church History Society* 22 (1986) 211–33.

Muirhead, Ian A. "The Revival as a Dimension of Scottish Church History." *Records of the Scottish Church History Society* 20 (1980) 179–96.

Mullan, David G. "Theology in the Church of Scotland 1618–c.1640: A Calvinist Consensus?" *The Sixteenth Century Journal* 26 (1995) 595–617.

Muller, Richard A. "Calvin and the 'Calvinists': Assessing Continuities and Discontinuities Between the Reformation and Orthodoxy." *Calvin Theological Journal* 30 (1995) 345–75.

———. "Calvin and the 'Calvinists': Assessing Continuities and Discontinuities Between the Reformation and Orthodoxy (2)." *Calvin Theological Journal* 31 (1996) 125–60.

———. *The Unaccommodated Calvin: Studies in the Foundation of a Theological Tradition*. Oxford Studies in Historical Theology. Oxford: Oxford University Press, 2000.

Murdoch, Alexander. "Campbell, Archibald, third duke of Argyll." In *Oxford Dictionary of National Biography*, edited by H. C. G. Matthew and Brian Harrison, 9:726–33. Oxford: Oxford University Press, 2004.

Murray, Derek B. "The Influence of John Glas." *Records of the Scottish Church History Society* 22 (1986) 45–56.

Needham, N. R. "Nairn, Thomas." In *Dictionary of Scottish Church History and Theology*, edited by Nigel M. de S. Cameron, 618. Downers Grove, IL: InterVarsity, 1993.

Niehaus, Jeffrey J. "An Argument Against Theologically Constructed Covenants." *Journal of the Evangelical Theological Society* 50 (2007) 259–73.

Orr, James. *The Progress of Dogma, Being the Elliot Lectures, Delivered at the Western Theological Seminary Allegheny, Penna., U.S.A. 1897*. London: Hodder and Stoughton, 1901.

Pearce, A. S. Wayne. "Erskine, Henry." In *Oxford Dictionary of National Biography*, edited by H. C. G. Matthew and Brian Harrison, 18:530–31. Oxford: Oxford University Press, 2004.

Pelikan, Jaroslav. *The Christian Tradition: A History of the Development of Doctrine*. Vol. 4, *Reformation of Church and Dogma (1300–1700)*. Chicago: University of Chicago Press, 1984.

Pettit, Norman. *The Heart Prepared: Grace and Conversion in Puritan Spiritual Life*. New Haven: Yale University Press, 1966.

Philip, William J. U. "'Federal Calvinism' Where Divergent Streams Meet?" *Theology in Scotland* 4 (1997) 41–53.

———. "The Marrow and the Dry Bones: Ossified Orthodoxy and the Battle for the Gospel in Eighteenth-Century Scottish Calvinism." *Scottish Bulletin of Evangelical Theology* 15 (1997) 27–37.

Rainy, Robert. *THREE LECTURES ON THE CHURCH OF SCOTLAND*. New rev. ed. Edinburgh: MacNiven & Wallace, 1883.

Reid, H. M. B. *The Divinity Professors in the University of Glasgow 1640–1903*. Glasgow: MacLehose, Jackson, 1923.

Richard, Guy. "Deus Qui Regnat in Excelso: Samuel Rutherford's Radical God-exalting Theology and the Grounds for his Systematic Opposition to Arminianism, with Special Reference to the *Examen Arminianismi* and the Question of Hyper-Calvinism." PhD diss., University of Edinburgh, 2006.

———. "Samuel Rutherford's Supralapsarianism Revealed: A Key to the Lapsarian Position of the Westminster Confession of Faith?" *Scottish Journal of Theology* 59 (2006) 27–44.

Roberts, Penny, and William G. Naphy. "Introduction." In *Fear in Early Modern Society*, edited by William G. Naphy and Penny Roberts, 1–9. Manchester: Manchester University Press, 1997.

Robertson, O. Palmer. *The Christ of the Covenants*. Philipsburg, NJ: Presbyterian and Reformed, 1980.
Ross, Kenneth R. "Patron, Patronage, Patronage Acts." In *Dictionary of Scottish Church History and Theology*, edited by Nigel M. de S. Cameron, 649–50. Downers Grove, IL: InterVarsity, 1993.
———. "Unions, Church, in Scotland." In *Dictionary of Scottish Church History and Theology*, edited by Nigel M. de S. Cameron, 835–837. Downers Grove, IL: InterVarsity, 1993.
Ryken, P. G. "Scottish Reformed Scholasticism." In *Protestant Scholasticism: Essays in Reassessment*, eds. Carl R. Trueman and R. S. Clark, 196–210. Carlisle, UK: Paternoster, 1999.
———. *Thomas Boston as Preacher of the Fourfold State*. Edinburgh: Rutherford House, 1999.
Sands, The Honourable Lord. "The Historical Origins of the Religious Divisions in Scotland." *Records of the Scottish Church History Society* 3 (1929) 81–95.
Saville, Richard. "Impasse and Potential in the pre-1707 Economy." Paper presented at Royal Society of Edinburgh, Conference on the Anglo-Scottish Union of 1707, 18 May 2007.
Schmidt, Leigh Eric. *Holy Fairs: Scotland and the Making of American Revivalism*. 2nd ed. Grand Rapids: Eerdmans, 2001.
Scott, David. *Annals and Statistics of the Original Secession Church: Till its Disruption and Union with the Free Church of Scotland in 1852. Chiefly Compiled from Official Records*. Edinburgh: Elliot, 1886.
Scott, Ebenezer Erskine. *The Erskine-Halcro Genealogy: The Ancestors and Descendants of Henry Erskine, Minister of Chirnside, His Wife, Margaret Halcro of Orkney, and Their Sons, Ebenezer and Ralph Erskine*. Edinburgh: Johnston, 1895.
Scott, Hew. *Fasti Ecclesiae Scoticanae: The Succession of Ministers in the Church of Scotland from the Reformation*. Edinburgh: Oliver and Boyd, 1915–1928.
Scott, Kenneth B. *Ebenezer Erskine, The Secession of 1733, and the Churches of Stirling*. Stirling: Viewfield Church, 1983.
Sefton, Henry R. "The Early Development of Moderatism in the Church of Scotland." PhD diss., University of Glasgow, 1962.
———. "Lord Ilay and Patrick Cuming: A Study in Eighteenth-Century Ecclesiastical Management." *Records of the Scottish Church History Society* 19 (1977) 203–16.
———. "Rev. Robert Wallace: An Early Moderate." *Records of the Scottish Church History Society* 16 (1969) 1–22.
———. "Revolution to Disruption." In *Studies in the History of Worship in Scotland*, edited by Duncan Forrester and Douglas Murray, 65–78. Edinburgh: T. & T. Clark, 1984.
———. "St Mary's College, St Andrews, in the Eighteenth Century." *Records of the Scottish Church History Society* 24 (1992) 161–80.
Sell, Alan P. F. "The Message of the Erskines for Today." *Evangelical Quarterly* 60 (1988) 299–316.
Shepherd, Christine. "University Life in the Seventeenth Century." In *Four Centuries: Edinburgh University Life 1583–1983*, edited by Gordon Donaldson, 1–15. Edinburgh: University of Edinburgh, 1983.

Sher, Richard, and Alexander Murdoch. "Patronage and Party in the Church of Scotland, 1750–1800." In *Church, Politics and Society: Scotland 1408–1929*, edited by Norman Macdougall, 197–220. Edinburgh: Donald, 1983.

Simpson, W. Douglas. *The Church of the Holy Rude: Stirling*. Stirling: Society of Friends of the Church of the Holy Rude, 1967.

Skoczylas, Anne. *Mr Simson's Knotty Case: Divinity, Politics, and Due Process in Eighteenth-Century Scotland*. Montréal, Québec: McGill-Queen's University Press, 2001.

———. "Professor John Simson and the Growth of Enlightenment in the Church of Scotland." PhD diss., University of Western Ontario, 1996.

———. "The Regulation of Academic Society in Early Eighteenth-Century Scotland: The Tribulations of Two Divinity Professors." *Scottish Historical Review* 83 (2004) 171–95.

Small, Robert. *History of the Congregations of the United Presbyterian Church 1733–1900*. Edinburgh: Small, 1904.

Smout, T. C. *A History of the Scottish People: 1560–1830*. London: Fontana, 1969.

Sprunger, Keith L. "Ames, Ramus, and the Method of Puritan Theology." *Harvard Theological Review* 59 (1966) 133–51.

Stanley, Arthur Penrhyn. LECTURES ON THE HISTORY OF THE CHURCH OF SCOTLAND. DELIVERED IN EDINBURGH IN 1872. London: Murray, 1872.

Stephen, Jeffrey. "The Kirk and Union, 1706–07: a Reappraisal." *Records of the Scottish Church History Society* 31 (2001) 68–96.

Stewart, M. A. "Wishart, William." In *Oxford Dictionary of National Biography*, edited by H. C. G. Matthew and Brian Harrison, 59:864–866. Oxford: Oxford University Press, 2004.

Stoever, William K. B. *"A Faire and Easie Way to Heaven": Covenant Theology and Antinomianism in Early Massachusetts*. Middletown, CT: Wesleyan University Press, 1978.

Struthers, John. THE HISTORY OF SCOTLAND, FROM THE UNION TO THE ABOLITION OF THE HERITABLE JURISDICTIONS IN MDCCXLVIII. TO WHICH IS SUBJOINED, A REVIEW OF ECCLESIASTICAL AFFAIRS, THE PROGRESS OF SOCIETY, THE STATE OF THE ARTS, &c. TO THE YEAR MDCCCXXVII. Glasgow: Blackie, Fullarton, 1827.

Tait, James. *Two Centuries of Border Church Life: With Biographies of Leading Men and Sketches of the Social Condition of the People on the Eastern Border*. Kelso, UK: J. & J. H. Rutherfurd, 1889.

Thomson, Andrew. HISTORICAL SKETCH OF THE ORIGIN OF THE SECESSION CHURCH. Edinburgh: Fullarton, 1848.

Todd, Margo. *The Culture of Protestantism in Early Modern Scotland*. New Haven: Yale University Press, 2002.

Torrance, James B. "The Covenant Concept in Scottish Theology and Politics and Its Legacy." *Scottish Journal of Theology* 34 (1981) 225–43.

———. Introduction to *The Nature of the Atonement*, by John McCleod Campbell. Grand Rapids: Eerdmans, 1996. Reprint, Eugene, OR: Wipf and Stock, 1999.

Torrance, Thomas F. *The School of Faith: The Catechisms of the Reformed Church*. London: Clarke, 1959.

———. *Scottish Theology: From John Knox to John McLeod Campbell*. Edinburgh: T. & T. Clark, 1996.

Tuck, Richard. Introduction to *Leviathan*, by Thomas Hobbes. Cambridge Texts in the History of Political Thought. Cambridge: Cambridge University Press, 1996.

United Associate Synod. "Historical Account of the Secession." *Christian Monitor* 1 (1821) 65–76.

Van Dixhoorn, Chad B. *A Puritan Theology of Preaching*. London: Pentecost, 2005.

"VINDICATION OF THE FIRST SECEDERS FOR NOT RETURNING TO THE ESTABLISHED CHURCH IN 1734." *Original Secession Magazine* 5 (1860–1862) 482–89.

Walker, James. *The Theology and Theologians of Scotland 1560–1750*. 2nd ed. 1888. Reprint, Edinburgh: Knox, 1982.

Ward, W. R. "Evangelical Awakenings in the North Atlantic world." In *The Cambridge History of Christianity*, edited by Stewart J. Brown and Timothy Tackett, 7:329–47. Cambridge: Cambridge University Press, 2006.

———. "The Evangelical Revival in Eighteenth-Century Britain." In *A History of Religion in Britain: Practice & Belief from Pre-Roman Times to the Present*, edited by Sheridan Gilley and W. J. Sheils, 252–72. Oxford: Blackwell, 1994.

Watt, Hugh. "Ebenezer Erskine, 1680–1754." In *Fathers of the Kirk: Some Leaders of the Church in Scotland from the Reformation to the Reunion*, edited by Ronald Selby Wright, 106–18. London: Oxford University Press, 1960.

———. "The Influence of Martin Luther on Scottish Religion in the 18th Century." *Records of the Scottish Church History Society* 6 (1937) 147–60.

———. *Recalling the Scottish Covenants*. Edinburgh: Nelson and Sons, 1946.

Webb, Clement C. J. *Pascal's Philosophy of Religion*. Oxford: Clarendon, 1929.

Weir, David A. *The Origins of the Federal Theology in Sixteenth-Century Reformation Thought*. Oxford: Oxford University Press, 1990.

Whatley, Christopher A. *The Scots and the Union*. Edinburgh: Edinburgh University Press, 2006.

Woodside, David. *The Soul of a Scottish Church: Or, The Contribution of the United Presbyterian Church to Scottish Life and Religion*. Edinburgh: United Free Church of Scotland, 1918.

Wright, David. "Aikenhead, Thomas." In *Dictionary of Scottish Church History and Theology*, edited by Nigel M. de S. Cameron, 7. Downers Grove, IL: InterVarsity, 1993.

———. "Hadow, James." In *Oxford Dictionary of National Biography*, edited by H. C. G. Matthew and Brian Harrison, 24:434–35. Oxford: Oxford University Press, 2004.

Young, John R. "The Scottish Parliament and the Covenanting Heritage of Constitutional Reform." In *The Stuart Kingdoms in the Seventeenth Century: Awkward Neighbours*, edited by Allan I. Macinnes and Jane Ohlmeyer, 226–50. Dublin: Four Courts, 2002.

Index

Abjuration Oath (1712),
    Juror position, 14–15
    Non-juror position, 13–14
Act 1730, 144
Act 1732, 132–35, 144
Act and Sentence 1733, 136, 144
Act anent the Planting of Vacant
    Churches (see Act 1732), 115
Act Concerning the Doctrine of Grace,
    178
Act of Indemnity, 3
Act of Uniformity (1662), 3
Aikenhead, Thomas, 4, 5
Airth, 40
Amyraldianism, 68n164
Anne (Queen of Great Britain), 7, 11, 15–16, 23
Antinomian Paradoxes, 83n226
Antinomianism, 30n7
Arminianism, 101n286
Associate Presbytery, 163, 169–81
Associate Synod, 163
Assurance, 94–101
Auchterarder,
    Creed, 29–30
    Presbytery of, 29

Ballingry, 132n83
Barth, Karl, 57n117, 58n119, 63n143, 97n275
Bathgate, James, 112n319
Bell, Charles, 218
Bisset, John, 207

Boston, Thomas, 30–31, 42, 60n127, 67n161, 72n183, 77n208, 104n298
Boyd, William, 1, 138, 159, 216
Breach, The, 197–211
Brown, Callum, 128–30
Bruce, John, 120n23
Buchanan, George, 186
Buchanan, James, 110
Burgess Oath, 197–99
Burntisland, 120n23

Cambuslang Work, 170, 174, 176
Campbell, Archibald, See "Ilay, Earl of"
Campbell, Archibald, 150
Campbell, Daniel of Shawfield, 117
Campbell, Robert, 221
Carson, John, 164, 184n74, 187n84, 195–96
Charles II, 1
Council of Peace, 103, 195–96
Covenant,
    Erskine's definition of, 42
    Hadow's definition of, 44
    Of Grace, 57–79
    Of Redemption, 54–57, 71–75
    Of Works, 47–53, 80–83, 85–87
    Of Work's relation to Covenant of Grace, 48–49
Cumberland, Duke of, 193
Cumming, Patrick, 168n18
Cunningham, William, 109
Currie, John, 126, 153, 159n179, 159n181

INDEX

Dickson, David, 41, 72n179, 76
Dunfermline, 120n23
Durham, James, 41, 46

Erskine, David, 192
Erskine, Ebenezer
    And covenant of grace, 57–62,
        66–70, 195–96
    And covenant of redemption,
        54–56
    And council of peace, 55, 58–59,
        60n127, 103
    Conversion of, 5–7
    Evangelical federalism of, xv
    Interpretations of, xiii-xiv
    Modified covenantalism of, xv-xvi
Erskine, Henry, 3
Erskine, James Lord Grange (see Lord Grange)
Erskine, James, 199
Erskine, Ralph, 39n39, 125n44, 126n54, 147n143, 169, 214

Federal theology, 37
Fisher, James, 39n39, 124, 142n126, 176, 200n130, 214
Fletcher, Andrew Lord Milton, 117
Fraser, Donald, xviii-xxi, 199n128, 207
Free Church of Scotland, 109

Gairney Bridge, 125
General Assembly,
    Of 1712, 15
    Of 1715, 37
    Of 1734, 125–26, 144–48
    Of 1739, 126
    Of 1740, 127
George I, 23
Gib, Adam, 221
Gillespie, George (Strathmiglo), 35–36
Gillespie, George, 192n105
Gillespie, Patrick, 41, 46, 51–53, 72–73, 76
Glasites, 161
Glorious Revolution (1688), xiv
Guthrie, James, 121n25, 151–52

"Gospel Commands", 63–67

Hadow, James, 31–32, 37–38, 39–40
    And covenant of redemption, 56–57, 63
    And covenant of grace, 62–70
Hamilton, Alexander, 38, 40, 119, 120–21, 147
Historiography
    Of the Disruption, xix-xxi, 32
    Of the Secession, xviii-xxi, 32
Hog, James, 6, 31, 39, 99n278
Howie, Robert, 40n41
Hume, Earl of, 192
Hutcheson, Francis, 166

Ilay, Earl of, 117–18, 122–23, 167–68

Jacobite Rising,
    Of 1715, 23
    Of 1745, 168, 192–95, 211
James VII, 1, 190
Justification, 87–94

Kidd, Colin, xvi
King's Confession, 182
Kinross, 120n23
Kirkcaldy, 111, 120
Knox, John, 189, 191n103
    On national church, 8–9
    On government, 186

Lachman, David, 33–35
Law of Christ, 83–87, 88, 92
Law of Nature (see also Moral Law), 42–45, 64
Lindsay, Henry, 125n47
Linning, Thomas, 1, 138, 159, 216
Lord Grange, 121
Lumsden, Charles, 40n41

Macculloch, William, 170n26, 176, 177
MacEwen, A. R., xviii, 207
Macmillan, John, 161, 183n70
McIntosh, John, 143
Mackie, James, 126, 135n97, 153n162, 158

INDEX

Mair, Thomas, 125n44, 126n54, 147n143
Malt Tax, 116
Marrow of Modern Divinity, 30–31
Mediate vs. immediate graciousness, 66–67, 75–77, 84–85
Mercer, James, 135
Ministerial Dissent, 138–40
Moncrieff, Alexander, 124, 142n126, 178, 200n130, 214
Moore, Charles, 119, 121, 125n47
Moral Law (see also Law of Nature), 42–47, 81–83
Muller, Richard, 34

Nairn, Thomas, 126n54, 183, 189–91
National Covenant, 181, 182–84

Olevianus, 40n41, 76n205
Overture anent the Planting of Vacant Churches (see also Overture 1731), 122–23
Owen, John, 93n258

Patronage, 2, 115–18, 122–23, 131–32
Patronage Act (1712), 11, 118, 122, 131–32
Penal sanctions, 44–47
Popular Party, 116
Porteous Act, 150, 160n186, 167
Portmoak, 5, 118
Presbytery,
    Of Kirkcaldy, 119–20
    Of Stirling, 120–21, 125n47
Protesters, 151

"Riding Committees", 122
Reformed Presbytery, 183n70
Renwick, James, 190–91
Representation and Petition (1721), 31
Revolution Settlement, 138
Rollock, Robert, 40, 51
Rule, Gilbert, 3
Rutherford, Samuel, 186–87, 189

Schmidt, L. E., xiv
Scrimgeour, Alexander, 38
Security Act (1706), 9–11, 16

Shawfield Riots, 117
Shields, Alexander, 1, 138, 152, 159, 190–91, 216
Simson, John, 29–30, 37–38, 113, 166n7
Solemn League and Covenant, 2, 10, 14, 170, 171, 173, 181, 182–84
Stirling, 118–22
Stuart, Charles Edward, 192
Sum of Saving Knowledge, 40–41, 45–46, 51, 71–72, 75–76, 77–78
Synod,
    Of Angus and Mearns, 130, 134
    Of Fife, 39, 120n24
    Of Perth and Stirling, 120n24, 124, 131, 135, 162

Thomson, James, 126n54
Todd, Margo, xiv
Toleration Act (1712), 11–12, 15
Torrance, T. F., 58n119, 60n127, 218
Tulliallan, 120n23
Turretin, Francis, 214n1
Tweeddale, Marquis of, 168

Union of 1707, xv, 7–11
Universal Redemption, 102–7
University of Edinburgh, 3–4, 34

Wallace, Robert, 168n18
Walpole, Robert, 117, 167–68
Webster, Alexander, 169
Webster, James, 29, 37
Westminster Confession of Faith, 28, 40, 71, 75
Whitefield, George, 164, 168–81, 186, 197, 209, 211
William III, 2
Willison, John, 33, 110–11, 116, 123n36, 130, 134–36, 140–43, 145–48, 153–56, 157
Wilson, William, 124, 142n126, 155n169, 200n130
Wishart, William, 150
Witsius, Herman, 41, 46–47, 53, 73–74, 76–77, 78–79
Wodrow, Robert, 118

www.ingramcontent.com/pod-product-compliance
Lightning Source LLC
Chambersburg PA
CBHW070242230426
43664CB00014B/2385